PASSION, POVERTY 客家 AND TRAVEL
Traditional Hakka Songs and Ballads

PASSION, POVERTY AND TRAVEL
客家

Traditional Hakka Songs and Ballads

Wilt L Idema
Harvard University, USA

Published by

World Century Publishing Corporation

27 Warren Street, Suite 401-402, Hackensack, NJ 07601

Library of Congress Cataloging-in-Publication Data
Idema, W. L. (Wilt L.)
　Passion, poverty and travel : traditional Hakka songs and ballads / authored by Wilt Lukas Idema, Harvard University.
　　pages cm
　Includes bibliographical references.
　ISBN 978-1-938134-65-4
　1. Folk poetry, Chinese. 2. Folk poetry, Chinese--History and criticism. 3. Hakka (Chinese people)--Poetry. 4. Hakka (Chinese people)--Music. 5. Hakka (Chinese people)--Social life and customs. 6. Ballads, Chinese. 7. Ballads, Chinese--History and criticism. I. Title.
　PL2519.F6I34 2015
　895.11008--dc23

　　　　　　　　　　　　　　　　　　　　　　　　　　2015008112

British Library Cataloguing-in-Publication Data
A catalogue record for this book is available from the British Library.

Copyright © 2015 by World Century Publishing Corporation

All rights reserved. This book, or parts thereof, may not be reproduced in any form or by any means, electronic or mechanical, including photocopying, recording or any information storage and retrieval system now known or to be invented, without written permission from the publisher.

For photocopying of material in this volume, please pay a copying fee through the Copyright Clearance Center, Inc., 222 Rosewood Drive, Danvers, MA 01923, USA. In this case permission to photocopy is not required from the publisher.

In-house Editor: Lum Pui Yee

Typeset by Stallion Press
Email: enquiries@stallionpress.com

CONTENTS

Acknowledgments   vii

Introduction   1

Part One   Mountain Songs   11
Introduction   11

Chapter 1   Mountain Songs collected by Huang Zunxian   25
Chapter 2   Mountain Songs collected by Zhong Jingwen   31
Chapter 3   Mountain Songs collected by Luo Xianglin   39
Chapter 4   Mountain Songs collected by Li Jinfa   53
Chapter 5   More Declarations of Love and of Despair   69

Part Two   Narrative Ballads   77
Introduction   77

Chapter 1   Ten-Mile Pavilion   81
Chapter 2   The Tale of Tang Xian   109
Chapter 3   Selling Lanterns   127

Part Three   Bamboo-Clappers Songs   187
Introduction   187

Chapter 1   Gao Wenju   191

Chapter 2   Liang Sizhen and Zhao Yulin   215
Chapter 3   Second-Hand Zhang Rents out his Wife   257
Chapter 4   Morals and More   283

Part Four   Migration and Emigration   295
Introduction   295

Chapter 1   Push and Pull   299
Chapter 2   Destination Taiwan   319
Chapter 3   Destination Singapore and Beyond   337

Appendix I   An Old and a New *Ten-Mile Pavilion*   357
Appendix II   An Alternative *Gao Wenju*   381
Appendix III   *The Slave Girl's Lament*: A Revolutionary
                Bamboo-Clappers Song   403
Appendix IV   The Lost *Romance of the Career of Yap Ah Loy*   425

Bibliography   437

ACKNOWLEDGMENTS

Without the assistance of many friends and colleagues this book could not have been written. I first of all want to thank Cynthia Brokaw. In her research on the Sibao printers of Western Fujian she collected a number of texts of traditional ballads which she kindly put at my disposal. One of these texts is translated in Appendix I, while other texts helped to make sense of problematical passages in other editions of the same story.

The staff of the Harvard-Yenching Library at Harvard University and the staff of the East-Asian Library at Leiden University were, as always, extremely helpful in locating primary and secondary materials. In this connection I would especially like to thank Ma Xiaohe and Sharon Yang. Of the many other people who provided me with materials at my request, I would like to mention Isabelle Ang, Guo Jie, Barend ter Haar, Nancy Hearst, David Helliwell, Sun Xiaosu, and Tian Yuan Tan.

Some of the texts translated in this volume deal with issues of migration and emigration, which is certainly not my field of expertise, so I bothered a number of more knowledgeable colleagues with my questions and they all took the time to write back to me at length. Here I would like express my thanks to Sharon Carstens, Leo Douw, Alison Groppe, Angela Leung, Elizabeth Shinn, Soo Khin Wah (Su Qinghua), Claudine Salmon, Michael Szonyi, and Wang Gungwu.

Needless to say, all mistakes in the translations and introductions throughout the book remain my responsibility.

The translation of the *Tale of Tang Xian* was earlier published in *Taiwanese Literature: English Translation Series* 31/32 (2013: 225–244). It is here reprinted with permission of the editors of that journal.

The translation by C.K. of the Chinese ballad on the life of Yap Ah Loy, first published in *The Selangor Journal: Jottings Past and Present* 1 (1893: 184–185) and reprinted in J. M. Gullick, ed. *History from the Selangor Journal.* Kuala Lumpur: Malaysian Branch of the Royal Asiatic Society (2007: 527–530), is here reprinted (in Appendix IV) with permission of the editors of the *Journal of the Malaysian Branch of the Royal Asiatic Society.*

Leiden, May 29th, 2014   Wilt L. Idema

INTRODUCTION

Among the Chinese (Hanzu 漢族), the Hakkas (Kejia 客家 or Keren 客人) are one of the most distinctive cultural subgroups.[1] They are distinguished first of all by their dialect,[2] but also set themselves apart from other subgroups of Chinese by some of their customs and habits (a few of which, such as details of clothing, were more visible in imperial times than at present). Many of the cultural traits that distinguish the Hakkas from other subgroups may be related to the main habitat of the Hakka. When, in the 16th century, the Hakka first become clearly visible in historical sources as a specific subgroup, they mainly lived in the mountainous and hilly terrain of

---

[1] Lozada 2005 provides a concise overview of Hakka history and culture in China and abroad followed by a selective bibliography. For an earlier overview, see Moser 1985, 235–255. Joniak Lüthi 2013 discusses the many processes of internal differentiation within the Han and chooses against applying the labels "ethnic" and "subethnic" to the resulting groups.

[2] Some linguists stress the link between Gan (the main dialect of Jiangxi) and Hakka, but Norman 1988, 210–244 classifies Hakka with Minnanese and Cantonese as offshoots of "old Southern Chinese," and stipulates a close link between Hakka and Minnanese. The grouping of Hakka with Gan is also rejected by Ramsey 1987, 111. *Zhongguo da baike quanshu: yuyan wenzi* 1988, 237–242 treats Hakka as one of the "seven great dialects" of Chinese. Nowadays the Hakka dialect of Meixian is often treated as a standard, but the differences between the various Hakka subdialects are substantial.

southeastern Jiangxi, southwestern Fujian, and northeastern Guangdong, on the margins of the main southern economic core areas. As mountain dwellers, the Hakka had developed several specialized skills such a hillside farming, logging, quarrying and mining, and also trade. Some of these skills the Hakka may have learned from the indigenous groups such as the She 畲 who are believed to have been the major population of these mountainous districts in earlier times.³ It was these skills that the Hakkas took with them when many of them migrated to other parts of China and beyond. Perhaps because so many Hakka men left their home villages to make their fortune elsewhere, one of the most visible characteristics of Hakka society in late imperial time was the participation of Hakka women in farm work outside their homes in the fields, which in turn may explain why Hakka women, in contrast to almost all other women in the final centuries of traditional Chinese society, did not bind their feet. Over the centuries, Hakkas not only migrated to many other areas on the Chinese mainland,⁴ but also to areas overseas. From the 18th century Taiwan was a popular destination and, in the 19th century, Hakkas also migrated to continental and insular Southeast Asia in greater numbers. In the twentieth century Hakkas not only played a major role in the Chinese revolutions,⁵ but also spread all over the world.⁶

---

³ Leong 1997.

⁴ In some areas tension between the pre-existing local communities and the new Hakka communities eventually led to violent conflicts. The most conspicuous example of such conflicts is offered by the Hakka-Punti Wars (1855–1867) in and around the Pearl-River delta of Guangdong, in which hundreds of thousands died on both sides. These conflicts (and their settlements) further contributed to Hakka migration. Earlier, strife between Hakkas and their neighbors also had contributed to the origin of the Taping rebellion (1849–1864). In the context of such conflicts in Guangdong the Hakka were often accused by their neighbors of not being true Han-Chinese.

⁵ Erbaugh 1992.

⁶ Depending on local circumstances, Hakkas have stressed their identity as Hakkas (as opposed to other groups of Chinese) or their identity as Chinese (as opposed to other ethnic groups). See Constable 1995.

In traditional and modern times Hakkas stood out both for their high degree of literacy (of the men)[7] and for their rich oral literature.[8] The genre of oral literature that first attracted scholarly attention is the Hakka "mountain songs" (*shange* 山歌). Most of these songs are quatrains, consisting of four lines of seven syllables each (in some cases the first line is replaced by a short three-syllable line, and there also are five-line mountain songs) and most deal with love. While such songs are also found in many other areas of China, the Hakka mountains songs stand out for their frank expression of passion and desire (inside and outside marriage). The Hakka mountain songs had already attracted the attention of the famous Hakka scholar, diplomat, reformer and poet Huang Zunxian 黃遵憲 (1848–1905), who not only transcribed a number of these songs, but even included them in his own collection of poetry. In the period of the May Fourth Movement, when modernizing Chinese intellectuals started to collect folksong as part of the Folklore Movement, three substantive collections of mountain songs were published by Zhong Jingwen 鍾敬文 (1903–2002), Luo Xianglin 羅香林 (1906–1978), and Li Jinfa 李金髮 (1900–1976). It is clear from their comments, however, that mountain songs not only circulated in oral form but also in manuscript and print — this seems to have applied particularly in the case of sets of mountain songs. The collection of mountain songs and the creation of new ones has gone on unabated in later decades, when larger and larger collections were printed — but editors also became more prudish in their selection and, after 1949, the frank discussion of passion and desire had to make place for fulsome praise of production. Some of these earliest anthologies of mountain songs also include other kinds of oral songs, such as children's songs and work songs. Later collectors of folklore also turned their interest to the rich store of oral tales that are part of the Hakka heritage.

As mentioned above, mountain songs might be organized into sets. One favorite organizing principle was question and answer

---

[7] Luo Kequn 2000 provides a detailed survey of Hakka writers and their works through the centuries.
[8] For a general survey of Hakka folk and popular literature, see Huang Ziyao 2003.

songs; another principle of organization was numerical, for instance according to the five watches of the night or the twelve months of the year. Longer sets could also develop into extended narratives. Such narratives existed alongside narrative ballads of a type which are encountered in many other parts of China. Whereas in mountain songs the first, second and fourth line rhyme, and the rhyme sound may switch from song to song, in these narrative ballads, also written in seven-syllable lines, only the even lines rhyme and the same rhyme sound may be maintained throughout the ballad, from beginning to end. These Hakka narrative ballads are known by a variety of names, such as *chuanben* 傳本, *guwen* 古文 (in Southern Jiangxi) and *zhuanzai* 傳仔 (on Taiwan). These narrative ballads deal with a great variety of topics. Some topics were popular all over China, while other topics enjoyed a highly regional popularity or were even specific to the Hakka-speaking communities. These narrative ballads circulated both in oral and written form and, in late imperial times, such ballads were printed by the many popular printing establishments in the region. In recent decades they circulate in simple cyclostyled editions, while performances are available on audiotape, on video, and on DVD. In the last few years an increasing number of performances have been uploaded onto the Internet.

The twentieth century also saw the emergence of a new genre of Hakka narrative ballad known as "bamboo-clappers songs" (*zhubange* 竹板歌).[9] This new genre, mostly performed by (semi) professional performers, drew on both mountains songs and narrative ballads for its music and subject matter. Its most distinctive formal characteristic is that the text is made up of five-line stanzas so the genre is also known as "five-line clappers" (*wujuban* 五句板). Most often these five-line stanzas are created by repeating all (or part) of the last line of the preceding stanza as the first line of the next stanza, a procedure which is also encountered in some of the question and answer sets of mountain songs. The subject matter of bamboo-clappers songs overlaps to a large extent with that of the narrative ballads, but some titles such as *Gao Wenju* 高文舉 and *Zhao Yulin* 趙玉麟 seem to have been especially

---

[9] In earlier translations I have rendered this term as "bamboo-beat songs."

popular as bamboo-clappers song. The traditional repertoire of the performers of bamboo-clappers songs was not limited to narratives, but also included love songs and nonsense songs, alongside moral songs that urged people to practice filial piety and to abstain from whoring and gambling. As a genre that was highly popular throughout local society, bamboo-clappers songs also attracted the attention of the new political and cultural authorities following the establishment of the People's Republic of China in 1949, which resulted in the creation of a number of new titles that broadly displayed the evils of the Old Society and enthusiastically sang the praises of the Communist Party and Chairman Mao. An example of such bamboo-clappers songs, composed in the context of the Socialist Education Movement (1962–1965) on the eve of the Cultural Revolution, is provided in Appendix III. Some of these new bamboo-clappers songs have a prosimetric format, meaning that passages in verse are interspersed by passages in prose. Such a format was not unknown in Hakka communities as the texts recited by Buddhist monks as part of Hakka funerary ritual often exhibited a prosimetric format.[10]

This collection of translations is focused on folk songs and popular narrative ballads. It therefore makes no attempt to cover Hakka traditional oral and popular literature in all its varieties and the geographical coverage is limited to northeastern Guangdong/southwestern Fujian and Taiwan. The main text has been divided into four parts. The first part is devoted to mountain songs. It is primarily divided by collectors as each of the early collections, despite some overlap amongst them, had their own emphasis. While Zhong Jingwen was focused on love songs, Luo Xianglin tried to collect as broadly as possible and also included texts in a wide variety of other genres. Li Jingfa also focused on love songs, but at the end of his collection included three long song sets which have all been translated in their entirety in this volume. The selections from these earliest collections are supplemented by some materials from more recent publications where these add to the variety of subject matter.

---

[10] For a short description of these Buddhist funeral texts, see Luo Kequn 2000, 377–385.

The second part is devoted to narrative ballads and presents three complete translations of ballads that would have enjoyed a special popularity in Hakka-speaking communities. This selection opens with *Ten-Mile Pavilion* (*Shili ting* 十里亭), which begins with the torrid description of a one-night stand of a couple who will never be able to marry, and concludes decorously with an extended account of the moral advice she gives to him as he prepares to travel to the capital to sit for the examinations (renditions of a shorter version of the same story from the 19th century and of an adaptation as a bamboo-clappers song, which turns the short affair into a tale of mutual love are included Appendix I). The second text selected is *The Tale of Tang Xian* (*Tang Xian ji* 唐賢記) which apparently enjoyed a considerable popularity on Taiwan, but is also known in southwestern Fujian. In this tale Tang Xian successfully participates in the metropolitan examinations, but then stays on in the capital. When he eventually returns home, his wife has already died from longing, but she appears to him in a dream to recount her travels through the underworld. The third narrative ballad translated in this section is *Selling Lanterns* (*Maideng ji* 賣燈記). This story is also known from Cantonese narrative ballads ("wooden fish books", *muyushu* 木魚書), but appears to have been quite popular in Hakka-speaking communities too. It tells the story of a young man, Che Long 車龍, who is reduced to such poverty upon the death of his father because of the machinations of powerful gentry that he is forced to sell flower lanterns. Eventually he successfully takes part in the examinations and takes revenge on his return. This is also the story of his fiancée, who insists on marrying Che Long despite the attempts of her father to dissuade her — Che Long has to mobilize all his social connections to make her his bride. The male protagonists in these three stories are all students. The first two of them can pursue their passions without any financial worries and, while Che Long may run into problems, his fellow students and his fiancée help him out with generous gifts — in the end it turns out he had been rich all the while because his father had hidden great treasure. In this respect these three male protagonists are quite different from the main male characters in the narrative bamboo-clappers songs of the next section, who are each as poor as poor can be.

The third part is devoted to bamboo-clappers ballads. It presents the full translation of three of such ballads, followed by a selection of non-narrative ballads in five-line stanzas. Among these moral ballads one finds *When Drinking from the Low River, Remember the High Ridge* (*Dihe yinshui nian gaogang* 低河飲水念高崗), which is widely listed as one of the best-known works in its genre. This urgent plea to practice filial piety and the recurrent warnings against whoring and gambling, have of course an added urgency in a society in which many men were on the move trying to make a living far away from their own family, who often relied on their remittances to survive. The narrative bamboo-clappers songs that I have selected for translation in this section are all said to be "traditional," which means that they have not been heavily edited after 1949 for ideological reasons, but as they have only been recorded in writing relatively recently, there is a possibility that they have been influenced by modern language and ideas. The selection of narrative bamboo-clappers songs starts out with *Gao Wenju*. The story told in this ballad is well-known from Ming-dynasty dramas. It deals with a topic that was very much beloved by Ming dynasty playwrights: the student as a bigamist. When Gao Wenju has passed the metropolitan examinations as Top-of-the-List, he is forced by the all-powerful prime minister to marry his daughter despite his protestations that he is married already. When his original wife later travels to the capital, his new wife, who keeps her arrival a secret, turns her into a slave (in the earliest version the original wife is even murdered), but when husband and wife are eventually reunited he proves that he has always remain loyal to her because he has never even touched his new wife. This story was widely popular on stage all over China and, in the course of transmissions, developed many twists and variations. In the Hakka-speaking areas too, the story was known in different versions and Appendix II presents an alternative version from 1990 as a regular ballad.

Liang Sizhen and Zhao Yulin (*Liang Sizhen Yu Zhao Yulin* 梁四珍與趙玉麟), the second narrative bamboo-clappers song in Part Two, would not have needed much editing after 1949 to be acceptable to the new ideological authorities as it is a mordant satire of the rich who despise and ridicule the poor. The destitute student Zhao Yulin even becomes a ballad-performer to beg his way to the capital where he will sit for the exams. Upon his return as Top-of-the-List he takes his revenge on his rich father-in-law and his three rich sisters-in-law as well as his three brothers-in-law, who all had taken great delight in humiliating him and his wife during their days of poverty. Poverty is also a major theme in the third bamboo-clappers song translated here, *Second-Hand Zhang Rents out His Wife* (*Zhang Gudong jieqi* 張古董借妻). In this farce the poor student Li Tingfeng 李庭風, whose fiancée has died, wants to borrow money (to go to the capital in order to sit for the examinations) from her father (still considered his father-in-law), who tells him he will provide him with the money if his new wife will call him "father." Because Li has no wife and is too poor to marry one, he want to borrow some money from his good friend Zhang, who has not got the money either, but who tells Li he can borrow his wife for the visit to his in-laws if he will return her before nightfall. Of course Li fails to do so and is forced to spend the night in one room with his best friend's wife. The resulting misunderstandings and complications are only resolved when Li returns home on passing the examinations. This story had been widely popular on stage from the 18th century onward.

Lack of money and forced absence are constant themes in the mountain songs, just as poverty and travel are recurring elements in these ballads in different genres. In the ballads, however, the travelers are primarily students who make their fortune by passing the metropolitan examinations and joining the bureaucracy.[11] The travelers in the final section of this volume, however, are not students but peasants. These peasants leave the mainland and travel overseas to Taiwan or the Southern Oceans to seek a better life and make some money. The texts about migration and emigration collected in Part Four focus not on those who succeed in their

---

[11] On the importance attached to the examinations in Hakka communities, see Puk 2009. On the organization of the examinations during the Ming and Qing dynasties and their impact on society at large, see Elman 2000 and Elman 2013.

ambitions, but on those who fail to achieve a better life away from home. The protagonists in these songs are not members of the elite, but simple folks who, depending on their destination, will work as farm laborers or miners. Many of these songs spell out in detail how these migrants are cheated out of their money by the snakeheads that organize their travel and then find on arrival that the only kind of work that is available is back-breaking labor in land reclamation or in tin mining. When these migrants have eventually managed to make some money, they will only too often spend it on whores or lose it by gambling. The chapter on migration to Taiwan mostly consists of a complete translation of *A Sad Song of Moving to Taiwan* (*Du Tai beige* 渡台悲歌). At the center of the chapter on migration to the "Southern Seas" (Nanyang 南洋) stands a very similar song reprinted by Luo Xianglin. While many of these migrants were attracted by the bright lights of Singapore, most of them would end up slaving in tin mines. Alongside these songs that tell the sufferings of migration from a male perspective, we also encounter songs that give expression to the feelings of the women who were left behind or decided to follow their men. While there exists a rapidly growing body of scholarship on Chinese migration and emigration, this type of material recounting the experience of migration from the perspective of the poor migrants is rarely consulted.[12]

This volume is first of all intended as a collection of translations of fascinating texts. As in my other publications of the same kind, these translations are primarily based on editions prepared and published by Chinese scholars. The sources of each of my translations are discussed in the introductions or referenced in the notes on each of the translations. Two books have been especially useful to me: Luo Xianglin's *Yuedong zhi feng* 粵東之風 (Airs of Eastern Guangdong) of 1936, which not only includes four hundred mountain songs, but also over a hundred other songs and ballads in a wide

---

[12] For a general survey of Chinese emigration see Kuhn 2008; Pan 1991; Pan 1999; Wang 2003. English-language publications on the poems and songs of migrants have focused on the productions of Cantonese-speaking immigrants in the US. See Hom 1987; Lai 1991; Zheng 1992.

variety of genres, and Hu Xizhang's 胡希張 *Kejia zhubange yanjiu* 客家竹板歌研究 (A study of the Hakka bamboo-clappers songs) of 2010, which is as much an anthology as a study and includes not only traditional and modern, narrative and non-narrative bamboo-clappers songs, but also several traditional narrative ballads. Despite the richness of these and other publications, my coverage of the subject is very much circumscribed by the available materials. There are some internal publications which I would have loved to inspect and utilize, but which remained inaccessible to me. I do not speak Hakka[13] and, to the extent that these published texts reflect that dialect, I have had to rely on the annotations and glosses provided by the editors of these texts. I have not conducted any fieldwork in Hakka-speaking communities, therefore many aspects of the performance of these texts will get short shrift.[14]

All texts translated in this volume are predominantly written in seven-syllable lines (in some cases a seven-syllable line is substituted by a three syllable line; there are also a few cases that a line is extend by one or more characters). In order to recreate for the reader some sense of this uniformity, I try to give each line in translation a roughly equal length on the page (shorter or longer lines in the original will stand out as shorter or longer lines on the page). This procedure will in some cases result in some minor padding, but as the original is not free from occasional padding I hope that this will be found permissible. Perhaps less permissible is that this procedure at times also results in the omission of detail, but I have done my best to keep those cases to a minimum. I have made no effort at rhyming.[15] While I take it for granted that the readers of this volume will at least have some background knowledge of Chinese culture and history, I have provided annotation where this was called for, but I have tried to keep the volume of these annotations limited.

---

[13] All characters are transcribed according to their pronunciation in Modern Standard Chinese.

[14] Performances of mountain songs and bamboo-clappers songs in a great variety of styles are easily found on the web.

[15] For examples of rhymed translations of mountain songs see Char and Kwock 1969, and Kwock 1988.

PART ONE

MOUNTAIN SONGS

Introduction

Short songs made up of four seven-syllable lines are probably the most wide-spread form of Chinese folksong. Such songs are encountered under different names in many parts of China, from North to South, and East to West. The term "mountain songs" (*shange* 山歌) is but one of the many designations for this type of song and is used in many regions; it is for instance applied both to the four-line songs of the Wu-dialect area (around Suzhou) and to the four-line songs from the Hakka-speaking communities. These songs are sung to a simple melody that may be the same for each song in any given locality. The most common theme tends to be love and passion in all its manifestations. To achieve their force they may either shock by their bluntness or display wit by a clever metaphor or an ingenious pun (as such, puns can rarely be satisfactorily reproduced in a foreign language. Songs that rely on such puns are very much underrepresented in translations, including this one).[1]

These four-line songs have a tradition that can be traced back in written sources for almost two thousand years, even though in the

---

[1] Huang Ziyao 2003, 55–67; Lin Geng 1944, 35–149; Ye Chunsheng 1996, 84–111; Zhong Junkun 2009.

earliest examples such as the "Midnight songs" and the "recital songs" from the third to the six centuries the lines still were limited to five syllables.² In pre-modern times the members of the intellectual elite (the literati) occasionally displayed an interest in such popular songs, which were most likely not so much folk songs as the repertoire of professional entertainers. Not only was it believed that some of the songs (mostly written in four-line stanzas) in China's earliest collection of poetry the *Book of Odes* (one of the Five Classics) had originated "among the people", it was also believed that in ancient times the sage kings of yore had collected the songs that circulated among the people to gauge the quality of the administration by their officials.³ At certain moments in Chinese history, interest in popular song was further stimulated when literary critics defined spontaneity as the defining characteristic of true poetry, claiming to find such poetry especially among unlettered peasants, women, and children. One of these periods was the last century of the Ming dynasty, when the Suzhou author and editor Feng Menglong 馮夢龍 (1564–1646) published a collection of popular song from the Wu-dialect area as *Mountain Songs* (*Shange* 山歌).⁴ When this collection was rediscovered in the 1930s it shocked many contemporary readers by its frank eroticism as they had often entertained rather romanticized notions of the folk.

From the 17th century onward some literati also occasionally recorded short four-line songs in the province of Guangdong, but it is not always clear whether the originals they transcribed were Cantonese songs or Hakka songs. The first time we can be sure the

---

²Birrell 2008.

³The *Book of Odes* contains slightly over 300 songs that date from the 10th to the 7th centuries BC, The collection has been translated into English a number of times. The most accessible translation is the one by Arthur Waley, reprinted in Waley 1996. For studies on the *Book of Odes* see McNaughton 1971; Wang 1974; Van Zoeren 1991; Rusk 2012.

⁴For a complete translation of this collection, accompanied by an extensive introduction, see Ōki and Santangelo 2011. For detailed musicological study of *shange* in the Wu-dialect area at the end of the 20th century, see Schimmelpenninck 1997. Single songs might be linked into large sets, producing narratives of epic length.

songs recorded must have been Hakka songs is when the Hakka intellectual Huang Zunxian, who hailed from Meixian, the center of the Hakka-speaking region in northeastern Guangdong, transcribed a number of songs from his hometown. Huang Zunxian was not only an important diplomat and reformer in the final decades of the Qing dynasty, but also a well-established poet who tried to revitalize classical poetry by writing on contemporary topics in contemporary language, and at one time even declared "My hand writes my mouth" (*Wo shou xie wo kou* 我手寫我口). His own practice in writing poetry may well have contributed to his interest in the popular poetry of his hometown, which he defended by referring to the canonical *Book of Odes*.

Huang Zunxian had no immediate successors. For the heyday in the collection and publishing of Hakka mountain songs we have to wait until the late 1920s, when Zhong Jingwen, Luo Xianglin, and Li Jinfa published their collections.[5] By this time the Qing dynasty had passed away and the Republic of China had been established. Following the Literary Revolution of 1917 and the May Fourth Movement of 1919, the call to do away with traditional Chinese culture and the classical language was accompanied by a call for all-out modernization/westernization and by a call to go to the people. The call to go to the people implied both the intention to raise the consciousness of the peasant masses and the desire to discover an authentic Chinese tradition among the rural population that had not been tainted by the moralism of Confucianism and the decadence and corruption of the traditional elite.[6] The Folklore Movement that emerged at Peking University started out by collecting folksongs in the city and in the Wu-dialect area, but soon spread its activities nationwide. It became especially influential in Guangdong when some of the leaders of this movement relocated to the Sun Yatsen University (Zhongshan daxue) in Canton. Zhong Jingwen

---

[5] Some smaller collections were published in newspapers and periodicals; some larger collections made at the same time were apparently never printed and remained in manuscript.
[6] Hung 1985; Schneider 1971.

(who would go on to become the doyen of Chinese folklore studies in the second part of the 20th century) and Luo Xianglin (who would go on to become the leading authority on Hakka history and culture) were still only students when they made their collections of Hakka mountain songs and considered their collecting activities to be a contribution to the Folklore Movement. Li Jinfa (a symbolist poet who would later pursue a career as a sculptor), however, claimed he had begun collecting mountain songs a decade before the Folklore Movement had started.[7]

Zhong Jingwen, Luo Xianglin and Li Jinfa collected their mountain songs and related materials from various sources — oral and written, manuscript and print, but despite the fact that mountain songs also circulated in written form, male and female singers were expected to rely on their powers of memory and improvisation. This is brought out in the legend of Liu Sanmei 劉三妹, which since the 1950s has become associated almost exclusively with the Zhuang minority in Guangxi, but which was widely spread throughout Guangxi and Guangdong, also among the Hakkas.[8] In one Hakka version of the legend, Liu Sanmei defeats the poet Luo Yin 羅隱 (833–909) in a singing match: when Luo Yin arrives with a boatful of books containing songs at the spot where the illiterate Liu Sanmei is washing clothes by the side of the river and challenges her to a singing match, she defeats him with the first song she sings:

> Since ancient times mountain songs proceed from the mouth.
> So how on earth can you fill your boat with mountain songs?
> Allow me, this Liu Sanmei who washes clothes by the riverside,
> To ask you, my brother, from where in the world do you come?

---

[7] For the publication and study of Hakka popular literature (oral stories and mountain songs) from Guangdong in the first half of the 20th century, see Wang Yan'an 2005 and Wang Yan'an 2006.
[8] For extensive studies of the legend of Liu Sanmei, see Lin Geng 1944, 133–148; Zhong Jingwen 1994. For the transformation of the legend of Liu Sanmei in the early years of the People's Republic of China, see Liu 2003.

In one version, Luo Yin immediately turns around and flees; according to another version he dumps his boatload of books into the river, and as a result since then:

The Five Lakes and Four Seas have all turned into songs![9]

Hakka mountain songs consist of four lines of seven syllables, of which the first, second and fourth lines rhyme.[10] One also encounters songs in which the first line consists of only three syllables, and songs which consist of five lines. The overwhelming majority of Hakka mountain songs are love songs, treating the whole range of emotions, from falling in love to the first kiss and from consummation to betrayal and resentment. Images are often taken from the concrete world at hand:

Entering the hills you see vines clinging to trees;
Leaving the hills you see trees covered by vines.
When the tree dies, the vine clings to it in death;
When the vine dies it will cover the tree in death.

The speaker in the songs can be male or female. While the male can be a husband, he is more often a lover — aspiring, happy, or rejected — and eager for sex:

When the tong-tree flowers, it has no leaves,
My dear, I've come here to have some fun:
These breasts were not sculpted from silver,
These pants don't need any key to come off.[11]

The female can be an unmarried girl, a wife, a mistress, or a prostitute. A central word in many of these songs is *liao* 聊. While dictionaries tend to translate this term as "to play with, to amuse oneself with, to fool around with, to tease, to pester". While

---

[9] Ye Chunsheng 1996, 85.
[10] In performance, depending on the melody that is used, individual lines may be followed by nonsense syllables to extend the melody.
[11] Zhong Jingwen 1991, 9–10.

the activities covered by this verb may not exclude banter and foreplay, they certainly aim for, and include, having sex. While this Hakka word nowadays is often transcribed with an innocuous character like *liao* 聊, the sexual nature of the verb is clearly indicated by the transcription used in these early collections that write *niao* 嬲, which shows one woman squeezed between two men. I have therefore at times used an appropriate four-letter word in my translations. If one thinks these songs are at times too blunt, one should keep in mind that their editors inform us in the prefaces that they have not included materials they deemed too explicit.

For all the praise in these early collections of the pleasures of *liao*, these songs are not a simple paean to the joys of free sex. To the extent that these songs reflect the actual circumstances of courting and relationships in Hakka society at the turn of the 20th century,[12] we have to be aware that those are very much intertwined with the relations of gender and power in Hakka society at that time. In this respect Li Jinfa's description of singing and courting is enlightening as it lets us know that, only too often, courtship came close to rape. Li, after he has stressed the educational achievements of Meixian in the early 20th century and has praised the high literacy of its men in the preface to his collection, goes on to deplore the low literacy of

---

[12] Many Hakka scholars have claimed that even the most explicit Hakka songs on extramarital relations cannot be read as reflections of actual behavior in Hakka communities because Hakka women at all times have been prim and proper exemplars of traditional Confucian morality. Ono Kazuko, however, basing herself on Luo Xianglin's collection of mountain songs, concluded: "The large number of Hakka songs of passion suggests that the relations between Hakka men and women who worked in the hills was extremely natural and open. Having attained an equal standing with men through participation in labor, Hakka women were not constrained by traditional Confucian norms and could express their love boldly". (Ono 1989, 4) She was criticized at length for this statement as late as 2007 by Liu Zuoquan for slandering Hakka women. Strangely enough, Liu supported his argument by highly selective quotations from Li Jinfa's preface to his collection (Liu Zuoquan 2007, 47). If One Kazuko's views are to be criticized, it should be because they present an idyllic and idealizing of Hakka gender relations and because they ignore the role of commercial sex in mountain songs.

its women and continues as follows:

> But in other places the mountains are many and the fields only few, with the result that many men leave for the Nanyang regions[13] to make a living. Because their annual income is large, the life of the people can be called rather prosperous. But because the men often stay away for eight or ten years without returning, the responsibility for maintaining the family and the lineage is completely entrusted to women, and as soon as there are persons who are emotionally dissatisfied with such a single life, they will engage in mutual singing and harmonizing "between the mulberry trees and on the river banks",[14] and this is the most important reason for the production of mountain songs.
>
> The women of Meixian are extremely capable of hard work and suffering. In their daily work they slave barefooted and bareheaded in the fields. Their clothing and food is extremely simple. On top of that the ritual restrictions are extraordinarily strict. In order words, their social position is that of slaves, and this is something from which they, overcome by pain and misery, wish very much to liberate themselves. Furthermore, the conceptions of surname and clan are extremely important. When women of large clans are hoeing or planting in the fields or collecting *lu* (a plant that is eaten by goats and that is used for heating) on the hills, you cannot approach them in a flippant or obscene way. As soon as she would be found out, the husband or her uncles and brothers can whip her at liberty, and if they catch the male culprit, not a piece of skin on his body will remain intact if he does not lose his life. Because of this there are constantly feuds between lineages, which usually originate in some utterly ridiculous and unimportant issue, but they are convinced that morals and truth are at stake, and that these conflicts can only be decided on the basis of principle and force. But when women of smaller surnames or weaker clans are working on the hillside fields, the lechers of strong sub-lineages and great clans will use the opportunity to flirt with them in the

---

[13] The Southern Oceans, i.e. continental and insular Southeast Asia.
[14] This is a classical euphemism for the places where young men and women meet to make love.

hope to seduce them. Those women whose husbands are absent are not controlled very much by the family elders — in smaller clans morals and truth are rather murky matters and they really don't have the leisure to be concerned about their "face" — that's the last thing they are after.

This is the way they get together. When those men know that the women of a certain surname are working out in the fields, they will roam the hills in groups of threes and fives, and from a distance they will sing mountain songs whose meaning will very much fit their position in order to seduce them. When the women are interested in getting together, they will reply to their songs in kind. Only as they slowly get closer will the men start to flirt with them or even forcibly fondle their naturally aroused breasts. If they are somewhat more reckless, they will lie down on the earth and engage in what they most want to engage in. This is what is called in these songs "getting the upperhand", "getting on top", "coupling", and "loving". This comedy in which heaven provides the bed-curtains and earth the mattress — how it fills one with longing! After that the woman will pretend back at home that she wants to visit her own mother and secretly hang out with that man for a few days. The place where they will hang out will not be at his house, but at one of the "assignation hostels/fornication sheds" (*liaopeng* 嫽棚) that are operated by certain people in the countryside. During the day their activities have to be kept secret (if women know of this kind of activities of their married husbands they often act as if they don't know a thing and they will only in secret complain about their poor fate — there's nothing to be done about!). At night they hold a banquet at which their friends can eat their fill. I remember that when I was thirteen I once participated in such an occasion with a cousin. There is yet another method, which is called "entering the hovel". This means that the man will stealthily enter the house of the woman and hide himself in her room without making a sound. If they are lucky they part after having fully enjoyed each other; if unfortunately he is caught, he will be in a terrible fix. He may be subjected to such cruel treatments as "pushed sand" (meaning he will be stamped to death with pebbles and stones), "flowing needles" (in this case needles are inserted into a small barbed loach that the adulterer is forced to swallow; when the fish will be digested in his belly, his guts will be pierced by the needles till he dies), "flowing tin", "sitting in the pig basket" (putting a man in a pig basket and throwing him into a river) or "eating shit". But these barbarous actions are only very rarely executed — perhaps they are only phrases.[15]

After this unflattering picture of local society and the powerless position of women, Li Jinfa proceeds with praise of the literary qualities of the songs as proof of the native intelligence of the Meixian Hakka and concludes with an appeal to improve the position of women:

> In these songs the expression of emotions is so sad and sentimental, the love is so true, and the situations are so miserable! This is often beyond the reach of the greatest poets. I have said that the people of Meixian are extraordinarily intelligent, and this is the crystallization of the popular culture — apart from this there is nothing in which they excel. The most marvelous aspect of these songs is their puns in their *xing* 興 as well as their *fu* 賦 to use the language of the *Book of Odes*.[16] But often these are extremely marvelous in the local dialect and lose most of their charm when reduced to writing. This is why I in certain places have made some corrections. Even so, I have to apologize: the impulses of the sexes in these songs attain the conspicuous and incisive expression of desire. These [women] either do not maintain their chastity when meeting with men or they disregard all family rules. When we read these songs, we seem to suffer their misery ourselves. We have a humanistic responsibility towards these women who toss and turn in the eighteen layers of hell and we should stretch out our hands to save them.
>
> There are many smart women who can sing while improvising in tune with the feelings they want to express as if they were rhyming seven syllable verse, and the marvelous beauty with which they arrange their words truly surpasses one's imagination.[17]

---

[15] Li Jinfa 1928, "Preface" 4–7.
[16] Critics of the *Books of Odes* refer to direct description as *fu*. Many songs in the *Book of Odes* start with an image (often taken from nature) that has no direct relation to the following content. Such a *Natureingang* is called a *xing* (stimulus). To this day literary critics in the PRC often discuss mountains songs using the critical terminology originally developed for the interpretation of the works in the *Book of Odes*.
[17] Li Jinfa 1928, "Preface", 4–7.

While these early collectors usually present the materials they gathered as single songs, mountain songs were often sung as part of larger challenge and reply, question and answer, complaint and comfort sets that could acquire great length. Individual songs might also be part of larger narrative sets. Among the early collectors, Li Jinfa provides us with three such sets (one of these is also included in the collection of Luo Xianglin). Some later collections provide more of these sets and some of them have been included in the final chapter of this part. More examples are provided in Part Four, in the chapters dedicated to songs and ballads on migration.[18]

Many publications on mountain songs from the People's Republic of China mention that before 1949 mountain songs often were prohibited by local political and moral authorities, even though the actual cases listed as examples tend to be very few in number. In view of the bawdy contents of some of the songs and the context of performance as described by Li Jinfa, such efforts are perhaps not so unsurprising, even though they will have been utterly effectual. As "songs of the laboring masses" (in the Marxist Jargon of the 1950s) the status of mountain songs was greatly raised after the establishment of the People's Republic of China by the Communist Party, which already before 1949 had made use of mountain songs to spread its message. Mountain songs were now performed in concert halls to the accompaniment of orchestras; new melodies were composed and new forms of singing were introduced. The melodies of mountain songs were even used in the creation of a new kind of "traditional opera" called

---

[18] Following the publication of the collections of Zhong Jingwen, Luo Xianglin and Li Jinfa in 1927, 1936 and 1928 respectively, the most important publication on Hakka folksong from China in the first half of the 20th century would appear to be the long chapter devoted to mountain songs in Lin Geng 1944. This publication in Japanese and printed in Shanghai just before the end of World War II has not enjoyed a wide distribution and is rarely quoted in later scholarship. Lin provides a topical survey of the content of mountain songs that is extensively illustrated by examples; he highlights both the physical aspects and the adulterous nature of love as described in mountain songs, which will not have endeared him to post-1949 critics even if they had had access to his work.

"mountain song opera" (*shange ju* 山歌劇).[19] These developments of the 1950s and 1960s up to the start of the Cultural Revolution were later summarized as follows:

> After Liberation, due to the brilliant enlightenment of Chairman Mao's line for revolutionary literature and arts, and due to the concern of the Party and the People's Government, the Hakka mountain songs achieved a new life of reform and development. Whereas mountain songs earlier only could be sung in the mountains, they could now be sung in villages, chanted at meetings, performed on stage, broadcast on radio, and reported in the papers. The form of mountain songs developed from solo singing, alternate singing, and duet singing into small-group singing, performance singing,[20] small-performance singing,[21] and even into mountain song opera. The melodies and the music of mountain songs also were continuously renewed and developed. The broad masses of the people used mountain songs to sing the praises of the Party and Chairman Mao, to sing the praises of Socialism, and to sing the praises of their happy life. They also tied mountain songs closely to the Three Great Revolutionary Movements[22] to propagate the Party's directives, policies and lines, to stimulate the fighting spirit of the masses, and to give full play to its huge function in struggle.[23]

As a result of this change of status and function, printed collections of Hakka mountain songs from the years following the establishment

---

[19] Zhang Zhiyao 1981.

[20] During "performance singing" the singer acts out the part of the singer through costume, actions and expression.

[21] "Small-performance singing" refers to short musical numbers in which a small number of singers act out the story of their song.

[22] The Three Great Revolutionary Movements may refer to the Land Reform Movement, the Movement for the Suppression of Counter-Revolutionaries, and the Resist America, Aid Korea Movement of the early 1950s, or (more likely) the Three Great Revolutionary Movements proclaimed by Mao Zedong in 1963: class struggle, production struggle, and scientific experimentation, a slogan that was revived in the aftermath of the Cultural Revolution.

[23] Huang Huoxing 1979, 6.

of the People's Republic of China did away with all "unhealthy songs"[24] and turned the genre into a saccharine expression of romantic love in the service of socialist production. The lovers in these songs are innocent young men and women who (educated by the Marriage Reform Movement) insist they don't need a lying go-between because they are free to choose their own marriage partners. In a collection of mountain songs published in 1957 one encounters for instance the following songs:

> A hoe that's made of iron is strong as can be,
> A sickle made of iron has many good uses.
> A girl made of iron and a guy made of iron
> Excel all in their hard work for production.[25]

> I love you and you also love me;
> We don't covet beauty or money.
> It is labor the two of us both love,
> For all eternity we'll never be separated![26]

> I cannot abandon that passionate lover,
> I cannot abandon you, so good in labor.
> When you harrow the field, I carry shit:
> Our mutual love is sweeter than sugar![27]

> When the songbird flees its cage if flies off to the hills;
> When the carp escapes the net, it swims off to the river.
> The great business of marriage is left to our own decision,
> So you and I together should sing the song of freedom.[28]

---

[24] Hu Xizhang and Yu Yaonan 1993, 93–98 distinguish between three kinds of unwelcome mountain songs: "those that reflect the rotten and decadent modes of thought, moral standards and value judgments of the old society"; "those that are low and vulgar in style"; and "those that are low-class and obscene".
[25] Niu Lang 1957, 13
[26] Niu Lang 1957, 71.
[27] Niu Lang 1957, 74.
[28] Niu Lang 1957, 76.

In those years, folklore studies were required to play their role in enhancing the consciousness of the masses by presenting them with enhanced versions of the songs and stories that had been collected from among these same masses.[29] This was even before the Great Leap Forward had called for a frenzied production of new folksongs in praise of production! Even for this type of mountain song, however, there was no place in China's Cultural Revolution (1966–1978) and the suppression of public performance of mountain songs was far more effective than any previous attempt.

Once the Cultural Revolution had come to an end, new collections of mountain songs were published that tried to undo the damage done during the years of the Cultural Revolution. Since then, the folklorization of mountains songs has continued unabated and, in the 1990s, mountain songs became a highly commercialized genre of singing. Mountain songs also have become the focal element in the objectification of Hakka culture for ethnic activists, and highly stylized performances of mountain songs are often included in the program of gatherings celebrating Hakka culture and ethnicity.[30] In 2006 two local varieties of local Hakka mountain songs (Xingguo shange 興國山歌 and Meizhou shange 梅州山歌), were placed on the national list of intangible cultural heritage by China's State Council.[31] As the intellectual climate continued to open up in the early years of the 21st century, scholars have started once again to study mountain songs in all their varieties.[32] If more recent collections, however,

---

[29] Emimov 1975.
[30] Lozada 2005, 100.
[31] Zhou Heping 2007, 65–66, 70; Liu Xiaochun, Hu Xizhang, and Wen Ping 2007. Zhou Heping 2007, 70 notes that mountain songs are quickly losing popularity with younger generations.
[32] For a survey of studies on Hakka mountain songs since the end of the Cultural Revolution, see Jie Yingli 2005. For a critical evaluation of these studies, see Zhong Junkun 2009, 1–7. In evaluating PRC scholarship on mountain songs of the decades from 1949–1989, one has to keep in mind that many publications of the Republican period were not easily available, especially when their authors had left China. Hu Xizhang 2007, 48 writes that he had not yet seen Luo Xianglin's *Yuedong zhi feng* when he and Yu Yaonan wrote in *Kejia shange zhishi daquan* in 1993.

do not necessarily contain materials that are as sexually explicit as the collections of the 1920s, one reason may be that singers have learned from their experiences during the Cultural Revolution to be more selective in their repertoire when performing in front of outsiders.[32a]

[32a] In his *Kejia shange shi yanjiu* 客家山歌史研究 (2013), 250–313, Hu Xizhang includes an annotated edition of the 120 *shange* in the *Chengkaiqi shange* 程楷七山歌 (Mountain songs of seven days on the road). This collection had been printed in 1985 in a cyclostyled edition by a certain Lai Yufeng 賴裕丰, a peasant from a village in Xingning district. According to local tradition, these 120 *shange* had been composed around the middle of the eighteenth century by Liu Jiankai 劉建楷, a student and famous litigation master, during a seven-day trip to Guangzhou in order to take part in the provincial examinations when that trip was aborted by a flood. The original manuscript had for decades been preserved in the lineage temple but was lost during the Taiping rebellion when the temple was destroyed by fire. The songs, however, had also been transmitted orally. Lai Yufeng had reconstructed the collection by visiting descendants of Liu Jiankai and other fellow villagers (Hu Xizhang 2013, 216–221). Hu Xizhang is convinced of the authenticity of this collection, but while the story of the origin of these *shange* is not inherently impossible, it is very similar to legends on the early history of other genres of popular literature that ascribe a major role to a locally well-known literatus or dignitary to enhance the status of the genre. The long period of oral transmission makes it impossible to determine which, if any, of the songs in this collection were originally composed by Liu Jiankai — some of the songs that are used by Hu to argue in favor of the authenticity of the collection, may well have been inspired by the legend of Liu Jiankai's failed trip. But even if the songs were not originally composed by Liu Jiankai, the *Chengkaiqi shange* are an important collection of *shange* that circulated orally in one specific location. *Kejia shange shi yanjiu* became available too late to be otherwise consulted in the preparation of this volume.

CHAPTER 1

MOUNTAIN SONGS COLLECTED BY HUANG ZUNXIAN

Huang Zunxian (1848–1905) hailed from Meixian (then called Jiayingzhou). From 1874 he lived in Beijing, and there passed the provincial examinations in 1876. He then joined the foreign service of the Qing empire and was posted to the Chinese embassy in Tokyo as counselor. In Tokyo he was greatly impressed by the quick modernization achieved by Japan since the beginning of the Meiji period, and his writings on this subject exerted a considerable influence back in China during the last two decades of the century. His later postings would take him to San Francisco (1882–1885), London (1890 — 1892), and Singapore (1892–1894). Shortly after Huang arrived in San Francisco in the spring of 1882, Congress enacted the Exclusion Act and public opinion in California at the time was virulently antagonistic to its Chinese immigrants.[34] In 1892 he arrived in Singapore as consul-general where he was greatly impressed by the

---

[34] Huang voiced his indignation at the treatment of Chinese immigrants in the US in a long poem entitled "Exiles" (*Zhuke pian* 逐客篇) (Huang Zunxian 1981, 350–365). For an English translation see Schmidt 1994, 242-247 (earlier published in Lo and Schultz 1986, 333–336). Also see Huang's "Memorandum no. 29 to Envoy Zheng", in Yung 2006, 43–47.

ostentatious wealth of overseas Chinese merchants,[35] but also worked hard to protect the interest of common Chinese workers.[36]

Huang is known as one of the greatest poets of the 19th century. He freely incorporated new subjects and new terminology into the classical genres and his exposure to the world outside China even made him a proponent of the adoption of the vernacular. His positive attitude towards the vernacular may well have contributed to his interest in the folksongs of his hometown. When his mother died in 1885 Huang returned to Meixian for the prescribed period of mourning, and it is most likely during those years that he first tried his hand at the transcription of local mountain songs. When his collected writings were first printed, they included a set of nine of these mountains songs where they are preceded by the following short preface:

> In my locality people love to do songs, and men and women sing to each other, very much in the style of the Midnight Songs and Recital Songs. Collecting those that I could reduce to writing, I came up with more than ten of them.[37]

The "Midnight Songs" and "Recital Songs" mentioned here are popular love songs from the third to fifth centuries. Like the mountain songs collected by Huang, such poems are all quatrains. As a rule they have a female speaker and this may well have influenced Huang to primarily select mountain songs with a female speaker too.

There also circulated manuscripts of songs collected by Huang that contained more items. Luo Xianglin, for instance, owned a manuscript containing the fifteen songs, followed by a number of notes.[38]

---

[35] Huang composed a long poem on the lifestyle of the Singaporean overseas Chinese merchants entitled "Overseas merchants" (*Fanke pian* 番客篇) (Huang Zunxian 1981, 608–640).

[36] For a general discussion of Huang's poetic encounter with the non-Chinese world, see Tian 2011, 239–277.

[37] Huang Zunxian 1981, 54–60; Ye Chunsheng 1996, 92–95.

[38] For a description of the manuscript and a full description of the text, see Wu Zhenqing 2007, 122–124.

In one of these, Huang again comments on the problems he encountered in recording these songs:

> ... But mountain songs use dialect to create puns, and also use dialect to rhyme. If you are not conversant with local customs, it is impossible to grasp their subtlety, and it is very difficult to reduce them to writing.

In perhaps the most influential of these notes he compares the mountain songs to poems in the *Book of Odes* and marvels at the beauty of these compositions of unlettered women:

> [The poems in] the fifteen sections of "Airs of the States" [in the *Book of Odes*] are the most marvelous compositions of past and present, precisely because they emerged from the oral declarations of women and girls. If scholars and officials would try to write such works plying their brushes they would be unable to do so, because human artifice is easy to practice but natural sounds are impossible to learn. I have been away from my hometown for a long period and have gradually forgotten the dialect, so in recording these songs and ditties I often had to wrack my brain and could not put down a single character for half a day, and I therefore pondered: how could these people who carry their loads from the top of the hill to the end of the brook, going back and forth all day while singing without end, have such great talents?

Huang was not a trained folklorist and the texts he provided are perhaps best characterized as recreations of mountains songs that would be accessible to his fellow literati.[39]

***

---

[39] Schmidt 1994, 225–226 (translates three songs). Also see Schmidt 1994, 62–67 for a discussion of Huang's views on the vernacular and Huang's transcription of mountain songs. For English translations of two songs selected by Huang that rely on puns for their effectiveness, see Liu and Lo 1975, 500–501.

1.

I saw my darling off up to Mt. Buffalo Horns,
And went back when he was hidden by the hill.
Now I cross it again today, I'm filled with regret:
The Buffalo Horns still are curved and round.[40]

2.

Other people want to tie the knot for a future life,
But I only want to tie a knot for the present, now:
I will never leave you, darling, any hour of the day,
Whether you walk or sit, I'll always be next to you!

3.

The rooster crows wildly, urging my lover to leave,
So I see him out and we part: water east and west.
I have no way to make the water flow to the west:
As of today I'll kill that cock that announces dawn.

7.

My neighbor came home with a letter in her hands;
I've no idea what the contents of that letter may be,
So I will go there and talk to her myself, asking her,
Asking her whether she is more emaciated than me.[41]

8.

Whenever one girl is brought over as a bride,
Ten girls look in the mirror, and wonder why.
Each roll of the drums that pass before the gate
Deeply moves their heart, booming "lover."[42]

---

[40] "Round" refers to the perfect union of lovers.
[41] Love sickness as a result of the absence of one's lover was believed to lead to weight loss.
[42] The word used for "lover" (*lang* 郎) is also used to describe the booming sound of the drum.

9.

I married you, my darling, thirteen years ago;
Now I do up my hair today, I fondly remember.
I recall that when I came I was still breast-fed:[43]
We slept close together in your mother's arms.

11.

If you are the moon, make sure to be a full moon;
If you are spring, make sure to be the full season;
If you are rain, make sure to be a long-lasting rain;
If you are a man, never be a man without passion.

12.

I see, my dear darling, that you are losing weight,
But I tell you, my darling, don't pursue that affair.
Inside a flower the butterfly sleeps with the flower —
Can it continue to sleep there safely also next year?

14.

People say the wind will blow the flowers from the branches,
But I want the wind to blow the flowers back on the branches.
So I myself affix the flowers to the branches with yellow wax,
Making sure that even in old age not a single flower will fall.

---

[43] This song reflects the wide-spread practice of infant marriage among the Hakka. Parents of an infant son would bring home an infant bride for him and raise the couple together. The marriage would of course only be consummated when both the boy and girl had reached a fitting age and the girl would do up her hair.

CHAPTER 2

MOUNTAIN SONGS COLLECTED BY ZHONG JINGWEN

Zhong Jingwen (1903–2002) hailed from Haifeng in Guangdong. Stimulated by the Folklore Movement he enthusiastically started to collect songs and stories from the early 1920s. Following his study at Lingnan University in Canton, in 1927 he joined the Sun Yatsen University (Zhongshan daxue) in the same city, which at that time could boast of some of the leading figures of the Folklore Movement on its faculty. Zhong moved to Hangzhou in 1930, and spent 1934–1936 at Waseda University in Tokyo for advanced study. After 1949 he taught at Beijing Normal University as the undisputed doyen of Chinese folklore and folk literature studies, but in 1957 he became a victim of the Anti-Rightist Movement, so he could hardly publish for the next twenty years.[1] In the last decades of his long life he was actively involved in the editing of the *Zhongguo geyao jicheng* 中國歌謠集成 (*Complete Collection of Chinese Folksong*) and other large scale projects to document traditional Chinese folk literature.[2]

---

[1] Yang Zhe 2004.
[2] The *Zhongguo geyao jicheng* is an ongoing project. Each Chinese province eventually will have its own large volume offering a representative selection of folksongs from the province concerned. Each volume is composed on the basis of earlier collections prepared at the district level. For Zhong's participation in this project see He Jia 2004.

31

Zhong's collection of Hakka mountain songs is one of his earliest publications.³ His *Keyin qingge ji* (*A Collection of Love Songs in the Hakka Dialect*), mostly consisting of songs gathered in Haifeng, appeared in 1927 and has also been reprinted as *Kejia qingge* (*Hakka Love Songs*). The main collection consists of 140 songs, though some more are added in his short study at the end of the volume. In his preface Zhong informs us that he had originally intended to transcribe the songs in a phonetic alphabet, but eventually decided against this. His collection presents the songs in Chinese characters, making ample use of dialectical expressions. Many songs are followed by glosses and, at the end, a long list of common Hakka words and expressions is provided. While Zhong points out that Hakka mountain songs also deal with topics other than love and desire, the title of his book makes it clear that his own collection is primarily focused on love songs. In contrast with Huang Zunxian's selection, in which the speaker in the poems was exclusively female, Zhong also includes many songs in which men passionately pursue love and sex. The songs in Zhong's collection are numbered so this selection from his collection follows that order.

***

2.

When I sleep I sleep till I'm darling-bewitched:
Even the pebbles on the ground I will call silver.
Even when dead for three days, I still won't die:
As soon as I hear her voice, I come back to life.

3.

When the sun sets on the hill, the moon appears;
Beans fold their leaves, but rice opens its leaves.
Rice widely opens its leaves to collect the dew:
At midnight I open the door to await my lover.

---

³ Chen Zi'ai 2004 provides a discussion of Zhong's folksong research throughout his career.

5.
When singing a song don't worry about your voice,
All that matters is that the four lines fit the beat.
When you love a girl don't worry about her looks,
All that matters is that you two share one mind.

7.
My dear darling has been that beautiful since birth:
Ink and brush of red pearls cannot depict her in full.
Ink and brush of red pearls cannot depict her at all;
A house that was rightly sited produced her beauty.[4]

30.
Since creation when taking a smoke, don't bring your own;
Since ancient times when loving a girl, don't carry any cash.
A good field does not need the water of an irrigation wheel,
And a good girl doesn't want any of her boyfriend's money.

31.
When the sun sets on the hill, it's been a day,
But for a girl without a lover, it's been a year!
The sun that sets in the west returns at dawn;
The river that runs into the sea can't return.[5]

36.
Tonight when I was leaving it wasn't my time:
I stumbled and I fell right into the henhouse.
It was a good thing my darling was so clever:
She called for the dog to catch the mean fox.

---

[4] This line reflects the widespread belief in *feng shui* 風水 in the Hakka-speaking communities. For introductions to these geomantic practices and the related writings, see Brun 2008 and Paton 2013.
[5] Literally: turn its head, change its mind.

43.

The rain has been pouring now for six months;
I count on my fingers: not one day was clear.[6]
Even if he with all his heart wants to be with me,
Water has flooded the street, there's no way.

44.

The moon shines brightly, my boy wants to come,
But there's a river outside and there is no bridge.
If you are true in your love and want to shag me,
I'll break this golden hairpin for your use as oars.

45.

Those seven stars in heaven are seven sisters;
Seven of the seven lotus flowers have opened.
No, six of the seven lotus flowers have opened:
One is still waiting for her own sweet darling.

46.

In the middle of the night I come to my darling;
My dear darling is fast asleep and has no clue.
Both my hands pull the red bed-curtains aside:
Her face, red as a flower, is round as the moon.

52.

One thousand miles I will walk to you,
Ten thousand miles I will walk to you.
I'll happily leave my wife to walk to you,
Will you leave your man to come to me?

60.

We separated —
How foolish I was in separating from you.

---

[6] "Clear" (*qing* 晴) has the same pronunciation as "love" (*qing* 情).

In other villages there is no girl like you,
Such a fine figure and also so smart!

69.

Because of you
I am filled with worries and pain you don't know.
At dawn I wash my face and I look in the mirror —
My face is nothing like it was in days now gone.

72.

That's a deal:
When you have died, I will go to the underworld.
With my money I'll manage to buy back your life,
So King Yama'll send you back to fuck your man.[7]

75.

When you drink wine, you should drink a lot;
The more you drink, the better you will feel.
If you love a nice girl, love one of seventeen:
The more you look, the more you'll be on fire.

76.

Partridges flying off are birds without a tail —
Don't ever get involved with a traveling man!
Once you get involved with a traveling man,
You're like a mad dog chasing birds in the air.

85.

With sore feet it is hard to climb a mountain there;
Hungry, it's hard to survive the lean Fourth Month.[8]
A pretty girl of eighteen that's chaste as a widow:
A boat made of paper can't cross the wide ocean.

---

[7] King Yama is the highest divinity in the underworld.
[8] The Fourth Month is a lean period because the winter supplies have been used up and the new harvest is not yet in.

101.

Having eaten my fill, I want to drink tea —
There never was a wasp that hated flowers.
There never was a girl that was so chaste —
Money moves hearts, and hearts love sin.

102.

My darling has gone out to the market,
Planning to buy young vegetable plants.
Having chosen the shoots, he has no plot,
But I have a garden — plant them with me.

105.

Tonight the light of the moon is clear like this;
I'm sure that my darling has already set out.
I pray that the moon may be covered by clouds,
So the two of us will be able to get together.

114.

Seventeen or eighteen is the proper time:
No garden flower will last a hundred days.
No garden flower will last a hundred days;
No human being stays in love for two lives.

120.

Don't see me off!
A broken heart cannot see off a broken heart.
In the present world people's eyes are mean:
Walk two steps together, and they will know.

126.

The duckling, small as it is, dares swim the pond;
My darling, young as she is, dares love her boy.
The winter melon, big as it is, is all only greens;
Peppers, small as they are, are hotter than ginger.

140.
From far away I see my darling coming:
Not too tall, not too short, a fine figure.
Not too tall, not too short, a fine figure —
It may take millions, but I'll make her mine.

CHAPTER 3

MOUNTAIN SONGS COLLECTED BY LUO XIANGLIN

Luo Xianglin (1906–1978) hailed from Xingning in Guangdong. Like Zhong Jingwen, he started to collect Hakka folksongs in his late teens. As a student at Tsinghua University in Beijing he too was stimulated by the Folklore Movement. Whereas Zhong Jingwen limited himself to mountain songs, Luo collected much more widely and his substantial collection, entitled *Dongyue zhi feng* (Airs from Eastern Guangdong) and completed in 1928 (but published only in 1936[1]), ended up containing heterogeneous materials. Luo went on to become a pioneering historian of Hakka culture, first at Yenching University in Beijing, and later in the 1950s and 1960s in Hong Kong, at Hong Kong University and at Chu Hai College. Luo is widely revered in Hakka communities because, mostly drawing on Hakka genealogies,

---

[1] All prefaces in this collection are dated to 1928 and, as a result, the catalogues of libraries that only hold a reprint of this title list 1928 as the date of publication. The few libraries that hold a copy of the original edition, however, list 1936 as date of publication. Originally published by the Beixin shuju in Shanghai, the collection was reprinted in Taipei in 1974 and in Shanghai in 1992. Even so, the distribution of the work in the PRC would appear to be quite limited. Hu Xizhang 2007, 48 states that he first read the collection as late as 2006 when a friend provided him with a manuscript copy.

he argued that the Hakkas are true Han Chinese who in various waves had migrated southward from northern China. His writings on Hakka history are often quoted as authoritative.

Luo's *Dongyue zhi feng* consists of two parts; a study and an anthology. The anthology consists of over five hundred items divided over a number of genres defined by subject, the largest of which is "love songs", comprising 400 items. The other categories are "life songs" (43 items), "moralizing and satirical songs" (8 items), "children's songs" (42 items), and "miscellaneous songs" (15 items). Almost all texts in the category "love songs" are mountain songs, but some of the items in the other categories are also mountain songs. Luo's annotations on individual items range from glosses to information about the origin of the item concerned and, on occasion, I have included these notes in my translation. Luo provided his songs with titles, maintained in this selective translation, which adheres to the sequence in which Luo presented his materials. Despite its size, Luo' study does not provide much concrete detail on the performance and function of mountain songs in the early twentieth century, but it does provide a fairly detailed survey of collecting activities up to 1928.[2]

***

Love Songs

1. Vines clinging to a tree

Entering the hills you see vines clinging to trees;
Leaving the hills you see trees covered by vines.
When the tree dies, the vine clings to it in death;
When the vine dies it will cover the tree in death.

8. Smell so sweet

Inside the moon there is no fire: how can it be so bright?
Inside the well there is no wind: how can it be so cool?

---

[2] For descriptions and evaluations of Luo's collection by contemporary scholars from the PRC, see Zhou and Zhou 2003, Hu Xizhang 2007, and Liu Zuoquan 2007. The last two articles were included in an issue of *Kejia yanjiu jikan* (2007 no. 2) which was devoted to appreciations of Luo's contributions to Hakka studies.

My darling this year has turned seventeen or eighteen:
How can she smell so sweet without one flower on her?

9. That first kiss

When earlier you were with me, my soul belonged to you;
But now you have abandoned me, my heart is in a mess.
You've lit a fire that now is burning in the muzzle of a cow:
How well I still remember, still remember that first kiss.

12. In earlier days you considered me a piece of gold

In earlier days you considered me a piece of gold;
Now today you treat me as a needle without hole.
Like the big storm that overturns the crows' nest:
That's how wrongly you treat me and how cruelly!

13. All in vain

Just recently you and I were one burning pit of fire;
Now today you are as cold to me as snow and ice.
If you put the torch to a shop that deals in silk,
All the silkworm's work day and night is in vain.[3]

14. Fooling with flowers

I don't fear death, and I don't fear anyone alive:
I dare make love to the king's youngest daughter.
Cut off my head: I'll say the wind blew off my hat;
Put me in jail and I'll say I'm fooling with flowers.

20. In love forever

In Songkou we pay a visit to the Sweet Dew Temple;
With sticks of incense in our hands, we both pray:
Dear god, my darling burns incense and I lit a candle,
Protect us so the two of us will be in love forever.

---

[3] "Thread" (*si* 絲) and "longing, love" (*si* 思) are homophones.

21. Welcomes her lover

Outside the gate the dog start to bark and to bay,
And when she in her room hears that clear signal,
She takes off her shoes and displays her bare feet,
And stealthily goes outside to welcome her lover.

26. Don't fear the distance ahead

On the fifteenth of the Eighth Moon I watch the moon,
And I keep observing the carps as they swim upstream.
These carps are not even afraid of the Yangzi's stream,
So one truly in love should not fear the distance ahead.

30. I will dare make love

My lover is on the other side, and I am on this side;
Separated by the wide river, we cannot get closer.
If you can build a bridge of straw and dare to cross —
If you dare to cross the river, I will dare make love.

44. I long for my darling

I long for my darling, one year and one more year:
An old well burns incense, secretly emitting smoke.
In the fifth watch my soul may make love to her,
But when I wake up, we're worlds apart as before.

64. Longing for you

When I wave this fan, it is round all over —
My husband beats me all because of you.
From the gate in front to the gate behind —
Before my tears have dried, I long for you!

70. What on earth

Yesterday when you saw me you were all smiles;
Today when you see me you feign not to know me.
When we meet face to face, you don't say a word:
What on earth have I said that made you so mad?

73. Three lovely young ladies come out in one group

Once bell and drum resound, the temple gate opens,
And three lovely young ladies come out in one group.
There's one who burns incense, and two who bow —
You're the one that's destined for me, the oracle tells.

78. Cannot get out

Everyone wears on his head a round bamboo hat;
Everyone's ambitions want to surpass even heaven.
But in the end it is heaven that covers each and all:
Jump as you may, you cannot get out of that circle.

87. The student on his way to the Capital

Student on the way to the Capital, how can you be so rash?
Once you set foot in Hengtang, you start asking questions.
I am the eldest daughter of a family unrelated to yours,
So why do you call me, again and again, "My dear niece"?

A student on his way to the Capital, I'm not rash at all.
Because I do not know Hengtang, I ask questions.
Now if you are the eldest daughter of that family,
How come you have these two protruding boobs?

89. Build a bridge

In the middle of the wide sea I have built a tower,
Surrounded on all sides by the ocean's high waves.
All those passionate friends cannot reach me here,
But I hope, my dear darling, you'll build a bridge.

91. Borrowing three things

When the plum flowers blossom, chrysanthemums wilt:
I would like to borrow three things from my dearest:
First of all I want to borrow a mandarin-duck cushion;[4]

---

[4] Mandarin-ducks are a well-known image for true and lasting love. A mandarin-duck cushion refers to a long cushion for a double bed.

Secondly I want to borrow a bed all inlaid with ivory;
Thirdly I want to borrow a recipe for saving my life.

My darling, sweet boy, how can you be so foolish?
How could I have the three things you mention?
The office for embroidery makes mandarin-duck cushions;
The office for woodworking makes beds inlaid with ivory;
And a medical doctor may have a recipe to save your life.

My darling, sweet girl, I am not all that foolish.
Your body can provide me with all these three things:
If you stretch out your arm, it's a mandarin-duck cushion;
Your belly resembles a bed inlaid with ivory;
And when the two of us make love, it's a life-saving recipe.

My darling, sweet boy, I do know all these things,
But right now my body cannot provide you with any fine things.
This body of mine cannot provide you with anything good.
But since I've been born I have had two pieces of skin,
That I, dear, if you want them, will happily let you have.

Note: This song is popular in Southern Jiangxi. These are question-and-answer songs.

99. The man who comes at night

The southern breeze is not as cool as the northern wind;
My husband is no match for the man who comes at night.
That man who comes at night really knows how to talk;
As soon as my husband falls asleep, he snores still dawn.

102. Of no use at all

Among the celestial stars there are the Seven Sisters;[5]
Here on earth down below we too have famous lovers.
If a young girl like me has to live a widow's chaste life,
Yellow gold and carved beams are all of no use at all.

---

[5] The Seven Sisters are the daughters of the Jade Emperor and the Queen-Mother of the West. Many legends tell of the love affairs of each of the Seven Sisters with mortal men.

104. I'd be happy

That newly made ring was made of sparkling gold,
I dropped it by accident into the middle of the sea.
Let's both go hand in hand and look for that ring —
And even if that would be my death, I'd be happy!

109. Never soak the shirt on the skin

A girl who fetches water runs as fast as she can;
Spilled water soaks her skirt and soaks her shirt.
If she soaks her skirt, there's still no harm done,
But never should she soak the shirt on her skin.

112. Why did you

As long as we were in love you wanted me to be happy,
But now we have broken up, I want you, my dear love.
If you never were true when you were fooling with me,
Why did you have to talk so sweet when first we met?

115. I'm really pissed off

In front of the gate the waves on the river are surging:
Darling, refrain from gambling but not from whoring.
If you talk about stopping with gambling, I'm pleased,
But if you refrain from whoring, I'm really pissed off.

146. I longed for you for many days

I longed for you for many days, my heart was full of you,
And there was not a single day I felt without a worry.
I wrote a letter but then feared you couldn't read it,
I sent a message but then feared it might sound wrong.

147. Hurry down here

A young girl of eighteen has opened a medicine shop;
Outside a golden-lettered plaque has been displayed:
You boys, if you by any chance fall ill because of love,
Hurry down here and you will all be cured for good.

149. At that age she still doesn't have a sweetheart

If the sun does not rise, the sky doesn't turn bright;
If summer doesn't pass, the rice will not turn yellow.
That girl has already turned seventeen or eighteen,
And at that age she still doesn't have a sweetheart.

150. No girlfriend

Two years ago I refrained from smoking opium;
Then last year I also refrained from gambling;
And since this year I have no girlfriend anymore —
I'm getting rich all because of these few years.

181. A southern wind

A southern wind has blown away that fiendish northern wind;
A new dragon is here to make his home in the old dragon pool.
When I see you, my girl, you're like a mattress of finest rushes:
Now please be so kind as to allow me to sleep on it for an hour.

201. Your love for me is beyond words

Many thanks, my dear husband, for your letter:
But from beginning to end, I see, it is blank.
It must be that you have no specific instructions
And that your love for me is beyond words.

207. None of us saw the sky

On the road I met my darling, by the road we made love:
A rock served as our cushion and the grass as the carpet.
Deep in the mountains the forest served as bed-curtains
That covered the two of us, so none of us saw the sky.

216. All rot away

Your teeth as white as snow have done me in —
Let me ask you, where do you buy toothpaste?
Next I'll put the torch to that toothpaste shop,
So your teeth will turn black and all rot away.

219. Thin coins and full coins

Thin coins and full coins are both ready cash;
A field sown with a winter crop is still a field.
Your flesh and mine flesh is flesh all the same,
Now why does your flesh take that much cash?

225. A pair of birds

A pair of birds flew past the mountain —
You have a partner, but I am all alone.
If in those hills you meet with a falcon
That grabs your partner, we are alike.

228. Beat the single bird[6]

We're playing cards, I have a full hand of aces,
So I tell my lover, stop gambling, not whoring.
If you stop gambling, you have a bright future;
If you stop whoring, you'll beat the single bird.

233. That beautiful girl

That beautiful girl has a body white as shoots;
Her lips are redder than pomegranate flowers.
Her nipples are as lovely as bamboo sprouts
And her fingers are tender like ginger shoots.

239. He is thinking of her and she is thinking of him

He is thinking of her and she is thinking of him;
These two are thinking like this — what a mess!
He ends up thinking I haven't yet had my meal;
She ends up thinking I haven't yet done my hair.

240. Break-up

A crane swoops down and picks up an earthworm,
Not knowing it actually has picked up a centipede.

---

[6] A euphemism for masturbation.

Had I known that you bastard had so many feet,
I shouldn't have aroused that evil beast of yours.

245. The door was locked

A mandarin is sweet to eat but its peel is bitter:
That pretty-looking girl has a cheating heart.
Forget about all the money that I spent on her —
She told me to come, but the door was locked.

254. Of ten roosters nine are crowing

From Luogang you arrive at Gancun market:
Of its ten roosters nine roosters are crowing.
Of its ten single guys, nine have a girlfriend;
The only one who is without one is poor me.

282. Don't let anyone else

Don't let people sing songs on the main road;
Don't let the buffalo eat the grain in the cellar.
My darling, now you're entertaining the world,[7]
Don't let anyone else ever stroke your nipples.

287. Because I dare entertain the world, what crowd do I fear?

When crossing the river barefooted, I don't fear the sand;
Because I dare entertain the world, what crowd do I fear?
If you have the desire to come over to have here some fun,
Don't be afraid to engage in our mutual joking and teasing.

292. Mouth on mouth

For quite a while I hadn't slept with my darling;
I heard that with others she slept back to back.
Last evening I went and slept one night with you:
When we woke up we still lay mouth on mouth.

---

[7] Seeing customers as a prostitute.

294. I had no date with my darling but still she arrived

Last night I had a dream and it was really strange:
I never had made a fire but the water was boiling;
I never had put in the rice but the rice was cooked;
I had no date with my darling but still she arrived.

297. Massage your belly

I see my sweet lover off all the way to Qingxi River,
And urge him never to drink any uncooked water.
From uncooked water you may get stomach cramps —
Out on the road who will gently massage your belly?

299. Sneering remarks

If I do not tell you, you will not know:
Everyone is talking about you and me.
I've eaten quite some empty-stomach rice,
I've heard quite a lot of sneering remarks.

304. Cannot be sung

Guangdong's mountain songs are quite famous,
And every mountain song contains your name.
And every mountain song is connected to you;
If one song lacks your name, it cannot be sung!

314. The way I like

You darling look the way that I like,
In all of Guangdong you're a rare find.
If you're destined to become my wife,
To live ten years shorter is also fine.

317. A coupling that is complete

My darling goes to the river to wash a white shirt;
As soon as I see her I go and I ask her a question.
I call out loudly to her and she answers me softly:
This love can lead to a coupling that is complete.

318. Thread is lost

If the lady is willing and the gent so inclined,
An iron ruler can be polished into a needle.
If she is the needle, then he is the thread —
But three steps of needle and thread is lost.

330. Fuck the moon

If you want to join me as mandarin-ducks,
You are leading a buffalo up a steep cliff.
If you want to become my partner in love,
You must up in the sky first fuck the moon.

334. Continue to haunt you

We harvest the grain before it's ripe because we are starving,
When I fall ill because of love longing it is all because of you.
If this butterfly will flutter about and die beneath the flowers,
Its shadowy soul will not dissolve and continue to haunt you.

336. Worlds apart

As soon as the lotus flower opens, is reaches for the sky;
When a good horse sets out, no need to apply the whip.
Since ancient times marriages are determined by Heaven,
So have no fear even though we are living worlds apart.

340. One dot of red

When the sun first rises it is one dot of red:
You ride a white horse, and I ride a dragon.
The horse up a hill, the dragon down a pool,
And no clue when we ever will meet again!

341. The heat is unbearable

In the Sixth Month of summer the heat is unbearable;
With that heat in my heart I don't know how to cool.
I fan my dear darling with a palm-leaf fan and ask her:
How is your heart feeling now? Has it grown cool?

342. At seventeen and eighteen

At seventeen and eighteen the flowers are blooming,
But a boy fears his father, and a girl fears her mother.
The two of them are both still controlled by others,
And so these couples don't yet dare become as one.

343. The girl has no sweetheart

At the start and the end of the month the moon lacks light;
At fifteen and sixteen the girl still hasn't got a sweetheart.
So at fifteen and sixteen the girl has to live a life of chastity:
If the pond lacks water, you cannot raise any fish.

350. I don't fear the rain and I don't fear the wind

I have covered the windows with translucent gauze,
Now I don't fear the rain, and I don't fear the wind.
I only want that the two of us remain united in love;
I don't fear that all of Guangdong knows our names!

358. My head is spinning

Once I drink spirits, my head is spinning,
And I need alcohol to douse my hangover.
Once one is drunk, only a drink will do;
Now I'm in love, you are my only cure.

361. Longing for you

Longing for you —
The butterfly's longing is all for the flowers,
It cares for the flowers, not for the weeds —
I care for my darling and not for my place.

362. Darling just think

Darling, just think:
Until when will you wait if you don't engage in romance?
I've only seen the wind blow flowers from the branches,
I never saw the wind blow flowers back on the branches.

382. No place to hide

Once the fifth watch has sounded the sky turns bright,
Gently so gently I shake my dear lover to wake him up.
With both my hands I open the door so he can get out:
In this cramped little house there's not a place to hide.

391. Sharing one coffin

As soon as I see my darling, my heart is elated:
This must be a marriage that's fixed by Heaven.
As long as we will live we will share one cushion,
And once we are dead we will share one coffin.

400. You need great gifts

For praying to Heaven for blessing you need great gifts;
When I see my pretty darling, it is hard to get together.
But now if it is fated that my dear darling will marry me,
I'll have a play performed to grandly thank all the gods.

Life Songs

3. Your songbird will fly into some other man's cage

White paper for the letter, red for the envelope:
I send it to that foreign country, to my husband.
If after another three years you still won't come back,
Your songbird will fly into some other man's cage.

CHAPTER 4

MOUNTAIN SONGS COLLECTED BY LI JINFA

Li Jinfa (1900–1976) established a reputation both as a poet and as a sculptor. He was born in Canton and raised in Meixian. In 1922 and 1923 he lived in Paris, where he not only decided to become a sculptor, but also encountered French decadent and symbolist poetry. During a subsequent stay in Berlin, he wrote his first collections of poetry. These poems have continued to baffle Chinese readers ever since because of their bizarre and irrational imagery.[1] Upon his return to China, Li not only produced a number of sculptures, but also taught in various art schools in Shanghai, Hangzhou and Nanjing. After 1937 he fled to the US by way of Vietnam, and later in the 1940s, served as a diplomat for the Republican Government in Iran and Iraq. In 1951 he moved permanently to the US, where he made a living raising chickens.

Li Jinfa had submitted his collection of mountain songs, entitled *Lingdong liange* (Love Songs of Eastern Guangdong), to the printer in 1926, but the printer's offices burned down, and his collection was not published until 1929. In the preface to his collection Li claims that he had started collecting mountain songs long before the

---

[1] For Li Jinfa's original poetry see the entries for his collections in Haft 1989, 150–159.

Folklore Movement appeared on the scene, and had at one moment entertained the hope of producing a set of French translations. We had already occasion to quote at length from his introduction for his description of the performance of mountain songs and their social context.[2] The main body of Li's collection consists of a large collection of unnumbered love songs (under the general title of "Mutual Songs of Love Longing"), followed by three large sets, each with their own title. These three sets have been translated in full.

***

Mutual Songs of Love Longing

p. 10

When cocks start fighting, they do so first with their spurs:
Before I have even slept with you, you already talk money.
I would be willing to shelve out even eighteen thousand,
But first of all, dear, it's you who must dare cross the line.

p. 13

A newly-constructed tea pavilion with four pillars:
Inside that tea pavilion I feel my darling's breasts.
After having felt her breasts, I then feel her thighs;
After having felt her thighs, I then give it my best.

p. 14

My dear darling, my dear little darling,
I know, my dear, that you have a pond.
I on my side, I have this fine goldfish:
I'll hand it to you to raise in your pond.

p. 15

Stiff bones are placed on the block to be cut;
Oiled fish is dropped in the wok to be cooked.

---

[2] Wu Xiaoli 2001. This short article quotes extensively from Li's preface.

You, boy, resemble dried bamboo sprouts:
Put them in my wok, have them fried by me.

p. 16
When you have a smoke, smoke only one pipe;
If you smoke two pipes, it's only a waste of effort.
When you love a girl, you'd better love only one;
When you love two, I'm afraid, you'll have fights.

p. 18
Dear, don't complain that I'm still a milk mouth,
Since my earliest teens I have slept around.
I have slept with women in all four districts,
But I've never yet slept with a remarried widow.

p. 20
When the pomegranate blooms, its flowers are red:
Dear, I see that your seal has not yet been broken.
Once your seal has been broken it's easy to see:
Your body stands taller, your boobies are firmer.

p. 26
A couple of mandarin-ducks is roosting in that tree:
Forming a couple, forming a pair in happy harmony.
Dear darling, I don't dare enter the front gate here,
So please hurry up, get the key and unlock the back.

p. 27
The roof beam is raised of your newly built house;
Firecrackers explode all day creating quite a noise.
Now I see, my sweet boy, that you've made it big,
I should ask the go-between to go and talk to you.

p. 37
As soon as the moon appears, I will fall asleep,
And each night in my dreams I lay next to you.

And when I dream at night I am on top of you,
Only to know when I wake up that we're apart.

p. 39

With many stars in the sky the moon won't be clear;
With many fishes in the pond, the waves won't stop.
Too many ministers at court will ruin the country;
A girl with too many lovers brings harm to herself.

p. 47

The thousands of flowers of the longan tree
Cannot match a single flower of the hibiscus.
Hundreds and thousands of days with my wife
Cannot match, my dear, a single fuck with you.

p. 50

Now you have taken my gift, you are my woman;
If you didn't want to, you shouldn't have accepted.
Once the carp has swallowed the hook made of gold,
It may struggle to escape, but will still lose its scales.

p. 52

My sweetheart, my flesh is frightened to death:
The house on all sides is surrounded by soldiers.
Mice making out are caught in the act by the cat:
Today we're doomed to die because of our love!

p. 65

From afar I saw my darling slowly coming my way,
And in my heart a hundred kinds of flowers opened.
But when she came closer, she was someone else:
I'm crushed by a stone slab of a thousand pounds.

p. 66

In ten gambling sessions I never once made money:
I took a hemp rope with me up to the second floor.

With all my heart I was determined to do myself in;
But once I saw my dear sweetheart, I failed to die.

p. 78

When you have no money to buy wine, the jug stays empty;
When you have the money to buy wine, the jug will be heavy.
If you have money and call your darling, she'll reply each time;
If you have no money and call her, she'll pretend to be deaf.

p. 80

I swore an oath to Heaven but all to no avail;
The gods are not concerned about our worries.
I pronounced all those many heart-felt curses,
But from the very beginning nobody ever died.

p. 81

When you were little baby I saw you play with a tile;
Now you're all grown-up, you've married a husband.
Each day I pass by in front of the gate of your house,
But I've never had even a single cup of tea from you.

p. 81

My dear girl, there is no need for you to act so coy:
You have been with half of the men of this district.
You've been with Minnanese from Chaozhou too,[3]
And you have been with Cantonese from Dabu.[4]

p. 82

At seventeen or eighteen years you rake in silver dollars;
Once you've turned twenty, you'll make smaller amounts.

---

[3]The dialect of Chaozhou is closely related to the dialects of Quanzhou and Zhangzhou in Southern Fujian (Minnanese). The song refers to the speakers of these dialects as *xuelao* 學老 (speakers of dialects that are so difficult to get used to that one has to study them till old age).

[4]The speakers of Cantonese are here referred to as *bendiren* 本地人 (locals). In older Sinological scholarship they were referred to as Punti.

Once over thirty, people complain you're asking too much,
Once past forty, it will be you who must pay in hard cash.

p. 96

I recently bought a mattress with nine main cords:
The mattress supports me, and I support my lover.
A brocade blanket covers him, and he covers me,
And whenever a flea bites me, I sure bite my lover.

p. 100

I see my lover off, I see him off as far as the city gate,
And I instruct my dear darling to buy me a headrest.
Buying one, make sure it's a mandarin-duck cushion;
On no account buy two of those separate headrests!

p. 119

When the sun sets on the hills, it sets on the hills,
But being a married wife is truly much harder work.
All during the day you have to slave like a buffalo,
Then during the night you are used like a mattress.

p. 120

She is only eighteen and now her husband has died;
Eyes swollen form crying, ears deaf from weeping.
She lifts her head, eats her rice, drops a chopstick —
Who is the man who picks it up to restore the pair?

p. 120

My sweet darling boy, I tell you, so listen:
How could it be that I wouldn't want you?
Take off your shirt and pants and let's fuck:
Then you'll see whether I've lost my mind.

p. 120

My sweet little darling is such a tender flower:
Her lips redder than the pomegranate flower;

Her nipples firmer than young bamboo sprouts;
Her thighs whiter than the shoots of red beans.

Dreams in the five watches of the night

pp. 131–132

In the first watch I dream of my lover, feeling so lonely:
While dusk is falling we two are walking out in the fields.
By the light of the moon we engage in clouds and rain,[5]
Just as Student Zhang who is having his way with Reddy.[6]

In the second watch I dream of my lover, tossing and turning;
Lying on the bed I pull in my legs, but I cannot find any rest.
I cannot find any sleep, I cannot even doze off for a moment,
Because I'm only waiting with all my heart for my sweetheart.

In the third watch I dream of my lover, already at midnight,
And when I dream of my darling lover he really shows up.
My lover is now in the prime of his youth and I am young,
So until when should we wait if we don't make love now?

In the fourth watch I dream of my lover, late in the watch,
And when I dream of my darling lover he comes back again.
But alas, the fourth watch doesn't last that long anymore —
If my dream could last one moment longer, that would
   be worth millions!

In the fifth watch I dream of my lover — the rooster crows:
It would be great to keep on sleeping till the sky is bright.

---

[5] "Clouds and rain" is a common euphemism for having sex.
[6] Student Zhang 張生 is the male protagonist in the famous love comedy *Xixiang ji* 西廂記 (*The Story of the Western Wing*) by Wang Shifu 王實甫 (ca. 1300). Student Zhang falls in love with the beautiful maiden Yingying 鶯鶯, but when she is unavailable he is happy to have sex with her maid Reddy (Hongniang 紅娘), who serves as the couple's intermediary. For an English translation of this play see Wang Shifu 1995. While in the original version of the play Reddy rebuffs the advances of Student Zhang, she becomes much more co-operative in later adaptations of the story in various genres.

Who is able to order my dear darling to come back to me?
I'll slaughter the cock and open the wine to wait for him!

I dream again thru the five watches till the east turns red;
Now my darling lover is in the west while I am in the east.
If we have a bond we will meet despite a thousand miles;
If we lack a bond we won't meet even when face to face.

I've dreamt thru the five watches and go back to sleep;
I close the door, count on my fingers, and am surprised:
When with both hands I pull aside the red bed-curtains,
I am one person short on the mandarin-duck cushion!

Ten pieces of advice for my girlfriend

pp. 133–136

First of all I urge you, my darling, please stay at home;
Don't hang around with the neighbors left and right.
The neighbor to your left is such a lazy old creature!
The neighbor to your right is so very lazy in spinning!
People who keep such lazybones harm themselves.

Secondly I urge you, my darling, please stay at home;
You must be diligent in your spinning and embroidery.
First of all you can dress your darling and yourself;
Secondly you can outfit the people whom you love.
What the two of us have, you must keep it hidden.

Thirdly I urge you, my darling, if we have a bond —
Make money by selling vegetables from the garden.
Don't be like those cheap whores on the streets
Who once past thirty are not worth one copper.
No one will turn young again once they are old.

Fourthly I urge you, my darling, please stay at home;
Don't think time and again of going back to your mother's place.
At the crossroads there may be people who will try and rob you,

And the people who rob you, they may also well try and rape you,
And once you'll have lost your honor, you'll realize your mistake.

Fifthly I urge you my darling, if you do love me —
Now you are with me, don't also be with others!
First of all, fights over favors may lead to beatings;
Secondly, I might beat those fighting over favors.
Without wind dust might rise from level ground.

Sixthly I urge you, my darling, now we are a couple,
You still must serve your old man really quite well.
Of all things I most fear the mean eyes of others;
Leeches are always lurking in the deepest waves.
What you and I have, dear, shouldn't be exposed!

Seventhly I urge, my darling, when it's Start of Fall,[7]
When I will be suffering and have too much to bear,
If you then have some money, please help me out.
If you help me, I'll help you, sharing what we have:
Each river will flow out into the one large stream.

Eighthly I urge you, my darling, if it is Mid-Autumn —
At Mid-Autumn you may well be compared to Immortal
   Maiden He up in heaven,
While I may then well be compared to Lü Dongbin.[8]
Dongbin still has his way with Immortal Maiden He —
But make sure to keep it hidden from your husband.

Ninthly I urge you, my darling, let me tell you this:
On no account go to the upper and lower markets!
At the upper market you will find a romantic rake;

---

[7] Start of Fall is one of the 24 half-months in which the Chinese lunar is divided. The first day of Start of Fall is August 7th, 8th, or 9th.
[8] Immortal Maiden He 何仙姑 and Lü Dongbin 呂洞賓 are two of the Eight Immortals. Lü Dongbin is well-known for his amorous adventures. On Lü see Katz 1999. For a simple introduction to the legend of the Eight Immortals see Lai 1972.

At the lower market you will find a piece of scum,
And I can't match them when it comes to money.

Tenthly I urge you, my darling, I strongly urge you,
Not to imagine all kind of problems and issues.
Get up early at dawn, do your household chores;
When evening falls, take good care of your baby,
And everything will work out fine, will be great.

(*Note: This song lacks surprising turns in its construction, but I have included it here anyway because it manages to give expression to local sentiments. It is not a widely popular work.*)

A Song of Love Sickness

pp. 121–129

Because of love longing I attracted an illness,
But in front of my parents I didn't dare say so.
In case the final moment for me has arrived,
Please tell my darling so she can wear white.[9]

When she heard that her boyfriend had fallen ill,
She took out a lantern and set out that very night.
With both hands she pulled aside the bed-curtains
And asked her lover how serious his illness was.

Now how serious it is, or how passing perhaps,
Let me thank you my dear for taking this trouble.
Take a seat on the low bench in front of the bed,
And I will explain my situation to you at length.

At daytime I have a fever, at night I'm delirious;
Heart and mind are adrift in a frightening way.
Love longing has turned into a pulmonary fire,
But no one, feeling my pulse, can read it fully.

---

[9] White is the traditional color of mourning in China.

When one suffers an illness, one knows the cause:
Call a doctor as quick as you can to make you better.
And if you, my lover, you lack the money for that,
I will now immediately pawn all my winter clothes.

My dear darling, please let me tell you the truth:
It is not possible for you to pawn your clothes.
That set of clothes has not been made by me;
If your parents will know it, you'll get a beating.

My dear sweetheart, there's no need to worry:
There's nothing special in pawning one's clothes.
Pawned clothes one can easily redeem again,
But if one day you are gone, no scheme will do.

When you want tea or water, you just let me know —
His sweetheart went to a shop to pawn her clothes.
With a slip of her shirt she wiped away her tears:
As long as my lover is cured, my heart will be happy.

In front of the pawn shop she called out loudly,
She called for the manager to pawn her clothes.
The manager asked me what I wanted to pawn:
One blue shirt, a pair of pants, and also a collar.

When the manager asked me how much I wanted,
I said: Exactly one thousand three hundred three.
The manager handed me nine hundred and nine:
If it's less, you pay back less in sum and interest.

At the market crossing she invited a medical doctor;
His fee for a visit was two hundred coppers sharp.
If you can cure him so my dear darling will be better,
I will tell all people here what a good doctor you are.

Dear lady, now you have come to my humble office,
Tell me what kind of illness your lover has attracted.

By the side of this table is this little folding chair,
Please take a seat and then explain the situation.

He has a fever, he is dizzy, and he is also delirious;
At the three meals, he doesn't want to eat anything.
During the day her runs a fever, at night he is thirsty;
He is deaf and dumb, and his pains are insufferable.

Once she had told the doctor, he displayed his craft:
Raising his golden brush, he wrote out a prescription.
A hundred kinds of medicinal herbs were all listed,
Together with half a bowl of water and some ginger.

His darling went out to market to buy the simples;
She had arrived at the market even before dawn.
Having selected the simples, she went back home;
She hurried back home to be with her dear darling.

She selected the simples at a furious, hectic pace,
Then went into his room, asking him for his health.
She took out a stone warmer and also charcoal
In order to brew a concoction, and waved a fan.

In her left hand she held that good healing water;
In her right hand she held a good healing brew.
Once you will have downed this miraculous drug,
My dear, the length of your life will be extended.

Let me tell you, my sweetheart, this cruel truth:
Even dragon liver or phoenix gall can't cure me.
If King Yama decrees you'll die in the third watch,
There's not a chance you can wait till the fifth.

My dear darling, you shouldn't say these things!
Tell that King Yama you have to go back again.
If you cannot talk yourself out of the underworld,
Tears will gush down, more than I can wipe away.

Her lover was lying in bed, and she sat in front of it,
When he impressed on her these last few words:
If I, my darling, by any chance would not recover,
Please continue to love me whatever will happen.

As her tears gushed forth, her guts were wrenched:
This house and its *feng shui* have really done you in.
Dear, from now on I never will have any other lover,
And those sour and chilly days will be hard to bear.

While the young man was speaking, his voice halted,
And when she saw this, she truly was in for a fright:
His soul had left him, the color was gone from his face,
And when she then felt his heart, it was cold already.

Only eighteen, dear, and you have lost all awareness!
Such a handsome young man, and now you have died.
In this world of light you have not engendered a son,
So who will carry the incense burner[10] during sacrifices?

Your elder and younger brothers want to honor you,
They have bought a fine coffin in which you are laid.
Your coarse cotton clothes they have taken away,
And you have been dressed in fine silks and satins.

Now he has died, please don't bury him quickly;
Now he has been encoffined, please wait for me.
With both hands I lift the cover from the coffin:
You are now at peace, having done me a wrong!

My darling sweetheart has died way before his time;
His elder and younger brothers now all burn incense.
When I count out your years, you were still so young;
I fall down on my knees — this karma is unbearable!

---

[10] The local term for the ancestral tablet with the name of the deceased.

Your elder and younger brothers want to honor you;
They clean out the great hall and make it a chapel.
They invite Buddhist monks and some musicians too;
At the Seven Sevens these perform their ceremonies.[11]

When gongs have sounded, his portrait is displayed:
We now miss my darling lover, that one single person.
In the underworld they now count one extra ghost,
But the world of light at present has one person less.

We have bought paper money, we have bought boxes;
We cut out paper money, darling, to provide you with.
When the combined monks summon back your soul,
It is none else but I who is carrying the incense burner.

You are now in the endless expanse of the underworld,
While I stay here in the world of light, broken-hearted.
I have used paper to make a spirit house for you to live;
Your traces are all broken off, while my heart is broken.

The neighbors and relatives truly want to honor you,
They have bought fine presents for my darling lover.
The three sacrificial animals are prepared for offering,
But eating a bite while alive would be so much better.

My dear darling you have died way before your time;
It must be that you were fated to die while still young.
This house is thronged but you don't live here anymore,
So I would happily move away and settle on some peak.

---

[11] The Seven Sevens refer to the seventh, fourteenth, twenty-first, twenty-eighth, thirty-fifth, forty-second, and forty-ninth days following a person's death. On each of these days the soul of the deceased has to appear before one of the judges in the underworld, and the merit of reciting sutras will help him or her in passing on to the next stage more quickly. On the ten courts of the underworld see Teiser 1994.

Your elder and younger brothers want to honor you,
So they invited a geomancer to determine the location.
He walks from the head of the ridge to the ridge's tail,
And on Nine-Dragon Ridge my dear lover is laid to rest.

The neighbors and relatives want to honor my lover,
They escort my lover all the way up to the very ridge.
In front of the grave I weep, behind it I go back home,
But each word is dear sweetheart, each word darling.

My darling sweetheart died way before his time,
The more I think of it, the more it breaks my heart.
Your darling may be compared to a perfume sachet:
Without my lover to wear it, it gives off no scent.

This capital of a million to me is like piled-up mud;
Without my dear darling, there also should be no me.
Despite my young age I will live the life of a widow:
The crowing cock before dawn will bring much pain.

The Sixth Month cannot surpass the high noon heart:
The bell sounded at dawn will bring pain to the widow.
If someone so young can stay chaste as a widow,
Even iron ships will be able to the cross the oceans.[12]

Fish find it hard to ascend the rapids' fast stream;
To live the life of a widow so young is quite hard.
When I sleep till the fifth watch, filled with longing,
I have ruined the finest new mattress by rubbing.

(*Note: Even though the construction of this song is not marvelous, the emotions intensify more and more and make one shed tears.*)[13]

---

[12] "An iron ship crossing the ocean" is a traditional image for something impossible.
[13] Luo Xianglin 1936, 158–165 also includes a version of this set of songs and notes: "This poem circulates as an independent text."

CHAPTER 5

MORE DECLARATIONS OF LOVE AND OF DESPAIR

In recent years the more the intellectual climate has opened up in the People's Republic of China, the more the mountain songs that are quoted in scholarly publications have become variegated and outspoken in tone. The following selection is based on a recent study by Zhong Junkun 鍾俊昆, *Kejia shange wenhua yanjiu* 客家山歌文化研究 (2009). While the first three single mountain songs translated here are simple declarations of love, the third one of these discloses that many relationships were extra-marital affairs.

A second group of individual mountain songs also reveals one of the reasons why many young women might be tempted to engage in such an adulterous relationship. In traditional society only well-to-do families could marry their children in the proper fashion because such a wedding involved a considerable financial outlay on the side of both the bride and the groom. Less well-to-do families therefore, often had recourse to other arrangements. One possibility was to adopt a young girl as soon as a son was born so the couple could grow up together and marry at an appropriate age (a practice that is reflected in one of the songs transcribed by Huang Zunxian). Another possibility was to adopt a young girl while waiting for the birth of a son, so the prospective bride also could serve as the nanny once the hoped-for son was born. This practice might of course lead to a considerable age difference between the partners. The frustration of brides who have to take care of toddler husbands is reflected in a group of songs translated here.

Whatever the reason for an affair, not all relationships ended happily. If lovers, male or female, felt betrayed by their partners, two matching sets of twelve songs each provided them with plenty of material to curse their former sweethearts.

***

p. 110

The more I fool around with you, the more foolish I get:
We've fooled around so much I refuse to go home.
I'll get a sharp knife and cut down a bamboo stake
That will prop up the sun so it can't sink in the west.

p. 112

My dear darling has from birth those many talents —
By virtue of what kind of geomantic conditions?
When she casts you a glance it's as sharp as a sickle:
It cuts out your heart, without one speck of blood.

p. 171

My dear darling, right now I don't have any other lover;
I never had any intention at all to love some other guy.
My dear darling, I implore you, put all your worries aside —
Apart from my husband, no one's dearer to me than you.

p. 174

She's a grown-up girl of eighteen, he's a husband of three:
Weeping and crying, she takes him to bed in her arms.
If I wasn't so afraid of the beating I'd get from my parents,
I'd send you off to King Yama with one well-aimed kick!

The rice sprouts I hold in my hands are so tender and tiny:
How can I make this this rice ripen so it can fill my hunger?
My husband is still soundly sleeping in his rocking cradle:
How can I live to see the day we'll become man and wife?

She's a grown-up girl of eighteen, he's a husband of three:
She's not only his wife, but she also serves as his mother.
During the day she plays with her husband so he won't cry;
At night she tells her husband to join her in their bedroom,
Hoping this night her dear husband won't pee on the bed.

p. 175
She's a grown-up girl of eighteen, he's a husband of three:
Each night she sleeps on the bed with the boy in her arms.
When she has slept till midnight her longings are aroused,
Wondering whether he is perhaps her son or her husband.

She's a grown-up girl of eighteen, he's a husband of three:
Night after night his shit and his pee are all over the bed.
If it wasn't out of consideration for your father and mother,
I'd throw you out of the bed with some stomps and kicks.

Cursing my Darling

pp. 245–247.
First of all I curse you darling so you'll know my curse:
You were the one to lead me on, to make the first move.
In the beginning I was the richest family here in town,
But I spent it all, darling, in feeding and clothing you:
Because of you I now am suffering this lonely misery.

Secondly I curse you darling and also thank Heaven:
Never go and love a whore who's bereft of feeling!
In the beginning you said this would last till old age,
But right now it hasn't even lasted for half a year
And you already despise me because I lack money.

Thirdly I curse you darling and I will curse you well:
A wife should be like a female sparrow in the hills —
When she has laid her eggs, she'll cherish her chicks,
And then the male bird will take care of the female.
But the way in which you act, dear, leads to fights.

Fourthly I curse you darling for being such a sleaze.
I'll call the dragons down so they will subdue you.
May tigers devour you in the hills during daytime
And may ghosts whip you when sleeping at night
Till blood flows from your seven bodily openings.

Fifthly I curse you darling for what you truly are:
You're a shameless slut who only wants money.
You're just like the butcher in the market place:
Half a pound is four *liang*, payable on the spot.
Your only concern is ready cash in your hands.[1]

Sixthly I curse you darling for putting yourself on sale;
Without being asked you're offering yourself for sale.
You're like the meat from a pig that died in a plague:
I am not coming forward but you are pulling me over,
And when I don't have the money you sell on credit.

Seventhly I curse you darling for being a whore:
In this world, I discover, your lovers are many.
You dredge them up in the east and the west.
May you end up as a wandering beggar woman,
Stretching out your hand in your dying days.

Eighthly I curse you darling so that it will hurt:
May you stay alive while your husbands die.

---

[1] The text literally writes: "as if your eyebrows were on fire you only care about what is right in front of your eyes."

As soon as you marry one, may that one die;
May they die until you whore are crying tears,
Cry till your eyes go blind, and suffer a stroke!

Ninthly I curse you darling, I'll curse you well:
May the children you bear all happen to die.
As soon as you bear a child, may that one die;
May they die until you whore go hopping mad:
From the evil you've done, no good can come.

Tenthly I curse you darling so you may hear well:
On this world, I find, there is none as lazy as you.
One day of work you drag out till over ten days,
Ten days of work you drag out till over a hundred;
Till your dying day you will wear a tattered shirt.

Eleventhly I curse you darling so you may hear.
As a whore you're like an old roadside pavilion.
You're like the rotten benches in that pavilion
On which wandering riffraff and beggars sleep,
So you will suffer seizures till the day you die.

Twelfthly I curse you darling in a most cruel way:
You resemble the duck that is coming down river;
You resemble the duck that's crossing the stream:
A strong gust of the storm is meeting you head on
And deposits your corpse by the side of the road.

Cursing my Friend

pp. 247–248.

First of all I curse you friend so you'll know my curse —
You were the one to lead me on, to make the first move.
I was originally a prim and proper virgin, chaste and all,
But because of your childish clamoring and shouting,
You have ruined my good name, leaving me no face.

Secondly I curse you friend as rotten coffin timber:
You'll die in the middle of the night, the third watch.
How you resemble the lowly snail on top of the cliff
That's bragging and posturing, that's talking so big:
Even if you die at home, there's none to bury you.

Thirdly I curse you friend as a good-for-nothing scum:
Without any feeling, without any honor — that's you!
At the start you wormed your way into my affections;
Wonderful stories you told to me without exception —
Death to hose two flaps of skin on your brazen face!

Fourthly I curse you friend for your improper acts:
Once you had someone else, you abandoned me.
You'll suffer retribution for the evil you committed:
If you're not in for luck, you will meet with disaster,
And when I will witness that, my eyes will brighten.

Fifthly I curse you friend, and I'll curse you loudly:
You must remember the time you acted the thief.
You were tightly tied to a pillar with hemp ropes.
"I broke the peace," you wrote again and again,
And you begged me to act as your guarantor.

Sixthly I curse you friend as a cheat and a fraud;
You are like a beggar that begs on the streets.
As soon as you get some food, you swallow it.
You'll die by the roadside, and be buried there,
Ending up, it's clear, in the way of a pig or a dog.

Seventhly I curse you friend, I lazily curse you:
May the dragons come down and subdue you.
With one pair of chopsticks and a single bowl
You'll be reduced to begging, imploring our pity,
And then I will watch you suffering in that way.

Eighthly I curse you friend, so you will hear it:
You are like a rotten shit bucket in the garden,
You're like the stinking pee in that shit bucket,
And I will pour it out all over you, my friend —
If there is no one to watch it, it would be bad!

Ninthly I curse you friend so you will know it:
Because I loved you I had to suffer quite a lot.
How often I have been beaten by my husband!
How often I have been scolded by his mother!
I gave you my heart but received a dog's guts.

Tenthly I curse you friend: when winter arrives
I wish that you will be without any descendant,
Wish that you won't have any money or goods,
Wish that your reputation will have been ruined
And I may see you begging for food as a beggar.

Eleventhly I curse you friend: damned coffin wood!
Who's the one who has a spell that makes you die?
All the things you promised to me you didn't have,
You took advantage of me because I'm so honest!
May you lack an heir in this life — wait till the next.

Twelfthly I curse you friend, I'll curse you fully.
I don't need any of your trickery and deception.
You may have good looks but your heart is evil:
When you cross a bridge, you take the planks.
I will stay with my husband till the day I'll die.

PART TWO

NARRATIVE BALLADS

Introduction

Narrative ballads written in rhyming seven-syllable lines were a common feature of popular culture in many areas of late-imperial China and the Hakka communities were no exception. Under a wide variety of names, such ballads circulated in both oral and written format. While oral performances would adapt themselves to the dialect spoken by the audience, the written versions, despite incorporating a limited number of dialectical expressions, stayed very close to the standard vernacular of late-imperial China. The written versions of these ballads were once one of the staples of the local publishing industry, as Cynthia Brokaw has argued in her study of the Sibao book printers — from their home base in Western Fujian they supplied readers throughout the Hakka communities with the books they needed and wanted.[1] In many other parts of China, such ballads reached even wider audiences in the late 19th and early 20th

---

[1] Brokaw 2007, 499–506. Apart from some of the titles included in this volume, the Sibao publishers also printed such perennial favorites such as *Liang Shanbo and Zhu Yingtai* (*Liang Shanbo Zhu Yingtai* 梁山伯祝英台) and *Meng Jiangnü* 孟姜女 (the version of the Meng Jiangnü ballad printed by the Jingxianzhai 敬賢齋 turns out to be basically identical to an edition put out in the early nineteenth century in Xiamen and translated in Idema 2008, 61–79).

centuries when imported printing technologies such as lithography made it possible to produce such popular reading materials both more cheaply and more attractively and also in much larger print runs.

Unfortunately, very little of such Hakka ballad literature survives because avid readers would read their copies to shreds and libraries did not collect such "vulgar" materials. During the struggle against the Four Olds of the Cultural Revolution (if not earlier) in the People's Republic of China, many copies were condemned and destroyed as they were deemed to be superstitious and obscene books. The continuing popularity of these ballads with common readers in Hakka-speaking communities, however, was attested by the appearance of cyclostyled copies of some titles as soon as the fury of the Cultural Revolution abated. Two of the texts translated in this section (the first and the third) are from a modern edition that is based on one of these cyclostyled copies, while the other text (the second) is based on a modern edition prepared in Taiwan. On Taiwan, the major publisher of Hakka ballads was the Zhulin shuju 竹林書局 in Xinzhu, which continued to be in business until the 1990s. In order to distinguish its Hakka ballads from the Minnanese ballads it also published, it identified the Hakka materialsas written in Guandongyu 廣東語, as most Hakka had arrived on the island from Guangdong Province. In the older texts the language is very close to the standard traditional vernacular of narrative ballads, but in the texts composed on Taiwan in the first half of the 20th century, the language became increasingly open to Hakka elements.[2]

The most common term for this type of narrative ballad in the Hakka-speaking communities is *zhuanben* 傳本 (story books). In southeastern Jiangxi, however, the common term for this kind of ballad is *guwen* 古文 (old texts), a term which in this context is probably best translated as "old tales."[3] In Taiwan, these Hakka ballads

---

[2] A catalogue of *zhuanzai* available on Taiwan is provided by Qiu Chunmei 2003, 147–189. Also see Huang Rongluo 2005. The texts of many *zhuanzai* are available on the *Kejiayu suqu changben ziliaoku* 客家語俗曲唱本資料庫, a website maintained by Wang Shunlong 王順隆.

[3] Chen Hong 2007; Huang Yuying and Yuan Dawei 2008.

were designated as *zhuanzai* 傳仔 (stories). The topics of such ballads derive from Chinese history and legend, drama and fiction and many are shared with other genres of popular literature in other parts of China. For this volume I have selected stories that are exclusive to the repertoire of *chuanben/zhuanzai* such as *The Tale of Tang Xian*, or that appear to have a special popularity with Hakka readers, such as *Ten-Mile Pavilion* and *Selling Lanterns*.

CHAPTER 1

TEN-MILE PAVILION

This ballad tells the story of a young man who falls in love with a beautiful maiden and forces himself on her for a night of torrid sex. On parting, she then provides him with sound moral advice on how to behave for the rest of his life while she sees him off to the first ten-miles pavilion. The ballad ends with the laments of the two lovers who never will be able to marry one another, as she has been promised already to another man — at their parting she actually gives her new-found lover a substantial amount of money so he can obtain a proper wife.[4] Ballads (and plays) with a storyline that adheres to this pattern are not only encountered in the Hakka-speaking areas of Southeastern China, but also (to judge by materials on the web) in areas as far apart as Shaanxi and Sichuan and Zhejiang and Jiangsu.[5]

---

[4] This long narrative ballad should be distinguished from a long set of mountain songs of the same title. In this set the songs are alternately sung by a wife and her husband when the latter is leaving on a business trip to sell tea. This extensive set is also included as one scene of the traditional Hakka opera *Zhang Sanlang Sells Tea* (*Zhang Sanlang maicha* 張三郎賣茶; also known as *The Tea Seller* [*Maichalang* 賣茶郎]).

[5] The place of action and the names of the protagonists may vary in these versions, but the main female character is usually named Liu Xiuxing 劉秀英. Her lover is often given the surname Ma 馬. The first accidental meeting of the lovers is often brought about when the young man goes flying his kite which then falls into the girl's flower garden when its string snaps. For a number of texts see http://bbs.

In some texts that belong to this family, the ballad ends with the despair of the parting lovers (one version even concludes with the girl's suicide[6]), but in some rewritings the detail of the girl's engagement is omitted, so they may become true lovers hoping for a speedy marriage.[7] There are also versions that conclude with the narrative of the couple's further adventures and their final happy reunion.[8]

The translation in this chapter of *Ten-Mile Pavilion* is based on the edition of one Hakka version presented by Hu Xizhang 胡希張 in his *Kejia zhubange yanjiu* 客家竹板歌研究 (2010: 357–368). Hu's edition is based on a mimeographed copy of the text originally bought in 1977 in Wuping District in Fujian by a nephew of the mountain-song singer Zhou Tianhe 周天和 and now in the possession of the latter.[9] The modern writer You Shengzhong 游生忠, who may

---

ahzyw.com/topic-91141.html (accessed June 13th, 2014). Some bloggers are so upset by the scandalous nature of the first parts of the ballad (the scenes of seduction and sex) that they are only willing to provide the text of the moral advice Liu Xiuying urges on her lover as she sees him off to Ten-Mile Pavilion (http://blog.sina.com.cn/s/blog_4a6e9e47010006ka.html; accessed June 13th, 2014). For photographs of an old manuscript copy of a *Ten-Mile Pavilion* ballad see http://book.kongfz.com/item_pic_1544_183183458/; accessed on June 13th, 2014).

[6] See *In Praise of a Kite* (*Fengzheng fu* 風箏賦). http://www.rmtd.com.cn/bbs/forum.php?mod=viewthread&tid=194 (accessed June 15th, 2014)

[7] For a modern adaptation of the story as a musical skit from Yunhe (Zhejing province) see Baidu.baike (http://baike.baidu.com/view/3516533.htm, accessed June 11th, 2014). This playlet is described as a revision of a traditional version from the Qing dynasty. The text is said to have been taken from Wu Wei 無為, *Xiangtu Yunhe* 鄉土雲和 (Zhongguo tianma chubanshe, 2007), a book which I have not seen. In line with modern sensibilities, the girl, on parting in the morning, urges the young man to have a matchmaker sent to her home so their affair will end in a marriage. In one untitled version available on the web Liu Xiuying even manages to talk her suitor in abandoning his plans of sleeping with her, after which she send him off with warmest feelings. (http://zhidao.baidu.com/lijk?url=gBISq1VarES4FxKF5Q-AtFILHpeQvhQgyB4e3Urn.Skwb35DerM6au4O6pe-NxNmPqUyAcOSKrtmhxea, accessed June 13th, 2014).

[8] See for instance *The Kite* (*Fengdeng Ji* 風燈記) that circulated among the Tu of Enshi district in Sichuan. http://bbs.enshi.cn/thread-505195-1-1.html (accessed June 15th, 2014). The happy ending is also encountered in the many dramatic adaptations from the Hakka areas entitled *New Ten-Mile Pavilion* (*Xin Shiliting* 新十里亭).

[9] Zhou Tianhe (b. 1930) has been a professional performer of mountain songs and bamboo clapper songs for most of his life. Born in Thailand, he came to China at

have seen this version of *Ten-Mile Pavilion* as well the old printed edition to be discussed below, had high praise for the moral advice dispensed by the girl while she sees her lover off, and commented as follows:

> The contents of *Ten-Mile Pavilion* are excellent; they are desirable. From the intent of the editor of *Ten-Mile Pavilion* one can gauge that the main point of the song is contained in the tenfold parting scene, but alas there have been some depraved people who have inserted quite a number of vulgar and low-class lines that are not only extremely unhealthy but also damage social morals. As a result, this work has been polluted, and *Ten-Mile Pavilion* has even become a work that people don't dare sing on public occasions.[10]

In his introductory comments, Hu too notes his amazement at the internal heterogeneity of the text, which he describes as follows:

> *Ten-Mile Pavilion* is very unique. As far as its contents are concerned it is different from ordinary ballads, because it is a composite of a ballad, an erotic text, a moral tract, and Hakka love songs, so it can be called a "four-unlike."[11]

Hu, who elsewhere argues that the bamboo-clapper songs developed in the early 20th century from the narrative ballads (*guwen*) as

---

the age of four and despite poverty managed to complete a lower middle school education. He had led an itinerant life as a peddler and performer in the early 1950s, then became a farmer, and eventually became a full-time professional performer in 1963, based in Xingning. His heydays as a performer were the 1980s and 1990s. Throughout his life he avidly collected materials that in one way or another might be of use to him in expanding his repertoire, also creating many new items. His *Second-Hand Zhang Rents out his Wife* is translated in the third part of this volume. Hu Xizhang 2010, 296–299 presents a brief biographical sketch. Hu Xizhang also composed a full-length biography as *Shange dashi Zhou Tianhe zhuan* 山哥大師周天和傳, Beijing: Zhongguo wenlian chubanshe, 2004, which I have not seen.

[10] You Shengzhong 2010. In this little article You states that he has produced a more decent rewriting but I have not seen this.

[11] Hu Xizhang 2010, 357. The "four-unlike" (*sibuxiang* 四不像) is mythical creature made up of parts of different animals.

performed by artists from southeastern Jiangxi, explains this heterogeneity as follows:

> But this is exactly the usual procedure of the *guwen* artists from Southern Jiangxi who insert moral tracts and mountain songs into their ballads when they perform them. As far as the form is concerned, it is not written in five-line stanzas and also not in four-line stanzas, but it is made up of couplets, just as Old Texts. It is a living fossil left behind when *guwen* were introduced into eastern Guangdong and provides rare evidence for the study of the development process of bamboo-clapper songs.[12]

Whether or not we follow Hu's historical explanation of the origin of bamboo-clapper songs, he correctly point out the affinity of some of the materials to other genres in Hakka popular literature.

Apart from the text edited by Hu Xizhang, we have least three different versions of *Ten-Mile Pavilion* from Hakka areas that are available in print.[13] Hu points out that in Wuping this story was also

---

[12] Hu Xizhang 2010, 358. Hu's statement here is influenced by his contacts with veteran *guwen* performers from southern Jiangxi such as Xiao Qiulin 蕭秋林, who discussed his performance of *Ten-Mile Pavilion* with Hu in an interview which Hu conducted in 2005. Xiao claims that there are many parts of *Ten-Mile Pavilion* he would not sing in performance because the content was too obscene. When Hu suggested that the original text might include language from *Eighteen Strokes* (*Shiba mo* 十八摸), Xiao answered in the affirmative. (Hu Xizhang 2010, 45). *Eighteen strokes* is an erotic song that was widely popular in traditional China and circulated both orally and in writing. It describes a man stroking his lover's body, starting from her hair and ultimately reaching her private parts. For a discussion of this type of erotic songs and their printed versions, see Kuzay 2009. One web-version of *Ten-Mile Pavilion* (http://blog.sina.com.cn/s/blog_530100qqbb.html; accessed June 13th, 2014) may well be a *guwen* version from Southeastern Jiangxi as it mentions the term *guwen* in one of its opening lines, but it is far more subdued in its description of the couple's lovemaking than the version edited by Hu Xizhang. This version is interesting because it includes a *shisonglang* 十送郎 (seeing off one's lover ten times) song before the couple's early morning departure from Liu Xiuying's house. In such songs, the female party accompanies her lover/husband from the bed in her chamber to outside the house, pausing at ten objects that each gives rise to one song.

[13] An additional version, this time from Ninghua, may be found at http://www.wuzuren.cn/simple/?t2943.html.

performed as a bamboo-clappers song. A bamboo-clappers version of *Ten-Mile Pavilion* from Wuping is reprinted by Liu Dake in his *Tianye zhong de diyu shehui yu wenhua* (*Local Society and Culture in the Fields*) 2007: 280–282. Liu based his version on a manuscript copy he had acquired in the course of his fieldwork. A bamboo-clappers song version, as performed in Yongding in 1990 by Lan Ruiteng, is included in the *Zhongguo geyao jicheng: Fujian juan*, and a translation of that version, which shows a clear textual link to Hu's edition, is presented in Appendix I.

Apart from these two recently published texts, there also exists a slightly damaged copy of a woodblock edition from the nineteenth century collected by Cynthia Brokaw.[14] A translation of that version is also included in Appendix I. The latter version is a narrative ballad like the version translated in this chapter, but considerably shorter. It very much focuses on the young man's seduction of the heroine, and her moral advice to him while she sees him off early in the morning after their night of love-making. Whereas the later versions develop the plot of the story by the addition of the characters of the servants of the two lovers and their complicity in their masters' affair, these characters are completely absent in the 19th century version. The version edited by Hu also greatly extends the ending of the story by adding songs of love-longing on the part of the separated lovers.[15]

A ten-mile pavilion is a simple covered structure along a major road, built to provide travelers with shelter against the sun and rain. Such structures were put up at regular intervals. The mile is here the

---

[14] Brokaw 2007, 502 mentions that (a) version(s) of this tale also was/were published by the Sibao publishers in Western Fujian. The copy she collected of an undated woodblock-printed edition is unfortunately incomplete. This version originally consisted of thirteen sheets, of which the first is missing and the second is damaged.

[15] In the Wu-dialect area too, modern editions of mountain song narratives based on oral performances tend to be much longer and much more circumstantial in their narrative than the woodblock-printed or manuscript versions of the same stories from the 19th and early 20th centuries. McLaren 2010 also notes that the earlier versions tend to be more explicit in their erotic descriptions because contemporary performers have learned to be cautious when outsiders are present. This may well apply to the bamboo-clappers song version of *Ten-Mile Pavilion*, which is based on a performance recorded in 1990, but would not seem to apply to the ballad printed by Hu. A translation of this bamboo-clappers song version is also included in Appendix I.

traditional Chinese mile (*li* 里), which measures slightly more than one third of an international mile. At about one hour's walking distance outside the city, the first ten-mile pavilion was a popular spot for seeing off departing travelers and many plays and ballads contain a scene of parting lovers set at a ten-mile pavilion.[16] One way to structure such a parting scene in ballads is by moving from the one-mile pavilion, to the two-mile pavilion, and on until the ten-mile pavilion is reached, the female party declaring her love and providing advice at each stop. This may then be followed by ten more songs in reverse order, in which the female party expresses her sadness and sorrow as she returns home.[17] The sequence can be further expanded by adding songs narrating the sadness and sorrow of the male party as he moves from the ten-mile pavilion to the twenty-mile pavilion.

***

Ten-Mile Pavilion

Ever since Pangu opened up heaven and earth,[18]
Each Son of Heaven has had his own ministers.
But let's not talk of the stories in earlier writings,
Let me start out by singing of Ten-Mile Pavilion.
   In Nanjing there lived a magnate surnamed Li,
Who was famed far and wide for his great wealth.
He not only had five sons but also two daughters;
These five talented sons had all passed the exams.

---

[16] For instance, the repertoire of Dunhuang opera (Dunhuang quzixi) from Northwestern Gansu includes a short play titled *Ten-Mile Pavilion* (*Shili ting*) which is an adaptation of the famous parting scene of Student Zhang 張生 and Yingying 鶯鶯 in Wang Shifu's 王實甫 *Story of the Western Wing* (*Xixiangji* 西廂記). In this playlet too, the lovers proceed from One-Mile Pavilion to Ten-Mile Pavilion as Yingting presses her advice on her lover now he is departing for the capital to take part in the examinations. *Dunhuang quzixi* 2010, 145–147.

[17] Li Guisheng 2013.

[18] According to one Chinese origin myth, heaven and earth were made out of the body of the giant Pangu 盤古 upon his death. Pangu is also widely venerated as the creator of the world and mankind in many of the non-Han ethnic groups of Southern China. See Schipper a.o. 2011.

The name of his elder daughter was Li Fengqin,
The name of her younger sister was Li Xiuying.
Xiuying had reached the sweet age of eighteen;
She looked as beautiful as a heavenly immortal.
   She excelled on the zither and in go, calligraphy and painting,
Was an expert in embroidering flowers, sketching phoenixes.
She was not only very kind and obedient but also very polite;
Her mind was quick, her hands were nimble: such a smart girl!

In the city of Nanjing there also lived a young man Chen:
With clear eyebrows and sparkling eyes he cut quite a figure.
His face was like that of Pan An and resembled the moon,[19]
He was as handsome as Song Yu with his sensual expression.[20]
   One day he went into the city just for his amusement;
The springtime weather was charming and very enticing.
From the eastern street he walked back to the western street,
Roamed the southern street, stopped on the northern street.
   His only intention was to pursue flowers like a butterfly,
To find out pampered girls from the inner apartments.
Romance always has been the business of young men;
A butterfly's love for flowers has always been our mind.
   As he was walking along he came to Yunhua courtyard,
And there he suddenly saw the body of that girl Xiuying:
Her eyes like autumn waves put even the moon to shame,
And her graceful figure was the very image of seduction.
   The hair on her head had been done up in a dragon-bun;
The red haze on her cheeks resembled peach blossoms.
As soon as our hero had seen her, he was dumb-struck;
Eyes staring blankly ahead, he didn't make any move.
   The young girl turned around, going back to her room;
The way in which she moved really aroused his desire:

---

[19] Pan An 潘安 is the epitome of male beauty. The character derives from that of the poet Pan Yue 潘岳 (247–300). Pan Yue is said to have been extremely handsome: when he rode through the capital in his carriage, it ended up being filled with the fruits amorous women threw at him in order to attract his attention.
[20] Song Yu 宋玉 lived in the third century BC. His handsome features made him attractive to women as he narrates in one of his own poems.

"If I could only be together with her behind bed-curtains,
I'd be happy to die and descend to the Yellow Springs!"[21]

When he had returned home, he was wasted by longing,
He was wasted by longing for that fine girl Li Xiuying.
During the day he desired her, at night he desired her,
And at mealtimes he couldn't swallow any tea or rice.
   His servant boy asked him what was bothering him,
Why his brow was furrowed, why he was depressed.
The young man opened up and told him the reason:
"I'm filled with longing for that nice girl Li Xiuying.
   If there's a flower and you don't pick it, you're no butterfly;
If there's a beauty and you don't seek her, your life is in vain.
Human life resembles a dream that urges spring to age,
How can I live through these fine days and not use them?
   But pondering the case from all sides, I can't find a solution,
That's why I show this sorrowed look and am filled with grief."
His servant boy whispered in his ear and told him softly
By which way, by what means he might get close to her.
   The young man nodded his head with a smile on his lips:
"The marvelous scheme you propose enlightens my mind.
Once I will have entered the pass that guards the beauty,
I will dredge up if needs be a needle from the ocean floor.[22]
   I don't fear how high the wind-swept waves may rise;
I'm not afraid of the many dangers waiting on the road.
If there is a method, it all comes down to hard work:
Even an iron pole can be polished into a tiny needle."

Now his mind was made up, he left as fast as he could,
Because he wanted to make love to that pretty girl.
As long as the string of love is tightly fastened,[23]
Blue Heaven will never betray a devoted person.

---

[21] The Yellow Springs are the world of the dead.
[22] That is, I will achieve the impossible.
[23] According to a well-known tale from the Tang dynasty (617–906), lovers who are predestined for each other are tied together with a red string by the Old Man in the Moon. For a translation of this tale, see Kao 1985, 271–274, "The Inn of Betrothal."

Quickly now the golden bird was sinking in the west
While the jade hare once again was rising in the east.[24]
On him he carried a dagger for his personal protection,
And he quickly hurried on so as to waste no time.
   When the young man came to the Li family garden,
He hid himself near the lotus pond's green bamboos.
Then he saw a servant girl appear, who lighted a lamp,
And his heart was filled with joy as he silently thought:
   "Tonight the moon is bright and the stars are few,
I cannot allow this good opportunity go by unused."
Without a sound he walked up to the servant girl,
And explained to her his purpose in coming there:
   "I beg you to help me as much as you can: my heart
Is pulled by the red string of the Old Man in the Moon.
If I can obtain a Magpie Bridge to make for a meeting,[25]
All my life I'll never forget your great favor and love."
   When that servant girl saw how true and sincere he was,
She very much wanted to help him to succeed in his plan,
So she told the young man: "You cannot be so impatient,
Hide yourself in the shade of flowers, below the willows.
   When the third watch has passed and no one is stirring,[26]
Come in through the back door, but don't make any noise."

When the young man heard this, he was filled with joy:
A stone had opened the heaven below the pond' surface!
   But he saw that the door to her room was firmly closed:
How could he ever come close to that young girl's body?

---

[24] The golden bird refers here to the crow that inhabits the sun; the jade hare is one of the inhabitants of the moon.
[25] According to one of China's most popular legends the Weaving Maiden (Vega) and Buffalo Boy (Altair) are a loving couple, but because they neglected their duties upon their marriage the Jade Emperor assigned them positions on opposite sides of the Heavenly River (the Milky Way); they are allowed to meet once every year, on the night of the seventh day of the Seventh Month (according to the lunar calendar) when magpies form a bridge for them across the river. See Idema 2009a, 79–99.
[26] In traditional China the night was divided in five watches. The third watch corresponds to roughly 11 pm to 1 am.

A snake that has entered a bamboo tube cannot wriggle;
A dumb man may have a mouth but cannot speak out!
   As he pondered his quandary, he saw no way forward,
His heart was in turmoil, and he didn't know what to do.
He was about to sound the gong and silence the drums —[27]
It seemed as if his mental anguish had all been in vain.
   While the young man stood there at a loss what to do,
He suddenly heard the servant girl who softly told him:
"If you want to make love to her, what's your problem?
Pry open the door to her room, and you can get near her."
   Then he thought of the dagger he was carrying with him:
"Why shouldn't I try to surprise her just like a falcon?"
So he took out that dagger he was carrying with him
And lightly, so lightly pried open the door to her room.

He pushed open the door, and then closed it behind him.
Inside the room the only light was that of an oil lamp.
He wanted to say some words to comfort the young girl,
But as a total stranger he had no idea what to say.
   He lightly so lightly pulled aside the red bed-curtains,
But then that girl all of a sudden turned herself around
And cried out: "Who are you, from where do you come
That you rashly dare enter into my private apartment?"
   The young man bowed down, wished her his blessings,
And said: "I love you, you're like a heavenly immortal!
I don't care about wealth and status in the world of men
Because I love only you, that precious body of yours!"
   When the young girl heard this, she felt truly ashamed:
"You little devil, what a daring temerity you display!
If you do not run off now, I will start to cry for help.
Then we'll see where you manage to hide yourself!"

---

[27] In the army the drum was sounded for the attack; when the gong was sounded the troops were ordered to retreat. Making love is often described in battle terms.

He addressed her very politely, saying, "Young lady Li,
Please listen to this honest declaration of my love.
I am not a bandit and I also am not a thief,
All my life I've been in thrall of your fame.

   I live in this city and am known as young man Chen,
I am eighteen years old and am filled with deep love.
I don't care for all the wealth and riches of my family,
All I want is to share couch and cushion with you!

   Yesterday when I passed by your flower garden,
I was smitten by love as soon as I caught a glimpse.
Day and night I was filled with longing for you;
My greatest happiness in life will be to tie the knot.

   Tea and rice at each mealtime I don't want to eat,
With all my heart I only seek your love and affection,
I implore you, young lady, please take pity on me,
Show compassion for me and my undivided heart."

   When the girl had heard this, she silently pondered;
With lowered head she kept thinking, without a word.
Then she lightly opened her lips and replied to him:
"You, a students of books, should behave correctly!

   My father Magnate Li loves me like a pearl in his hand,
He has promised me as bride to a man surnamed Wang.
Since ancient times a good horse refuses two saddles;
How can one thread pass through two needle holes?

   Threefold obedience and fourfold virtue are old norms,[28]
So, guarding my body like a jade, I stay free from dust.
It's common sense to stick to these ancient teachings,
How could I as a decent girl throw away my virginity?

   You are the son of a family with a scholarly reputation,
I implore you, consider this carefully, don't commit rape.

---

[28] As a daughter a woman should obey her father; as a wife her husband, and as a widow her grown-up son. The four virtues expected of a woman are chastity, proper speech, a pleasant expression, and diligence in spinning and weaving.

A crime committed in the dark still invites disaster, and
He who breaks the law is bound to suffer the punishment."

The young man knelt on the floor and implored the girl:
"Please, smart and intelligent girl, please listen to me.
    The honey bee visits the flowers and so makes honey,
Even empresses and palace ladies have secret lovers.
Chang'e in the moon has found a partner and a mate,[29]
The Weaving Maiden sleeps with the Buffalo Boy Star.
    Fourth Sister came down to sleep with Cui Wenrui,[30]
Seventh Sister slept with the man surnamed Dong,[31]
Lotus-Blossom fell in love with Yang Wenguang,[32]
And the Immortal Maiden longed for Lü Dongbin.[33]

---

[29] Chang'e 嫦娥 is the goddess of the moon. When her husband Hou Yi 后羿 had obtained the elixir of immortality, she stole it from him and drank it all, whereupon she rose into the sky. In the Palace of Spreading Cold she now lives a life of eternal loneliness, longing for a partner.

[30] Fourth Sister is one of the celestial seven sisters, who are described as the daughters or granddaughters of the Jade Emperor in Heaven. In a widely popular legend Fourth Sister secretly leaves heaven to join the poor but filial student Cui Wenrui 崔文瑞. When a rich man frames her lover for theft, she defeats all government troops; when the Jade Emperor summons her back to heaven she defeats all celestial troops sent against her until she is allowed to bring Cui Wenrui (and his mother) with her to heaven. See Idema 2012.

[31] Seventh Sister is the youngest of seven celestial sisters. When the filial son Dong Yong 董永 sold himself into servitude in order to be able to provide his deceased father with a decent burial, the Jade Emperor ordered her to descend to earth and assist him in paying back his debt. In a hundred days she had woven enough silk to obtain Dong Yong's release. See Idema 2009a.

[32] Yang Wenguang 楊文廣 is one of the generals of the Yang family, who acquired their fame in the wars of the Song against the Liao at the end of the 10th century. See Idema and West 2013. In one of the 16th century novels on the exploits of the generals of the Yang family, Yang Wenguang on a mission to Mt. Tai is forced to marry three bandit princesses after he has been defeated by them, but none of them is called Lotus Blossom (Hehua 荷花).

[33] Lü Dongbin 呂洞賓 is a member of the group of Eight Immortals. He is well-known for his many flirtations with mortal and divine women. The immortal maiden mentioned here may refer to Immortal Maiden He 何仙姑, the only female member of the group of Eight Immortals. See Katz 1999.

Third Sister secretly promised herself to Liu Wenxi,[34]
And Green-Coat had his way with those girls of Liu;[35]
Wang Ying secretly married a maiden of high heaven,[36]

---

[34] Third Sister is one of the children of the divinity of Mt. Hua. She forced the student Liu Wenxi 劉文錫 to become her lover. When their affair was discovered by her brother Erlang 二郎, she was imprisoned under a mountain, from which she was eventually freed by her son Chenxiang 沉香. See Dudbridge 2005; for a full translation of one of the many versions of this legend see Idema 2011b.

[35] One of the best known exemplars of male chastity in Chinese history is Guan Yu 關羽 (d. 219), one of the sworn brothers of Liu Bei 劉備 (161–223). At one stage of the civil wars at the end of the Han dynasty, Guan Yu. while in charge of Liu Bei's wife and concubine, is separated from Liu Bei and forced to take service with the rival warlord Cao Cao 曹操 (155–220). One of the conditions of Guan Yu's surrender to Cao Cao is that he will be given an accommodation with a divided courtyard, so he and the women will all have their privacy. Later, when Guan Yu has learned the whereabouts of Liu Bei, he leaves Cao Cao and returns Liu Bei's wives to his brother without ever having touched them even in the slightest. This episode in the career of Guan Yu was popular on stage from an early date. See Idema and West 2013, 105–151. The story of Guan Yu's chastity is told at great length in the 16th century novel *Romance of the Three Kingdoms* (*Sanguo yanyi* 三國演義), Ch. 25–27. See Luo Guanzhong 1991, 192–212. Guan Yu was conventionally depicted dressed in a green coat. Our male protagonist here makes the outrageous claim that Guan Yu of course must have taken advantage of the situation to have sex with the two women.

[36] Wang Ying 王英 (my emendation for Yuying 玉英) is a member of the famous band of righteous robbers based at Liangshan, whose activities are described in the 16th century novel *Water Margin* (*Shuihu zhuan* 水滸傳). Wang Ying is described as an ugly and lustful dwarf. During an attack on the Zhu Family Manor he is captured by Hu Sanniang 扈三娘. In the novel Hu Sanniang is described as beautiful young woman and a fierce female warrior. When she has been captured by the Liangshan heroes and when Wang Ying has been freed, the leader of the band assigns Hu Sangniang as wife to Wang Ying. See Shi Nai'an and Luo Guanzhong 1980, 755–817. In some other versions of this legend this line refers to the relation of Wang Lanying 王蘭英 and He Wenxiu 何文秀. The latter is the male protagonist of *The Jade Hairpin* (*Yuchai Ji* 玉釵記) an extremely complicated *chuanqi* play of the Ming dynasty. In some versions of later adaptations of this play one of He's female partners is called Wang Lanying 王蘭英. After this high-born young lady has bestowed her favors on He Wenxiu, the lovers are separated to be reunited only after many adventures. The three characters for "a maiden from high heaven" (*jingtiannü* 京天女) might conceivably be a mistake for the Chinese characters that make up the name of He Wenxiu if written in (poorly legible) running script. If we

Whereas Zongbao secretly made out with Mu Guiying.[37]
   Master Peng's life was set to end at eight hundred;[38]
Ancient Zhang still had affairs at twenty thousand.[39]
When yesterday I happened to pass by a monastery,
I overheard an arhat flirting with bodhisattva Guanyin.[40]

---

would follow that reading, the line would have to be rendered "Wang [Lan]ying secretly gave herself to He Wenxiu."

[37] Yang Zongbao 楊宗保 is one of the junior generals of the Yang family. While still a very young man he is defeated by the barbarian princess Mu Guiying 木桂英 (穆桂英) who then falls in love with him and forces him to marry her, whereupon she joins his side and becomes one of the most famous women warriors of Chinese tradition. See Idema and West 2013, 182; 194.

[38] Peng Zu 彭祖, known as the most long-lived mortal, lived to over 800 years. For a translation of one of the versions of the modern legend that explains why he attained that age, see Anonymous 2013. In Hu Xizhang's edition the last three characters of this line read *yan gying si* 陽應死 (his life in this world had to end). Other versions instead write *yin bing si* 淫病死 (he died because of lechery) or a very similar phrase.

[39] Ancient Zhang (Zhang Gu 張古) probably refers to Zhang Guolao 張果老, the oldest of the Eight Immortals. He was a white bat at the beginnings of time that eventually achieved human form. See Lai 1972. Here his legend would appear to be conflated with the Tang-dynasty tale of Old Zhang (Zhang Lao 張老). Zhang Lao is an old and poor gardener, but when a local noble family seeks a groom for their daughter, he is easily able to pay the ridiculously high bride price they demand. Later the couple moves away. When the bride's brother comes to visit them, he finds they are living in utter luxury, and he is later sent home with great gifts. For a translation of the Tang tale see Kao 1985, 281–287. A vernacular retelling was included by Feng Menglong 馮夢龍 (1574–1646) in his *Stories Old and New* (*Gujin xiaoshuo* 古今小說, 1620/1621), a collection of forty vernacular short stories. For a translation of that version see Yang and Yang 2000, 572–589.

[40] The bodhisattva Guanyin 觀音 (Avalokitesvara) may take on any shape when he answers the prayers of those of her believers who appeal to him to be rescued from acute distress. Since the 10th century the bodhisattva has been venerated especially in her female manifestation as the White-Robed Guanyin or the Guanyin of the Southern Sea. In her female manifestations the bodhisattva is the perfection of female beauty, and the bodhisattva will not hesitate to use this beauty to convert men. Eventually Guanyin would become one of the most widely venerated and most powerful deities of the Chinese pantheon. See Yu 2001. In the Chinese legends of Princess Miaoshan 妙善 the future bodhisattva will display a conspicuous chastity throughout her human life. See Dudbridge 2004 and Idema 2008. Arhats are those

If even gods and immortals engage in amorous affairs,
How can you blame young men in the prime of youth!
It is only Buddha in heaven who is clear like a mirror —
But who knows whether that is a lie or perhaps a fact.

If the butterfly doesn't love flowers it's a silly moth;
If a man doesn't desire women, he is only a silly fool.
If a snake doesn't swallow a man, it is only an eel;
If a wasp doesn't sting men, it is only a buzzing fly.

Even horses follow their saddle to pursue their masters,
There're those that guard the lowly to pay back their owners.[41]
If animals still act in accordance with their own feelings,
How can you blame me, this young man, for loving you!

If you, dear girl, refuse to take pity on me for my love,
I can only slit my throat here and now to prove my love."
The girl now was riding a tiger and couldn't step down,
He had stirred her heart: she truly was moved to concern.

Even mandarin-ducks know they have to form couples,
Migrating geese, flying high, don't abandon each other.
And blushing all over she comforted him in these words:
"Moved by your affection, I cannot refuse your love!

I am now of a mind to prove you my love and affection,
But please, my dear lover, please don't brag about it.
A swallow, carrying loam, has to keep its mouth shut;
A spider that spits out thread feels it belly all hurting.[42]

If one person informs ten, ten will inform a hundred,
And even an idle rumor then becomes established fact.
A hemp cloth washing the face: it's our first meeting;
Don't tell idle stories, please preserve my reputation."

---

persons who achieved enlightenment upon hearing the preaching of the Buddha. Buddhist monasteries often contain statues of both Guanyin and a group of arhats.
[41] The meaning of these two lines is not clear to me and the translations are tentative. The *guwen* version of the ballad mentioned in note 7 here has the following two lines: "A horse, born without a saddle, will seek a rider/ And a dog has the loyal spirit to save its master."
[42] The word for "thread" (*si*) is has the same pronunciation as the word for "thought/longing" (*si*).

With both hands he opened the red gauze bed-curtains;
They lay together and flew together like mandarin-ducks.
The body of the fellow was sparkling white like snow;
The body of the maiden was sparkling white like frost.

    The brocaded blanket covered him, and he covered her;
The straw mattress supported her, and she supported him.
One human being on top of another: sky covering earth;
Flesh was hidden inside flesh when yin enveloped yang.

    As long as the golden disk had not yet appeared,[43] none
Was willing to retreat his troops and abandon the battle.

    "On Mt. Shamanka clouds and rain disappear in a moment,[44]
But please, my dear lover, please never betray my love.
Falling flowers may want to follow the flow of the stream,
But you can never be faithless like those flowing streams."

    In the first quarter of the first watch their love is intense,
As if they are dragon and snake departing from Dongting.[45]
In the second quarter of the second watch they're in a rage:
They resemble ravenous tigers that are leaving the hills.

    And if those tigers can dine on the flesh of swine or sheep,
They don't care whether they live or die, lose their lives.
In the third quarter of the third watch their love is an ocean:
None can recall his troops from the fiercely-fought battle.

    In the fourth quarter of the fourth watch their love is intense,
The sky turns bright when the golden rooster announces dawn.[46]

---

[43] The golden disk refers to the sun.

[44] In ancient times the goddess of Mt. Shamanka (Wushan 巫山) appeared in a dream to a king of Chu and shared his couch. When she left she told the king that she manifested herself in the morning as rains and in the evening as clouds. "Clouds and rain" (*yunyü* 雲雨) has been the most common euphemism for sex ever since.

[45] Lake Dongting is a large lake in Hunan, near the confluence of the Yangzi and the Xiang. All rivers and lakes are home to dragons that often manifest themselves as snakes.

[46] The golden rooster is the heavenly bird that announces dawn and whose call is echoed by all roosters on earth.

Lightly so lightly she shakes her young lover and wakes him,
So he will not end up as an enemy captive taken in dreams.
   She tells her lover: "Please do not leave now immediately!"
And she, Xiuying, gets her key and she opens a storage box.
She takes out one big ingot of yellow gold, [and she says:]
"This I present to you, my lover, for your love and affection!
   I urge you don't waste it on whores once you're back home,
But preserve it so you can at a later date marry a decent wife.
Threefold obedience and fourfold virtue shackle my feet
So in this life we cannot become flowers on a single stem."
   She took her lover by the hand and led him to the kitchen,
In the kitchen the rice and vegetables smelled very good.
They raised golden cups and drank, facing each other,
Silently, without saying a word, both hurt by emotions.
   She took her lover by the hand and took him outside:
Intense emotion and great love made it hard to part.
"My dear lover, make sure to take good care of yourself,
 So we may have chance of meeting on Magpie Bridge."

She accompanied her lover to the One-Mile Pavilion,
Silently, without a word — a love that can't be cut off!
The singing birds, the fragrant flowers: a love for ever;
It is utterly impossible for her to abandon her loved one.
   "On the one hand I'm thinking of my parents, already so old,
On the other hand I am thinking of you, my one dear lover.
I urge you, my darling, don't covet flowers and willows;[47]
The flower and willow lanes harbor bewitching monsters.
   In rising and staying, drinking and eating be circumspect;
Also when having a good time, do never forget your health.
When you have had a fight, you two still will share a couch:
One night as husband and wife is a hundred nights of love.
   When you plant a flower on a rock, it cannot grow roots;
It all depends on love and affection and mutual passion.

---

[47] "Flowers and willows" are a common euphemism for courtesans and prostitutes.

A fine flower by needs depends on diligent watering;
By diligent watering you'll breed flowers sharing a stem.
    If you want to bring home a bride, inspect her yourself;
Don't trust the words of matchmakers, those old crones.
They will deceive you with glib speech and fancy words,
Who knows how many young people they have killed!
    My dear darling, in your daily life please be thrifty,
Don't waste your good money on flowers and willows.
My dear darling, this is the truth that I now tell you,
Please, darling, remember this forever in your heart."

She accompanied her lover to the Two-Mile Pavilion,
Where she explained to him the ways of the world:
"A young man, you shouldn't go whoring and gambling;
Once you fall into that pit, it's hard to mend your ways.
    Your parents' love and affection is as deep as the sea,
Once you are a grown-up, you have to pay them back.
Study the Odes and the Documents, grasp the Rites;[48]
If you understand the scriptures, you will be respected.
    By pursuing flowers and willows you'll harm yourself,
Please my dear lover, never develop a lecherous heart.
In all actions think thrice and act with circumspection,
Don't behave in a reckless manner, never speak wildly.
    When you have wine and money, you'll have friends,
But when you are in trouble, you'll not see one of them.
If you don't believe me, just pay attention at banquets:
People first of all toast to the man who has the money.
    Riches and wealth are obtained by diligence and thrift,
Despite a hundred clever schemes not by human cunning.

---

[48] The Odes refers to the *Book of Odes*, an ancient collection of over three hundred songs that is counted as one of the Five Classics. The Documents refers to the *Book of Documents*, an ancient collections of speeches and treatises ascribed to the ancient kings and their advisors. This collection is also counted as one of the Five Classics. The Rites is the common designation for three ancient texts on statecraft and ritual prescriptions for all aspects of upper-class life. These three texts are together counted as one of the Five Classics.

Never go against the instructions of your two parents:
A dumb person who doesn't speak acts most properly.
    Even if they strike you once in a while, don't strike back:
As their son you must show an obedient and filial attitude.
Please be aware that the words of the crowd are a threat;
In that way you'll avoid that unpleasant trouble arises.
    If in your daily life you never commit any offence,
A nighttime knock on your door will not scare you.
What I am telling you now is the truth, nothing less,
So please let it be carved in your heart at all times."

She accompanied her lover to the Three-Mile Pavilion
Where she explained to him the ways of the world:
"Be a filial son who respects his father and mother;
Be a good man who comes to the aid of those in need.
    My lover, you are the respected son of a rich family,
So don't put on airs to take advantage of the poor.
At home old and young must live in good harmony,
And brothers should not fight over a small profit.
    If you get into a fight, never battle your brothers,
Swords and lances have two faces, you share one heart.
If brothers get into a fight, please think of your mother:
Those ten thousand red flowers all grow on one tree.
    Disputes all arise out of speaking out way too often;
Trouble follows from interfering in the affairs of others.
So I urge you, my lover, often commit good deeds,
And you will have friends all over this wide world.
    If you commit a crime, they will take you to court;
The king's law is like an oven and shows no mercy.
On a place where a fire has raged, no grass will grow;
If you steer your boat into the waves, danger looms.
    So I urge you, my lover, to always be circumspect,
Remember the sayings of those who were sages.
If you know that a mountain houses a fierce tiger,
Don't court danger by insisting on visiting the place."

She accompanied her lover to the Four-Mile Pavilion,
Where she explained to him the ways of this world:
"Don't go to places where they engage in gambling,
Don't pass in front of gates where evil is hatched.

I fear you'll lose your footing and make a mistake;
Once you've lost life and fame, regret will be useless.
If you've reached a lofty spot, you can see far ahead:
In all actions one must stick to one's proper position.

Dissolute and illegal behavior is never allowed,
Leading on bees and butterflies also is not permitted.[49]
If one day the warrant arrives from the courthouse,
You are yourself to blame for your troubles and woes.

A violent gust of wind will uproot the solitary tree;
Corrupt officials squeeze money from good people.
What I am telling you today are words from the heart,
Words from the heart to serve as a warning for you."

She accompanied her lover to the Five-Mile Pavilion
Where she entrusted her innermost feelings to him:
"When you travel you must follow the Yang Pass road;[50]
Take care to avoid dangerous rapids and narrow lanes.

Do not visit the flower streets and the willow lanes;
Those beauties carry a heart of disaster at their waist.
Painting a tiger, the stripes are easier than the bones;
In case of a man, one knows the face, not the heart.

I only fear that if one day you commit a mistake,
Your regret will be too late and your grief in vain.
It's still a minor matter to have lost one's money,
But once you've ruined your reputation, it's gone.

---

[49] "Bees and butterflies" is a common designation for men who seek sex outside marriage.
[50] "The Yang Pass road" (*yangguandao* 陽關道) originally refers to the road to Central Asia ("Outside Yang Pass you will have no friends" is the oft-quoted line from a parting poem by the Tang poet Wang Wei 王維), but here the expression obviously refers to the bright and straight road in contrast to the "narrow lanes" of the next line, which are known as the location of houses of ill repute.

In every thought think you are facing the enemy;
When crossing a bridge, always be on your alert.
In this human life one most fears the aging of spring;
Each hour and minute of youth is worth a million!"

She accompanied her lover to the Six-Mile Pavilion
Where she explained to him the ways of the world:
"The gibbon's wail and the crane's cry startle people,
They're also frightened by wind-blown waving grass.
 In deep mountains one fears a fierce tiger's emergence,
On level land the appearance of a bewitching monster.
Don't insist on crossing a swollen river's high waves;
Don't travel without a companion in moonless nights.
 I'm afraid that one day some accident might happen,
So in my inner apartments I will be filled with worry.
Even before the sky turns dark I will already go to bed;
When the rooster announces dawn, I will watch the sky.
 Riding a boat or a horse are both fraught with danger;
When crossing districts and lakes you must be careful.
But even the Yellow River will on occasion run clear,[51]
So you too at one moment will be bound to succeed.
 No need to cherish a brocade gown, precious as it is;[52]
What you should cherish most are your days of youth.
If you can pick the flower, you definitely should do so,
But don't only pick a branch when there is no flower.
 True love and affection are most important in life,
While glory and wealth resemble a flowering branch.
If you want a bridal room night of flower and candle,
Your name has first to appear on the golden plaque."[53]

---

[51] The Yellow River is known for its muddy brown water because of the quantity of silt the river contains.
[52] A brocade gown is the gown of an official.
[53] The golden plaque contains the list of the students who have not only passed the metropolitan examination, but also the subsequent palace examination and who could look forward to a brilliant bureaucratic career.

She accompanied her lover to the Seven-Mile Pavilion,
Where she explained to him the ways of the world:
"My dear lover, now allow me to tell you the truth:
Never become intimate with a woman without love!

    When she sees you have money, all things are fine,
But when you have no money, she changes her mind.
Those lascivious women have hearts like a scorpion,
And with feigned devotion they'll seduce your heart.

    They want you to provide them with golden hairpins,
They stretch out their hands when they want fine rings.
They want you to provide them with brocade and silk,
But when your money is all gone, they will stay away.

    That beauty of barely sixteen is craftily made up,
But all she displays is only a show of deep feeling.
She hides her blush behind her tender white hand
And has been trained to shed those tears of longing.

    In her winning smile she hides a vicious scheme;
A brew to seduce your soul she hides in her belly:
From ancient times to the present day — who knows
How many young men she has trapped and harmed?"

She accompanied her lover to the Eight-Mile Pavilion,
Where she explained to him the ways of the world:
"The drum of the fifth watch wakes mandarin-ducks,
But the most loveless creature on earth is a woman.

    To your face she will tell you the prettiest words,
But in secret she also harbors a treacherous heart;
Deceiving you with fine words and a glib tongue,
She seduces your heart with her bewitching figure.

    Her tongue resembles that of a sleek-haired snake,
Her heart resembles the poisonous sting of a wasp.
There are cures for a snake's bite and a wasp's sting,
But it's hard to recover from the poison of seduction.

    Corrupt officials have hearts like tigers and wolves,
But evil women are even more harmful monsters.
I want you to be extremely careful and circumspect,
So their bewitching miasma won't violate your body."

She accompanied her lover to the Nine-Mile Pavilion,
Where she explained to him the ways of the world:
"I implore you, my lover, to always pay attention;
Take good care of yourself, even more than of gold.

   A seven-story pagoda on fire may be a great sight,
But is not as good as a single lamp in providing light.
When you concern yourself with your own business,
No storm-swept waves will emerge out of the blue.

   If you want to serve others, they must first serve you;
For a tree to grow luxuriously, its roots must be firm.
As long as your own intentions are honest and true,
You don't have to fear the forces of wind and waves."

She accompanied her lover to the Ten-Mile Pavilion,
Where she explained to him the ways of the world:
"I would have liked to escort you for twenty miles,
But alas, my feet are tired and my waist is hurting.

   I'm also afraid that my parents may learn of this —
I would feel way too ashamed to have to face them!
What we have done tonight only the two of us know,
So I implore you, darling, don't tell it to anyone else.

   The world may be filled with fleeting acquaintances,
But how many can there be who'll be your true friends?
Don't go and pluck those flowers out in wild fields —
Wild flowers contain a poison that can bring harm.[54]

   Don't covet the wives and daughters of other men;
If you slip into a muddy pit, you will be disgraced.
And don't drink the running water of a cold spring:
If cold water hits your stomach, you'll be in pain.[55]

   My lover, stay away from whoring and gambling;
Devote yourself to your studies, seek advancement!
With firm roots a tree needn't fear a violent storm;
With a straight trunk its shadow will not be crooked.

---

[54]"Wild flowers" is another common euphemism for courtesans and prostitutes.
[55]Travelers are consistently warned to drink only cooked water so as to avoid diarrhea.

I cannot tell you the thousand words I'd like to say,
So I entrust, my dear lover, this one true heart to you.
I want you, my lover, to take good care of yourself;
On my side I'll be happy to suffer bitter desolation.

The flush of sex and of wine are both equally a flush;
Spring bud and fall chrysanthemum are equally fragrant.
My soul has attached itself to your body, my lover;
I implore you, my lover, please never ever forget!

I had hoped to live together with you till old age,
But in an earlier life I burned a short incense stick.
Our love and affection today ends in separation —
I've no tears left for weeping — it breaks my heart.

"I accompanied my lover, but will go back all alone:
Without a flock, a lonely goose suffering desolation.
A kite with a snapped string — where will I drift to?
My heart's overcome by emotions of sadness and woe.

With every single step that I go, I look back once —
How hard it is to let go, to be separated, how painful!
It is as if a knife is scraping the skin from my body:
The pain has no limits while my tears course down.

I urge you, my lover, to take good care of yourself,
Don't wreck your career prospects because of me.
My sweetheart, you're like a swallow leaving the nest:
Soon you will spread your wings and fly to the skies.

In this existence we failed to accomplish our wishes,
But in a next life we will tie the marriage knot again.
I have comforted you with well-intentioned words,
So cut off the threads of passion, don't leave roots.

"Having seen off my lover I return from Ten-Mile Pavilion,
Ten-Mile Pavilion which increased my feelings of sorrow.
Having seen off my lover I now go back home —
Even a man made of iron or stone would be hurt.

Having seen off my lover I return from Nine-Mile Pavilion,
I now resemble a kite the string of which snapped.

When we came here we were a couple and a pair,
But now I leave I am only a lonely shadow, alone.
    Having seen off my lover I return from Eight-Mile Pavilion;
When I think of my lover, tears gush from my eyes.
I wish my dear darling lover a safe and speedy return;
I may have lost my honor now, but still I am happy.
    Having seen off my lover I return from Seven-Mile Pavilion,
And while I think of my dear lover, I go back home.
I pray my lover may be listed on the golden plaque
And so also will bring comfort to me and my love.
    Having seen off my lover, I return from Six-Mile Pavilion
And in my heart I only think of my darling lover.
Our duckweed affection resembles morning fog,[56]
Each day by the early sun turned into a light mist.
    Having seen off my lover, I return from Five-Mile Pavilion;
When I look back, I don't see my lover anymore.
Wanting to call my lover I cannot open my mouth,
Just like a dumb person who has eaten *huanglian*.[57]
    Having seen off my lover, I return from Four-Mile Pavilion,
And the more I long for my lover, the more it hurts.
Last night those rains and clouds at Mt. Shamanka:
That memory beats my heart to shreds — and again!
    Having seen off my lover, I return from Three-Mile Pavilion:
My lover longs for me while I long for my lover.
Buffalo Boy and Weaving Maiden parted tonight:
When will a Magpie Bridge let us declare our love?
    Having seen off my lover, I return from Two-Mile Pavilion,
But when I lift up my head, I don't see my lover.
My heart is in utter turmoil, at a loss what to do;
My shoes hurt my small feet as I lament my woes.

---

[56] "A duckweed affection" is a temporary relationship, as short-lived as the meeting of duckweed leaves on flowing water.

[57] *Huanglian* 黃蓮 is Chinese goldthread (*Coptis chinensis*), a herbaceous perennial. Its root and stem are used in Chinese medicine and known for their bitter taste. "A dumb person who has eaten *huanglian*" is a common image for a person who is unable to give expression to his or her bitter sufferings.

Having seen off my lover, I return from One-Mile Pavilion
And resemble a lonely goose that sadly cries out.
I pull up the wick in the lamp before the Buddha:
In this existence I'm done with all duckweed love."

(sung by the young man)
"While I now return to Pavilion Number Eleven,
I remember that passion of my darling, my love:
Peach Blossom Pool may be a thousand feet deep —
It's not as deep as her passion in seeing me off.[58]

  While I now return to Pavilion Number Twelve,
I remember there in the pavilion her love for me.
But a heartless cudgel separated the mandarin-ducks —
Alas, my darling lover now is left behind all alone.

  While I now return to Pavilion Number Thirteen,
I ponder there in that pavilion the ways of the world.
Whatever you may think of can be easily obtained,
But it is hard to find a woman passionate like her.

  While I now return to Pavilion Number Fourteen,
My heart is filled with sadness, without any joy.
A thousand threads and knots can easily be untied,
But it is impossible to undo the love of my darling.

  While I now return to Pavilion Number Fifteen,
All these events of the past surge up in my heart.
A peony may be a fine flower but I don't look,
It cannot compare to the dazzling beauty of her!

  While I now return to Pavilion Number Sixteen,
I ponder in that pavilion the ways of the world:
Ten thousand ounces of gold I can renounce,
But I cannot renounce my darling's affection.

  While I now return to Pavilion Number Seventeen,
I cannot catch any sleep as I think of my darling.

---

[58] These two lines are based on a well-known quatrain by the famous Tang-dynasty poet Li Bai 李白 (701–762).

During daytime I think of her till late at night,
During nighttime I long for her till early dawn.

 While I now return to Pavilion Number Eighteen,
I remember my darling — she is really to be pitied.
She is a lotus flower that is just about to bloom,
But she is cruelly locked up in inner apartments.

 While I now return to Pavilion Number Nineteen,
A single lamp accompanies her in her loneliness.
The man who understood her heart has departed —
To whom can she tell all her sorrow and grief?

 While I now return to Pavilion Number Twenty,
I don't see anyone in the darkness around me.
My body is in this pavilion, my heart is with her:
Buffalo Boy and Weaving Maiden tied by love.

"Here at Ten-Mile Pavilion I feel so very lonely;
When I lift up my head, I don't see my lover.
If only those lucky magpies could build a bridge
Across the Silver River, so we could make love.[59]

 Here at Ten-Mile Pavilion the scenery is fine,
But all sights stir my emotions, a limitless pain.
The green hills are the same, but she has left —
A lone goose far from the flock, utterly lonely.

 Outside Ten-Mile Pavilion the moon is dark;
An icy wind hits my face, I'm feeling so cold.
Separated by only a foot — at the world's edges:
Her clear eyes are staring, her tears come down.

 Outside Ten-Mile Pavilion wild flowers blossom,
But she has gone to her room, and I wander about.
The clouds and rains of Mt. Shamanka are gone,
But this mutual longing is breaking our hearts."

---

[59] The Silver River is one of the many alternative names of the Celestial River (the Milky Way).

CHAPTER 2

THE TALE OF TANG XIAN

The plot of *The Tale of Tang Xian* is very simple. Tang Xian is a brilliant student. After he leaves home to pursue a career, he does not come home for nine years, despite his promise to come back after three. Eventually his wife, Tenth Daughter Zhang, dies of loneliness and grief and appears to him in a dream. When Tang Xian hurries home, he discovers that his wife has died. King Yama allows her to appear to him in a dream, on which occasion she explains to him the organization of the underworld and the punishments of sinners. The most original element here may well be her description of the triumphal progression through the underworld of those who are not only destined to be reborn as a human being because of their virtue but also are fated to become high officials in the world of men.

The Tale of Tang Xian, which also circulated in other Hakka-speaking areas,[1] appears to have enjoyed a special popularity in the Hakka-speaking communities on Taiwan. The following translation is based on the edition provided in Qiu Chunmei 邱春美, *Taiwan Kejia shuochang wenxue zhuanzai yanjiu* 台灣客家說唱文學傳仔研究 (2003: 259–278). Qiu based her edition on a comparison of five different manuscripts.

***

---
[1] Huang Changsheng 2004.

The Tale of Tang Xian

Please allow me, elders and brothers, to give some advice,
I will tell you all what happened from the very beginning.
Since olden days there exists the famous tale of Tang Xian,
Who was living in the region of Luoyang in Chuanzhou.

From his earliest youth Tang Xian was a perfect pupil,
And from the age of seven he loved literary composition.
After a number of years, bye and bye, he turned fifteen,
And when he had reached that age, he was without a wife.

When he had reached the age of fifteen, he had no wife,
But the Zhang family of Western Bank had a daughter.
When his parents learned about the daughter of the Zhangs,
They discussed, in the hall, the matter with a matchmaker.

When the matchmaker heard this, she was filled with joy,
And went off to the Zhang family to deliver the message.
This daughter of the Zhang family was very beautiful,
She had reached the age of fifteen: this was the right time!

Furniture, gardens and fields were not an issue at all,
And Tenth Daughter was quite willing to marry Tang Xian.
The wedding letters thereupon were compared together,[2]
And his only desire was to make Tenth Daughter his bride.

This one daughter of the Zhangs had reached the proper age,
In the sequence of sisters she was counted as number ten.
Her eyebrows resembled willow-leaves in the Third Month,
And her lips were just as red as the pomegranate's flower.

Ritual gifts such as wine were sent to seal the engagement,
They brought pigs and lambs and goods of gold and silver.
A good hour and a lucky day were thereupon selected
For him to bring her home as bride, to serve his parents.

A lacquered bed, a sedan chair, a silver stepping stool:
So then she made her toilette with rouge and powder.
For the three years after he brought her home as bride
The couple served his parents filially and obediently.

---

[2] The dates of birth of the prospective bride and groom are compared to make sure they will be compatible partners.

But then suddenly one day Tang Xian made up his mind
That he wanted to take the exams and obtain a function.
With all due respect he asked for his parents' permission
And then returned to their room to hear from his wife.
  "I want to leave home to search for fame and function,
While you stay here at home to take care of my parents."
When Tenth Daughter had heard him say these words,
The tears that poured from her eyes soaked her clothes.
  "If you leave to find a function, go for a thousand days,
You leave me behind to guard this empty room all alone.
In the capital there all those many girls like red flowers —
On no account desire those flowers once you've left me!
  If you obtain a function, be sure to return in three years,
And if you fail, return to the village within six months!"
  Husband and wife deliberated the affair face to face:
"This golden hairpin I give you to keep and carry with you!
My red shoes and my precious mirror I will all store away
Until you come home, until we will be happily reunited!"
  His father and mother repeatedly told their son Tang Xian:
"Whether you obtain a function or not, come home quickly!"
After Tang Xian had heard these words from all of them,
He took with a bow his leave from his parents and his wife.
  The latter saw him off through the three gates of the mansion,
Tears continued to course down from her eyes, without end.
As her hands clutched the balustrade she watched him go —
There was no knife in her belly, yet her innards were cut!

Let's not sing of Tenth Daughter and her gloomy sorrows,
But let's sing of Tang Xian who had left for the capital.
When he arrived in the capital, he was very happy indeed,
Because the capital city had so many fine sceneries to offer.
  There was no end to enjoying the capital's many attractions,
And the thought never occurred to him of wanting to go home.
Each day at the imperial court brought many new pleasures
And he had no desire to go and see his father and mother.

Let's not sing of Tang Xian and all his many pleasures,
Let's change the subject and sing again of Tenth Daughter.
When she returned to her room, she was filled with longing;
The tears that streamed from her eyes were without number.
    Inside the bed-curtains of red gauze, filled with longing,
She prayed to Heaven and Earth and the Three Bright Lights:[3]
"May my husband's name be listed on the golden poster,[4]
And may he come home to express gratitude to Heaven!"
    As time went by after husband and wife had been separated,
Tenth Daughter's heart was increasingly filled with longing.
Ever since his departure she had received not a single letter;
She didn't apply rouge and powder, didn't make her toilette.
    She didn't apply any red to her lips, didn't paint on eyebrows,
And she had no desire to select some clothes from her chests.

After her husband had been gone for a full three years,
Tenth Daughter day and night watched out for her husband.
But after five years not even one letter had been sent home,
While at night the bird of Yang announced spring's dawn.[5]
    She waited for her husband for eight years, but he didn't return,
Even after nine years she did not see him return to the village.
During night time, filled with longing, she could not sleep —
Day and night she was filled with longing: it broke her heart.
    She did not long for gold and she did not long for silver,
Her only thought was of her husband who didn't come home.
Longing for her husband day and night she ruined her beauty,
Longing for him without end gave her a sallow complexion.
    Day in day out she longed for her husband who didn't return,
Out of longing for her husband she fell ill and took to her bed.

---

[3] The Three Bright Lights are the sun, the moon, and the stars.

[4] The golden poster is the poster on which the names are listed of the students who have passed the metropolitan examinations and have achieved the *jinshi* 進士 degree.

[5] The "bird of Yang" refers to migrating geese.

Having been ill for three days, she breathed her last and died:
Her soul left for the Underworld to appear before King Yama.[6]

Her parents-in-law approached the bed and wept loudly,
The whole family, old and young, wept till their hearts broke.
Longing for her husband Tenth Daughter fell ill and died —
They bought a coffin, dressed the body, placed it in the hall.
   Tang's parents went out and hired a number of priests and monks,
And on the Seven Sevens they came over and read the scriptures.[7]
Then his parents hired a geomancer to select a site for her grave
Where the layout of the land would be suitable for a tomb.
   When they had found a place where she might be buried,
Amidst the hills on four sides and rivers from eight directions,
They buried Tenth Daughter there in her tomb and grave,
A perfect site for a grave on top of a Nine-Dragon Ridge.
   His mother, remembering Tenth Daughter who died of illness,
Wept on and on in front of her tablet — a burner full of incense!
"Husband and wife of naked bodies: an unbreakable love!
Now she has gone to the realm of shade, she must feel bad!"

Tenth Daughter went to the capital by means of a dream,
From the realm of shade she dispatched a dream to Tang Xian,
And so Tang Xian, faraway in he capital, experienced a dream,
A dream in which Tenth Daughter told him of her broken heart:
   "Two trees were blossoming, but one tree has died,
Of the two burning lamps, only one is still shining.

---

[6] King Yama is the ruler of the underworld, in charge of the Ten Courts of Hell. Upon death the soul of the deceased is judged by the underworld judges to determine his or her future fate.

[7] As the soul passes through the Ten Courts, sutras are read to ease his or her passage. The soul appears before the first court on the seventh day following death, before the second court on the fourteenth day, and so on, appearing for the seventh court on the forty-ninth day. These sutra-reading sessions are designated as the "Seven Sevens." Further ceremonies follow on the one-hundredth day following death, a year following death, and twenty-seven months following death, as the soul appears before the eighth court, the ninth court and the tenth court. Teiser 1994.

Of the two green pine trees, one tree now has died,
Of the couple of mandarin-ducks, one bird has died."
　When he awoke from his dream, he was upset and frightened:
"This must mean that my mandarin-duck has met with disaster!"
So he immediately asked the national teacher to read his dream,[8]
And the national teacher explained this dream as "separation."
　"This dream, I am afraid, is highly inauspicious,
Husband and wife will definitely be separated."
When Tang Xian heard this, he was filled with gloom,
And he immediately thought to himself all silently:
　"When I departed I said I'd return in three years,
But by now I haven't been home for nine years.
I'm not only afraid that my parents have fallen ill,
I'm also afraid something has happened to my wife."
　The next morning he handed in a petition to the Emperor,
In which he asked the Emperor permission to go back home.
When the Emperor read the report, he was very pleased,
So he granted Tang Xian permission to go back home.

Riding a dragon-like horse with a silver-encrusted saddle,
Tang Xian left behind all those many officials of the capital.
Throughout his trip he traveled each day as fast as an arrow,
And in an instant his trip had brought him back home.
　When he arrived at the gate he descended from his horse,
But when he saw his mother, her tears flowed down.
Touching the floor he bowed before his father and mother:
"It is nine years ago since I took my leave of my parents.
　But why do you weep, my dear mother, when I greet you,
What is the reason that you weep and cry without end?
I went off to find a function, and have succeeded since long,
So why do you today still weep with heart-broken grief?"

---

[8] It is unclear to me to which high office the words "national teacher" (*guoshi* 國師) refer in this context, but in other tales too this official is called upon to interpret dreams. In the 16th century novel *Romance of the Three Kingdoms* (*Sanguo yanyi* 三國演義), *guoshi* is the title of Zhuge Liang 諸葛亮, who stands out by his knowledge of the mantic arts.

His father and mother promptly cursed their son Tang Xian:
"Dear son, what you are saying is very thoughtless and rash!
When you left, you said you would return within three years,
So why did you never come home for nine years on end?
　　Your wife here at home was filled with gloom and sorrow,
She waited for years and months but you never returned.
Out of longing for you Tenth Daughter fell ill and died,
And her body has been buried atop Nine-Dragon Ridge."

When Tang Xian had been told this, his tears coursed down,
Sadly weeping and shedding tears, her entered her chamber.
All he saw in the room were the bed curtains of red gauze,
All he saw now was the empty bed — he didn't see his wife.
　　In the interior chamber Tang Xian long wept miserably,
With each cry and each sob he was weeping for his wife.
In the interior chamber Tang Xian wept quite miserably —
His wife was not there to reply to his broken-heart weeping.
　　"Forever separated is this one couple of red gauze cushions,
Below the earth now rests one side of the red-lacquered bed.
In this room I do not see Tenth Daughter's face,
I do not see Tenth Daughter to tell me her story."
　　Sadly weeping, shedding tears he wept quite miserably,
As he did not see Tenth Daughter anymore in that room.
"Husband and wife since earliest days, a love for ever —
How could you leave me all alone without a thought?"
　　Before her soul-tablet he prayed to his wife to return:
"If I only could see you in my dreams I'd be satisfied!"
In the first watch of the night he did not see her in a dream,
In the second watch he guarded the empty room all alone.
　　In the third watch he was all alone with the lonely lamp,
In the fourth watch he did not see his Tenth Daughter.
In the fifth watch he heard the rooster announcing dawn,
But he did not see Tenth Daughter come and tell her story.
　　He considered all the facts from the very beginning:
"I'll never see her again in this life unless in a dream!"
Out of longing for Tenth Daughter his heart broke in two,
And he did not care at all for any of the day's three meals.

His thrice repeated loud weeping alarmed the underworld,
It alarmed the underworld and frightened King Yama,
Who promptly shouted to the ghosts of the Three Bureaus:[9]
"Who is that man who is weeping in the world of light?"

The Three Bureaus stepped forward and replied together,
And they reviled Tang Xian for his lack of decorum.
"How does he dare alarm and frighten our King Yama!"

The Three Offices again answered the King by saying:
"The person weeping in the world of light is Tang Xian.
While he, the husband, served as prime minister at court,
His wife at home attracted an illness and passed away.

When he came back home, he did not see her face.
Crying and weeping he now calls for Tenth Daughter."
When King Yama had heard of this state of affairs,
He hastily gave orders to transmit this information.

He promptly instructed Alas-river's soul-commissioner:[10]
"Now get a golden ferry and ferry her across the river!"
When Tenth Daughter's soul had been brought back:
[He said:] "You will now return to meet with Tang Xian."

He then gave her a single bowl of soul-soup to drink,
And immediately she was transformed into a living being,

Let's not narrate how Tenth Daughter returned to light.
Within a moment her soul had returned to her village.
Her husband at home was sadly shedding his tears,
When in front of the gate the wife called out: "Tang Xian!"

---

[9] The Three Bureaus (*sansi* 三司) probably may be identified with the Three Offices/Three Officials (*sanguan* 三官) of Heaven, Earth and Water that since the beginning of the first millennium are believed to be in charge of the registers of good and bad deeds and the judgment of souls. By the end of the first millennium they were incorporated in the underworld bureaucracy headed by King Yama and the Ten Courts of Hell. The Three Offices were widely venerated in Southeastern China in late imperial times. For the veneration of the Three Offices among the Hakka on Taiwan see Li Hengdao 1983.

[10] The Alas-river is a river in the underworld. Sinners will be swallowed by the waves of the river when they try to cross but those who lived a virtuous life can pass it easily.

And when Tang Xian heard his wife calling his name,
He promptly left his room and welcomed Tenth Daughter.
   When she saw her husband, her heart broke in two!
When he saw Tenth Daughter, his heart broke in two!
When they two saw each other, they bowed to each other.
"Now explain to me all the facts from the very beginning:
   You departed to find a function, we said a thousand days,
But for nine years in a row you never once came home.
From the day you left, we never received any letter —
How could you leave me alone without any thought?
   Out of longing for you I attracted an illness and died,
My soul left for the underworld, met with King Yama."
When Tang Xian heard her tell him her story like this,
How she attracted an illness and died, his heart broke in two.
   The wife then continued speaking to her husband and lord:
"In an earlier life I must have burned second-hand incense!
Husband and wife since earliest days, we were a couple,
So why did you leave me alone without any thought?
   You departed to find a function, we said a thousand days,
And you had me guard the empty chamber all alone.
It must be because in an earlier life I lacked in virtue
That today husband and wife are widely separated."
   When Tang Xian heard his wife speak like this,
Tears flowed from his eyes and soaked his clothes:
"Husband and wife are birds from the same forest,
How could you leave me alone without any thought?"

"King Yama fetches his victims, whether old or young,
The infernal judges ply their brushes without any feeling.
Before your date of birth is fixed, your death is fixed,
And your miserable poverty is all determined by fate.
   King Yama has no fear of even the mightiest heroes,
He has no fear of high officials or people of position.
He will take an elderly grandfather of over eighty,
As well as a stripling boy of only eighteen years.

He takes the high and mighty according to their fate,
He takes the unborn infant still in its mother's womb.
Each living being eventually will have to go that way,
And good deeds while alive don't make a difference."

The wife replied to her husband and lord as follows:
"Listen to me as I will provide you with an explanation!
In the underworld there are no districts and no courts,
There are also no neighborhoods and no villages.
  Upon death we all have to pass the Dark Mansion,
And on the gate of that place it is spelled out clearly:
Upon death a person's souls are all dispersed, as the
Three souls and seven spirits each go their own way.
  One soul goes off to appear before King Yama,
One soul goes off to stay in the ancestral shrine,
One soul goes off to reside in the tomb and grave,
While the seven spirits go to the kings of darkness."
  Tang Xian then asked his wife the following questions:
"Which sin is seen as most heinous in the Underworld?
  For which sin are people burned by raging fire?
For which sin are people cooked in seething oil?
For which sin are people pulverized in mills?
For which sin are people nailed to an iron bed?"

The wife replied her husband and lord as follows:
"Let me tell you the facts from the very beginning.
  On the First Seven, it's the Great King of Qin's Plains,
On the Second Seven, the King of Chu's Rivers presides.
On the Third Seven, one comes before the Emperor of Song,
And on the Fourth Seven, it's the King of the Five Faculties.
  On the Fifth Seven, it's the hall of His Majesty King Yama,
Whose karma-mirror shows all one's karma, without fail.
It shows all evil one has committed in the world of light —
Upon death the underworld punishment is unbearable!
  On the Sixth Seven, the King of the City of Bian presides,
On the Seventh Seven, the Tiger Lord and King of Mt. Tai.

Upon death one has to pass them all in the world of shade:
On the hundredth day it is the court of King Right and Equal.
After one full year all people see the King of Dark Obscurity,
After three years they see the King of Good and Evil Rebirth.
If you committed a murder in the world of light, undetected,
It is clearly written down in the registers of the underworld!
There are also those who with cruel heart abuse the poor,
There are also those who with evil intent calumniate others:
Upon death their thousands of crimes will be clearly displayed,
Their thousands of tortures will be an unbearable punishment.
My husband and lord, if you want to know the underworld,
Please allow me to provide you with a detailed explanation:
There are people who commit evil and murder with words:
Locked in shackles and chains they're stripped of their skin.
People are escorted to the Alas-river to cross its bridge,
Where the thousands of lamentations are insufferable!
People who practiced good will cross over that bridge,
Those who practiced evil disappear under the bridge.
The lamentations in the river are of those who did evil,
Irrespective of their age, old and young all suffer disaster.
Those who have passed away all are bound to suffer,
For each evil deed one will meet with misfortune.
They pass through the eighteen hells, again and again,
Interrogations in the realm of shade show no mercy.
The hell of spears and knives lacks no torture at all,
And the hell of the fiery pit is one blazing red fire.
The worst sufferings are found in the hell of iron beds,
One's body is flayed and burned: an unbearable punishment.
Monks and priests are pulverized in mills made of iron,
Lustful monks but no buddhas — nailed to the iron bed!
Commit a murder in the realm of light, and in the shades
You're shackled and strangled and stripped of your skin.
Pollute and defile gods and buddhas, or commit a murder,
And you'll be flayed, your tongue ripped out: a cruel pain!
Commit evil in the realm of light, and once in the shades
King Yama's karma-mirror will display your sins clearly.

And once it displays the evil you committed on earth,
He'll call out buffalo-headed and horse-faced demons.
　The buffalo-headed and horse-faced demons are without honor,
They'll interrogate you under torture in darkness without mercy."

Tang Xian answered his wife: "Now listen…"
"I urge you to burn incense, even when fine!"[11]
　First of all, never commit vicious arson!
Secondly, never eat the money of the gods!
Thirdly, never feed meat to vegetarian monks!
Fourthly, never consider committing murder!
　Fifthly, never burn incense while polluted!
Sixthly, never put the torch to a piece of land![12]
Seventhly, never seek other people's fields!
Eighthly, never incur other people's enmity!
　Ninthly, never rely on the power of others!
And tenthly, never spend the money of others!
If you can maintain these ten rules while alive,
You'll be fine down below, even when accused.
　Irrespective of other crimes in the world of light,
Never covet flowers, never pollute buddhas and gods.
All sinful crimes you commit in the world of light
Are punished without mercy in the realm of shade."

Tang Xian asked his wife: "If so, in which way
Will one enjoy what good time in the realm of shade?"
His wife replied: "My husband and lord, please listen,
I will tell you all the facts from the very beginning.
　What will be the office of those who keep the law?
Men and women, in office and titled, have a good time.

---

[11] One of the manuscripts provides the following four lines here: Tang Xian answered his wife, saying:/"By which acts can I avoid such misfortune?"/The wife answered her husband saying:/"I urge you to burn incense, even when fine." In this last line she urges her husband to pay his respect to the gods at all times, also when he is doing fine and doesn't need to make any request.

[12] Because in that way many innocent animals will be killed.

Once you have received King Yama's notification,
Your office and function on earth is divinely shown.

    Myriads of mounted troops will throng about you,
Ivory benches and sedan chairs are carried behind you.
Blazing red flags enhance my mansion's might, and
Troops lined up shout and clear the road on both sides.

    Cannons reaching to heaven resound like the thunder,
Paralyzing King Yama, shattering his heart and gall.
Myriads of mounted troops come and welcome you,
And people assist you when meeting shade-officials.

    In the underworld's hells you'll display your power,
And King Yama will not dare inquire into your case.
When a man obtains rebirth and will have an office,
He finds there a silver bridge he will cross on horseback.

    When a woman obtains rebirth and will have an office,
The blood-bowl hell will turn into a blood-lily pond.[13]
The nine times nine essence soldiers guard them at night:
Men and women, in office and function, take their ease.

    So I urge people while alive to change their thinking,
So they will obtain rebirth as a man and have an office.
There is no end when speaking about the underworld —
My husband and lord, keep to the rules while alive!

    Commit vicious arson with vicious hand and evil heart,
And you'll be punished with a bloated body and belly.
Do not read the canonical books and do not keep the law:
You'll end up a hunchback villain with a bloated belly.

    Despite a fate of poverty they do not 'practice and sow,'[14]
With naked and exposed bodies they offend the divinities,

---

[13] The blood-pond hell (or blood-bowl hell) is a Chinese addition to the Buddhist system of multiple hells. Belief in the blood-pond hell started in the Song and Yuan dynasties, when the *Blood Bowl Sutra* (*Xuepen jing* 血盆經) started to circulate. This short apocryphal sutra insists that women upon their death will be assigned to the blood-bowl hell as a punishment for the pollution that has been caused by the blood they spill in menstruation and childbirth. See Cole 1998, 197–214, and Soymié 1965.

[14] Practice goodness and sow the seeds for happiness in a future existence.

In their reckless rashness they don't respect the divinities,
Ugly and evil miscreant men, they don't respect Heaven —
  The power of His Majesty King Yama is vast and great,
In the registers of his infernal judges their sins are listed.
Those who observe the ten virtues will prosper for ever,
But those who distort the Way will not prosper for long.
  If you want to ensure your family's lasting prosperity,
Persist, while rich, in religious practice for generations.
The one to excel in reading sutras was Woman Wang,[15]
The only one to persist in practice was the Perfected Li.[16]
  Mulian went to the Western paradise to save his mother,[17]
For seven years persisting in practice he obtained the fruit.
If you don't believe, just look at the water from the eaves:
Drop after drop continues to fall to the ground, without fail.
  If you don't believe, look at Tripitaka of the Tang dynasty:
Carrying sutras to the Western paradise he saved his mother.[18]

---

[15] Woman Wang 王 is elsewhere known as Woman Huang 黃. The legend of Woman Huang originated in the Song dynasty and had become widely popular by the 16th century. When Woman Huang urges her husband, a butcher, to abandon his sinful profession, he informs her that her sins by polluting the gods with the blood she sheds in menstruation and childbirth are much greater. From that moment, Woman Huang refuses to share her husband's bed and devotes her time to reciting the *Diamond Sutra*. Her piety attracts the attention of King Yama, who invites her to the underworld and allows her to be reborn as a man, in which reincarnation she achieves enlightenment. Grant 1989; Grant and Idema 2011.

[16] It is unclear to me which person may be intended here as there several famous Daoist masters who have the surname Li 李, to begin with the Old Master himself.

[17] The legend of Mulian 目連 has been widely popular in China since the Tang dynasty. When Mulian has become a monk, he is surprised to learn that his mother has been condemned to hell upon her death. In order to save her he appeals to the Buddha, who resides at the Thunderclap monastery in the Western Heaven. Grant and Idema 2011; Guo Qitao 2005; Hou Jie 2002. Starting from the transformation texts from Dunhuang the ballads and plays on the Mulian legend tend to contain extensive descriptions of the underworld and the gruesome punishments to which sinners are submitted in hell. Mair 1983, 87–122. The Mulian legend was the foundational myth of the Ghost Festival in the middle of the Seventh Month. Teiser 1988.

[18] Tripitaka of the Tang dynasty usually refers to Xuanzang 玄臧, the protagonist of the 16th century novel *Journey to the West* (*Xiyou ji* 西遊記). See Yu 1977–1983. But

Only these three people were able to truly practice virtue,
To persist in practice with full devotion, not harming others.
   When you are an official, make sure to be pure and fair,
When you are a monk, make sure to recite the true sutras.
When your body is defiled and polluted, practice purification;
Make sure you never allow yourself to slacken your mind.
   Whether you are pure and clean or still defiled, all this
Is clearly listed in the registers of the realm of shade.
If you refuse to donate bridges and pave roads,[19] how can
You dare bow down to express gratitude to Blue Heaven?
   If you are filial and persist in practice, your merit is great;
Donate to the gods, donate to the buddhas, burn incense!
Whenever there is a hungry man, make sure to donate rice,
When you meet with a freezing fellow, donate some clothes.
   I urge you under all circumstances to practice donations,
They are clearly listed in the registers of the realm of shade."
But before Tenth Daughter was done advising her husband,
Her guard outside the gate warned Tenth Daughter to leave.

When Tang Xian had heard these words, he lighted a fire
In the kitchen, and got ready to slaughter pig and sheep.
He prepared for her three dishes of well-prepared foods,
And he poured her three cups of wine at their separation.
   Tenth Daughter replied to her husband and lord thusly:
"There is no need now today to slaughter a pig or a sheep,
Because you are a living being and I am only a ghost, so
Even if you offer me pork or mutton, I could not eat it.
   All I want is one bowl of coarse rice, to be offered
Before my soul-tablet, and then I will be off on my road."

Xuanzang traveled to the Western regions in order to fetch sutras, whereas it is Mulian who in later adaptations of his legend carries both sutras and the ashes of this mother when traveling to the West to appeal to the Buddha for help. At a loss to decide whether he should carry the sutras in front of him or the ashes of his mother, he decides to carry these two loads to his left and his right.

[19] To donate money for paving roads and building bridges is one of the good works expected of rich people.

The guard who escorted her soul called her name outside,
And the lad who guides the soul pressured her to depart.
 When the hour had arrived, he saw Tenth Daughter go,
As she left her lover in order to meet with King Yama.
When Tenth Daughter took her leave of him and left,
He felt as if a sharp sickle cut right through his guts.
 Husband and wife both bowed towards each other,
Tears flowed from their eyes, an unstoppable flood.
She took a golden hairpin and gave it to Tang Xian:
"For all eternity, as long as you live, never forget me!
 My husband, once I have left, I will follow that soul,
Once I have left, I will follow him to the Yellow Springs.
My husband, in the blink of an eye I will have disappeared,
Within the shortest moment you will not see me anymore!"
 Tang Xian wept to such a degree his heart was broken:
"My dear wife, you leave me to enter the Yellow Springs —
If I had known from the very beginning this would pass,
I would have come home at least nine years ago!
 I would not have served as an official at court, and
There would have been no need for my wife to die!"
Supporting himself on the balustrade he wept piteously,
Without a sickle in his belly, his guts were cut through!

This is my advice to all you gentlemen in this world:
Without a wife you suffer desolation by day and night!
Filial and obedient couples always stay together, but
Fighting and scheming couples will not last long.
 So I have written this book on the *Tale of Tang Xian* —
When he had reached the age of seven, he spoke of affairs.
Even though my work may not be "sentences like pearls,"
Yet, when narrated, it may serve as "counsel to the world."
 Each paragraph and sentence was finished timely,
In the hope that the purport would be deep and far-reaching:
May fighting and scheming couples turn into filial couples,
And may the people who commit evil end up doing good.

When you have finished reading, give the text to others;
Let millions love Tang Xian and Tenth Daughter Zhang.
Whether a bright day or a rainy one, read it regularly, so
You'll cultivate your mind by reading and not harm others.

Women who hear this tale will respect their husband,
Men who will hear this tale will dearly love their wife.
If there are educated people who can memorize the text,
They may often repeat the text as if it were a scripture.

Men should all want to be like Master Tang Xian,
Women should love to emulate Tenth Daughter Zhang.
Out of longing for her husband she fell ill and died:
Tenth Daughter's virtuous chastity will live forever!

CHAPTER 3

SELLING LANTERNS

Che Long Sells Flower Lanterns tells the tale of the destitute student Che Long 車龍 and his faithful fiancée Yu Jiao 余嬌. Che Long is the single son of a high official, but when his father dies, the family is soon reduced to poverty because local bullies cheat them out of their money. Eventually Che Long is even forced to sell flower lanterns on the occasion of the Lantern Festival (celebrated on the first full moon of the year).[1] As a child, Che Long has been engaged to Yu Jiao, the daughter of one of his father's fellow officials who now, however, plans to renege on the engagement. But when Che Long comes to his mansion peddling his lanterns, he is noticed by Yu Jiao who secretly lets him have some money and urges him to pursue the marriage. Soon afterwards, when her father promises her hand to the son of the rich Zhao family and an appeal to the provincial governor comes to naught, Che Long requests the aid of the original match-maker, now a high official in the capital, and eventually abducts his bride by force. The story ends happily when Che Long later passes the metropolitan examinations with high honors and his wife discovers the hidden family fortune.

---

[1] The Lantern Festival is celebrated on or around the middle of the first lunar month of the year, which is also the first full moon of the year.

Che Long is an example of the many poor students we will encounter in bamboo-clapper songs, who all succeed in restoring their family fortune by making the long journey to the capital (making their way by begging if needs be) and passing the metropolitan examinations as Top-of-the-List. In that way such stories reflect the importance attached to study and the examinations as a means of social mobility and enhancing local prestige and power in the Hakka communities of the last imperial dynasty. Yu Jiao is a representative of the young women in many of such tales who will stay loyal to their fiancés or husbands despite their poverty and is contrasted to all those men and women who only focus on wealth. The account in this story of the humiliation of the poor, of broken engagement promises and of swindles, bribes and raids also may have held a special fascination to Hakka readers because of the endemic feuds that characterized many regions inhabited by Hakka (as well as regions inhabited by Hakka and speakers of other dialects).

The following translation is based on the modern edition of this ballad by Hu Xizhang, *Kezjia zhubange yanjiu* (2010: 326–357). That edition is based on a cyclostyled copy of the text in simplified characters, probably dating from the 1960s or 1970s, a prized possession of the mountain song performer Zhou Tianhe. Hu states as his opinion that this edition must go back to a *guwen* from southeastern Jiangxi.[2] Cynthia Brokaw, however, collected a cyclostyled edition of this ballad which was based on a woodblock edition produced by the Zhou Rixin tang 周日新堂 (the Rixin tang of the Zhou family or the Firm of Zhou Rixin) in Ting city (Changting) in western Fujian.

---

[2] The two *guwen* stories that are introduced as representative of the genre in Cheng Hong 2007, 196 also both focus on the loyalty of a young girl from a rich family to her impoverished childhood fiancé despite her family's pressure to marry a wealthy suitor — both stories end happily when the original fiancé passes the metropolitan examination as Top-of-the-List, is appointed to high office, and marries his fiancée. In one story the impoverished student is reduced to peddling water, in the other he is thrown into jail. The first story, known as *The Water Peddler* (*Maishui ji* 賣水記), is also encountered in the repertoire of other genres (Huang Wenhua and Liu Xiaolan 2006, 212).

In this edition (in which the text has been transcribed in simplified characters) the text is divided in two *juan* 卷 (scrolls); the original edition had been cut in the year *renshen* (most likely 1872). To judge from the xerox copy kindly made available to me by professor Brokaw, the text of this two-*juan* version is very similar to the text presented by Hu. A slightly earlier edition is mentioned in *Zhongguo quyi zhi: Fujian juan* (2007: 156), which lists a *Che gongzi zhuan* 車公子傳 (The tale of young master Che) printed in Tingcheng (Changting) in 1869 by "the Jiujingtang 九經堂 in front of the Prefectural School". According to Zhou Tianhe, this story was also part of the repertoire of bamboo-clapper songs in Xingning. Zhou claimed he had heard that version as a child and that its text was different from the version he provided to Hu, but no further information on these differences is provided.

The story of Che Long selling flower lanterns also circulated as a "wooden-fish book" (*muyu shu* 木魚書). "Wooden-fish books" is the common designation for narrative ballads in Cantonese.[3] In that edition too, the text is divided into two parts, and these parts are each are divided into six chapters. The first part is divided into the chapters: "Introduction," "The marriage of the Che and the Yu families," "Abusing one's power to cheat an orphan," "Che Long sells lanterns," "Sending silver by a clever trick," and "Wrongly blaming Yu Jiao." The second part is divided in the following six chapters: "The marriage proposal of the Zhao family," "A wrong verdict because of bribery," "The bitter complaint against the governor," "Departure for the examinations," "A successful entry into the bureaucracy," and "Returning home in glory."[4] These chapter headings suggest that the story in that genre must have been very similar to the version translated here.

***

---

[3] Kim a.o. pp. 171–173; Zeng and Zhu, pp. 49–51.
[4] Also see Brokaw 2007, 504–505. She states that the Sibao version must have been much shorter than the *muyushu* version.

Che Long Sells Flower Lanterns

Ever since Pangu first opened up heaven and earth,
Each Son of Heaven has had his group of ministers:
Some of them, loyal and good, supported the state;
Others, however, were evil traitors inside the court.
 First of all there was Grand Secretary Minister Lin;
Secondly there was the prime minister named Zhang;
And thirdly there was at court a man surnamed Chen;
Who in charge of the mainstays managed the people.
 Let's abandon this idle talk — I will not sing about it.
At the start of this book I will sing of a famous man:
This man lived in Ji'an prefecture of Jiangxi province,
In the district capital of Dahe, and was surnamed Che.
 But because in the high hall he lacked a son, an heir,
And had no boy as successor, he was pained at heart.
Husband and wife decided to engage in good deeds,
The couple most diligently engaged in good deeds.
 They distributed their gifts in all streets and wards;
They also donated gold for the gods in temple halls.
If some temple was dilapidated, they had it restored;
They also delivered grain to temples and nunneries.
 On hot days they distributed clothes for hot days;
On cold days they distributed warm winter clothes.
They distributed their gifts in all streets and wards;
They personally gave gifts to the poor to save them.
 They doled out food in years of famine and starvation,
On high hills without any water they built tea pavilions.
Where the mountains lacked roads, they built roads;
Where rivers lacked bridges, they constructed bridges.
 The associate judges reported this to Heaven's Court;[5]
Reporting this to the Jade Emperor, the Jade Sovereign.

---

[5] The associate judges belong to the bureaucracy of the underworld that meticulously keeps track of the good and bad deed of every single individual in the Registers of Life and Death.

When the Jade Emperor saw this, he happily smiled,
And he ordered the judges to bring out the registers.
   The judges opened the Registers of Life and of Death,
And checked out those doing good deeds while alive.
They found that lord Che was doing many good deeds —
But his father had harmed people by heinous crimes!
   In this life lord Che was fated to remain without issue:
No son was to be bestowed on him as was only proper.
But the judges then all crowded together, addressing
The Jade Emperor with the following sincere request:
   "If Your Majesty even in this case will not bestow a son,
Then who on earth will be willing to do good deeds?"
Hearing this, the Jade Emperor followed their advice:
"A golden boy and jade maiden will descend to earth:[6]
   The golden boy will descend to the Che family mansion,
And the jade maiden will be a member of the Yu family.
When they will have grown up, they will be married,
And tied together as husband and wife for all eternity."

Let's not sing of the Jade Emperor sending down infants,
Let's sing again of lord Chen and his wife surnamed Jin.
   Having slept till the third watch the lady saw in a dream
How a dragon took up residence in the ancestral temple.
And when all of a sudden she woke up from that dream,
She was covered in a cold sweat that soaked her clothes.
   When she got up, she thereupon informed her husband:
"My dear husband, please listen to what I have to say.
Yesterday night in the third watch I witnessed in a dream
How a dragon took up residence in the ancestral temple."
   At the Yu family, the lady of the house also had a dream,
She also had a dream in which she saw a fresh red flower.
   Her husband explained the meaning of the dream to her:
"A red flower is the symbol of a beautiful young girl!

---

[6] Servant boys and servant girls in the celestial realm are often described as golden boys and jade girls (jade in these cases always refers to white jade).

It doesn't matter whether it will be a boy or a girl;
It's up to Heaven to make that decision on our behalf.
   But once we will have raised the girl to the proper age,
We will hire a teacher for her to teach her her letters.
If we instruct her in female skills and in the Classics,
Even such a little girl can well be a match for any boy."
   Let's not sing of lord Yu and his words to his wife;
Let's change the subject and return to the Che family.
After she had been pregnant for ten months in total,[7]
Lady Jin gave birth to a son who was quite healthy.
   Husband and wife cradled him in turn in their arms;
They loved their son as if he were a treasure, like gold.
When he was brought out on the third day for naming,
The name they chose for their son was Che Long.[8]
   On cold days they held him in their arms inside curtains,
On hot day they waved a fan for the little boy's comfort.
The four seasons, light and shadow, easily passed by,
And without any disaster or problem the boy grew up.
   When Che Long in a flash had reached the age of seven,
They sent the boy to a school to study books and Classics.
But let's not sing about how Che Long read his books,
Let's change the subject to sing of those surnamed Yu.
   When the wife of lord Yu had carried out her pregnancy,
She gave birth to a baby girl who was quite healthy.
Husband and wife cradled her in turn in their arms,
And they treasured her like a pearl on one's hand palm.
   When she was brought out on the third day for naming,
The name they chose for their daughter was Yu Jiao.
The four seasons, light and shadow, easily passed by,
And without any disaster or problem the girl grew up.
   When Yu Jiao in a flash had reached the age of seven,
She surpassed others in her embroidery and needlework.

---

[7] In traditional China a pregnancy was said to last ten months, counting from the moment of fertilization to the month of birth.
[8] "Long" means dragon, so the name is a reference to lady Jin's auspicious dream.

In every skill she was just as smart as all her teachers,
Excelling in music and go, in calligraphy and painting.

Let's not sing of the many joys of those surnamed Yu,
Let's sing of the emperor who was appointing officials.
His Majesty the Son of Heaven made his appointments,
And he appointed lord Che as an investigating censor.
  When lord Che learned that he had been appointed
To Yunnan province to administer the common people,
Husband and wife were both filled with happy joy, and
Having performed a sacrifice to the river, they set out.[9]
  Throughout the long journey they met with no obstacles,
And very soon they had arrived in the capital of Yunnan.
When he had chosen a lucky day to assume his office,
Lord Yu also arrived there as the intendant of education.
  Let's not sing of lord Yu as the intendant of education,
Let's sing of the emperor who was appointing officials.
He appointed lord Zeng as the military governor, to be
In charge of military personnel in all of Yunnan province.
  Now it was the Mid-Autumn Festival of the Eighth Month.[10]
Lord Che and lord Yu were both from the same district,
And Lord Yu also loved the military governor lord Zeng,
Because he hailed from the same region and prefecture.
  "At present I'm serving here as the intendant of education,
And he is here in the same province in charge of the army.
So let me now go and invite Military Governor Lord Zeng,
And also go and invite the investigating censor Lord Che."
  When Lord Che arrived there in the high festive hall,
The two of them bowed to each other as host and guest.
Once Lord Che and Lord Yu had started drinking wine,
They toasted each other in turns, all wrapped in smiles.

---

[9] As they will be traveling by boat, the couple sacrifices to the river to pray for a safe and speedy trip.
[10] The Mid-Autumn Festival is celebrated on the fifteenth of the Eighth Month, because of the full moon on that night.

While they were drinking and engaged in a conversation,
Lord Yu addressed the following question to Lord Che:
"Dear colleague, please allow me to ask, how many sons,
How many fine sons do you have? Please let me know."

When Lord Che was asked this, he replied in this manner:
"My dear wife originally was a daughter of the Jin family.
We have only one son, and that boy just has turned nine.
At present he accompanies us here at my official posting."

When Lord Yu had heard this, he was overcome by joy,
He congratulated him on having such a fine boy, and said:
"I on my side have a daughter who has also turned nine,
Let her be engaged to your son for a future marriage.

Now I have orally promised her here as officials together,
I'll never dare renege on my words to seek another match."
Lord Che answered him repeatedly: "I cannot accept this —
How can my stupid son be a match for your fine daughter?"

But Lord Yu interrupted him, and answered as follows:
"Dear brother Che, what you say makes no sense at all!
At present you are a high official as investigating censor,
How can I reject you as too poor as my in-law relation?"

Lord Zeng rose from his seat and congratulated them,
Congratulating the two gentlemen on this engagement.
"I'll serve as matchmaker and go-between for you both,
Now with one word confirm this match from both sides!"

As soon as Lord Yu heard this, he, overcome with joy,
Picked up a brush to write down the date of her birth:
"Our little daughter became nine years old this year;
She was born at midnight on the fifteenth, First Prime."[11]

When he had written out the eight characters of her birth,[12]
He handed that piece of paper to Military Governor Zeng,

---

[11] First Prime is the fifteenth day in the First Month of the year in the lunar calendar.

[12] The eight characters are the four combinations of two cyclical characters for the year, month, day and hour of birth of prospective marriage partners. As one step in the engagement procedure families exchange the eight characters of their children so a soothsayer may predict the compatibility of the future couple. If the soothsayer advises against a marriage, the engagement can be rescinded.

And when the latter had received it with both his hands,
He in his turn handed it over to Investigating Censor Che.
 When Lord Che had received it, he was quite pleased,
And promptly performed the engagement wine ritual.
Three hundred ounces of silver were the engagement gifts,
And Military Governor Zeng served as the go-between!

Let's not sing of Lord Che finalizing the engagement —
Let's sing again of the emperor appointing his officials:
Lord Zeng was called to court to become grand secretary,
And Lord Yu went home upon the completion of his term.
 Let's not sing of Lord Yu who returned at the end of his term —
Lord Che was reappointed again to administer the people.
Because he was advanced in years, his duties caused him
Such illness and pain that he suffered a debilitating stroke.
 The heart of his wife was filled with trepidation and fear,
And the filial son invited a doctor to examine his father.
When that specialist had felt his pulse, he explained:
"Your father's illness, I'm afraid, is very serious indeed.
 Even if I would possess a medicine that works miracles,
A miracle medicine cannot cure people destined to die.
If anyone would be able to restore Lord Che to health,
No one would descend to the Yellow Springs anymore."
 The doctor then went home after he had taken his pulse.
Lord Che's wife wept and cried, her tears gushing down.
When Che Long saw that his mother was awash in tears,
He realized that his father's illness was extremely serious.
 "If my father now passes away here at his official posting,
How will it be possible for him to return to his native village?"
When Lord Che saw his son was awash in tears, [he said:]
"My son, my dear boy, now please listen to your father.
 If at any moment now I will leave for the realm of shade,
There is nobody left who can take care of you, my boy.
So if I will have passed away here in my official quarters,
Bury me temporarily here in these distant, foreign parts.
 In case you will be lucky enough to grow to manhood,
Transport my remains then back to my old native village.

I don't know whether this illness of mine is for true or not,
But once the realm of shade invites me, I will have to go."
    Even before he had finished imparting his instructions,
He turned into a dream phantom from Southern Branch.[13]
    When Che Long saw that his father had breathed his last,
He loudly wept, overcome by grief, dissolving in tears.
Lord Che's wife also wept in a most heart-rending way,
And the servant girl piteously wept, crying her eyes out.
    Now Lord Che had passed away in his official quarters,
The whole family lacked a master — on whom to rely?
They then bought a coffin in preparation for the funeral;
They kept to the fast for seven days and had masses read.
    When they had had masses read for the full seven days,
Their relatives all heaved a heavy sigh and came to visit,
Heaved a sigh because Lord Che as investigating censor
On quite some occasions had saved a poor man's life.
    "Now he has passed away here in his official quarters!
August Heaven is truly unfair toward good-hearted men.
It shows no consideration for Che Long, this young man,
Nor for his fine father Lord Che, the investigating censor."
    The assembled mourners donated two hundred ounces[14]
For the transportation of Lord Che back to his hometown.
When the relatives donated two hundred ounces of silver,
Che Long made a deep bow to thank these benefactors.
    "When later I will have gloriously passed the examinations,
I will pay you back for your largesse, my dear benefactors!"
He thereupon selected a good hour and also a lucky day,
Sacrificed to the river and transported his father back home.

---

[13] In a well-known tale from the Tang dynasty a man who falls asleep in a drunken stupor has a brilliant career, culminating in his appointment as prefect of Southern Branch. When he wakes up he realizes that it all had been a dream that had taken place in the world of the ants on the southern branch of the acacia tree in his courtyard. For a translation of this tale see Nienhauser 2010, "An Account of the Governor of Southern Branch."

[14] Ounces of silver.

Traveling by water and by land he met with no obstacles,
And straightaway returned to the home of the Che family.
As soon as he entered the east gate, at the foot of the wall
The relatives came and visited them, offering their sacrifice.
  Let's not sing how the relatives offered their sacrifice —
Che Long went to the court and invited the national teacher.[15]
The national master identified the location of the grave:[16]
There at the foot of the east gate Lord Che was laid to rest.
  The national teacher had identified the mouth of a dragon:
Later generations were bound to produce a Top-of-the-List![17]
Once Lord Che had been buried at the foot of the city wall,
The national master wished him well and went back home.

Let's not sing how Lord Che was buried with all due honor,
Or how at home his widow lady Jin lived a life of mourning;
Let's not sing of lady Jin living the chaste life of a widow —
Let's sing of their tenant who conceived of a devilish plan!
  Without further ado he came to the Che family mansion,
Shouting and screaming, screaming and shouting, on and on.

---

[15] "National teacher" (*guoshi*, also translated as preceptor of the state) was an honorific title applied to the highest ranking officials. In traditional vernacular fiction the title is often applied to a senior personal advisor of the ruler and master of esoteric knowledge. Later in the text the national teacher will be called upon to interpret a dream.

[16] In many parts of China it was firmly believed that the geomantic location of a grave could greatly influence the fortune of the deceased's descendants. Reading "the winds and streams" (*feng shui* 風水) of a landscape was a highly developed art, which was practiced widely, not only by professional *feng shui* masters but also other educated people. One of the landscape formations the practitioners of this art looked for was that of a "dragon" and the "mouth of a dragon" counted as an extremely auspicious location. See Bruun 2008 and Paton 2013.

[17] Students who had passed the triennial metropolitan examination in the capital subsequently took part in the palace examination that was nominally presided over by the emperor in person. The person who obtained the first place in the final ranking at the palace examination was known as the "Top-of-the-List" (*zhuangyuan* 狀元) and destined for a brilliant career in the imperial bureaucracy.

"Plowing the three hundred *mu* of your fields and land[18]
I've always paid my full rent, never the tiniest bit short.
   But your father's office had to put such pressure on me
That I was forced to sell my son and to sell my daughters.
They took one thousand ounces of silver away from me —
Main sum and interest, I find, are now exactly the same.
   If you now are willing to pay back the full amount to me,
All problems are settled, and I will not pursue this matter."
Che Long thereupon answered him in the following way:
"You tenant, you're such a mean cheat you're not human!
   When earlier my father served as an investigating censor,
He was a man known in Yunnan for practicing goodness.
The silver we spent at home were the expenses of office;
He was a pure official who didn't abuse his power for gain.
   Now if I may still be too young to know all business deals
My mother should have a full and complete understanding.
So go and take your case to the district magistrate's court,
So who's right and who's wrong can be clearly established."
   When the tenant heard these words, he became frightened:
"I will die here right now in the courtyard of your mansion:
May a few inches of soil be scraped from all of your fields,
And may you end up as a prisoner, a rat bound in shackles!"
   But the widow lady Jin addressed her son in these words:
"My dear son, my darling boy, now please listen to me.
Two thousand ounces of fine silver are not that important;
It's far better to seek peace and quiet than to seek wealth."
   Let's not sing of that tenant swindling them out of money —
Lord Lin also paid them a visit to swindle them out of money.
Without further ado he came to the Che family mansion,
With each and every word cursing them without any pause.
   "When your father had become an investigating censor,
He borrowed silver from me in order to live in grand style.
He borrowed thirty thousand ounces of fine white silver;
Main sum and interest, I find, now are exactly the same.

---

[18] A *mu* 亩 is roughly one seventh of an acre.

If you now are willing to pay back the amount to me in full,
All problems are settled, and I will not pursue this matter."
Che Long thereupon answered him in the following way:
"Lord Lin, you're such a mean cheat you're not human!

Borrowing silver — this issue was never even discussed!
You're only here to swindle some money out of my family,
Even if that might be because I am still too young in years,
My father would still have told my mother about the deal."

Lord Lin thereupon threatened him at the top of his voice
In these words: "Che Long, you are no human being at all.
My father presently serves at court as a grand secretary,
One word from him to the Emperor, and you'll be killed!

You will be arrested, taken to court, meet with misery,
And you'll end up as a prisoner, a rat bound in shackles!"
This scared Che Long so much his courage was shattered,
And his mother on hearing these words dissolved in tears.

With tears in her eyes she addressed her son as follows:
"My dear child, please listen to what I will tell to you now.
At present that white silver is really not all that important;
It's far better to seek peace and quiet than to seek wealth."

When they had sold all their fields and also all their farms,
When they had sold their male servants and female slaves,
They pawned their garden pavilions to the Zhang family,
And so scraped together thirty thousand to pay Lord Lin.

Once they had sold their house, they had no place to live,
So they rented a thatched shed as their temporary shelter.
Mother and son were truly living in miserable conditions
And from early dawn they wept until the western sunset.

Che Long blamed his father for having died before his time:
"Because my father died we are now reduced to poverty;
Here at home I presently suffer extreme cold and misery,
And there is nobody to take care of me, this lonely orphan!"

At home they didn't have any money, had no rice to cook;
They passed their days, suffering hunger, enduring misery.
Che Long did his best to relieve his dear mother's misery:
"Dear mother, please put your worries and sorrows aside.

Please put your worries aside and don't suffer vexation,
At your age such vexation may very well harm your health."
After he had dispelled his mother's one thousand worries,
He went to the school to study his books and the Classics.

When Che Long arrived at the school and went inside,
His study friends asked him what had happened to him.
Che Long immediately addressed them in these words:
"My dear friends, please listen to what I will have to say.

My father died early and we were swindled by Lord Lin,
Because of his scheme we are now reduced to poverty."
When his friends heard this, they all heaved heavy sighs,
And exclaimed: "That Lord Lin is less than a human being!"

They admonished Che Long not to give in to his miseries:
"You should still spend your days in a bright, happy mood.
The essays you write are, we all see, the best of the class,
So at some future date you are fated to serve at court.

We will give you three hundred ounces of white silver,
Take them with you back home to pay for daily expenses."
When Che Long received this money, he was very happy,
And profusely thanked his good-hearted fellow students.

"If ever at some later day I will enjoy riches and glory,
I will pay you back for this favor, as deep as the ocean!"
Straightaway he went back to the high hall, having bought
Some firewood and rice to provide his mother a fine meal.

When his mother saw him coming back, she asked him:
"Why are you so happy and pleased now you come home?"
Che Long stepped forward and answered her as follows:
"Dear mother, please listen to what I now will have to say.

When today I went to the school and told what happened,
My fellow students and friends turned into my benefactors:
Because they gave me three hundred ounces of white silver
To take back home with me to pay for our daily expenses."

When his mother heard this, she was overcome by joy:
"You are deeply indebted to your fellow students for this.
My son, if you pass the examinations at some future date,
You must pay back your friends, these great benefactors!"

Che Long stepped forward and addressed her as follows:
"My dear mother, please listen to what I now have to say.
For the moment we are living here at home in dire poverty,
So for the time being this year I'll become a lantern seller.
Tomorrow happens to be the day of the Lantern Festival —[19]
Without a skill one will consume even the largest capital!"

His mother then addressed him in the following manner:
"My dear boy, now please listen to what I have to say.
My baby, sweet boy, you only turned twelve this year,
So how would you know how to stich flower lanterns?"

Che Long then addressed her in the following manner:
"Please give me a free hand to take care of this business."
He went out to the market and bought brushes and glue,
And he also bought every kind of colored paper for sale.

At the same time he also bought two flower lanterns;
By the light of these flower lanterns, he made his own.
On his lanterns he didn't depict bookish wise sayings,
But he depicted famous people from earlier dynasties.

He depicted Han Xiangzi, who enters playing the flute,[20]
And the Eight Immortals performing songs in the streets.[21]
He depicted the Divine Husbandman creating the grains,
The five grains that, once harvested, feed the people.[22]

---

[19] The Lantern Festival was celebrated on the fifteenth of the First Month of the year. Because it often included the display of elaborate and specially constructed lanterns and illuminations, the festival often stretched out over a few days.

[20] Han Xiangzi 韓湘子 was a grand-nephew of the staunch Confucian Han Yu 韓愈 (768–824). Later legend turned Han Xiangzi into a wonder-working magician who even managed to convince his uncle of the truth of Daoism and convert him to the cult of immortality. From the 13th century onward Han Xiangzi was counted as one of the Eight Immortals. Lai 1972; Yang Erzeng 2007.

[21] The Eight Immortals were a popular group of immortals in visual arts and on the stage from the 13th century on. Lai 1972; Wu Yuantai 1993.

[22] The Divine Husbandman (*Shennong* 神農) from a mythic past is said to have discovered the use of grains and medicinal plants by tasting them all. He is credited with the invention of agriculture. The five kinds of grains are variously defined, but are often believed to refer to wheat, two kinds of millet, rice and beans.

He depicted the Sage Confucius in the act of creation,
The Sage Confucius, forever famous for his wise books.[23]
Despised by his wife and ignored by his brother's wife:
A man lonely and cold and miserable just like Su Qin.[24]
    He depicted Liu Zhiyuan who, addicted to gambling,
Had to seek shelter in horse stables or in old temples;[25]
Lü Mengzheng who in his hovel had the great fortune
Of being selected by young miss Liu as her husband.[26]
    He depicted the Three Kingdoms of earlier dynasties:
Guan Yu, Zhang Fei and Liu Bei, all sharing one heart.

---

[23] Kong Qiu 孔丘 (Confucius, 551–479 BC) is often credited if not with authoring then at least with editing the Classics.

[24] Su Qin 蘇秦 (ca. 300 BC) had studied strategy and rhetoric, but his first attempt to make a career ended in a dismal failure, so when he returned home he was despised by his wife and his sister-in-law. Later in life he would become prime minister in the state of Qi and lead an alliance of the eastern states against the emerging power of Qin. Accused of treason he eventually was quartered. The tale of his initial failure and later success was widely popular on stage.

[25] Liu Zhiyuan 劉智遠 (895–948) was the founder of the Posterior Han dynasty (947–950), one of the short-lived Five Dynasties in Northern China in the 10th century. When in his youth he was only a simple farmhand, his employer became convinced of his future greatness and gave him his daughter Li Sanniang 李三娘 as wife, but he was despised by her brothers for his dissolute behavior. Following the death of his father-in-law Liu Zhiyuan did not dare return home after he had messed up once again. He then secretly took his leave of Li Sanniang and left to pursue a career in the army. Following his departure, Li Sanniang, who stayed loyal to her husband and refused to remarry, suffered greatly at the hands of her brothers, but eventually the couple was reunited. The story of Liu Zhiyuan and Li Sanniang was widely popular on stage in late imperial China. See Doleželová-Velingerová and Crump 1971.

[26] Lü Mengzheng 呂蒙正 (946–1011) rose to the highest ranks of the imperial bureaucracy after having gained entry into it by passing the examinations. Later legend stressed his poverty during the days of his youth. When his future wife miss Liu 柳 was asked to select a husband by throwing a ball into the crowd of assembled suitors, it was Lü Mengzheng who caught the ball. When she refused to repudiate the match as demanded by her father, he threw the couple out, and they were reduced to such poverty that they had to live in a dilapidated kiln. When Lü Mengzheng eventually passed the examinations with highest honors, his father-in-law informed him that he had only thrown them out to spur him on to greater effort. This story was widely popular on stage in traditional China. see Wang 1984/1985.

In the Peach Orchard they swore an oath as brothers,
Surpassing full brothers born of the same mother.²⁷
    He depicted An'an while delivering rice to his mother,
An'an delivering rice in order to feed his dear mother.
He depicted Jiang Shi in his practice of filial piety,
And Pang Sanniang suffering many kinds of misery.²⁸
    A good wife seeking her husband: this Meng Jiangnü
Brought down the Great Wall for miles by her weeping.²⁹
He depicted Mulian who came to his mother's rescue,
Saving his mother from hell so she ascended to heaven.³⁰

---

²⁷ The Three Kingdoms refers to 3rd century when the Chinese empire was divided between the three kingdoms of Wei (220–265), Wu (220–280), and Shu-Han (220–263), following the collapse of the Eastern (or Later) Han dynasty (25–220). The civil wars leading up to this tri-partition and the continuing wars between the three kingdoms were very popular with professional storytellers and on the stage. While canonical historiography considered the Wei (founded by the warlord Cao Cao's 曹操 son Cao Pi 曹丕) as the successor to the Han, popular opinion accorded legitimacy to Shu-Han, because it had been founded by Liu Bei 劉備 (161–223), a distant relative of the Han ruling house. Liu Bei and his two sworn brothers, the heavy and impulsive Zhang Fei 張飛 and the tall and proud Guan Yu 關羽, became the central characters in the ballads, plays and novels devoted to this saga. See Luo Guanzhong 1991; Idema and West 2012.

²⁸ When the filial son Jiang Shi 姜詩 at the behest of his mother divorces his wife Pang Sanniang 龐三娘 she moves in with a poor relative. In order to support her in her poverty her young and loving son An'an 安安 provides her daily with rice. When he cries because he misses his mother, she tells him not to do so, so as not to upset his father. Eventually the family is happily united when Jiang Shi's mother realizes she has been deluded by slander. Under a wide variety of titles this story was quite popular on the traditional stage.

²⁹ During the reign of the cruel First Emperor (221–210 BC) Meng Jiangnü's 孟姜女 husband is called up as a corvée laborer to work on the construction of the Great Wall, but soon dies because of exhaustion and his body is buried inside the wall. When winter approaches and Meng Jiangnü travels to the work site to bring her husband a set of winter clothes, she learns that her husband has died. She then weeps until the wall collapses where her husband had been buried, so she can collect the bones and provide them with a proper burial. See Idema 2007.

³⁰ Mulian 目連 was one of the disciples of the Buddha. When he learned that his mother had been condemned to suffering in the deepest hell because of her many sins, he traveled down to the bottom of hell in order to liberate her and to ensure

Meng Zong wept over bamboos, so winter grew shoots;[31]
Wang Xiang searched for carps and lay down on the ice.[32]
He depicted Guo Hua who was seeing off guests,
And Yueying, who was selling rouge in her shop:
Because he bought rouge there for so many days,
The two of them fell in love, and hoped for a wedding.[33]
Ding Lan carved wooden statues of both his parents,[34]
Guo Ju buried his son, so Heaven gifted him with gold.[35]

---

her rebirth in heaven. This myth was used to explain the origin of the Ghost Festival in the middle of the seventh lunar month when people made offerings to Buddhist monasteries to ensure a speedy rebirth of their ancestors. Greatly developed, the story was widely performed as a ballad already in the Tang (617–906). Mair 1983. In later times it was widely performed as a play that might take three days or more for its complete performance. Guo 2005; Grant and Idema 2011; Hou Jie 2002.

[31] The story of Meng Zong 孟宗 is included in *Ershisi xiao* 二十四孝 (*Twenty-Four Exemplars of Filial Piety*), a widely popular primer in late imperial China. When his evil step-mother demands fresh bamboo shoots to eat, the young boy lies down on the ground — moved by his extraordinary filial piety bamboo shoots thereupon miraculously emerge. Jordan 1986.

[32] The story of Wang Xiang 王祥 is also included in *Ershisi xiao*. His evil step-mother wants fresh carp in the middle of the winter when all rivers are frozen over. When Wang Xiang lies down on the ice to melt it with the warmth of his body, two carps jump into his hands. Jordan 1986.

[33] Guo Hua 郭華 falls in love with Wang Yueying 王月英, a shop assistant in her mother's rouge shop, and comes back repeatedly to buy rouge. Yueying promises to meet him on the night of the Lantern Festival in the Xiangguo Monastery, but when she gets there Guo Hua, who had been out drinking with friends, is fast asleep and she cannot wake him up. As love tokens she leaves a shoe and a handkerchief with him. When Guo Hua wakes up, he is overcome by remorse and suffocates upon swallowing the handkerchief. When the body is discovered the next morning, the shoe is traced to Yueying. When she is confronted with Guo Hua's body, she pulls the handkerchief from his mouth, whereupon he revives. The judge thereupon orders the couple's marriage. The story was widely popular on stage.

[34] Ding Lan 丁蘭 is an exemplar of filial piety whose story is included in *Ershisi xiao*. Upon the death of his parents, he had wooden statues made of his parents. When his wife damaged these, he divorced her. Jordan 1986.

[35] Guo Ju's 郭巨 story is also included in *Ershisi xiao*. Guo Ju and his wife are so poor that they cannot provide for both his elderly mother and their infant son. When Guo Ju notices that his mother gives her food to his infant son, he decides to bury

He depicted Yulian throwing herself into a river to die,[36]
And Xuemei who out of chastity moved to her in-laws.[37]
  He depicted Rihong while searching for her husband,
And also the wooden fish that announced her begging.[38]
He depicted Li Sanniang who had to push the mill,
Who had to push the mill in its room till break of day.[39]

---

the little body, but when he digs a hole, he finds a pot with gold, saying "for the filial son Guo Ju." Jordan 1986.

[36] Qian Yulian 錢玉蓮 is the female protagonist of *Jingchai jJi* 荊釵記 (*The Thorn Hairpin*), one of the four famous early *chuanqi* 傳奇 plays. She is the wife of the poor student Wang Shipeng 王十朋. When Wang passes the examinations with highest honors but refuses to marry the daughter of a prime minister, he is appointed to a low post in a remote region. When he entrusts a friend with a letter to his wife, the friend substitutes it with a writ of divorce because he wants to make Yulian his concubine. Yulian knows that the writ of divorce is false but to escape pressure to remarry, she tries to commit suicide by jumping into the Yangzi. She is, however, rescued by a passing high official who adopts her as his daughter. When that man later becomes Wang Shipeng's superior, he engineers the couple's happy reunion. Birch 1973.

[37] Qin Xuemei's 秦雪美 parents have engaged her at a very young age to Shang Lin 商林, but while her father rises to high position at court, Shang Lin's family falls on hard times. Qin Xuemei's father invites Shang Lin to the capital for his studies, but when he falls ill, he has Xuemei's servant girl marry him under her mistress' name. When Shang Lin discovers he has been tricked, he soon dies. Xuemei's father wants her to marry the new Top-of-the-List, but she adamantly refuses to do so and moves to the Shang family in order to raise the boy borne to Shang Lin and the servant girl. This story was widely popular in traditional popular literature.

[38] Meng Rihong 夢日紅 is the wife of the student Gao Yanzhen 高彥珍. After he has left for the examinations, she takes care of his parents in the most virtuous fashion. After they have died, she travels to the capital, supporting herself by begging, singing her begging songs to the accompaniment of a "wooden fish" (a hollowed-out piece of wood carved in the shape of a fish and used as a rhythmical instrument). Her husband had, upon passing the examinations, been forced to marry the daughter of a prime minister who had not allowed him to contact his family and has Meng Rihong poisoned when she shows up in the capital. Meng Rihong revives, receives a divine sword, established great merit for the state, and eventually achieves revenge. This story is widely popular in traditional drama.

[39] After Liu Zhiyuan has left to join the army, her evil brothers force the pregnant Li Sanniang to work all through the night pushing the mill. In the mill room she will eventually give birth to her son and, as she is all alone, she has to bite through the umbilical cord. Doleželová-Velingerová and Crump 1973.

He produced flower lanterns with ancient characters,
The flower lanterns he produced were quite original.
The different kinds of flower clusters were well done;
The lantern skirts and lantern belts also were perfect.[40]
    When he had hung these lanterns up in the high hall,
He asked his mother to come out and to have a look.
And when his mother saw these fine flower lanterns,
She praised him for his ingenuity in making lanterns.
    But secretly she thought: "In the past he was a student,
But today he has become someone who sells lanterns.
How bitterly my dear son has to suffer now at present:
He has to sell lanterns in order to feed me, his mother!"

Che Long stepped forward and addressed her thusly:
"Dear mother, please stay here at home, seated at ease.
I will take my lanterns outside, to the market streets,
And right now turn myself into a man who sells lanterns."
    He offered them for sale on the eastern and western streets;
He offered them for sale on the western and eastern streets.
He offered them for sale on every corner of those streets,
But there was nobody who bought any lantern from him.
    Pondering the matter from all sides he had no choice,
But to raise his voice and call to the people in the market:
"Whoever buys my flower lanterns and lights the candle,
Will see all his wishes fulfilled as soon as they are uttered.
    If an elderly man buys my lanterns and lights the candle,
All those who lacked energy will find they have energy;
If an elderly woman buys a lantern and lights the candle,
Her eyesight will be restored and her ears will hear well.
    If an official buys my lanterns and lights the candle,
His appointment at court will be further increased in rank;
And if a student buys my lanterns and lights the candle,
He'll pass the capital examinations as the Top-of-the-List.
    If a young man buys my lanterns and lights the candle,
He will buy fields and build houses, forever prosperous;

---

[40] I do not know to which part of a lantern "lantern skirts" and "lantern belts" refer.

And if a farmer will buy my lanterns and light the candle,
Grain will fill his granaries — gold measured by the peck.
  If a merchant will buy my lanterns and light the candle,
He'll make great profits on even the tiniest investments;
And if a pupil will buy my lanterns and light the candle,
He'll enter the prefectural school, becoming a student.
  If a widow will buy my lanterns and light the candle,
Heaven will quickly send down a unicorn son and heir;
If a servant girl buys my lanterns and lights the candle,
She'll end up as a lady too behind a screen of pearls."
  But even when his throat was coarse, no one bought,
And by chance he had reached a memorial archway.
He saw how neatly the archway had been constructed:
The scenery outside the gate was all gilded with gold.
  Che Long sat down there for a while to take some rest,
His rack of flower lanterns put down under the archway.
And while he sat there on a rock with nothing else to do,
He composed a poem to dispel the gloom from his heart:

The poem reads:
I see from afar the green hills, encircled by a hundred birds;
Eaves of houses face each other at the time of going home.
Today I'm exposed to suffering because I sell these lanterns,
But next year at court I'll be dressed in the gown of my rank.

Let's not sing of Che Long while he is intoning his poems,
Let's change the subject and sing again of the Yu family.
Lord Yu had taken his seat in the high hall of the Yu family,
And as he raised his voice, he called for his one daughter.
  "Tomorrow happens to be the day of the Lantern Festival,
Make sure to buy everything needed for the celebration.
In your private room you've nothing else to do right now,
So put together flower lanterns to offer to the ancestors."
  As soon as Yu Jiao had heard this command of her father,
She called for Meixiang, her personal servant girl, and said:
"Tomorrow happens to be the day of the Lantern Festival,
And my father has told me to put together flower lanterns.

But today I'm not feeling too well, I'm also quite listless,
And I have no intention to depict those ancient figures.
So I order you to go and buy some outside in the market,
Come back with flower lanterns to offer to the ancestors."

When Meixiang heard this, she was filled with great joy;
Having received her orders, she immediately started out.
But as soon as she was outside the mansion's main gate,
She already saw there a person who was selling lanterns.

She saw the many different scenes on the flower lanterns,
Each flower, each cluster capable of stirring one's feelings.
So she asked for how much the flower lanterns were on sale:
"Please tell me how much the price for a lantern may be."

When Che Long heard this, he addressed her as follows:
"Meixiang, dear girl, now please listen to what I will say.
Now one flower lantern will cost you two *qian* and a half,[41]
So two flower lanterns together make five *qian* of silver."

Meixiang thereupon addressed him in this manner:
"Dear brother lantern seller, please listen to my words.
Our mansion now will buy two of your flower lanterns,
But I must ask you to carry them inside, into our house."

When Che Long heard this, he was filled with great joy,
And carrying the flower lanterns, he set out on the road.
He straightaway went to the mansion of the Yu family,
And sat down in the southern loft, inside the courtyard.

Meixiang went and reported to her mistress Yu Jiao;
In the inner apartments she informed the young lady:
"Young mistress, you told me to buy flower lanterns,
So I've bought flower lanterns to offer to the ancestors.

These two flower lanterns are quite exquisitely made,
The workmanship and various colors of highest quality."
When the young lady heard this, she was filled with joy:
"Let me get properly dressed, then I'll have a good look."

---

[41] A *qian* 錢 as a measure of weight equals one tenth of a *liang* 兩 (ounce).

She combed her hair into a heavy dragon-phoenix bun,
And in her hair she stuck many precious baubles of gold.
The long golden hairpins were divided in left and right,
And the pearly rings in her ears were richly bejeweled.
  On top she wore a red silk jacket quite exquisitely made,
Over a brocaded embroidered skirt made of white satin.
The golden lotuses of her feet were less than two inches;[42]
Eyebrows and autumn waves were truly quite startling!
  Properly dressed from head to toe she was so beautiful!
Accompanied by Meixiang she walked through the gate.
In quite a hurry she hastened to the courtyard's center
To have a look at the flower lanterns — and their vendor.
  She noticed that he was not a lantern-selling type at all;
His fingers were slender and tapered: a sign of greatness.
She remembered that last night she had seen in a dream,
Had seen that a yellow dragon had entered the courtyard.
  The dragon's head in her dream rested on the balustrade,
And now today this lantern seller had come to pay a visit.
The yellow dragon in her dream was a sign of greatness,
And in the future this person would be seated at court!

The young lady went to her room, filled with longing,
And there she called for Meixiang, her own servant girl.
"My dear girl, I have a matter I want to entrust to you:
Now go back and question that person selling lanterns.
  Ask him from which prefecture he is and which district,
Ask him or his surname and name without any mistake.
Such a superbly talented person and still not a student!
This lantern selling debases a man of culture and style!"
  When Meixiang heard this, she answered as follows:
"Why should I go to the courtyard and question that guy?
When buying lanterns one talks about lantern business,
So why do I have to go and question that lantern seller?

---

[42] Small bound feet are conventionally compared to golden lotuses.

And in case any outsider would come to know about this,
This might greatly damage your reputation, young lady!"
The young mistress immediately loudly cursed her out:
"You brazen hussy, you are not even a human being!

You are my servant girl here in the inner apartments,
So why are you so argumentative and disobey orders?
If you do not put these questions to that lantern seller,
Thirty lashes of a leather whip will ruin your tendons!"

When Meixiang heard this, she was truly frightened,
And she left in a hurry to question that lantern seller.
And when Meixiang entered into the great high hall,
She promptly started to question the lantern seller.

"My young lady ordered me to ask these questions:
From which prefecture, from which district are you?
What is your surname and name, which your family?
Why are you selling lanterns and not studying books?"

Che Long thereupon addressed her in this manner:
"Dear Meixiang, my sister, please listen to my words.
I do not hail from some different district far away,
I am registered in this prefecture and in this district.

My surname is Che, my name Long, and my father
Administered the people as an investigating censor.
When my father died, we were robbed of our money;
That rapacity of others reduced us to direst poverty.

Pondering the matter from all sides, I saw no way
But to become a person who sells flower lanterns."
The young lady, stealthily listening behind a screen,
Clearly heard that this man was her husband to be!

"I will not blame Heaven and I will not blame Earth,
I can only blame my fate for causing this hindrance.
While still at home, my husband is no student at all,
But because of poverty has become a lantern seller.

Now today you have come here selling your lanterns —
If my father would know that you are now so poor,
That you are so poor and have fallen on hard times,
He definitely will renege on this marriage contract.

Our mansion already bought two flower lanterns,
Let me buy two more lanterns to be delivered."
When Meixiang entered the young lady's room,
She informed her young mistress in a soft voice:
   "He is not from a different prefecture or district,
He is a man from this prefecture and this district.
His surname is Che, he told me, his name is Long,
And his late father was an investigating censor."
   The young lady immediately addressed her thusly:
"Meixiang, now listen to what I will have to say.
We already bought two flower lanterns from him,
Let's add two more flower lanterns to be delivered.
   You say that his flower lanterns are very well made,
So I have weighed out the silver to take back to him.
Two flower lanterns make for five ounces exactly,
But I add two ounces of silver for him to come back."
   Taking the silver, Meixiang hurried to see him off,
And personally handed the silver to Che Long, saying:
"The young lady says that your lanterns are perfect,
So please come and deliver two more of your lanterns.
   Deliver those flower lanterns to our house tomorrow,
And we'll weigh out the silver to take home with you."
When Che Long got this silver, he was filled with joy;
He returned home as fast as his feet could carry him.

He went straightaway to the house of the Che family,
And filled with joy and elation he greeted his mother.
When his mother saw he was filled with such joy,
She immediately asked him the following question:
   "How much money did you make selling lanterns?
How come you are so happy, all wrapped in smiles?"
Che Long stepped forward and addressed her thusly:
"Dear mother, please listen to what I'll have to say.
   Today I was able to sell two of my flower lanterns,
And for those I received five ounces of white silver.
They also said that my flower lanterns were perfect,
And that I should deliver two more to their mansion.

Today, when selling lanterns, I had a stroke of luck:
I came across a young lady of the inner apartments,
Who, weighing silver in the dark, made a mistake,
And so weighed out two ounces too many for me."

When his mother heard this, she started guessing,
And she said, "My dear boy, now please listen to me.
That young lady did not make a mistake in weighing,
But she took pity on you because you are so poor.

She was concerned because of your many sufferings,
So she weighed out some extra silver to give to you."
But let's not sing of his mother's words on this topic —
Che Long took his leave of her and went to his study.

Without further ado he entered his study, and there,
Having lighted a lantern, he made his flower lanterns.
He did not depict any idle tale or scandalous story,
But he depicted famous figures from earlier times.

He depicted the maiden Zhang Shuying, who remains
Famous in every household for cutting off her hair.[43]
Busily, busily, he worked on them till midnight,
Until he had finished these two flower lanterns.

Che Long considered that he could not go to sleep,
Because otherwise he might not wake up at dawn.
When in the fifth watch the sky finally turned bright,
He heated some water in the kitchen, all in a hurry.

Having fried some cold rice and taken a quick bite,
He shouldered the flower lanterns and set out fast.
Straightaway he hastened to the Yu family mansion,
Where he knocked on the gate, calling repeatedly.

When Yu Jiao heard that he had arrived already,
She called for Meixiang, her personal servant girl.

---

[43] Zhang Shuying 張淑英 is most likely is a mistake for Pei Shuying 裴淑英, a well-known example of female loyalty of the early 7th century. She remained loyal to her banished husband, and when she was pressured to remarry, cut off her hair. Eventually she was reunited with husband. The story was adapted for the stage in the 16th century and continued to enjoy great popularity.

Meixiang immediately went out to welcome him,
And the first thing she said was: "Lantern seller,
　Our mansion will buy these two flower lanterns,
But the master of the house cannot know of this.
I will now take you with me to the flower garden,
And then we'll quickly weigh out the silver for you."
　When Che Long heard this, he was filled with joy;
Shouldering his flower lanterns, he entered the garden.
Without further ado he walked into that flower garden,
And once inside the garden sat down amidst the rocks.
　Sitting there in the flower garden, he was told to wait;
They kept him waiting till noon, so he couldn't but cry.
They kept Che Long waiting till darkness started to fall:
He waited there from early dawn till the sun set down.
　Che Long's heart by now was filled with resentment:
"You shouldn't be fooling me till dusk is coming down."
He blamed the young lady for lacking human decency,
For causing all these problems for him, for Che Long!
　"Perhaps you don't have the money to buy my lanterns,
But I am starving from hunger and my eyes give out."
The young lady heard how her husband was blaming her —
"Where do I now find the white silver for paying him?"
　The young lady immediately came up with a scheme,
And promptly called Meixiang, her personal servant girl.
　Meixiang approached her to listen to her instructions.
"Tomorrow is the festival of the First Night of the Year.[44]
Yesterday his lordship my father ordered me to buy
Whatever was needed for the sacrifice to the ancestors.
　So I now order you to buy those goods in the market,
Bring back some sweet candy and Hangzhou peanuts.
Now make sure to go to the market as fast as you can,
So we can offer these to the ancestors on your return."

---

[44] The First Night is a year's first night of a full moon, and so coincides with the night of the fifteenth of the First Month in the lunar calendar.

When Meixiang had obediently left for the market,
The young lady was very much pleased in her heart.
Her secret intention was to write a letter to Che Long,
But then she was visited by her two sisters-in-law.

The young lady asked her sisters-in-law to sit down,
And poured the two of them an excellent cup of tea.
When they had drunk their tea and put down the cup,
Her two sisters-in-law addressed her in this manner:

"Dear sister, how come you are not yet fully dressed?
Why are you still wearing some of your old clothes?
Tomorrow is the feast of the First Night of the Year,
Everything everywhere has a completely new look.

Dear sister, as you and we have nothing else to do,
Let's all go to the flower garden and have some fun."
The young lady thereupon addressed them as follows:
"My dear sisters-in-law, please listen to what I'll say.

Tonight, alas, I am not feeling all too well, I'm afraid,
So I cannot accompany you now to the flower garden.
Let's wait till tomorrow, when I will be feeling better,
To go all three sisters together to the flower garden."

When her sisters-in-law heard this, they very happily
Took their leave of the young lady and left her alone.

Let's not sing of the sisters-in-law going back again —
The young lady Yu Jiao now started writing her letter.
She lifted her brush and set out to write a letter
Addressed to her mother-in-law of the Che family:

"Earlier my father-in-law was an investigating censor,
So for what reason are we now suffering such misery?
From now own you cannot sell lanterns anymore,
Your talented son is not meant to be a lantern seller.

I hereby send you three hundred ounces of silver,
So you, my mother-in-law, will have enough to live.
Two hundred ounces will cover household expenses;
One hundred ounces are for your son's study costs.

Today he came to our house, selling flower lanterns,
But fortunately my father did not learn of that fact.

If he would know how poor your family has become,
He is bound to renege on the marriage engagement."

When she had finished writing this one letter of hers,
She enclosed it in an envelope and she was all done.
She thereupon found herself two wicker rice baskets,
And placed the silver and the letter in these baskets.

She covered silver and letter with white rice on top;
She didn't even let Meixiang know what she'd done.
And when her maid came back home from the market,
The young lady gave Meixiang the following order:

"You now go and carry this rice to the flower garden,
And send this lantern seller off with this load of rice."
When Meixiang heard this, she replied as follows:
"So you do not give any silver to that lantern seller?"

The young lady thereupon told her: "This rice is fine,
It will allow him to get through the day back at home.
You just tell him that his lordship had invited guests,
That's why we have to send you home with this rice."

When Meixiang carried the rice she could barely walk,
So she immediately complained about the young lady,
So when Yu Jiao heard her, she loudly cursed her out:
"You brazen hussy, you are not even a human being!

If you do not carry these baskets of rice to that man,
Thirty lashes of a leather whip will ruin you tendons!"
This scared Meixiang so much that she was frightened,
And hurriedly she carried the baskets to the garden.

When Meixiang had taken them promptly to the garden,
She straightaway told that seller of flower lanterns:
"Today his lordship had invited guests for a banquet,
And we do not have the silver to pay you right now.

These three pecks of rice are as good as white silver,
Take them with you back home to pass your days."
When Che Long heard this, he was very much upset:
"This young lady in her chambers in less than human!

Without money she still wants to buy flower lanterns —
Why on earth does she send me off with white rice?

I had to wait from early dawn till late evening dusk,
I've suffered such hunger all day my eyes lack sight!"
One load of white rice weighs several tens of pounds:
When Che Long saw this, his eyes brimmed with tears.

When he shouldered the rice, he hardly could walk,
And he promptly complained about the young lady:
"Yesterday when I sold my lanterns, you paid all right,
But today you're causing problems because I am poor."

Meixiang immediately addressed him in this manner:
"You brother lantern seller, now you listen very clearly.
Tomorrow it is the feast of the First Night of the Year,
So his lordship will come to the garden for his enjoyment.

Now if you are discovered by him, you will be arrested.
You'll be tightly bound with hemp ropes, and no mercy!
His lordship will have you locked up in the prison room,
And he definitely will say that you're a common thief."

When Che Long heard these words, he was frightened;
Shouldering the white rice, he left that flower garden.
With the heavy load on his shoulders he wept piteously,
Complaining that the young lady had no human feelings.

After one stretch of the road, the next stretch waited,
And because of the load his shoulders were bleeding.
"Young lady, if you marry this year, may your husband die next year,
So you will have to live all alone each year of your life!"

After he had crossed one hill, another hill was waiting,
And because of the load his back was covered in blood.
"Young lady, if you marry this year, may your husband die next year,
So you will have to be a widow for the rest of your life."

Let's not sing of Che Long complaining about the girl —
Eventually Che Long arrived at his own house again.
Putting down the baskets of rice, he breathed deeply,
And raised his voice to weep and cry, awash in tears.

When his mother saw her son weeping in this way,
She promptly asked her son: "My dear boy, my baby,

Why did you only return so late from selling lanterns,
And why are you weeping and crying, awash in tears?"
    Che Long stepped forward and addressed her thusly:
"Dear mother, please listen to what I will have to say.
That young lady in her room lacks all natural decency,
So she has been causing all kinds of problems for me.
    She kept me waiting from early dawn till evening dusk,
Causing me such hunger that she almost had me killed.
Without any money she still wanted to buy lanterns,
And then she sent me back home with this load of rice.
    Today this young lady acted with deliberate malice,
This heavy load of white rice has almost done me in!"
    His mother thereupon addressed him in these words,
Saying to him: "My dear boy, now listen to my words.
Tomorrow will be the feast of the First Night of the Year,
This white rice comes in handy as food for the festival.
    Now we have the bridge, we can break down the road:
White rice can also be exchanged against yellow gold.
The young lady acted from the goodness of her heart:
This white rice is perfect to save us from our poverty."
    But when his mother poured the rice into a container,
She found no end of white silver inside those baskets.
This scared his mother so much she was frightened,
And she immediately addressed her son in this way:
    "My son, it was pitch black when you came home,
You definitely must have joined a band of robbers,
And have bored through fences, dug through walls,
To steal white silver from people and bring it home."
    She loudly cursed out her son as a good-for-nothing:
"Good people you don't imitate, only the evil kind!
Yesterday night lord Cao's mansion was burglarized,
So I will now take this white silver back to his place."
    When Che Long heard this, he addressed her thusly:
"I definitely am not some kind of common criminal!
I don't know what the young lady may have intended.
She's wanting to cause problems for us, poor people.

She sent me back home, saying she had no silver —
Perhaps it was her who put the silver in the baskets."
When his mother heard this, she looked more closely,
And found a letter inside one of the wicker baskets.

Che Long of course immediately opened the letter,
And as soon as he had read it, his tears came down.
"Had I known that she was my very own wife to be,
I never should have complained against my wife.

The words of grievance and expressions of hatred,
All those words that I spoke, may they turn to dust!"
When his mother saw her son so all awash in tears,
She promptly asked her son: "What is the reason?

What are the extraordinary words in that letter?
Why are you are you even more sad upon reading?
Are there any characters in the letter you don't know?
Please read it again, very carefully, so it will be clear."

Che Long thereupon addressed his mother thusly:
"My dear mother, please listen to what I have to say.
The one who bought my lanterns today was my wife,
She gave the silver so we may get through the days."

He read out the letter to his mother for her to hear:
"To my respected mother-in-law of the Che family.

Earlier his lordship served as an investigating censor,
But today your son has fallen on hard times indeed.
As of today don't allow him to go and sell lanterns;
Your talented son is not meant to sell lanterns.

When today he came to our house selling lanterns,
My dear father did fortunately not learn of that fact,
Because if he would know how destitute you all are,
He definitely would renege on the marriage contract.

I now have here three hundred ounces of fine silver,
Three pecks of white rice and also some yellow gold.
Two hundred ounces are for your household expenses,
One hundred cover the costs of your fine son's study."

When his mother heard this, her tears coursed down:
"Rare are the wives that are even more wise than she!

My son, if you in the future achieve glory and riches,
You should bring home this bride as fast as can be."

Let's not sing of his mother still sighing in admiration —
Che Long devoted himself to his studies even more.
Let's not sing of Che Long devoting himself to his books,
Let's change the subject, sing of the man surnamed Yu.
   Lord Yu was seated in the high hall, and when he saw
The flower lanterns, he was very pleased in his heart.
One flower lantern had been hung up in the upper end,
One flower lantern had been hung up in the lower end.
   One lantern had been hung in the southern pavilion,
And one lantern had been hung in the northern building.
When lord Yu saw the sight of these lanterns, [he thought:]
"My daughter, to judge by these lanterns, is smart indeed."
   Let's not sing of lord Yu who was watching the lanterns,
Let change the subject and sing of his precious daughter.
The young lady went over to her sisters-in-law, saying:
"My dear sisters-in-law please listen to what I will say.
   Tonight is the feast of the First Night of the Full Moon,
So let us all three sisters together go over to the garden."
Her two sisters-in-law were filled with joy at these words,
And accompanied her as they enjoyed those new flowers.[45]

Let's not sing of those young women enjoying the scenery,
But let's sing of a man surnamed Zhao, a man with money.
This full name of this lord Zhao was Zhao Chengwei,
And he had only one son, who was named Zhao Long.

---

[45] The cyclostyled edition in the possession of Cynthia Brokaw here adds the following two lines: "If you want to learn about Che Long's happy marriage/Let me sing the second part and you will know." This is followed by a line stating "Here ends the first part of *The Tale of the Flower-Lanterns of Che long and the Young Lady Yu Jiao*." The second part then starts with the two lines: "The earlier text has told you all the facts about Che Long, / So now read the second part that continues the story." The text then continues with the lines: "Let's not sing about the sisters-in-law in the flower garden,/ But let's sing of a man surnamed Zhao…"

At the age of fifteen he entered the prefectural school,[46]
And at present he had already turned into a grownup.
Quickly he had then reached the sweet age of sixteen,
But even so no marriage deal had been made for him.

This evening happened to be the feast of First Night,
So he went out into the streets to watch the lanterns.
And when he passed the gate of the Yu family house,
He caught a glimpse of Yu Jiao, that precious darling.

And once he had seen the stunning beauty of Yu Jiao,
He kept thinking of her as he walked on, and thought:
"If I could be united in wedlock with this girl as a couple,
That would surpass the first place on the golden list!"

When Zhao Long had returned and gone to his study,
He fell ill within one day — he couldn't rise from his bed.
But let's not sing of Zhao Long and how the boy fell ill,
But change the subject and sing once more of Che Long.

The emperor announced the metropolitan examinations;
The time of the triennial examinations had come again.
When Che Long heard this news, he was filled with joy,
And after he had bought paper, he sat for the exams.

In the district examinations he placed number one,
In the prefectural examinations he got the first place.
The provincial examiner listed him as head of the file;
He was admitted to the prefectural school as a student.[47]

The provincial examiner saw he looked exceptional:
"This man definitely is bound to serve as an official!"
A band of pipes and drums played loudly in his honor
And escorted the new student back to his own house.

---

[46] By passing the lowest level of examinations at the prefectural level, one was admitted to the prefectural school as a student (*xiucai* 秀才).

[47] The examinations at district level were preliminary examinations. Passing them allowed one to sit for the prefectural examinations but gave no status. The prefectural examinations were administered by the educational intendant of the province concerned. By passing the prefectural examinations one was admitted to the prefectural school as a student and achieved the status of *xiucai*, which allowed one to sit for the provincial examinations.

When he had come home and entered the high hall,
His mother was filled with joy on seeing this situation.
"As today my son has been listed on the tiger poster,
The old mirror, polished again, shines brightly anew."

Let's not sing how Che Long bowed to the ancestors —
The crowd spread the news widely in all directions:
"Earlier that Che Long was only a mere beggar boy,
But today he is a student in the prefectural school!"

Lord Yu also pricked up his ears in order to listen:
"What I now hear people tell is so confusing to me.
People say that Che Long is listed on the tiger poster,
So I must have misheard he begged in the streets.[48]

That day I shouldn't have misplaced our daughter,
It was stupid to wrongly promise her to those Ches.
If I ponder this matter from all sides, I cannot but
Find her another fine talent in some major lineage."

When his wife hear these words, she grew angry,
And said: "My dear lord, you're devoid of gratitude!
Since ancient times a marriage is fated by Heaven,
How can one daughter be promised to two grooms?

When she was nine, you promised her personally,
And Military Governor Zeng served as go-between.
Lord Zeng now serves as grand secretary at court:
One word of him to the emperor, and you're dead."

Lord Yu thereupon shouted at the top of this voice:
["Indeed, wife, you never became a human being!"][49]
Even though lord Zeng may be a grand secretary,
He will never trouble himself about such a beggar!

Now if you say one more word and refuse to listen,
I will have you trussed up and beaten, you broad!"
He spoke in such a way that his wife grew angry:
"Then follow your own advice, you old bastard!"

---

[48] Selling goods out in the streets, going from door to door, was considered little better than begging.

[49] This line is missing in the edition provided by Hu Xizhang and has been added on the basis of the photocopy of the cyclostyled edition collected by Cynthia Brokaw.

Let's not sing of lord Yu and his vicious intentions,
But let's change the subject and sing of Zhao Long.
When lord Zhao saw his son was suffering a disease,
He went to his son's room, asking him for the cause.

"Why have you fallen ill so seriously upon returning,
My son, from watching the lanterns on First Night?"
Zhao Long then told him the whole story, saying:
"My father, please listen to what I will have to say.

When watching the lanterns, I passed by the Yus,
And there I caught a glimpse of my darling Yu Jiao.
If only Yu Jiao and I could become a couple, a pair,
That would surpass a first place on the golden list."

When lord Zhao heard this, he was filled with joy,
And he told his son, "My dear boy, now don't worry!
One shop down the road lives that Huang Haizhen,
Who all his life has busied himself as a go-between.

I will immediately send the servant boy over to him,
And ask that Mr. Huang to serve as the go-between."
Mr. Huang soon arrived at the Zhao family mansion,
And after a cup of tea (and wine) set out on the road.

When straightaway he arrived at the Yu family house
Lord Yu invited him inside and they entered the hall.
He invited Mr. Huang inside and once they sat down,
He treated his visitor to an excellent cup of tea.

Having finished their tea, they put down their mug,
And lord Yu then asked him the following question:
"For quite a while now you haven't paid me a visit,
So what brings you today to my humble abode?"

Mr. Huang immediately replied in these words:
"I have come to your house to play the go-between.
You must know lord Zhao, His Excellency Zhao —
He has only one son, who is named Zhao Long.

Fifteen years old he entered the prefectural school,
But up to today he still has no marriage partner.
I've heard, Sir, that you have a precious daughter,
So I would propose that she join the Zhao family."

When lord Yu heard this, he was filled with joy,
And said: "The Zhao family is much to my liking."
He opened a box, and took out a sheet of red paper,
To write her eight characters with his gilded brush.
  "My little daughter right now is fifteen years old,
She was born at midnight of the fifteenth, First Prime."
When he had written the eight characters of her birth,
He handed the piece of paper to go-between Huang.

Let's not sing of lord Yu conceiving this evil design —
When the servant girl of Yu Jiao knew about this,
She hastened to the room of her young mistress
And, speaking softly, informed the girl of her fate.
  "Young lady, while you were engaged in embroidery,
Your father has conceived of a mean and evil scheme.
You will now be married off to a Young Master Zhao;
And Associate Judge Huang is serving as go-between."
  When Yu Jiao heard this, her tears coursed down:
"That detestable father of mine is less than human!
  At the age of nine I was promised to the Che family,
But now he covets their wealth, dumping the poor.
In case he wants me to marry a quite different man,
I had better jump in the river and join the shades."
  She did not do up her hair, she did not put in jewelry,
She did not want tea or food, didn't catch any sleep,
All because this vexation about her marriage partner
Lay heavily on her heart like a thousand-pound rock.
  Meixiang stepped forward and tried to cheer her up:
"Young lady, it serves no purpose to be so depressed.
You've been promised in marriage to that Che Long,
So write now a letter to inform your husband-to-be.
  If you tell the Che family to send the wedding gifts,
We can see what your father's state of mind will be.
In case he does not accept their wedding gifts at all,
Then go to the magistrate and insist on an inquiry!"

When Yu Jiao heard this, she was filled with joy,
So she took up her brush and composed this letter.
In this letter she did not discuss any trifling matters
But only wrote: "My father lacks a clear conscience!

He now wants me to marry some Young Master Zhao,
And Associate Judge Huang is serving as go-between.
I now write this letter to you in the hope that you will
Present the wedding gifts and come to fetch the bride.

If my father will refuse to accept these wedding gifts,
Then submit an accusation, demand an investigation!"
When she had completely finished writing this letter,
She called for Meixiang, told her to deliver the letter.
When Meixiang took this letter, she was filled with joy;
She left, running as fast as her two feet could carry her.

Straightaway she arrived at the Che family mansion,
And there handed the letter to a Che family servant.
When Che Long opened the letter in order to read it,
His tears coursed down once he had read the content.

With tears in his eyes, he thanked Meixiang, saying:
"Many thanks, Meixiang, you're a good-hearted person.
When in the future I will have achieved glory and riches,
I will thank you for this service as deep as the ocean.

Now go back to your house and implore the young lady
To take good care of herself and not to worry too much.
As long as I am a man, I stand out far beyond the crowd:
The Zhao family won't necessarily dare compete with me."

When Meixiang had heard this, she was filled with joy;
She hastily took her leave and returned to her house.

Let's not sing of Meixiang who delivered Yu Jiao's letter,
But of Che Long who entered the school, awash in tears.

He straightaway went to the school and entered the room,
His face beclouded by worry, and his tears coursing down.
His fellow students stepped forward and asked him thusly:
"Dear brother Che, why are you melting down in tears?

Yesterday when we saw you, you were still filled with joy,
But now today on your arrival your tears are heart-rending.
Please tell us today what the cause of the matter may be,
So we all together can help you out in this bad situation."

Covered in tears, Che Long addressed them as follows:
"My dear fellow students, how could you know the cause?
I am engaged to the daughter of Educational Intendant Yu,
But he is coveting riches and dumping me as way too poor.

My wife is now to marry instead some Young Master Zhao,
And Associate Judge Huang is serving as their go-between.
My dear wife wrote me a letter to tell me of this matter,
And tells me to present the wedding gifts and fetch her.

And if her father will accept none of my wedding gifts,
She tells me to lodge an accusation, demand an inquiry!"
When his friends heard this, they pondered it silently,
And they concluded: this girl has indeed a virtuous mind!

His fellow students thereupon decided to help him out
And give him enough so he could go and fetch the bride!
Young Master Cao contributed a donation consisting of
Various fruits such as betel nuts and Hangzhou peanuts:

All together these various fruits filled exactly ten boxes;
He also donated three hundred pounds of cooked pork.
Young Master Chen also helped out with a donation;
He made a donation of a thousand pounds of fat pork.

He further made a donation of a hundred fat chicken,
And on top of that he sent ten big jugs of finest wine.
Young Master Yang came and contributed a donation;
He donated fifty baskets all filled with country chicken.

He further sent five hundred ducks producing down,
He also sent three thousand ounces for the bride price.
Young Master Zheng came and contributed a donation
Of golden hairpins and finger rings, alongside yellow gold.

All the required wedding presents were donated in full,
To help out Che Long, so he could go and fetch the bride.
They selected a good day and also an auspicious hour
To present these wedding gifts and to fetch the bride.

But it was not only the Che family that sent its gifts,
The Zhao family also arrived with their wedding gifts.
    The two families went both to the Yu family mansion,
Each family claimed the right to bring Yu Jiao home.
The bride-fetchers of the Che family cried for justice,
And went off to the magistrate, demanding an inquiry.
    The magistrate, locking his gate, didn't hear this case,
So they went on and appealed to ever higher offices.
The three families fought their case up to the province,
They fought their case right in the governor's court.

Now when the governor came to investigate the case,
He first of all submitted Che Long to his questioning.
Che Long stepped forward and addressed him thusly:
"Your Honor, please listen as I will sketch the facts.
    Long ago my father served as investigating censor,
My father-in-law, Lord Yu, as educational intendant.
The two of them were drinking wine in their office,
And discovered that Yu Jiao and I were of equal age.
    At that banquet she was promised to me as my wife,
And Military Governor Zeng acted as the go-between.
At present he serves at court as a grand secretary,
But still lord Yu conceived of a mean and evil plan.
    Yu Jiao was promised as wife to young master Zhao,
And Associate Judge Huang acted as the go-between.
I very much hope Your Honor will come to my rescue,
Come to the rescue of me, this insignificant person."
    The governor said that there was no need for a panic:
"Just wait for my investigation and then I'll decide.
In the meantime the three families should go home,
I will later let you know what decision I've reached."
    One way or another lord Yu got the silver together
And sent a full one thousand ounces to this governor;
The Zhao family also sent him one thousand ounces,
One thousand ounces of silver to buy some drinks.
    On receiving this silver the governor was very pleased,
And the very next day he was set to sentence the case.

At noon of that day all people had indeed all arrived:
The three families had come to the governor's office.

The governor took his seat and started his interrogation,
First feigning to put the blame on young master Zhao,
So he said: "You, Zhao Long, are bereft of all reason!
How can you rob a man of his wife? Tell me clearly!"

Zhao Long stepped forward and replied as follows:
"Sir, please listen to my detailed account of this case.
There is a go-between to preside over this marriage,
And there is also my father-in-law, Intendant Yu."

The governor thereupon questioned Intendant Yu:
"How can you promise one daughter to two grooms?"
Lord Yu immediately spoke up to rebut this question:
"Your Honor, please listen to what I will have to say.

I do not know that young man of the Che family at all,
I've never met that Che Long, that damned poor devil.
I have never even seen the face of that young man Che,
So why should I want to promise my daughter to him?

My daughter is promised in marriage to Zhao Long,
Zhao Long is the future husband of my dear daughter."

When Che Long heard this, he hastened to kneel down:
"Your Honor, please now listen to what I have to say.
Grand Secretary Zeng was go-between and witness
That Yu Jiao was promised to me as my wedded wife.

If you don't bother about me because I'm a student,
You should think of my father, the investigating censor.
If you don't care for the face of all these young men,
You should think of lord Zeng, the grand secretary.

Lord Zeng now serves at court as a grand secretary:
One word of him to the emperor, and you're doomed.
You will be locked in prison and there leather whips
Will not be able to show any forbearance or mercy!"

Let's not sing of Che Long who cursed the governor out —
The governor exploded in rage and ordered his underlings
To chase that Che Long out of the governor's office —
"You'll never again be allowed to utter such lies!"

These underlings hastened to chase Che Long away;
In a fit of rage he collapsed right there on the ground.
The eighteen scholars returned and went home;[50]
Not a word they put in had been of any assistance.
 They carried Che Long with them back to his house;
He had nowhere where he could vent his frustration.
Accepting bribes the governor had ruined his marriage;
He inflicted great shame on Che Long and his friends.

His fellow students discussed the situation together
And urged Che Long to ask help from the go-between:
 "Even though lord Zeng may not presently be at home,
You still should go and pay a visit to his own mansion.
And if you, brother Che, lack the money for that trip,
We'll give you the silver needed to go to the capital."
 When Che Long heard this, his tears coursed down,
Filled with gratitude toward his kind fellow students,
And he straightaway went to the Zeng family mansion,
Where he was received by the grand secretary's son.
 He welcomed Che Long and once they were seated,
The young master addressed him in the following words:
 "For quite a while you have not come to our mansion,
So what is the reason that you have come here today?
If it's not for the capital's metropolitan examinations,
What then may be the cause that brought you here?"
 Only then did Che Long address him in these words:
"To raise this issue fills one with shame and dishonor.
I was engaged to Educational Intendant Yu's daughter;
When he served in office, she was promised to me.
 But after my father's death, we were robbed blind;
We had to sell all our landed estates and our house.
Now lord Yu is saying that I have become a beggar
Who'll not be able to provide for his dear daughter.

---

[50] The "eighteen scholars" must refer to Che Long's fellow students.

Lord Yu despises my family for being so destitute,
And so has promised his daughter to someone else.
Since ancient times marriages are fated by Heaven,
But lord Yu, coveting riches, rejects me as too poor.

I have entered the prefectural school as a student,
I never made a living by begging for food outside!
When I was nine, he made that promise in person,
And Military Governor Zeng served as go-between.

At present he serves in court as a grand secretary,
And there is now nobody else who can rescue me.
So I hope very much that His Excellency will intervene
And make sure that the young lady is returned to me."

The young master of the Zeng family replied thusly:
"You should have informed me earlier of these facts.
My father serves the emperor as a grand secretary,
So who dares wrongly decide this matrimonial case!"

When Che Long heard this, he replied in this way:
"Young Master, please listen to what I'll have to say.
He had promised my wife now to young master Zhao,
Associate Judge Huang serving as the go-between.

The young lady wrote me a letter to inform me,
And told me to send the gifts and fetch the bride.
But lord Yu refused to accept my wedding gifts,
So I went to the magistrate, demanding an inquiry.

But that man, locking his gate, didn't hear the case,
So at present I have even appealed to the province.
The three families fought all the way to the province,
But the governor accepted bribes to decide the case.

I was thrown out of the Council and chased away,
And my fellow students were not allowed to speak.
Pondering the matter from all sides I see no way
But to implore your father to intervene in this case."

When the young master heard this, he angrily said:
"This detestable lord Yu cannot be counted as human!
He gave his promise long ago when serving in office;
One daughter should not be matched to two grooms.

And what kind of provincial governor has the temerity
To take bribes and misjudge such a matrimonial case!"

He promptly wrote a letter to his father, which read:
"My dear father, please be informed of these facts.
Yesterday I here at home was visited by one Che Long,
Who is meeting with problems in matters of marriage.

His bride is the daughter of Educational Intendant Yu;
That man has the gall to covet riches and dump the poor.
He has now promised his daughter to one Zhao Long,
Falsely claiming that Che Long is a destitute beggar.

When they were nine, he made the promise in person,
And at that banquet, you, father, served as go-between.
But Yu Jiao has now been given to young master Zhao,
And Associate Judge Huang serves as the go-between.

The young lady sent a letter to the Che family mansion,
And she told the Che family to come and fetch the bride.
'If the wedding gifts of the Che family are not accepted,
Then lodge an accusation and demand an investigation.'

The three families have put their case to the province,
But that governor accepted bribes and bent his verdict.
He made the claim that Che Long was a good-for-nothing,
And he also repeated the lie that he was a mere beggar.

He had Che Long thrown out and chased from his office,
And in his verdict awarded Yu Jiao to that Zhao Long."
When he had finished writing this one very long letter,
Family servants took the letter to the national capital.

Let's not sing of the family servants delivering the letter —
At the capital Lord Zeng, serving at court, had a dream.
In his dream plum blossoms were scattered by a storm,
An evil storm that swept through groves and gardens.

He then invited the national teacher to read his dream,
And the national teacher arrived to interpret his dream.
He promptly said: "This dream is inauspicious indeed.
Grand Secretary Zeng, please listen to my explanation.

A salaried official served in the past as go-between,
But today this marriage has been turned into a mess.

Not only has this marriage at present been annulled,
The case may even bring damage to your noble mind."
　When lord Zeng heard this, he replied in these words:
"Never in all my life have I acted as a match-maker!"
While these two men were still discussing the dream,
The two family servants arrived from his hometown.
　They handed him the letter sent to him by his son,
They handed this letter to Grand Secretary Lord Zeng.
When the latter had opened and read his son's letter,
When he had read all its content, he started to curse.
　He also said: "My son, how can you be such a child!
Why didn't you come to the rescue of this Che Long?"
　Lord Zeng immediately produced paper and a brush,
And in this letter criticized the provincial governor.
"What kind of provincial governor has the brazen gall
To abort justice in his administration of the people!
　While I am serving now at court as a grand secretary,
He has the temerity to bend the facts of this case!
That he has accepted some money is not a big deal,
But his brazen gall hides Heaven and obscures reason.
　If you award the bride once again to young master Che,
You will be forgiven and without crime stay in office.
But if you award the bride to that young master Zhao,
You'll be deprived of your rank and reduced to zero."
　He also wrote that lord Yu was deprived of reason:
One daughter should not be promised to two grooms.
　If Yu Jiao indeed is married to that young master Zhao,
The law of the land will not allow any pardon for you.
Your daughter has to be married to young master Che,
That is the only possibility for you to escape execution."

When he had fully finished writing this one long letter,
He ordered these family servants to take it back home.
When his son had opened and read that long letter,
He had himself carried to the office of the governor.
　The provincial governor welcomed young lord Zeng,
And treated him most civilly to a cup of strong tea.

But the young master cursed him out in this manner:
"You detestable governor, you're a cheat and a bully!
Today I received this letter from the national capital,
Please read it for yourself with your own mean eyes!"
When the governor had opened and read that letter,
He was so frightened at heart his tears coursed down.

The provincial governor discussed this with lord Yu:
"Lord Zeng is placing all the blame on the governor!"
Lord Yu again sent him one thousand ounces of silver
So the bride would be awarded to young master Zhao.

The son of lord Zeng thereupon truly exploded in rage,
He ordered his people to arrest lord Yu and tie him up.
They gave lord Yu such a beating he couldn't escape;
They kept on beating until he was covered in blood.

Lord Yu suffered such pain that tears coursed down,
And he hated young lord Zeng for showing no mercy.
"It may not matter I served as educational intendant,
But you still should have taken my age into account."

Pondering the matter from all sides he had no way
But to go to the provincial governor to explain it all.
The latter said: "Lord Yu, you were bereft of reason,
One daughter should not be promised to two grooms.

Lord Zeng, the grand secretary, has now sent a letter:
Even I will only barely be able to escape punishment!"
Lord Yu thereupon also was asked to read the letter;
When he had read the letter, he too was frightened!

The provincial governor thereupon spoke as follows:
"I will now question your daughter Yu Jiao in person.
I will write a letter to invite you daughter to this court,
Which you will have to place in her hands in person."

That old bastard lord Yu also received such a letter,
And yet another letter invited Che Long to be present.
One more letter summoned young master Zhao too;
Four police officers were dispatched to his house.

Lord Yu, once back home, took his seat in the hall,
And called for his daughter, the young lady Yu Jiao.

Yu Jiao came from her room and entered the hall,
Bowed, and asked her father how he was doing.
   Lord Yu thereupon addressed her in these words:
"My dear daughter, please listen to what I will say.
Today a private letter has arrived from lord Zeng,
Who accuses your father of a very serious crime.
   The governor orders us to be in court tomorrow;
Tomorrow he'll decide the case of your marriage.
I have spent two thousand ounces of silver on this,
And he wants to hear from you whom you'll marry!"
   Her two sisters-in-law also chimed in by urging her:
"Dear sister of us, you cannot but cover up the facts.
As for your marriage, you must choose Zhao Long:
He is wealthy, he's loaded — and a student to boot!
   But in case you decide to marry into the Che family,
We'll never come to the aid of such destitute people."
When Yu Jiao heard this, she answered as follows:
"I will not let you guys make my decision for me!"
   Let's not sing of the sisters-in-law and their advice —
The mother also provided advice to her daughter:
   "My dear girl, you must honestly follow your heart;
On no account can you cover the facts of this case.
Since ancient times marriages are fated by Heaven,
On no account can you out of greed dump the poor."
   When Yu Jiao had heard this, she was very pleased:
"These words of my mother conform to my heart.
If ever I later in life will achieve riches and glory,
I will never, my dear mother, forget your favors."

Let's not sing of her mother, her words of advice —
Yu Jiao arrived at ease at the governor's courtyard.
She straightaway walked into the governor's court;
She lowered her head and knelt down on the floor.
   The three parties there were not questioned at all,
The only one to be questioned was the girl Yu Jiao.
   "Do you want to marry the son of the Che family,
Or do you want to marry the man surnamed Zhao?

Now make sure to tell the truth and nothing else,
On no account are you allowed to bend the facts!"
    Yu Jiao immediately replied in the following way:
"Your Honor, please listen to what I now will say.
This all is determined by karma, fated by Heaven,
So I would not dare dump the poor out of greed.
    If you now decide I will marry young master Che,
I will preserve my life to take care of my mother.
But in case you award me to young master Zhao,
I'd rather die and not live in this world anymore."
    Hearing her words the governor couldn't but smile:
"This girl Yu Jiao is indeed a most virtuous woman."
His verdict was that she should marry Che Long;
He ordered the Zhao family to find another bride.
    The Zhao family was fined one thousand ounces
For disrupting a marriage and stealing one's wife.
Mr. Huang was also fined one thousand ounces
For acting as a go-between against all propriety.
    Lord Yu was fined one thousand ounces of silver:
One daughter shouldn't be given to two grooms.
These three parties all were fined the same fine,
And these three families were equally put down.
    Lord Yu and young master Zhao both were carried
In their sedan chairs and so went to their homes.
    Let's not sing of how they went back to their homes,
Let's sing again of the governor back in his office.
Now he had received these thousands of ounces,
He forwarded all this silver to the imperial court.

Let's not sing of the governor not keeping the silver,
Let's change the subject and sing again of lord Yu.
He shouted: "That daughter of mine is of no use!
With each word she wanted to marry Che Long!"
    Right then and there he wanted to throw her out,
To throw her out of the house, that common slut!

When Yu Jiao heard this, her tears coursed down,
And she called Meixiang, saying: "My dear girl,
  You now have to deliver a letter on my behalf,
You have to deliver this letter to my Che Long.
Today your mistress is thrown out of the house;
My father's violence is beyond human bounds."
  When Che Long read this letter, he had to cry:
"That detestable lord Yu is no human being at all!"
  But when young master Zeng had read the letter,
He immediately spoke to Che Long in this manner.
"You must adapt your plans to the circumstances;
There's no need now to offer lord Yu a fine banquet.
  There is no need for any gifts now to fetch the girl,
I will come along with you to bring home the bride.
And if that lord Yu still refuses to admit his defeat,
We will tell the bride-fetching party to beat him up."
  They then collected a party of three hundred men,
Together with four sedan chairs to carry the bride.
The music of pipes and drums resounded so loudly;
Gongs and drums resounded to heaven without end.
  The major and minor functionaries filled the streets,
Flaming banners formed the head of the procession.
But when they arrived at the house of the Yu family,
The Zhaos too had arrived in force to kidnap the girl.
  Young master Zhao loudly shouted his commands,
Telling his sedan chair carriers to mount an attack.
Che Long's bride-fetching party was soundly beaten;
Their drums were shattered and reduced to rubble.[51]

Let's not sing of the Zhaos trying to kidnap the girl —
At both sides her sister-in-law kept on cursing her.

---

[51] In the cyclostyled version of this story collected by Cynthia Brokaw it is the party from the Zhao family that is beaten. That would appear to be the correct version of the story.

"The drums in front of the gate sound so heavily,
Which family is this late conducting a funeral?"
    Yu Jiao immediately answered them as follows:
"Dear sisters-in-law, what you say lacks all sense!
When the music and drums sounded so clearly,
That was the Che family's bride-fetching party.
    The drums of the Zhao family sound so heavily:
They're taking a coffin, it seems, to the funeral."
    Let's not sing about Yu Jiao putting it to them —
Che Long fetched his bride and took her home.
Yu Jiao, dressed up in all her finery, was as pretty
As the bodhisattva Guanyin of the Southern Sea.[52]
    In the hall they bowed to the various ancestors,
Then turned around and bowed to his mother too.
They also bowed to the third son of lord Zeng;
Exchanging a cup of wine they were man and wife.
    They lit the colored candles in the bridal chamber:
The joys of happy husband and wife had no end.

Let's not sing of the marriage of these people —
Che Long went again to school to read the books.
And as soon as he had arrived back at school,
His fellow students addressed him in this way:
    "This is the year of the imperial examinations,
And everyone is preparing to go to the capital.
If you don't have the money to go to the capital,
We will donate it to you so you can seek fame."
    When Che Long heard this, he was very pleased,
And he promptly went back to speak to his mother.
Having spoken to his mother, he next saw his wife,
And with tears in his eyes he entered her room.
    When Yu Jiao saw him, she addressed him thusly:
"My talented husband, why are you so sad at heart?

---

[52] The bodhisattva Guanyin as revered on the island Putuoshan (Guanyin of the Southern Sea) is often mentioned as the epitome of female beauty.

Is it perhaps because you despise me as too ugly?
Do you hate me because of my meager trousseau?"
　Che Long immediately answered her as follows:
"My dear wife, please listen to what I will say now.
I do not despise you because you are way too ugly,
I don't hate you because of your empty trousseau.
　This is the year of the metropolitan examinations,
And all people tell me I should take these exams.
But we have only been married for these few days,
So I find it unbearable to leave my love here behind.
　Also, my white-haired mother is advanced in years,
And it's you who'd have to take care of my mother."
Yu Jiao answered him: "I understand the situation.
My husband, there's no need for you to be worried.
　I will look after my mother-in-law with greatest care,
So you can without a worry take these examinations.
Now I will take this golden beaker and offer a toast;
I offer a golden beaker of wine to my dear husband.
　One cup of fine wine — it is Bamboo Leaf Green —
My dear, drink this wine now you go to the capital.
My husband, now you drink my first cup of wine,
I wish you may pass the exams with great success.
　This second cup of wine I present to my husband
Who goes to the capital to take the examinations.
My darling, now you drink this second cup of wine,
I wish you will quickly return as the Top-of-the-List.
　This third cup of wine is Chrysanthemum Yellow;
Your silly wife offers this wine to her talented beau.
My darling, now you drink this third cup of wine,
I wish you will come home as the Top-of-the-List!"
　When Che Long heard this, he was filled with joy;
He said goodbye to his mother and wife and set out.

Let's not sing of Che Long on his way to the capital,
But let's rather talk about the young lady, Yu Jiao.
"Now my husband has left and gone to the capital,
I've no idea when he may come back home again."

During those long days at home she felt quite bored,
So she went to her mother-in-law to have a chat.
"When my father-in-law served as grand secretary,
He must have constructed some garden pavilions."

The widow thereupon answered her as follows:
"We have pawned the garden to the Zhang family."
When Yu Jiao had heard this, she was filled with joy
And wanted to borrow the key to enjoy the garden.

She told Meixiang to go borrow it from the Zhangs,
And Meixiang very obediently went on her way.
Meeting with Mr. Zhang, she explained to him:
"The young master has left to go to the capital.
Because the young lady today is very depressed,
She'd like to visit the garden for her amusement."

[Mr. Zhang was very happy to grant her request,][53]
And allowed the young lady to borrow the key;
When Mr. Zhang heard this, he was very pleased,
And handed the key to the garden to Meixiang.

When Meixing had received it, she was pleased,
And said goodbye to Mr. Zhang to go back home.
Straightaway she went home and in the high hall
Handed the key of the garden to the young lady.

The young lady and Meixiang went over there
To enjoy the garden and so dispel their worries.
When the young lady entered the flower garden,
She saw that the pavilions displayed fresh colors.

She also saw that one pavilion still hid treasure:
"Too bad that my husband was so short on luck!"
But before Yu Jiao could finish saying these words,
Lord Che manifested himself, scaring them greatly.[54]

He scared Meixiang so much she was frightened
And screamed: "Young lady, let's go back home!"

---

[53]This line is absent in the edition prepared by Hu Xizhang and has been supplied on the basis of the edition collected by Cynthia Brokaw.

[54]The ghost of Che Long's father manifests itself to Yu Jiao in order to instruct her how to find the hidden treasure.

But Yu Jiao answered her: "No need to be afraid!
I see that a letter is hidden inside this pavilion."
 She then told Meixiang to fetch her a ladder:
Yu Jiao climbed that ladder to find the letter.
When her hand entered the dragon's mouth,
She indeed retrieved a letter from that place.
 When Yu Jiao opened that letter and read it,
She read that treasure was buried right there.
When Yu Jiao read this, she was quite pleased
And told Meixiang to close the garden's gate.
 She locked the gate to retrieve the treasure,
She dug through the stones and found the gold.
She retrieved a few jars filled with white silver,
And a few jugs filled with betel nut shaped gold.
 Yu Jiao stepped forward and asked her mother:
"Dear mother-in-law, please let me ask a question.
For how much money was this garden ever sold?
I would like to redeem it by paying white silver."
 The widow thereupon addressed Yu Jiao thusly:
"I will now tell it to you so will know all details.
The garden was pawned for one thousand ounces;
Main sum and interest should be exactly the same."
 When Yu Jiao heard this, she was very pleased,
And she promptly ordered Meixiang, her servant:
"Go to the Zhang family mansion and tell them
We've got two thousand to redeem the garden."
 Meixiang then obediently left with the silver,
Going straightaway to the Zhang family house,
And there she addressed Mr. Zhang as follows:
"Dear Mr. Zhang, please listen to what I'll say.
 The new bride of the Ches has plenty of money,
So I bring two thousand to redeem the garden."
When Mr. Zhang heard this, he was very pleased;
Both interest and contract he handed to Meixiang.
 "I will keep the one thousand of the main sum,
The interest I hereby give back to the young lady.

Take it back to the young lady to buy some silk,
And also inform the old lady, her mother-in-law."
   Receiving the silver Meixiang was filled with joy;
She said goodbye to Mr. Zhang and went home.
Straightaway she returned to the Che family place,
And there she told the widow what had happened.
   "Mr. Zhang took one thousand ounces of silver;
Both interest and contract he returns now to you."
When the widow heard this, she was very pleased;
Mr. Zhang's kind action filled her with gratitude.
   "When my son will have achieved riches and glory,
He must show his gratitude to this fine benefactor."

Let's not sing of the widow redeeming the garden,
Let's sing of Che Long entering the examinations.
On the ninth of the Third the examinations started:[55]
Students from all provinces went to the grounds.
   The candidates were three thousand seven hundred,
From which the grand secretaries selected the talents.
From the three thousand seven hundred candidates
They selected the three hundred men of lofty talents.
   From these three hundred men they made a selection:
They selected the thirty men with the highest talents.
From these thirty men they made a further selection:
They selected the three men with the highest talents.
   Their essays were then placed inside a golden urn,
And the emperor lit incense and bowed to the gods,
And then took out the essay that was the best of all,
To decide which of the essays would take first place.
   Che Long passed the examinations as Top-of-the-List;
A man surnamed Chen passed as the Number Two.
A man surnamed Lin passed as the Number Three,
And these three people all hailed from Dahe district.
   The Top-of-the-List paraded the streets for three days:
Outstanding men emerge from the students of books!

---

[55] The examinations start on the ninth day of the Third Month of the lunar calendar.

Copying the list, people spread the news everywhere;
Runners on fast horses reported the Top-of-the-List!
  Changing their boats and also changing their horses
They quickly arrived at the official reception pavilion.
There lord Yu immediately asked these messengers:
"Who is the person who passed as Top-of-the-List?"
  The messengers immediately answered thusly:
"Che Long passed the examinations as Top-of-the-List,
A man surnamed Chen passed as the Number Two;
A man surnamed Lin passed as the Number Three."
  Let's not sing of lord Yu who asked this question —
The messengers arrived at the Che family mansion.
When the widow heard this, she was filled with joy;
And when Yu Jiao heard this, her face was all smiles.
  "Today my son has been listed on the golden poster:
The old mirror, polished anew, is bright once again!"
Everyone who heard this was filled with great joy,
And they sent the messengers off with their reward.

Let's not sing of the messengers who went back,
Let's tell about lord Yu, the educational intendant.
When Yu Jiao had been married for a full month,
Her two sisters-in-law visited her at her new home.
  They brought her a box of betel nuts, rotten inside,
Only to spite Yu Jiao for being such a poor person!
Now when Yu Jiao saw this, she exploded with rage:
This was the doing of her father, that cruel bastard!
  He has sent me these betel nuts just to spite me,
But my sisters-in-law also lack all human feelings!
"Don't think that the Che family is utterly destitute,
We here have nine jugs of betel nuts made of gold.
  And if you, my sisters-in-law, do not believe me,
I will take you along so you can see for yourself."
The sisters-in-law went upstairs to have a look:
It was no lie at all, what she said was the truth!
  Her two sisters-in-law immediately said goodbye,
And straightaway returned to the Yu family house,

And there the two women told lord Yu the facts:
"Today your daughter is truly loaded with money.
Today she took us upstairs to have a good look,
There were nine jugs of betel nuts made of gold!"

When lord Yu heard this, he was very much upset
And cursed that Che Long as a scoundrel and thief.
"If he now at present has plenty to eat, I'm afraid
That that will spell trouble for me down the road!"

Let's not sing of lord Yu and his many complaints,
Let's sing of the Top-of-the-List meeting his ruler.
In the fifth watch the emperor ascended the hall,[56]
And the Top-of-the-List expressed his gratitude.

When the emperor read his statement, he smiled,
And he gifted the Top-of-the-List a gown and a cap.
He gifted him one cup of fine Dragon-Phoenix tea,
And he also treated him to a cup of imperial wine.

Each month his salary would be three thousand,
His wives were ennobled as Ladies of the first rank,
Each received three hundred ounces for cosmetics,
And all were ennobled as Ladies of the first rank.

On their head they could display crowns of gold,
They could wear dragon-phoenix brocade gowns.
The Top-of-the-List was pleased with these gifts,
But he promptly addressed the emperor once again:
"I want to pay back my benefactors with favors,
My enemies I will pay back in the same measure."
His lord and master quickly approved his request
And gifted the Top-of-the-List a sovereign sword.[57]

The Top-of-the-List was pleased with these gifts
And thanked the emperor with twenty-four bows.

---

[56] The emperor received his ministers in audience at dawn, so he had to ascend his throne in the fifth watch of the night.
[57] "Sovereign sword" should more literally be translated as "the sword of a liege lord." The sword (only encountered in fiction) allows civil officials to execute death sentences without prior permission from the emperor.

Thrice he shouted "A myriad years to the emperor,"
Then was granted permission to return back home.
   The civil and military officials came to see him off,
Governors and dignitaries attended his departure.
The music of fifes and drums resounded to heaven;
At the gate nine cannons were fired in succession.

When he came to hills, new roads were constructed,
When he came to rivers, new bridges were erected.
As he traveled by water the journey took many days,
But eventually he arrived back at his old house.
   Officials arrived each day to offer congratulations;
The well-wishers and officials were treated well.
   Let's not sing of Che Long treating his many visitors,
Let's sing of lord Yu, congratulating his son-in-law.
   He had selected three hundred *mu* of fertile fields
And a pair of golden dragons to offer as presents.
Three hundred rolls o satin, three hundred of silk
He presented to his son-in-law, the Top-of-the-List!
   Let's not sing of lord Yu who was bringing presents,
Let's sing of Yu Jiao, the young lady his daughter.
   She instructed the family servants, more than ten:
"You have to guard the main gate of this mansion.
The presents of other people you can allow inside,
But presents of the Yu family are not allowed inside!"
   The presents of the Yu family very soon did arrive,
And these were spotted by these family servants.
They went to her room and reported the situation,
Whereupon the young lady appeared and declared:
   "A good son will not use the fields of his father,
A good daughter will not use her dowry clothes:
Burn the property deeds of those fields to ashes,
Turn those satins and silks into smoke and dust."
   Lord Yu was so shamed that he had no face left,
And in his sedan chair he promptly returned home.
Once he was back home he felt a pain in his breast:
That very moment he collapsed because of a stroke.

Let's not sing of lord Yu who then died of a stroke,
Let's sing about Che Long who saw his guests off.
After a while all guest at the banquet had dispersed,
And the Top-of-the-List thanked all his benefactors.

   He recommended Mr. Zhang to the royal court,
Recommending him for promotion to high office.

   He stripped lord Yu of all his official appointments,
And in this way reduced him to commoner status.
Zhao Long was forbidden to take the capital exams,
All his life he remained a student till his dying day.

   He had Associate Judge Huang killed by the sword:
He should not have wrongly served as go-between;
He also had lord Lin killed by this sovereign sword:
He shouldn't have robbed them of all their money.

   He also made sure that the tenant was executed,
And then went to the school to thank his friends.

   On the left he constructed a Top-of-the-List house,
On the right he erected a Top-of-the-List pavilion.
The plaque above the gate had golden characters;
In addition he also had a new school constructed.

   For three years no one ever visited the Yu family:
The house was overgrown, the road filled with dust.
The Yu family went downhill, as if scoured by water;
Their fields and their houses were completely sold.

   They sold wine in the streets to make a poor living;
Now Che Long stepped forward, explaining to them:
"I was selling flower lanterns to feed my old mother,
And so offended lord Yu, the educational intendant.

   My brothers-in-law, now you are selling this wine,
But you never offended me, the Top-of-the-List.
I now here have three hundred *mu* of fertile fields
Which I give to you, my brothers-in-law, for a living."

   The Top-of-the-List went home and told his wife
That she should send people to invite her mother,
They invited her mother and served her most filially;
Thanking her for her favors, they treated her well.

The Top-of-the-List became the father of five sons
Who passed the exams and became Hanlin scholars.[58]
I have reached the end of the *Flower Lantern Tale* —
People should read it thoroughly to grasp its intent.

---

[58] During the Qing dynasty the Hanlin Secretariat was the most prestigious advisory and academic institution in the central government. Students who had passed the metropolitan examinations with high rankings often received a first appointment as Hanlin scholars.

PART THREE

BAMBOO-CLAPPERS SONGS

Introduction

While the narrative ballads translated in the preceding section do not have any distinctive formal features that set them off from ballads in many others parts of China, the bamboo-clappers songs translated in this section distinguish themselves by their typical five-line stanzas. In these stanzas the opening line usually repeats (part of) the last line of the preceding stanza. The rhyme pattern, however, suggests it is not the first line that has been added to a four-line stanza, but rather the final line of the stanza that should be considered an addition: in a standard four-line stanza the rhyming pattern is AAXA, but in the five line stanza the rhyming pattern is AAXAA. The pattern of borrowing the first line from the preceding stanza is also encountered in some sets of mountain songs and it is most likely that bamboo-clappers songs borrowed the practice from there. It is also most likely that five-line mountain songs provided the model for the five-line stanza. The close link between bamboo-clappers songs and mountain songs is further suggested by the fact that the performers of bamboo-clappers songs call themselves performers of mountain songs.[1]

---

[1] For brief introductions to bamboo-clappers songs, see Xue Shan 1985, 118–120; Luo Kequn 2000, 385–392; Huang Ziyao 2003, 114–120. For a comprehensive

Bamboo-clappers songs are named after the musical instrument (the bamboo-clappers) that is typically used to accompany the singing. Whereas mountain songs could be sung by anyone at any time, bamboo-clappers songs were very much the specialty of (semi) professional performers, who would go from door to door singing their songs, hoping for a small donation in money or food. One of the other common designations for the genre therefore was "beggars' songs" or "begging songs" (*jiaohuage* 叫化歌; *qishige* 乞食歌). In the late nineteenth century, such begging songs still employed a four-line format, as is clear from a note on the subject by Huang Zunxian:

> And then there are beggar songs. [These beggars] go from house to house, beating their clappers. It is especially people from Xingning who excel in this. I recorded one of these songs:
>
>> One day only has twelve full hours;
>> In one hour I only do a few houses;
>> In each house I only get one penny:
>> Blue Heaven, how truly miserable!
>
> It sounded tragic and mournful, so I generously gave [the performer] a hundred coppers and also said some comforting words. That is why I still remember the song.[2]

It would appear that it was only in the early 20th century that these performers adopted the five-line stanza and expanded their repertoire by adapting the stories of narrative ballads. Hu Xizhang, in his *Kejia zhubange yanjiu* (2010), argues that these performers mostly borrowed their subject materials from the ballad singers from southeastern Jiangxi, who performed widely in northeastern Guangdong in those days, but, in view of the wide availability of

---

monograph on the subject that also includes a number of complete texts, see Hu Xizhang 2010.
[2]Huang Zunxian 1981, 55.

narrative ballads in both oral and written form in traditional society, his hypothesis may well be too exclusive.[3]

The repertoire of bamboo-clappers songs was (and is) quite variegated. Until the middle of the 20th century many performers sang songs narrating the events that had reduced them to poverty and the vagrancy of begging. In order to induce their patrons to greater generosity they also might flatter them by singing songs in praise of their home or amuse them by performing outrageous nonsense songs. Their repertoire included not only slightly risqué materials, but also long moral ballads warning against the evils of whoring and gambling and urging people to practice filial piety. All modern scholars who have written on bamboo-clappers songs comment on the widespread popularity of the moral ballad *When Drinking from the Low River Remember the High Ridge* (*Dihe heshui nian gaogang* 低河飲水念高崗), and a translation of one version of this song in praise of filial piety has been included together with other non-narrative items in Chapter 4 of this section.

The narrative items in the repertoire of bamboo-clappers songs cover a wide variety of stories from a great variety of sources. The most popular narrative bamboo-clappers songs would appear to have been *Liang Sizhen and Zhao Yulin* (or simply *Zhao Yulin*).[4] *Gao Wenju* and *Second-hand Zhang Rents out his Wife* also are often listed among the most popular titles. These three narratives have been translated here on the basis of the editions provided by Hu Xizhang in his *Keja zhubange yanjiu*. Hu classifies these three texts as "traditional scripts," in contrast to "newly composed scripts." The latter

---

[3] In view of their late date of origin, it is not surprising that bamboo-clappers songs are not encountered in the Hakka-speaking communities on Taiwan.

[4] While this title is listed as the most popular item in descriptions of bamboo-clappers songs from northeastern Guangdong and southwestern Fujian, the title is not listed in the only description of bamboo-clappers songs from Guangxi that I know of, which mentions such perennial favorites of popular literature as the stories of Meng Jiangnü 孟姜女, and of Liang Shanbo 梁山伯 and Zhu Yingtai 祝英台 as the most commonly performed titles. Huang Shan 2012. On the story of Meng Jiangnü, see Idema 2007; on the story of Liang Shanbo and Zhu Yingtai, see Idema 2010a and Idema 2011a.

category refers to scripts that were written after 1949, often at the instigation of cultural cadres who had organized performers of bamboo-clappers song into propaganda teams and wanted their performances to make a contribution to the political consciousness of the masses.[5] Hu characterizes the "traditional scripts" in the following words:

> When I speak of "traditional," it is not only in contrast to "newly composed", but also in contrast to "edited" and "revised". These three texts are the "original true goods" as recorded from the mouth of old artists.[6]

Hu adds that "these three items were all particularly liked by the masses and very well display the characteristics of bamboo-clappers songs, so they are very representative of traditional scripts."[7] In Appendix IV, I present a translation of *A Slave Girl's Lament* (*Binü Hen* 婢女恨) as an example of the "newly composed scripts."

---

[5] For a listing of traditional and post-1949 titles, see Hu Xizhang 2010: 318–325. Hu Xizhang states that before 1949 texts of bamboo-clappers songs were mostly orally transmitted. Materials collected in Meixian in the years 1951–1956 were all lost in a flood.
[6] Hu Xizhang 2010: 368–369.
[7] Hu Xizhang 2010: 369.

CHAPTER 1

GAO WENJU

The story of Gao Wenju 高文舉 originated in the Ming dynasty and is known from two stage adaptations of that period. The story remained a favorite in many genres of local opera throughout the subsequent Qing dynasty, also in Hakka-speaking areas. The story is named after its title hero Gao Wenju, a poor student who is deeply indebted to his father-in-law because the latter first saves him from prison and later has him marry his daughter. But when Gao Wenju travels to the capital and passes the metropolitan examinations as Top-of-the-List, he is forced by the powerful prime minister Wen 溫 to marry his daughter and, as the minister claims the authority of the emperor, Gao Wenju has no option but to go through with the ceremony. The dilemma of a successful but married student who is pressured to marry an all-powerful minister's daughter held great fascination for the playwrights of the early Ming dynasty and is encountered in many *chuanqi* plays of that period, starting with *The Story of the Lute* (*Pipa ji* 琵琶記) by Gao Ming 高明 (c. 1307–371). In *the Story of the Lute* the main hero marries the minister's daughter, but when his original wife shows up in the capital his second wife is so moved by her story that the two women become sworn sisters and both serve the play's protagonist as his wives.[8]

---

[8] Mulligan 1980.

Gao Ming's play was an adaptation of an earlier version in which the bigamous protagonist was struck dead by lightning because of his moral laxity. While Gao Ming tried to save his male protagonist from the accusation of immorality by claiming that he acted under pressure (first from his father in leaving his wife to sit for the examinations, and later from the emperor who ordered the second marriage),[9] later playwrights tried to save the reputation of their protagonists in other ways, for instance by having them steadfastly stand up to all pressure, even if it means banishment to the border in wartime.[10] Gao Wenju saves his virtue by never touching his second wife during three years of married life. In most plays on bigamous students the second wife is portrayed as a meek daughter who follows her father's orders in marrying the student, but Gao Wenju's second wife is portrayed very much as a jealous shrew: when his original wife also travels to the capital after three years of waiting for her husband, the second wife treats her as a slave (in the earliest version she even has her murdered), and it takes further developments before the original couple can meet. Because the story is set in the reign of Emperor Renzong (r. 1023–1063; the Humane Ancestor) of the Song dynasty (960–1278), the final solution and judgment in the case can be entrusted to the famous Judge Bao (Bao gong 包公). The character of Judge Bao was based on that of the official Bao Zheng 包拯 (999–1062) who, during his lifetime, established a reputation for his strict incorruptibility and who, in later centuries, became a famous judge managing to bring even the most baffling cases to a proper conclusion.[11]

The following translation is based on the edition of a traditional bamboo-clappers song script provided by Hu Xizhang in his *Kejia zhubange yanjiu* (2010: 399–415). Hu based his edition on a manuscript prepared by Fang Weiqing 房偉清 and provided to him by Lan Peiye 藍培業.[12] The story was not only performed as a bamboo-clappers song but also as a regular ballad. The *Fujian geyao jicheng: Fujian juan*

---

[9] Mulligan 1980, 9–12.
[10] Birch 1973.
[11] Hayden 1978; Idema 2010b.
[12] Hu lists the performer as "unknown."

includes, for instance, the text of a ballad as performed in 1987 at Kanshizhen by Lu Shoumin 盧壽民 and recorded by Chen Yanrong 陳炎榮.[13] In order to show how the plot of a single story can vary even within the same dialect area, I provide a translation of that text in Appendix II.

***

Gao Wenju

I *Selling Oneself to Bury One's Mother*
I noisily beat out the beat with my bamboo-clappers,
Please listen at leisure so you will clearly understand:
In the Song dynasty there lived a certain Gao Wenju;
When he turned seven, he recited classics and books;
Devoted himself to his books, and studied the Sage.[14]

He studied the Sage
When at the age of nine he was struck by disaster:
His family's fine fields were washed away by a flood;
Their house caught fire, and so was turned to ashes —
That one family, old and young, suffered great misery.

They suffered great misery,
But once the roof is leaking, rain keeps on falling.
His father and mother also fell ill because of this.
Once they stopped breathing, they passed away:
Within seven days two deaths as both had died!

As both had died
Wenju, still so young, had truly fallen on hard times:
His father had passed away, then his mother had died.
He had not a penny left to pay for his mother's burial.

---

[13] The summary of this story as presented in the *Zhongguo quyi zhi: Fujian juan* 2006, 168–169 is based on the ballad performed by Lu Shoumin.
[14] Confucius.

Suffering a grievous injustice he had to sell himself.

He had to sell himself
And so sold himself as of then to the Zhang family.
As if serving as a slave was not yet suffering enough,
He was out of the blue struck by disaster once more
As unexpectedly he was involved in a major incident.

A major incident:
One day at night when it was as dark as dark can be
A thief had sneaked into the house of the Zhangs.
The thief had run off with some ounces of fine silver,
But Master Zhang thought it must have been his slave.

It must have been his slave!
But Wenju who was innocent replied to his master:
"True gold doesn't fear the fire of the red-hot oven:
I didn't steal your white silver and that is the truth —
Beat me to death if you want as you are my owner!"

"You are my owner!"
That cruel Master Zhang showed no consideration,
Beat him with a cudgel and kicked him with his feet.
He also had him arrested and locked up in his jail,
Where he was shackled in chains of tens of pounds.

Several tens of pounds!
Now next door there lived a man surnamed Wang,
And Master Wang had a daughter, called Jinzhen.
Now she and Wenju were very close to each other —
The girl was spontaneous, lively, and pretty smart.

She was pretty smart
And when she had heard that Wenju was locked up,
She was at a loss what to do and hurried back home.
Once there, blushing for shame, she told her father:

"You have to save that boy who is now in danger!"

"A boy in danger!"
When Master Wang heard this, he promptly agreed.
With silver in hand he went over to the Zhang family,
And with a gift of three hundred ounces of fine silver
He ransomed Wenju who had suffered such an ordeal.

II *Passing the Examinations as Top-of-the-List*
In front of the gate the magpies[15] called without end:
A pleased Master Wang was all wrapped in smiles.
Wenju was quite intelligent and also very diligent.
With all his mind he worked on the Sage's classics,
And at eighteen he obtained the degree of *xiucai*.[16]

He obtained the degree —
Master Wang was truly a kind-hearted person,
So one day he called his daughter Jinzhen over,
And told her that as she was so close with Wenju,
Shouldn't the two of them tie the marriage-knot?

Tie the marriage-knot?
With a blush on their face the two people agreed.
Mice wanting to climb up a wall — no way to succeed![17]
Bowing before the ancestors they became a couple:
A hundred yard of silk thread, such was their love.[18]

Such was their love,
More than that of Buffalo Boy and Weaving Maiden!
But that year exams were to be held in the capital city.

---

[15] The call of the magpie is believed to foretell good fortune.
[16] *Xiucai* 秀才 (flourishing talent) was the title of those who had passed the prefectural examinations and had been admitted into the prefectural school as students.
[17] A phrase said of something one has longed for for a long time but has been unable to obtain: their greatest wish.
[18] The word for "thread" (*si* 絲) has the same pronunciation as the word for "love/longing" (*si* 思).

Wenju made up his mind to go to the empire's capital,
And the whole family, old and young, supported him.

They all supported him,
So Wenju gathered his luggage in order to depart.
In his hand he held a pearl that he broke into halves.
At parting, husband and wife, overcome by emotion,
Both hid one half of that broken pearl on their body.

Hiding it on his body
Wenju travelled to the capital and arrived at court.
On the ninth of the Third Month the exams began
And in each session his essays surpassed all others,
So he passed as Top-of-the-List, gaining first place.

He gained first place,
So His Majesty the Humane Ancestor received him at court.[19]
He awarded this talented person nine golden flower stems;
He awarded this noble person golden boots and a fast horse,
A dragon robe and a jade belt — every article perfectly new!

Every article perfectly new,
Drums resounded to heaven with a deafening noise!
He paraded the streets, famous throughout the world.
In front and in back surrounded by oh so many people:
Throngs of people wanting to see the Top-of-the-List!

III *The Forced Marriage*
The Top-of-the-List paraded the streets in high spirits;
Master Wen, the prime minister, observed him clearly:
He wanted to get the Top-of-the-List as his son-in-law

---

[19] The Humane Ancestor (Renzong 仁宗) was the posthumous title of the Song emperor who reigned from 1023–1062. As this long reign was a period of peace and prosperity it became the setting of many stories in later times.

But was afraid that he might not agree to his proposal,
Yet when he furrowed his brow he came up with a plan.

He came up with a plan:
He devised a devious scheme to put pressure on him.
He immediately went to court and told the emperor:
"As my daughter wants to marry the Top-of-the-List,
I beg Your Majesty to serve as the matchmaker here."

To serve as matchmaker —
The Humane Ancestor happily accepted his request.
"If that latest Top-of-the-List meets your expectations,
We'll allow your daughter to make him her husband
And We will take charge, serving as the go-between."

"Serving as the go-between."
When Master Wen heard this, he was very pleased.
He blocked the road and invited the Top-of-the-List:
"My daughter wants to marry you, Top-of-the-List,
So quickly come along to the Wen family residence."

At the Wen family residence
The Top-of-the-List replied and explained the facts:
"At present I have a wife, waiting for me at home.
I definitely will not marry again here in the capital.
This marriage you propose cannot be concluded."

"Cannot be concluded":
When Master Wen heard this, he cursed without end:
"His Majesty serves as the matchmaker, he is in charge,
So for what reason can this marriage not be concluded?
Do you dare, here in court, disobey an imperial order?"

"Disobey an imperial order?
I, this top-of-the-List, will not accept your proposal.
Abandoning one's wife out of love for a concubine

Isn't done, even if the emperor acts as go-between.
I don't want to be Top-of-the List, rather a student."

"I prefer to be a student!"
Master Wen, that evil dog, was full devious cunning.
Hurriedly he hastened to court to inform the emperor.
When the emperor heard of this, fire raged in his heart,
As again and again he said: "Kill that Top-of-the-List!"

"Kill that Top-of-the-List!"
This frightened Number Two and Number Three.
These two, out of their friendship for Gao Wenju,
Went to court to speak up for the Top-of-the List:
"Don't kill, we implore you, such a good person!"

"Kill such a good person?"
The emperor slapped his table and cursed them at length:
"Disobeying imperial orders you dare act as his guarantors,
So the two of you also will suffer the ultimate punishment:
Behead them outside the south gate, without any clemency!"

"Without any clemency!"
When the Top-of-the-List heard this, he couldn't bear it:
"It's more than bad enough if I'm killed without any guilt,
But how can I involve the two of them in this case of mine?
I can only give in and state that I'll be happy to marry her."

"I'll be happy to marry her."
Now he had to think of a way to deal with the situation.
During daytime he acted the part as husband to his wife,
But at night when sleeping they rested in separate beds:
This annoyed his bride Wen Jin, who became very upset.

She became very much upset
But the Top-of-the-List didn't dare tell her the truth,
And so he told Wen Jin the following deceptive story:

"This is because I am suffering from an ugly illness,
And if we would sleep together, I might infect you."

"I might infect you."
That young lady Wen Jin still harbored her doubts:
"The Top-of-the-List says he suffers from an illness,
But I don't know whether that is the truth or a lie,
So I'll have a doctor submit him to an examination."

Submit him to an examination!
Now the doctor turned out to be a kind-hearted man.
Wenju honestly explained the full situation to him,
And the doctor expressed his sympathy to him, saying
That he happily would help such a true-hearted man!

A true-hearted man —
So he provided this explanation of his illness to Wen Jin:
"The Top-of-the List is suffering from a venereal disease.
I implore you on no account to sleep together with him —
Sitting next to him on a bench may transmit the infection!"

May transmit the infection —
The Top-of-the-List was only thinking of Wang Jinzhen.
He wrote a letter and thereupon ordered his major domo
To instruct a mounted messenger to go and tell his wife
To set out that very same day and join him in the capital.

Join him in the capital —
But that major domo was a devious and treacherous fellow.
In front of the Top-of-the-List he agreed to do as he asked,
But the took the letter and showed it to his mistress Wen Jin;
She destroyed the letter and made up a lie to harm Jinzhen.

She decided to harm Jinzhen —
The Top-of-the-List day and night was wracked by worries,
And when eventually the letter-carrier came back again,

He was told that his parents-in-law had both passed away
And that Jinzhen already had married some other person.

Had married some other person —
The Top-of-the-List didn't know what he had to believe.
He would like to ask someone to go and inquire again,
But, alas, he lacked a person he could truly trust in this:
Pondering this day and night he was wounded by grief.

IV *Trekking to the Capital in Search of her Husband*
Let me explain this clearly:
Master Wang was waiting for his son-in-law to return.
Having waited for three years, there still was no news.
At night he admonished his daughter not to be grieved,
On no account to damage her figure of a young woman.

The figure of a young woman —
The more Jinzhen longed for him, the more she suffered:
"My husband has been gone now for three years already,
How come we never received any letter or news from him?"
Each and every night she wept and cried till break of dawn.

Till break of dawn —
Her serving girl named Caijiao admonished her mistress:
"Milady, if you find it so hard to forget young master Gao,
You should at the earliest opportunity set out to find him.
I'll most happily come along when you trek to the capital."

"When you trek to the capital":
These were the words that moved Wang Jinzhen to action.
Immediately she discussed the matter with Master Wang.
Jinzhen gathered her luggage without any further delay;
Together with Caijiao she promptly set out on the road.

They promptly set out on the road
And day and night they traveled on despite all hardships.
They rested in god knows how many abandoned temples;

They slept in god knows how many dilapidated pavilions.
How much sadness and suffering for these two people!

These two people
One day arrived in the middle of a huge mountain forest.
The girl servant Caijiao was the one who walked in front,
But she slipped, lost her footing, and fell into a tiger trap,
And that left Jinzhen all alone there as the only survivor.

As the only survivor
Jinzhen wept in a heart-rending way till break of dawn.
When early on the hunter's wife checked the tiger trap,
She met there to her utter surprise with Wang Jinzhen.
But as soon as they had met, they became best friends.

They became best friends:
The hunter's wife understood once she heard her tale.
When she realized that Jinzhen did not know the road,
She happily agreed to accompany her and be her guide.
The two of them, old and young, continued the journey.

They continued the journey,
But alas, the hunter's wife was already advanced in years.
Because of the hardships on the road she fell ill and died,
Becoming a person in a Dream of the Southern Branch.[20]
How very much to be pitied now was our Wang Jinzhen!

Wang Jinzhen:
A single body, a single shadow: alone and forlorn —
After she had travelled god knows how many roads
She arrived by happenstance in the imperial capital,

---

[20] In a well-known tale from the Tang dynasty the protagonist has a splendid career, but when he wakes up from his drunken stupor he realizes it had all been a dream. In his dream he had been appointed as prefect of South Branch. For a translation of this tale see Nienhauser 2010, 131–188, "An Account of the Governor of the Southern Branch."

Where she became a drifting ballad-singing beggar.

A ballad-singing beggar,
Investigating the precise whereabouts of her husband.
She learned he was living at the Wen family mansion;
On top of that she heard he had married the daughter.
So she hastily hurried to the home of the Wen family.

To the home of the Wen family,
Where Wen Jin turned out to be a mean lowlife:
As soon as she knew that this woman was Jinzhen,
She started to curse her without any compassion,
With each word wanting to kill that Wang Jinzhen.

That Wang Jinzhen!
But then again Wen Jin feigned to be a nice person:
"On the basis of your crime you should be executed,
But in consideration of your long and distant journey
I will only condemn you to servitude in this mansion.

"Condemned to servitude:
So it is not fitting anymore to call you Jinzhen.
From today on we will change your surname
And will call you by the name of Latest Arrival.[21]
Only in that way can I spare your rotten life."

Your rotten life —
Now Jinzhen was a very smart woman and knew
That is was best if she stayed at the Wen mansion
And eventually found a way to see her husband —
Having made up her mind, she accepted the deal.

V *Lamenting Throughout the Five Watches*
Once Jinzhen had entered the Wen family mansion,
She again slept alone — a cold couch, a single cushion.

---

[21] *Xinlairen* 新來人.

She hated the watches: too long; the night: too short!
She barely wanted to close her eyes, when light broke;
Throughout the watches she lamented her husband.

The first watch was sounded — what a booming roll!
"Once long ago when you had been locked up in jail,
It was my father who ransomed you with his money,
Who ransomed you so you could become my husband,
So why are you such a despicable creature now today?"

The second watch was sounded — what a dreary roll!
She cursed that Wenju as a man without any decency.
"Once long ago you swore an oath, calling on Heaven:
You would never marry another woman as your wife!
Do you remember that keepsake of the broken pearl?"

The third watch was sounded — what a booming roll!
Her tears coursed down, more than she could wipe away.
"Let me pose the question to the doorgods of this house:
The doorgods too must know you are married to me.
So how can you, my dear husband, be devoid of love?"

The fourth watch was sounded — still no sign of dawn!
"How can my husband be so devoid of love or affection?
As I sit here on this couch and lament my bitter fate,
Even this headrest knows that you are married to me.
How could my dear husband dare be such a traitor!"

The fifth watch was sounded — the sky turned bright.
She angrily vilified Wenju as less than a human being.
"You may be able to face Heaven — you can't face Earth;
You may be able to face Earth — you cannot face man:
Will you ever be able to face your wife Wang Jinzhen?"

Throughout the watches she sadly lamented till daylight,
So people in other rooms could hear her most clearly.
The sound of her lament spread in all four directions:

Yingchun when she heard was filled with compassion,[22]
So she walked over to her and she comforted Jinzhen.

She comforted Jinzhen:
"Your husband presently is staying at Nine-Loft Pavilion.
Sighing and whining here in your room is of no use at all.
You should go out and sweep the floor in his courtyard,
And then find out his feelings for you by singing a song."

VI *Sweeping the Courtyard Ten Times*
Black clouds cover the whole sky, no star to be seen:
Husband and wife are separated, cannot come close.
Early in the morning Jinzhen goes and sweeps the floor,
Before the broom touches the floor, tears gush forth,
And as she sweeps, she curses that faithless fellow.

When she sweeps the courtyard a first time, she curses a rooster:
"Don't disdain me just because my fate is so poor.
This rooster may well be compared to Gao Wenju:
We ransomed you but you cause me such misery —
As you fly over southern hills, the northern hill cries."

When she sweeps the courtyard a second time, a heavy task,
The only animal there in the courtyard is a tommy cat.
"This tommy cat may well be compared to Gao Wenju:
We ransomed you but it was all a waste of money —
You cannot catch any mice and turned out a traitor!"

When she sweeps the courtyard a third time, there is a bird:
"Little bird, how come you do fly so high in the sky?
This little bird may well be compared to Gao Wenju:
He married again, took a concubine — what cruelty!
He sure will be hacked to death with a thousand cuts!"

---

[22] Yingchun is a serving girl in the Wen mansion.

When she sweeps the courtyard a fourth time, there is a flute:
"You started out a green young bamboo in the village,
But as this flute you may be compared to Gao Wenju.
He married again, took a concubine, such pleasure!
Be prepared that one day you'll be burned to ashes."

When she sweeps the courtyard a fifth time, she sees some geese,
With their wings all preened they swim across a ditch:
"Today you together may be compared to Gao Wenju
As one gander is here followed by two female geese —
But do you understand the pain of that other person?"

When she sweeps the courtyard a sixth time, there's a single shoe:
"Let me tell you the terrible fate of this old shoe.
Earlier it was one of a pair that was hot like on fire,
But today it is all alone and forlorn exactly like me:
Wind-blown, rain-drenched, and yet nobody cares."

When she sweeps the courtyard a seventh time, she confronts a dog,
And as she points at the dog she gives it a scolding:
"You now may well be compared to that Gao Wenju.
We ransomed you but all that money was a waste,
You don't remember the love of husband and wife."

When she sweeps the courtyard an eighth time, she finds a book:
"That husband of mine is so muddle-headed with books!
Once he loved to read you and feasted his eyes on you;
Now he doesn't read you anymore, you're tossed away.
I too am just like an old book that's been tossed away!"

When she sweeps the courtyard a ninth time, she found there a pig,
And as she points at the pig, she curses her husband:
"You may well be compared now to that Gao Wenju.
All these years of your life you're so muddle-headed,
All you ever care for is your own comfort and pleasure."

When she sweeps the courtyard a tenth time, she sees there a flower:
"Who may have dropped you now here in the mud?
Don't let it be that rotten scoundrel Gao Wenju:
For all the love of the flower, he treats it like mud.
Right flowers he doesn't pick, only wild flowers.

"I have cursed him once and I've cursed him twice;
All kinds of beasts and birds I have cursed at length.
I may be compared to a little boat on the waves:
Whatever way I may try, I cannot reach my goal.
Who knows on which day we'll be united again?"

VII *The Broken Pearl Reunited*
Jinzhen vilified her husband in such moving manner,
Each and every word entered the Nine-Lofts Pavilion.
The Top-of-the List therefore wondered in his heart:
"This voice resembles that of my wife Wang Jinzhen,
Can it be she has come to the capital, looking for me?"

"Did she come to the capital?"
When Yingchun came up the stairs to bring him his tea,
The Top-of-the-list didn't order her to put down the cup,
But immediately asked: "Who is that woman down below?
All morning she kept on cursing without any interruption!"

All morning long —
Yingchun didn't dare tell him the facts of the case in full,
So she said, "It's that sweeping woman. I don't know her,
I have no clue what kind of person she perhaps may be.
The others in this household just call her Latest Arrival."

"Latest Arrival?"
The Top-of-the-List pondered this in his mind,
Then, opening his mouth, he ordered Yingchun:
"Now go to the kitchen and there tell the cook
To make me a rice cake — I'm eager to have one."

"I'm eager to have one!"
Now this was a tall order that perplexed the cook.
The cook didn't know how to prepare such a cake.
So he questioned Latest Arrival about this topic:
"You're from the same place, so you must know!"

"So you must know!"
When Jinfen heard this, she was filled with joy.
She told people to buy some flour from a shop
And she also needed two pounds of white sugar.
But she had to make the cake with her own hands!

She would make it,
So the cook then and there accepted her proposal,
The flour and the sugar were bought and brought in.
Jinzhen played her role of kitchen maid to perfection
And hid her half of the broken pearl inside the cake.

Hid it inside the cake —
When the bun was steamed it tasted so very sweet.
Yingchun took it with her and delivered it upstairs.
When the Top-of-the-List had inspected the cake,
He pulled it apart to have a look and understood all.

He understood all:
One half of a broken pearl was one half of a heart.
And when he also took out his half of the pearl,
These two halved pearls fitted perfectly together,
So he knew that his wife had come to the capital.

She had come to the capital:
Yingchun only now could tell him the facts of the case.
Hearing this, the Top-of-the-List was filled with grief.
He wanted to rush downstairs and meet with Jinzhen,
But was afraid of that black-hearted woman Wen Jin.

That black-hearted person —
But Yingchun turned out to be the smarter of the two.
As she opened her mouth she said to the Top-of-the-List:
"We must be careful in coming up with a successful plan.
You must patiently, patiently wait for the right moment
And then a magpie bridge[23] will bring you lovers together."

VIII *Meeting but Separated by a Window*
As the sun sank on the hills, night's darkness descended;
From all directions the birds now returned to their woods.
Back to the woods, the birds flew in pairs and in couples,
But the boy and girl were still separated, each living alone,
Constantly filled with longing for that other, their lover.

Filled with longing
They waited for the moon, for the sun, and for the stars.
Then one day the Emperor celebrated his sixtieth birthday
And Master Wen and his whole family went to the palace,
But the Top-of-the-List feigned an illness, staying in bed.

He stayed in bed,
But the young lady Wen Jin had a most devious mind:
If the Top-of-the-List would get up and wander about,
He might of course very well encounter Wang Jinzhen,
So she devised a marvelous scheme to keep them apart.

To keep them apart
She scattered chalk powder on the steps of the staircase;
The nine gates of the pavilion too were securely locked,
And upstairs and downstairs she had people keep watch:
Even the greatest capacities would be unable to succeed!

---

[23] Buffalo Boy and Weaving Maiden, two stars on opposite banks of the Celestial River (the Milky Way) are only allowed to meet on the night of the seventh of the Seventh Month, when magpies construct a bridge across the stream on their behalf.

Unable to succeed —
But Yingchun suggested a clever scheme to Wang Jinzhen:
"There is no point in screaming from below the staircase.
It's much better for you to go to the flower garden pavilion.
If we put a short ladder in place, you can meet your lover."

"You can meet your lover."
Separated by the window they met and cried without end.
The Top-of-the-List then instructed his dear wife Jinzhen:
"Make sure to leave the Wen family mansion immediately;
If you are murdered here, that injustice cannot be avenged.

"It cannot be avenged,
So quickly go and find an inn where you can stay for a while
And wait for the return to the capital of Lord Bao, the judge.[24]
Then block his road, lay a plaint and recount your suffering:
Lord Bao is the one who's able to hand down a clear verdict."

Hand down a clear verdict —
Jinzhen immediately climbed down from the garden pavilion.
She went without further ado to the inn of granny Wang,[25]
Hoping for the return to the capital of Lord Bao, the judge,
Who could reunite husband and wife and undo their grief.

IX *Husband and Wife Reunited*
Now tell that His Excellence Iron-Face Bao, having completed
His term of office in Yunnan, returned to the imperial capital,
Where Jinzhen blocked his road and submitted her complaint.
The stirring words of her complaints provided a clear exposé —
It scared His Excellency Iron-face Bao squarely out of his wits!

---

[24] In many stories that feature Judge Bao the crimes in the capital are said to have taken place during his temporary absence from the capital, implying that criminals would not have dared to act if he had been around.
[25] In other Judge Bao stories too, granny Wang provides hospitality in her inn to women seeking justice.

"Your Excellence Bao,
Firstly, I accuse Master Wen of forcibly acquiring a son-of-law;
Secondly, I accuse Gao Wenju of abandoning his wedded wife;
And thirdly, I accuse His Majesty of serving as the matchmaker.
I implore you, Lord Bao, please settle this case by your verdict."

"Settle this case by your verdict."
Lord Bao, accepting the accusation, promised to take on the case.
He ordered his assistants Zhang Long and Zhao Hu immediately
To conduct a full investigation into the facts of this false marriage —
Tomorrow he would decide on this matter at the court audience.

At the court audience
Bao Zheng had made preparations in an experienced way.
He had requested His Majesty to join him in judging the case
And the Humane Ancestor had readily agreed to his request,
Bestowing the precious sword of authority on Minister Bao.[26]

Bestowing it on Minister Bao.
Behind the bench Lord Bao had taken his seat to judge the case,
But on his head he did not wear his cape made of blackest gauze.
Four coffins had been prepared and placed outside in courtyard:
This scared all civil and military officers at court out of their wits.

It scared them out of their wits
When Lord Bao promptly started to explain the facts of the case:
"Gao Wenju who abandoned his wife out of love for a concubine
Is, based on the law, condemned to suffer a capital punishment:
The first coffin has been readied to encoffin his bodily remains."

To encoffin his bodily remains.
As for the second culprit, he also explained the facts of the case:
"Prime Minister Wen used extreme force to acquire a son-in-law;

---

[26] The sword of authority will allow Judge Bao to execute criminals without prior authorization from the emperor.

Therefore he too deserves to receive the ultimate punishment.
The second coffin has been readied to hold his bodily remains."

To hold his bodily remains.
As for the third culprit, he also explained the facts of the case:
"Your Majesty, as matchmaker you exerted excessive pressure,
So your person too deserves to suffer the ultimate punishment:
The largest coffin has been readied to hold your bodily remains."

To house your bodily remains.
As for the fourth culprit, he also explained the facts of the case:
"While deciding a case, I, Bao Zheng, brazenly murder my ruler,
So it is only fitting that I also will suffer the ultimate punishment:
The fourth coffin has been readied to hold my mortal remains."

To house my mortal remains —
This scared the Humane Ancestor so much he begged for mercy,
But Lord Bao ordered that the criminals involved be arrested
So they might be interrogated all together there in the palace:
Those civil and military officers — their eyes popped wide open.

Their eyes popped wide open for fright!
Wenju knelt down and addressed His Excellency Bao as follows:
"I would never dare to drop my wife out of love for a concubine,
But I had no choice as His Majesty served as the matchmaker —
If I did not accept the proposal of his, he might have me killed.

"He might have me killed!
But I never consummated this marriage to my bride Wen Jin.
For three long years I feigned I was suffering from an illness,
And at night we never shared the same couch for sleeping.
Immaculate, chaste and pure, I never ever touched her body."

I never touched her body —
That deviously cunning Wen Jin made her appearance in court.
She feigned to be pregnant, she feigned to be heavy with child,

And as she knelt down on her knees, she wept copious tears;
She sadly clamored that she was the victim of gross injustice.

Clamored she was suffering injustice,
So Lord Bao gave order that she be exhaustively investigated.
He ordered the guardsmen with golden blades and jade axes
To arrest Wen Jin then and there in the middle of the court hall
And take her away so an investigation might settle this clearly.

To settle this clearly —
Cut in two a little god might perhaps have made his escape,
But Wen Jin was so scared that her cheeks turned all purple;
When she wanted to make her escape by taking big strides,
The old rags she had stuffed inside her shirt all fell to the ground.

Old rags indeed!
Everybody had a good laugh at the expense of Master Wen;
Wen Jin felt so mortified she didn't know which way to turn.
There in the hall she bashed her head against a solid pillar —
For no good reason at all a young girl had died all in vain.

This young girl had died.
Now Master Bao set about to sentence His Excellency Wen:
"Forcing a man to become one's son-in-law violates the law.
Stripped of your office you will become a common citizen;
You are allowed to show remorse and become a good man."

Become a good man —
Next he sentenced His Majesty for acting the matchmaker.
"Without the faintest idea about blue or red, black or white,
You had the temerity to order a marriage under pressure.
You will parade the streets, mend your ways, and do good."

You will do good —
Next he also sentenced the Top-of-the-List Gao Wenju:
"For three years oppressed, you maintained your chastity,

So for a thousand years your pure fame will be renowned.
It is only fitting that you will be raised one step in rank."

This is only fitting:
The Humane Ancestor loudly voiced his approbation;
Civil and military officers wished him "a myriad years!"
And their thousand voices thanked His Excellency Bao,
Wenju and Jinzhen were happily all wrapped in smiles.

Were all wrapped in smiles
And knelt down on their knees to thank their benefactor.
Lord Bao raised them up and addressed them as follows:
(*speak:*) "Men should all follow the example provided by Gao Wenju,
(*sing:*) Women should all follow the example set by Wang Jinzhen.
Even if seas dry out and rocks rot away, don't forget your love."

CHAPTER 2

LIANG SIZHEN AND ZHAO YULIN

The story of *Liang Sizhen and Zhao Yulin* may well have been the most popular title of all bamboo-clappers songs. The song must have held a special appeal for the performers as it told how the poor student Zhao Yulin made his way to the capital to sit for the examinations begging his way as a street performer and how he, upon his return as Top-of-the-List, dressed in a beggar's rags to find out what his father-in-law truly thought about him. The story is at least as much about Zhao Yulin's long-suffering wife Liang Sizhen who stands by her man despite the taunts of her three sisters, who all have married rich husbands. The origin of the story, which does not appear to have circulated outside Hakka-speaking communities, is unknown, but a version as a ballad has been (almost entirely) preserved in an undated but most likely 19th-century woodblock edition.[1] The following translation of the version as a bamboo-clappers song is based on the edition provided in Hu Xizhang, *Kejia zhubange yanjiu* (2010: 369–398). Hu based his edition on the text included in *Wujuban chuanben ji* 五句板傳本集, published in January 1997 by the Cultural Office of Wuhua district, which itself was based on performances by

---

[1] Brokaw 2007, 503–504.

Wen Songman 溫松滿 and Zheng Yuying 鄭玉英 as recorded by Peng Qiang 彭強.[2]

In Fujian the tale of Liang Sizhen and Zhao Yulin was performed as a bamboo-clappers song in Wuping and as a ballad in four-line stanzas in Yongding. The *Zhongguo geyao jicheng: Fujian juan* (2007: 609–620) includes the latter version as *Zhao Yulin*. The text is based on the performances by Lu Shoumin, Jiang Qian 江謇 and Su Tianfa 蘇天發, as recorded by Chen Yanrong in 1998 at Kanshizhen. The editors of that work added the following note:

> "Zhao Yulin" is a traditional narrative song that is popular throughout the Hakka-speaking districts of Fujian. Each district has its own traditional version, that each has its own characteristics in terms of literary format and performance shape. We have selected the song in the volume from Yongding district that is named "Zhao Yulin," which is made up of stanzas of four lines of seven syllables and counts 700 lines. The song in the volume from Wuping district is called "Zhao Yulin and Liang Sizhen"; it is made up of bamboo-clappers stanzas of five lines of seven syllables, and counts 1006 lines. Even though they are different in performance and even though there are minor plot items that are different between the two districts, the theme and the plot of the two songs are very much the same as they both satirize those who cheat the poor and love the rich, both castigate the mean people who are led by power and profit, and both praise a love that is strong and cannot be breached. Because the songs propagate the beautiful virtues of our nation's tradition, they are deeply loved by the broad masses, and therefore its performance has not diminished in popularity over the years.

---

[2] Wen Songman (1921–1997) and his wife Zheng Yuying (b. 1936) were both professional performers of bamboo-clappers songs from Wuhua. Wen, who was lame in one leg ad basically illiterate, had started to train as a performer from the age of eight. Zheng had finished high school but later gone blind. The *Wujuban chuanben ji* consists mostly of text performed by Wen and Zheng (Hu Xizhang 2010, 285). Peng Qiang (b. 1964) is a musicologist who, since 1992, has served in the cultural bureau of Wuhua, most lately as its director. He is an accomplished musician and singer and played a leading role in the collection of the bamboo-clappers songs that were collected in *Wujuban chuanben ji* (Hu Xizhang 2010, 315–316).

More information on the popularity of this tale in southwestern Fujian is provided in *Zhongguo quyi zhi: Fujian juan* (2006: 155–156).

> This item is a moralistic work. The story is well-made with a proper beginning and ending. It was one of the items that was performed by the group representing the Longyan region when they went and participated in the Fujian Province First Collective Performance of *Quyi* in June 1958 in Zhangzhou. Popular artists like Li Tiansheng 李天生 from Yongding and Lin Jinbiao 李金標 from Caixi in Shanghang also performed this item at the same period. A shortened and edited text was included in the *Zhongguo geyao jicheng: Fujian juan — Yongding fenjuan* by the editorial committee for popular literature of Yongding district. The item also used to be popular in the area of Meixian in Guangdong, where they have DVDs and audiotapes to meet the demands of the market. That version has the added episodes of Zhao Yulin begging his way by performing songs when trekking to the capital to take the examinations, and staying at the Yuelai inn, where the female owner granny Wang treats him very generously, whereupon he tells her that he wants to make her his foster mother (*ganniang* 干娘) once he will have passed the examinations.[3] At the same time these [DVD's and audiotapes from Meixian] omit episodes such as how upon Zhao Yulin's return to Wuzhou his father-in-law Millionaire Liang is so ashamed that he flees to the kitchen and covers his face with a ladle, and how his three brothers-in-law and his three sisters-in-law respectively carry a sedan chair for him or serve as maids in his house.

The text presented in the *Zhongguo geyao jicheng: Fujian juan* is very similar to the text in a mimeographed copy, also entitled *Zhao Yulin,* probably dating from the 1970s and collected by Cynthia Brokaw in the context of her research on Sibao publishing.[4]

---

[3] In yet another version of the tale this helpful innkeeper is surnamed Liu 劉. When Zhao Yulin has passed the examinations and returns home, he takes her with him so he can take care of her for the rest of her life.

[4] Brokaw 2007, 503–504 briefly compares this text to an earlier undated woodblock-printed version, noting the substitution of many characters by simplified characters or completely different characters. Texts of *Zhao Yulin* also circulated on Taiwan. Qiu Chunmei 2003, 187–188 lists two manuscripts.

Whereas the ballad text as found in the *Zhongguo geyao jicheng: Fujian juan* is very much focused on the relation of Liang Sizhen to her three elder sisters, the mimeographed text also contains a long description of Zhao Yulin's trip to the capital. It also further includes the details of Zhao Yulin buying worn clothes from the captain of his ship. The main difference in plot between these ballads and the bamboo-clappers song is that the latter makes great effort to distinguish clearly between Liang Sizhen's kind mother and her mean father, while the ballads do not. When in the bamboo-clappers songs she asks her father for a loan so her husband can travel to the capital and is rebuffed, whereupon her mother gives her a golden hairpin, in these ballads Liang Sizhen does not ask for a loan and the hairpin she gives to Zhao Yulin is part of her own dowry. The ballads do, however, contain a description of the rich husbands of Liang Sizhen's elder sisters making fun of Zhao Yulin when, upon his return, he appears before them in rags at his father-in-law's birthday celebration. This scene is curiously lacking in the bamboo-clappers version. A translation of this scene from the ballad and of the slightly different punishment of the three young men is appended to this translation.

The bamboo-clappers song version of Zhao Yulin and Liang Sizhen from Wuping is reprinted by Liu Dake in his *Tianye zhong de diyu Shehui yu wenhua* (2007: 268–279). Liu Dake based his edition on a manuscript copy he had bought in the course of his local fieldwork. That version has been compared to the ballad from Yongping by Lian Jian'an 2009.[5] One of the original elements in the version from Wuping is that Zhao Yulin does not buy a three-stringed banjo, but is given one by an immortal fairy while he is making his way to

---

[5] Lian Jian'an, who claims to have heard performances of this tale by blind performers in the 1980s, mentions that male performers tended to call this tale "Zhao Yulin and Liang Sizhen", whereas female performers preferred to call it "Liang Sizhen and Zhao Yulin". Lian adds the information that when a performer would arrive in a village he or she would visit each of the houses to collect a donation during the daytime, singing only a few stanzas and then at night would perform a full-length tale such as "Liang Sizhen and Zhao Yulin" for the whole village at a suitable venue (Lian Jian'an 2009, 209).

the capital. In many other respects it would appear to be closer to the text presented by Hu Xizhang.[6]

***

Liang Sizhen and Zhao Yulin

When I tell a hundred stories it is all only idle chatter;
Now I start out on this song, I'll sing of ancient times,
A story from Wuzhou prefecture in Guangxi province.
Wuzhou prefecture was the home of the Zhao family;
Investigating Censor Zhao Duanming was living there.

Investigating Censor Zhao Duanming was living there,
The wife to whom he was married was surnamed Chen.
The couple of husband and wife lived in utter harmony.
They were blessed with the birth of a very bright son;
At the Full Month celebration they named him Yulin.[7]

At the Full Month celebration they named him Yulin.
He grew up without any problems, with no disaster.
When very quickly he had reached the age of seven,
His father and mother entrusted their son to a school,
And his teacher taught him to read the Book of Odes.

And his teacher taught him to read the Book of Odes.
That so very smart and intelligent pupil Zhao Yulin

---

[6] A short text entitled "Liang Sizhen Sees Her Husband off as he Leaves for the Examinations" (*Liang Sizhen song lang fukao* 梁四珍送郎赴考) is included in *Zhongguo geyao jicheng: Guangdong juan* 2007, 656. According to a short note at the end, it was performed by Li Bingxiang 李炳祥, recorded by Liu Yuanwei 劉苑薇 and Liao Li 廖莉 (in 1987 in Lianping district and Xingning district) and edited by Wu Zhen 吳鎮. This text is composed of a mix of five-line stanzas and four-line stanzas.
[7] The Full Month ceremony is celebrated one month after the birth of a baby (if it has survived).

Studied from the age of seven to the age of twenty.
His belly was stuffed with fine texts; rich in talents
He passed the prefectural exams and became a *xiucai*.[8]

He passed the prefectural exams and became a *xiucai*,
But times turned against him and his fortune declined.
A flood destroyed his fields and a fire burned his house.
His whole family, old and young, all met with disaster,
And there were only two who escaped with their lives.

And there were only two who escaped with their lives.
Those who escaped were Zhao Yulin and Liang Sizhen.[9]
They were reduced to poverty and, at a loss what to do,
They built a shed on the Southern Hills as a place to live;
Poorly fed, almost starving, they lived from day to day.

Poorly fed, almost starving, they lived from day to day.
But now my song must turn to that district's Mr. Liang.
In that district there lived a rich man, Magnate Liang,
Who had married as his wife a woman surnamed Jin,
And she had born her husband four daughters in total.

And she had born her husband four daughters in total.
Now let me tell you the names of these four daughters.
The couple's eldest daughter was called Liang Caifeng;
The couple's second daughter was named Liang Yuying;
She was not only quite beautiful but also very intelligent.

She was not only quite beautiful but also very intelligent.
Without making any mistake I will tell you the true facts:
Now the couple's third daughter was named Liang Sangui;

---

[8] *Xiucai* 秀才 (flourishing talent) is the title that is commonly used to designate those who have passed the prefectural examinations and have been admitted as students to the prefectural school.

[9] As we will learn later, Liang Sizhen is the wife of Zhao Yulin.

The youngest daughter was given the name Liang Sizhen[10]
And she surpassed all other women in Wuzhou prefecture.

And she surpassed all other women in Wuzhou prefecture.
As a father Mr. Liang was very serious in seeking matches:
First of all, the future in-laws had to report at least a million;
Secondly, as sons-in-law he rejected men without a degree.
Without a degree even with a million it still was no deal.

Without a degree even with a million it still was no deal:
He married his eldest daughter to a man surnamed Chen;
He married his second daughter to one Millionaire Xie;
He married his third daughter to a man of the Lin family;
His fourth daughter he gave in marriage to Zhao Yulin.

His fourth daughter he gave in marriage to Zhao Yulin.
Now the Zhao family was originally a very fine family,
But alas, a heaven-sent disaster burned down their house,
So the family was destroyed, leaving only that couple.
They eked out an existence of such bitter hardship!

They eked out an existence of such bitter hardship!
As a result, Yulin addressed Liang Sizhen as follows:
"Here in my house we live now in such bitter poverty
That I will write out a writ of divorce on your behalf,
So you may marry another man, one who has money."

So you may marry another man, one who has money.
Sizhen thereupon answered him in the following way:
"A loyal servant will never betray a righteous master;
A virtuous woman will never marry a second husband.
Even in this dire poverty I will stay with Zhao Yulin."

---

[10]The names of the third and fourth daughter contain the elements "three" (*san* 三) and "four" (*si* 四).

Even in this dire poverty I will stay with Zhao Yulin.
Zhao Yulin's wife discussed the situation with him:
"You can go to the market to make money as a scribe,
While I will go out and cut rushes I'll offer for sale —
Don't worry we'll lack the food we need to survive."

Don't worry we'll lack the food we need to survive.
Yulin followed the advice of his wife Liang Sizhen.
He went each day to the market, working as a scribe,
And she went out and cut rushes she offered for sale:
Husband and wife worked hard without ever resting.

Husband and wife worked hard without ever resting,
And sun and moon passed by as quickly as a shuttle.
Very quickly the term of the examinations arrived:
A poster summoned students throughout the empire:
"If your writings excel, you'll be promoted to office."

If your writings excel, you'll be promoted to office.
Yulin addressed Liang Sizhen in the following way:
"At present we are suffering such bitter poverty here.
I want to go to the capital to sit for the examinations,
But alas, I don't have the money so I cannot set out."

But alas, I don't have the money so I cannot set out.
Liang Sizhen thereupon spoke to Zhao Yulin, saying:
"If you want to go to the capital and take the exams,
I will go and see my father to discuss this with him
And borrow some money for your trip to the capital."

And borrow some money for your trip to the capital.
Sizhen thereupon went to the Liang family mansion.
Upon entering the room, she there greeted her father,
Who was disgusted by his youngest daughter Sizhen:
At a glance his sharp eyes[11] identified her as a beggar!

---

[11] The Chinese here reads *yan hu yan zhen* 眼忽眼針. The translation is tentative.

At a glance his sharp eyes identified her as a beggar!
Liang Sizhen softly addressed her father as follows:
"Your son-in-law wants to sit for the examinations,
So we would like to borrow some money from you
For his trip to the capital, so that's why I came here."

For his trip to the capital, so that's why I came here.
Her father, Mr. Liang, answered Sizhen as follows:
"Presently your family is as poor as a naked demon,
So where would you find the money to pay me back?
I may have money, but don't make loans to beggars."

I may have money, but don't make loans to beggars.
"Let me tell you the truth," he said to Liang Sizhen,
"Staying with that poor devil will lead to nothing.
Wouldn't it be better to marry some other fine gent,
So you don't have to worry you've nothing to eat?"

So you don't have to worry you've nothing to eat —
Sizhen answered her father in the following words:
"Since ancient times it's one husband till old age,
Despite his poverty I'll always stay with Zhao Yulin,
I'll never be one who hating poverty covets wealth."

I'll never be one who hating poverty covets wealth.
Her father, Mr. Liang thereupon said to his daughter:
"If you refuse to listen to the advice of your father,
Then stay with that poor devil of yours, Zhao Yulin,
But for all eternity never again set foot in my house."

But for all eternity never again set foot in my house.
Sizhen thereupon answered her father in this manner:
"A good son doesn't make his father work the fields,
A good daughter doesn't make him take care of her.
In life and death I will always stay with the Zhaos."

In life and death I will always stay with the Zhaos —
Lifting her feet, Sizhen was about to take her leave,
But her mother lady Jin who had noticed her arrival,
Pulled Sizhen, her youngest daughter, over to her
To have a conversation with her, holding her hand.

To have a conversation with her, holding her hand —
Now this lady Jin was a very kind mother, and said:
"This hairpin made of seven point two *qian* of gold
Let me give it to you to take back with you to your home.
Let that pay for your husband's travel to the capital."

Let that pay for your husband's travel to the capital.
Sizhen took it with her and immediately returned.
She straightaway went back to the Southern Hills,
And as soon as she saw her husband, she told him:
"Zhao Yulin, my father despises all of your family.

"Zhao Yulin, my father despises all of your family,
But to my good fortune my dear old mother gave me
This hairpin made of seven point two *qian* of gold;
She told me to give it to my husband Zhao Yulin
As travel money to pay for your trip to the capital."

As travel money to pay for your trip to the capital.
Now Zhao Yulin trusted the advice of Liang Sizhen
And straightaway went to the gold-exchange shop,
Where he called for the manager Huang Guangxing,
As he wanted to exchange a golden hairpin for cash.

As he wanted to exchange a golden hairpin for cash.
Huang Guangxing addressed Zhao Yulin in this way:
"Aren't you suffering from poverty and deprivation?
So how did you get a gold hairpin to take to others?
If you have one, show it to me so I can have a look."

If you have one, show it to me so I can have a look.
Yulin then handed the hairpin to Huang Guangxing,
And the manager Guangxing immediately told him:
"This is seven parts copper and three parts gold —
Dull bronze and scrap iron for fooling the crowd!"

Dull bronze and scrap iron for fooling the crowd!
Guangxing also told the following to Zhao Yulin:
"This golden hairpin of yours is not of good value,
But I'll give you three hundred and sixty coppers.
Are you willing or not willing to accept my offer?"

Are you willing or not willing to accept my offer?
Yulin heaved a sigh and then answered as follows:
"In the hands of the poor even gold turns to iron;
In the hands of the rich even iron turns into gold.
These words of the ancients are each and all true.

"These words of the ancients are each and all true.
Whatever the amount of money, I'll take the offer."
With the money he went away, passing the market,
And there he saw an old man strumming the banjo;[12]
He strummed the banjo and sang to its clear sound.

He strummed the banjo and sang to its clear sound.
Yulin went up to that old performer and asked him:
"When I listen to your banjo, its sound is very good.
What's the price you ask for it? Please tell me clearly,
And sell that three-stringed banjo to me, Zhao Yulin."

And sell that three-stringed banjo to me, Zhao Yulin.
The old man answered him in the following words:
"To others I would never sell it for so little money,

---

[12] The musical instrument intended here is a three-stringed banjo-shaped instrument called *sanxian* 三弦 (three strings).

But considering how destitute you are, Zhao Yulin,
It will be yours for three hundred and sixty coppers."

It will be yours for three hundred and sixty coppers.
When Yulin heard this, he happily smiled and said:
"If it had been one more copper, I couldn't pay you,
But I have three hundred and sixty coppers with me."
He handed the money to the professional performer.

He handed the money to the professional performer
To take the three-stringed banjo with him back home.
Straightaway Yulin went back to the Southern Hills,
But when he took out the banjo and tried to strum it,
When he tried out the banjo, the sound wasn't clear.

When he tried out the banjo, the sound wasn't clear.
Now let's sing about Liang Sizhen who was inside.
When she heard the sound of the three-stringed banjo,
She thought: "From where did that beggar appear?
How come he doesn't know how destitute we are?"

How come he doesn't know how destitute we are?
When she went outside, she there saw Zhao Yulin:
"You left with a golden hairpin to go to the market,
To exchange it for money to travel to the capital —
So why did you buy a three-stringed banjo instead?"

So why did you buy a three-stringed banjo instead?
Yulin answered Liang Sizhen in the following way:
"Don't think that gold hairpin was such a big deal —
Three hundred and sixty coppers was all that I got,
That's not even enough to buy one dish of pickles.

"That's not even enough to buy one dish of pickles.
But let me explain to you the true state of affairs:
Now I have bought me this three-stringed banjo,
I'll be fine even after three days without any food,
Singing my songs I'll beg my way to the capital."

Singing my songs I will beg my way to the capital.
When Sizhen had heard this, she felt truly saddened:
"Others go to the exams riding a horse or a sedan chair,
But my husband goes to the capital begging his way."
She respectfully offered her husband a cup of water.

One cup of water, as clear as chrysanthemum flowers,
She respectfully offered in both her hands to her man:
"My dear husband, please drink this one cup of water:
May you speedily reach the capital and there become
The Number One Person before the emperor's gate."[13]

The Number One Person before the emperor's gate.
She repeatedly told Zhao Yulin to heed this advice:
"While on the road never drink any uncooked water,
And ever lie down for sleep on a spot that is soaked.
As a beggar you have to show respect at all times."

As a beggar you have to show respect at all times.
Yulin thereupon told his wife in very clear words:
"You've always been very kind to me and when I
Have passed as Top-of-the-List and come home,
You'll be ennobled as a Lady of the First Rank."

You will be ennobled as a Lady of the First Rank.
When husband and wife had said adieu, he set out.
He ate the food begged from hundreds of families;
He slept at night in roadside pavilions and temples,
Suffering the full measure of misery: Zhao Yulin.

Suffering the full measure of misery: Zhao Yulin.
He travelled one stretch and then another stretch,
And while he walked the roads he sang his songs.
Eventually, after a long time, he came to the capital,
Where he made his way to the examination grounds.

---

[13] The cyclostyled copy of the ballad collected by Cynthia Brokaw writes for this line "The Number One person of all the students of the Son of Heaven."

Where he made his way to the examination grounds.
Ten thousands of students had arrived at that place:
Three hundred and sixty names were listed as *jinshi*;[14]
Eighteen persons were appointed as Hanlin scholars;
Last of all were selected the Top-of-the List, the Number Two,
    and the Flower-Snatcher.[15]

Last of all were selected the Top-of-the-List, the Number Two,
    and the Flower-Snatcher.
The Number One, the Top-of-the-List was Zhao Yulin;
The Number Two on the list was a man surnamed Lin;
The Number Three, the Flower-Snatcher was a Chen,
And these three men were all received by the emperor.

And these three men were all received by the emperor.
They performed twenty-four bows in front of the ruler,
And His Majesty bestowed on them black gauze caps;
Dragon gowns and jade belts he bestowed on them too.
On horseback these three paraded through the capital.

On horseback these three paraded through the capital:
On horseback, for three days — it was quite a new sight.
Fiddles were played on horseback, drums followed:
The five tones and six instruments resounded loudly
As everyone wanted to see the new Top-of-the-List.

As everyone wanted to see the new Top-of-the-List.
After parading for three days, they returned to court.
His Majesty bestowed on them a sovereign sword,
And allowed the Top-of-the-List to go back home
With license to kill,[16] to take revenge on his enemies.

---

[14] *Jinshi* 進士 (presented scholar) is the title of those who have passed the metropolitan examinations.

[15] The Flower-Snatcher (*tanhua* 探花) occupies the third place on the list of those who have passed.

[16] The Chinese text reads *xian zhan hou zou* 先斬後奏 (reporting to the throne only after execution). In traditional China civil authorities had to report every death

With license to kill, to take revenge on his enemies.
The Top-of-the-List received permission to go home.
The high and low officials all came to see him off;
Civil and military officers all joined to see him off,
And nine cannons were fired when he left the palace.

And nine cannons were fired when he left the palace.
On the bustling bank of the river, he boarded a boat.
Let's not talk about the Top-of-the-List on his boat,
But let's sing of that Wuzhou man surnamed Liang:
He was to celebrate his birthday in a grand manner.

He was to celebrate his birthday in a grand manner.
Master Liang, that rich man, gave clear instructions:
"My three eldest daughters, those all are wealthy,
So quickly send an invitation to all three of them.
Forget about my youngest daughter, Liang Sizhen."

Forget about my youngest daughter, Liang Sizhen.
Now let's talk about those three women with money.
"Tomorrow when our daddy celebrates his birthday,
We will pass the Southern Hills when we go there
With all our presents, so let's shame that poor devil.

"With all our presents, so let's shame that poor devil.
We, her three sisters, will catalogue all our presents.
Each of us will give three hundred ounces of silver,
And all kinds of new garments of silks and gauzes —
That will shame that poor devil, that Liang Sizhen."

That will shame that poor devil, that Liang Sizhen!
The three sedan chairs then set out on their journey,
And straightaway they arrived at the Southern Hills.

---

sentence to the court and the condemned criminal could only be executed after the case had been reviewed and the verdict confirmed.

Sizhen welcomed the threesome of her elder sisters;
Pouring tea and fetching benches she knew no rest.

Pouring tea and fetching benches she knew no rest.
Her eldest sister thereupon addressed her as follows:
"People with money are seated on chairs of gold,
I have no need for your branch of some dead tree.
Poor beggar, don't show off your fake hospitality!"

Poor beggar, don't show off your fake hospitality!
Now that quite quick-witted Liang Sizhen replied:
"Please, dear, sit down on your folding chair of gold,
And I'll sit down on this branch of some dead tree.
It is the righteous who will be seated most solidly."

It is the righteous who will be seated most solidly.
The three of them thereupon asked Liang Sizhen:
"Tomorrow our daddy will celebrate his birthday,
How come you are still acting as if in no hurry?
You should go along together with us as sisters!

"You should go along together with us as sisters!
Just have a look at the presents of the three of us.
We will give him three hundred ounces of silver
And all kinds of new garments of silk and gauze.
Poor beggar, what will you give him as a present?"

Poor beggar, what will you give him as a present?
Sizhen provided them the following clear answer:
"You who have money, go on ahead, wish him well.
Don't compare yourself to me who has no money,
I don't have any present now to give to my father.

"I don't have any present now to give to my father.
I will have to wait for my dear husband, Zhao Yulin.
When he returns from the capital as the Number One,

We'll make longevity candles of a thousand pounds
And with some extra bows we'll congratulate daddy."

And with some extra bows we'll congratulate daddy.
Her eldest sister thereupon explained to Liang Sizhen:
"Your husband may be tall but his belly hangs down,[17]
If he won't become a beggar, he'll carry sedan chairs:
That man doesn't have the looks of a Top-of-the-List!"

That man doesn't have the looks of a Top-of-the-List.
Sizhen countered her eldest sister's words as follows:
"My dear husband is tall and his belly hangs down,
He surely is destined to ride a horse or a sedan chair.
The Top-of-the-List in this round will be Zhao Yulin."

The Top-of-the-List in this round will be Zhao Yulin.
The second sister tried to put Liang Sizhen in her place:
"If your dear husband indeed will pass with high honors,
A carrying pole may fall to the ground and sprout roots;
A manikin made of loam may become a human being!"

A manikin made of loam may become a human being.
Sizhen also countered this sister, in the following way:
"It may be a carrying pole, but it is made of bamboo,
And that tender bamboo will earlier have grown roots.
The Top-of-the-List in this round will be Zhao Yulin."

The Top-of-the-List in this round will be Zhao Yulin.
Her third sister tried to put Liang Sizhen in her place:
"Your dear husband resembles the water in a well —
How can it ever surge and reach the heart of the sea?
How can it be possible for scrap iron to turn into gold?"

How can it be possible for scrap iron to turn into gold?
Now this very eloquent Liang Sizhen replied as follows:

---

[17] Physiognomy was a highly developed art in traditional China and it was widely believed that a person's fate could be foretold from his or her physical features.

"My dear husband indeed resembles the water in a well:
When there's plenty of water, it will easily reach the sea,
And when fortune changes, scrap iron may turn to gold."

The four of them were fiercely arguing with each other;
The three sisters tried to put her in her place all together:
"If your husband this time passes with highest honors,
Banana trees will be dressed in gowns, and even dogs
Will wear hats, while pigs will be covered by blankets!"

Will be wearing hats, pigs will be covered by blankets.
Sizhen once again replied to them, this time declaring:
"If my husband this time returns with highest honors,
I will dress banana trees in gowns, and even dogs
Will wear hats, while pigs will be covered by blankets."

Will wear hats, while pigs will be covered by blankets.
Her third sister once again tried to put her in her place:
"Your husband resembles low-quality loam I'm afraid:
When plastered on walls it won't stick, you must know.
If he wants to be Top-of-the-List, he's wide of the mark."

If he wants to be Top-of-the-List, he's wide of the mark.
A spirited Sizhen countered her in the following manner:
"My dear husband perhaps resembles low-quality loam,
But rice straw mixed with lots of loam will stick together.
He'll be the one who wins the place of Top-of-the-List."

He'll be the one who wins the place of Top-of-the-List.
Her third sister once again tried to put her in her place:
"Your dear husband resembles the shape of a shoe knife:[18]
Crooked this way and that, it's the world's ugliest thing.
There's no way they will appoint him Top-of-the-List!"

---

[18] *Xiedaozi* 鞋刀子 (shoe knife) is not attested in dictionaries. I assume it is another word for shoehorn, but I have preferred to keep the word "knife" in my translation because of Liang Sizhen's later threat.

There's no way they will appoint him Top-of-the-List.
Sizhen loudly counterattacked and answered her thusly:
"My husband may resemble the shape of a shoe knife,
But you have no idea how utterly terrifying he can be:
He'll skin the three of you, flay that dead buffalo hide."

He'll skin the three of you, flay that dead buffalo hide.
The three sisters again tried to put Sizhen in her place:
"If your husband has indeed passed with high honors,
Your eldest sister will serve you as your kitchen maid,
Your second sister set out benches and sweep the yard.

"Your second sister set out benches and sweep the yard.
Your third sister will be the one to fan you with a fan;
All day long she will fan you till the dark night arrives,
And at night she will fan you till the sky will brighten.
Your three brothers-in-law will be the ones to carry your sedan chair."

Your three brothers-in-law will be the ones to carry your sedan chair.
Sizhen then clearly told them to their face: "Sisters,
"When my husband comes back as the Top-of-the-List,
You must remember the words you have just spoken —
Don't say that I, your sister, will show you no mercy."

Loudly shouting together, they confirmed their words,
And her three sisters also addressed her as follows:
"Your house is even too poor for a ghost to live in;
Bamboos planted at dawn provide afternoon shade.
Get out as long as you haven't yet died of hunger.

"Get out as long as you haven't yet died of hunger.
You are clear about the situation in our mansions.
During daytime the kitchen fires all burn until dusk,
At night the kitchen fires all burn until bright dawn,
Stewing fish and cooking meat without interruption."

Stewing fish and cooking meat without interruption.
Sizhen thereupon answered her three sisters, saying:
"Burning fires during daytime is all right and proper,
But the only ones to keep the fires burning at night
Are those who conduct a funeral or cope with death."

Are those who conduct a funeral or cope with death.
With this rebuttal she silenced her sisters, who said:
"Rich people never should argue with poor beggars;
Don't try to explain to the poor their lowly position.
The three of us should not have come here to visit."

The three of us should not have come here to visit.
The three decorated sedan chairs set out on the road.
When Master Liang from afar saw them coming,
He went out to welcome these three rich women:
"At my birthday tomorrow this adds to the mood."

At my birthday tomorrow this adds to the mood.
But his wife lady Jin also observed the situation:
"These three sisters with money have come early,
But I do not see the youngest one, Liang Sizhen.
It must be she has no money and so didn't come."

It must be she has no money and so didn't come.
She thereupon informed Chunlan of the situation:[19]
"Your youngest young mistress has not yet come,
So you have to go to the Southern Hills, find her,
And invite the youngest young mistress, Sizhen."

And invite the youngest young mistress, Sizhen.
The servant girl Chunlan then answered her, saying:
"The youngest young mistress is as poor as can be,
So get her a blue jacket and a pair of black trousers,
Which she can wear when she has to meet people."

---

[19] Chunlan is the name of a serving girl.

Which she can wear when she has to meet people.
With these clothes Chunlan then set out on the road.
Straightaway she made the trip to the Southern Hills,
And when she met with the youngest young mistress,
Liang Sizhen had a whole set of questions for her.

Liang Sizhen had a whole set of questions for her.
The servant girl Chunlan provided her with answers:
"Tomorrow you dad celebrates his sixtieth birthday,
So why are you as youngest daughter not yet there?
Please identify the reason and let us know the facts."

Please identify the reason and let us know the facts.
Sizhen then answered the maid Chunlan as follows:
"Because my three elder sisters are all so wealthy,
They heartily despise me for being a poor beggar,
And therefore I will not go because I lack money."

And therefore I will not go because I lack money.
Chunlan changed Liang Sizhen's mind by saying:
"All that talk is just like wind passing by one's ears!
Liang Sizhen, you are so blessed and magnanimous,
You should not blame those three for their words."

You should not blame those three for their words.
Chunlan was quite efficient in whatever she did.
She helped her lock up her straw-thatched hovel,
And holding the youngest mistress by the hand,
They set out as she pulled her and dragged her.

They set out while she pulled her and dragged her.
Very soon they arrived at the Liang family mansion.
When Master Liang looked up and saw them coming,
He ordered his servant boy to bolt the main entrance
And not to allow that beggar woman into the house.

And not to allow that beggar woman into the house.
Now Chunlan was quite intelligent in all her actions.
When she saw that the main gate had been bolted,
She led Liang Sizhen into the house by a side door,
So she could meet with her dear mother, lady Jin.

So she could meet with her dear mother, lady Jin.
Her mother thereupon told her daughter Sizhen:
"Tomorrow your father is celebrating his birthday.
Because he despises you because of your poverty,
Don't go and congratulate him out in the main hall."

Don't go and congratulate him out in the main hall.
Sizhen thereupon answered her mother in this way:
"Relatives and guests will offer their congratulations,
So I too will wish him long life out in the main hall.
If I would not make my bows, it wouldn't be proper."

If I wouldn't make my bows, it wouldn't be proper.
Soon, the five watches done, the sky turned bright.
The sisters with money went in to make their bows,
Their heads beating the floor, and bowing on and on,
They truly bowed to Master Liang's full satisfaction.

They truly bowed to Master Liang's full satisfaction:
They bowed to him as if they were bowing to a god.
Master Liang was therefore very pleased in his heart
And promptly rewarded them with silver and gold;
He also rewarded them with some sets of silk clothes.

He also rewarded them with some sets of silk clothes.
Chunlan informed Liang Sizhen of these goings-on.
She advised Liang Sizhen to speak auspicious words:
"When you go out into the main hall and bow to him,
The master will reward you with silver and with gold."

The master will reward you with silver and with gold.
Sizhen made her bows out in the main hall, and said:
"With this first bow I wish my father blessed longevity,
With this second bow I wish my father extra energy,
With this third bow I wish him clearer eyesight and
   better hearing.

"With this third bow I wish him clearer eyesight and
   better hearing.
With my fourth bow I wish him a promotion in rank;
With my fifth and sixth, I wish him riches and honor;
With my seventh and eighth, lordship over the village,
That he may surpass all people of Wuzhou prefecture."

That he may surpass all people of Wuzhou prefecture.
But Master Liang was utterly disgusted, and thought:
"To be congratulated by such a poor devil looks bad."
The more she bowed to him, the more he was angered,
Until his head felt dizzy because of her multiple bows.

At her first bow, a fire burned the heart of Master Liang,
At her second bow, Master Liang angrily pursed his lips.
At her third bow, Master Liang's heart was all aflame,
And at her fourth bow, his heart was consumed by rage:
"You had better present your bows to that Zhao Yulin!"

"You had better present your bows to that Zhao Yulin!"
Master Liang loudly spoke in reply to her felicitations:
"Poor beggar, for all your bows you bring no present,
All your many wishes are only so many empty words!"
For all to see he handed her as his reward an old rag.

For all to see he handed her as his reward an old rag,
And tears coursed down the cheeks of Liang Sizhen.
"Those with money receive satins and silks from you,
But all I receive from you today is this dirty old rag!"
Throwing it down, she returned the rag to her father.

Throwing it down, she returned the rag to her father.
Her three sisters thereupon spoke to Sizhen, saying:
"You'd do better in taking that rag home with you.
Several layers of rags can cover your body nicely,
You are a poor beggar, so you can't be so finicky."

You are a poor beggar, so you can't be so finicky.
Sizhen then replied to those unforgiving women:
"Even though my house may be utterly destitute,
You never have seen at my place such an old rag.
My father really despises me way beyond measure."

My father really despises me way beyond measure.
Liang Sizhen was overcome by a bitter depression.
"If my three sisters despise me, I couldn't care less,
But that my father despises me, me this poor beggar!
Nine and a half cup of rice will never fill out a pint."

Nine and half cup of rice will never fill out a pint.
She thought hard, seriously, about her bitter misery.
The river's three feet of water was not fit for drowning;
Half an hour wasn't enough to die by hanging herself,
Because it was impossible to abandon her Zhao Yulin!

Because it was impossible to abandon her Zhao Yulin.
The servant girl changed her mind by saying to her:
"Youngest mistress Sizhen, there's no point in dying.
Your husband will soon come home with high honors.
Bamboos planted by ancestors will benefit their heirs."

Bamboos planted by ancestors will benefit their heirs.
Master Liang hosted the banquet and was no end busy.
Those who had money were all seated in the high hall,
But all through the day he detested that Liang Sizhen,
She ate her meal in the flower garden behind the wall.

She ate her meal in the flower garden behind the wall.
Because her mother lady Jin deeply pitied Liang Sizhen,
She didn't take part in the banquet held in the high hall
But she also went to the flower garden behind the wall
Where she joined her youngest daughter, Liang Sizhen.

Where she joined her youngest daughter, Liang Sizhen.
Her sisters made fun of Liang Sizhen by informing her:
"We who have money have our banquet in the high hall,
But father despises you because you're such a poor devil —
Who has her food in the flower garden behind the wall."

Who has her food in the flower garden behind the wall.
Sizhen replied to her three sisters in the following way:
"Hurry and take your seats over there in the high hall,
And I'll take my seat here in the hidden flower garden.
I will never take after you — you're too nasty and mean."

I will never take after you — you're too nasty and mean.
Her three sisters once again spoke to Sizhen, and said:
"People who have money all receive a glass that is full,
But even the serving girls despise you for being so poor,
And only will pour you half a cup, filling but one half."

And only will pour you half a cup, filling but one half.
Sizhen thereupon answered her three sisters as follows:
"People who drink without measure are given full cups,
But the serving girls respect those who have some style,
And that is the reason why they will pour us half a cup."

And that is the reason why they will pour us half a cup.
Now let us talk about that Top-of-the-List, Zhao Yulin.
Riding his boat he had arrived in Wuzhou Prefecture,
And there asked the boat's captain, the man at the helm:
"Who there is celebrating such a magnificent event?"

Who there is celebrating such a magnificent event?
The boat's captain answered Zhao Yulin in this way:
"His Excellency Master Liang is having his birthday,
So he has invited all local officials and his relatives.
The plays performed before the gate are spectacular."

The plays performed before the gate are spectacular.
Now Zhao Yulin had quite an extraordinary thought:
"Master Liang may be my own father-in-law perhaps,
But I now will masquerade as a one begging for food,
To find out what my father-in-law really is thinking."

To find out what my father-in-law really is thinking.
So he then addressed the man at the helm as follows:
"Inside your boat you have three precious treasures,
You don't have to give them to me for nothing at all:
Three hundred and sixty coppers I will pay for sure."

Three hundred and sixty coppers I will pay for sure.
The boat's captain thereupon answered Zhao Yulin:
"On board of this boat there're no precious treasures.
Please tell me clearly what you are thinking about —
I'll be happy to give it to you for free, Zhao Yulin."

I'll be happy to give it to you for free, Zhao Yulin.
The Top-of-the-List then told the man at the helm:
"One straw hat without crest, shoes without soles,
And a jacket repaired with half a pound of thread:
Hand these three articles over to me, Zhao Yulin."

Hand these three articles over to me, Zhao Yulin.
The man at the helm, the captain, had a good laugh:
"I can sell all these rags for three hundred coppers
Now I met with the Top-of-the-List, this noble man.
Had I known earlier, I would have kept all my rags."

Had I known earlier, I would have kept all my rags.
The Top-of-the-List put them on — truly ridiculous:
On the inside he wore a golden gown, court shoes;
On the outside he was completely covered by rags.
Picking up his banjo he was all set to make a visit.

Picking up his banjo he was all set to make a visit:
He went to the gate of the mansion of Master Liang.
Holding his banjo in his hands he played and sang;
Strumming and plucking, plucking and strumming
He drew the attention of quite a number of people.

He drew the attention of quite a number of people.
All these people came forward to have a good look.
They asked the vagrant for his name and surname,
And the Top-of-the-List provided a clear answer:
"I am Master Liang's son-in-law, that Zhao Yulin."

I am Master Liang's son-in-law, that Zhao Yulin.
When Master Liang heard this, it hurt his brains:
"All other vagrants have to the good sense to die,
So how come this Zhao Yulin still hasn't croaked?
Now today he has to return to my mortification!"

Now today he has to return to my mortification!
He thereupon instructed his servants as follows:
"That vagrant before the gate, that singer of tales —
Make sure to push him outside, chase him away!
Don't let him bring misfortune to everyone here!"

Don't let him bring misfortune to everyone here.
Yulin then answered him in the following words:
"Other vagrants you can beat up at will perhaps,
But don't arouse the anger of me, Zhao Yulin —
You'll be wearing a cangue of a hundred pounds.

"You'll be wearing a cangue of a hundred pounds.
You have to know that I, Zhao Yulin, have been
Appointed by His Majesty as the Great Vagrant
Of the Twenty Four Provinces to sing my songs.
If you dare beat me, you and your family are dead."

If you dare beat me, you and your family are dead.
When Master Liang heard this, he laughed no end:
"His Majesty only appoints men to official position.
Now His Majesty should have appointed a vagrant?
How could the emperor ever go to such extremes?"

How could the emperor ever go to such extremes?
He then gave the cook the following clear orders:
"Bring three bowls of tofu as sour as pure vinegar,
And add a bowl of buffalo guts and a buffalo penis.
This we will have him eat so he can visit others."

This we will have him eat so he can visit others.
The cook prepared the dishes as he was instructed.
He prepared three bowls of sour-as-vinegar tofu,
And he also added buffalo guts and a buffalo penis.
In a rice sieve he carried this out through the gate.

In a rice sieve he carried this out through the gate.
Now Yulin acted as if he was a poor starving devil.
He put three rocks together to serve as his table.
With its feet upside down it also served as bench.
No bench or table was offered to him, a vagrant.

No bench or table was offered to him, a vagrant,
Zhao Yulin acted in quite an extraordinary way.
Holding his chopsticks, he picked up his food;
Each time he also picked up that buffalo dick,
And chewed till his eyes popped out of his head.

And he chewed till his eyes popped out of his head.
He ate the buffalo guts, chewed on the buffalo dick.
He chewed and he chewed, and then flew into a rage.
With bowl and all he beat it all into smithereens,
The dogs fought over the bits and created a mess.

The dogs fought over the bits and created a mess.
The Top-of-the-List thought hard and hard again.
He threw down he bowls of rice and vegetables
And went inside and entered the reception hall,
Ready to bring ruin on the whole Liang family.

Ready to bring ruin on the whole Liang family.
But his fellow student Chen recognized him,
And immediately called out to him, saying:
"Top-of-the-List! Top-of-the-List Zhao Yulin,
You've come back quite early upon passing."

You've come back quite early upon passing.
The three sons-in-law addressed him as follows:
"Dear Student Chen, why do you have to blabber?
If you continue to call that vagrant Zhao Yulin,
We will also chase you away through the gate!"

We will also chase you away through the gate.
But student Chen addressed them as follows:
"The clothes you wear may be far better indeed,
But as for essays you're no match of Zhao Yulin.
It makes no sense to detest him for his old rags."

It makes no sense to detest him for his old rags.
Yulin was dead serious in making a fool of them:
His suddenly placed his five fingers on the table,
He then grabbed a piece of pork of half a pound,
And without taking a bite he threw it on the floor.

And without taking a bite he threw it on the floor.
The dogs fought over the meat and also bit guests.
The dogs fought over the meat, a fight broke out;
Inside the hall people then started pushing people,
And the tables with all their food were overturned.

And the tables with all their food were overturned.
Master Liang that moment was consumed by rage,
And he angrily cursed that vagrant singer of tales:
"How did you dare disturb the banquet in this hall!
A leather whip — thirty lashes will leave you dead."

A leather whip — thirty lashes will leave you dead!
Yulin was in all his actions quite bright and clear.
A stalwart hero avoids a beating he sees coming —
Before he could be whipped, he made his escape!
It's not that he took to his heels, he said goodbye.

It's not that he took to his heels, he said goodbye.
With his banjo in his hands, he left by the gate.
When he servant girl Chunlan saw him coming,
She called out to him: "Young master Zhao Yulin,
How come you returned so early upon passing?"

How come you returned so early upon passing?
Yulin then said to them: "This I would like to know:
I have seen all her sisters and my brothers-in-law,
But so far I haven't yet seen my Liang Sizhen.
So servant girl, please be so kind as to tell me."

So servant girl, please be so kind as to tell me.
The servant girl Chunlan thereupon said to him:
"Young Master, this is very awkward to tell you.
Because your father-in-law despises Liang Sizhen,
She is eating in the flower garden behind the wall."

She is eating in the flower garden behind the wall.
When the Top-of-the-List heard this, he felt very hurt.
"Please, Chunlan, be so kind as to go over there to her
And ask the youngest young mistress to come outside;
Tell her to come and meet me, her dear Zhao Yulin."

Tell her to come and meet me, her dear Zhao Yulin.
The servant went in all hurry to the flower garden,
And while she was walking, she also called Sizhen:
"Your husband has succeeded as the Top-of-the-List,
He is completely dressed in a fine set of new clothes."

He is completely dressed in a fine set of new clothes.
Liang Sizhen was overjoyed on hearing these words,
So she dropped the bowl in her hands on the ground,
And left the back flower garden in leaps and bounds,
Only to find her husband still covered in dirty rags!

Only to find her husband still covered in dirty rags!
While tears coursed down her cheeks she asked him:
"When you left your clothes were no rags like these,
So how come your clothes are now such scary rags?
How could you have become the Top-of-the-List?"

How could you have become the Top-of-the-List?
As Sizhen thought about this, she was deeply hurt:
"Had I known that my husband indeed had not passed,
I would have hung myself there in the flower garden,
Because my three sisters detest me to such a degree!"

Because my three sisters detest me to such a degree!
Suppressing the pain in her stomach she asked Yulin:
"Because you have been away from home for so long,
I, your wife at home, barely have been able to survive.
Do you have any money with you now you are back?"

Do you have any money with you now you are back?
Yulin pulled Liang Sizhen's leg by telling her in jest:
"Don't you see what I am eating, what I am wearing?
Look! Your husband is dressed in these dirty old rags,
So how could I have any money to bring home today?

"So how could I have any money to bring home today?
Dear Liang Sizhen, let me tell you the true situation.
If you want to have money, that's a very easy matter.
I will write you a writ of divorce so you can marry someone else
And won't have to worry about your food and clothes."

You won't have to worry about your food and clothes.
With tears in her eyes Sizhen replied to Zhao Yulin:
"As long as I live I'm a daughter-in-law of the Zhaos,
And upon my death I'll be a ghost of the Zhao family.
Zhao Yulin, as poor as you may be, I'll stay with you."

Zhao Yulin, as poor as you may be, I'll stay with you.
When the Top-of-the-List heard this, he was pleased:
"My dear wife, if you are truly so firmly determined,
Stretch out your hands and then feel all over my body,
So you will find out, what kind of man is my husband?"

So you will find out, what kind of man is my husband?
Sizhen then let her hands wander all over Zhao Yulin:
With her left hand she discovered his yellow-gold seal;
With her right hand she discovered his formal court gown,
   completely new.
So she thanked Heaven and Earth without interruption.

So she thanked Heaven and Earth without interruption.
When her three sisters came and saw this, they said:
"It would appear as if Sizhen is possessed by a ghost,
Beating her head to the ground, she keeps on bowing,
Bowing to that husband of hers who's dressed in rags."

Bowing to that husband of hers who's dressed in rags.
Sizhen answered her three sisters in the following way:
"My husband is dressed in satins and dressed in silks.
Now if one of you would be his lawfully wedded wife,
You also would bow to him without any interruption."

You also would bow to him without any interruption.
Sizhen also addressed her three sisters in these words:
"My husband doesn't ape the example of your men.
If your men would be able to resemble Zhao Yulin,
They would be able to turn into man-eating tigers."

They would be able to turn into man-eating tigers.
When the three sisters had understood this clearly,
None of them had any desire to make comments,
Because if they would go on so for another hour,
Their three husbands would become sedan chair carriers!

Their three husbands would become sedan chair carriers.
Sizhen went back to the flower garden in the back,
And the Top-of-the-List went back again to the boat,
Where he took off his outer garments made of rags
In preparation for taking revenge on his enemies.

In preparation for taking revenge on his enemies.
Inside the house Master Liang had heard all this:
"First it was 'that singer-of-tales surnamed Zhao',
Now they talk about him as 'the Top-of-the-List'.
How on earth can there be that many Zhao Yulins!"

How on earth can there be that many Zhao Yulins!
Inside the kitchen the cook also had heard all this:
"Yulin may well have passed as the Top-of-the-List,
But why did he have to break the buffalo penis bowl,
Throw down my pots and pans before running off?"

Throw down my pots and pans before running off?
Master Liang's whole house now was in an uproar:
The three sisters were hiding themselves upstairs,
Their husbands were so scared they wanted to flee,
But they had no idea where they could safely hide.

But they had no idea where they could safely hide.
In that large mansion they frantically milled about.
They pushed open the windows, hoping to flee,
But the two iron nails were truly quite sharp
And drew furrows through their fleshy buttocks.[20]

And drew furrows through their fleshy buttocks.
Now let me tell about that mean Master Liang.
Nowhere in the house, he figured, he could hide,
So he stepped into the water vat in the kitchen;
Covered by the lid, he was soaking in the water.[21]

Covered by the lid, he was soaking in the water.
Now let me sing about his daughter Liang Sizhen.
She also entered the kitchen, where she washed
Pots and pans without any interruption, saying
Repeatedly she needed hot water to take a bath.

Repeatedly she needed hot water to take a bath.
Sizhen pretended that she had absolutely no clue,
She opened the lid of the vat to ladle out water.
Master Liang was sitting there inside the water vat;
By chance she hit him over the head with the ladle!

By chance she hit him over the head with the ladle!
As fast as he could Master Liang came out of the vat,
And knelt down on the floor in front of his daughter:

---

[20] The translation of these last two lines is tentative. I take it that the nails had been used to fasten the windows.
[21] The translation of this line is tentative.

"Liang Sizhen, you are so blessed and magnanimous,
You, my daughter, are now a lady of the first rank!"

You, my daughter, are now a lady of the first rank!
Sizhen thereupon addressed her father as follows:
"'His Majesty only appoints men to official ranks,
Since when does His Majesty ennoble vagrants?'
About that Top-of-the-List I don't have any idea."

About that Top-of-the-List I don't have any idea.
The Top-of-the-List that moment entered the kitchen.
Master Liang was bound and shackled at his order:
"In years gone by you detested me without restraint;
This precious sovereign sword beheads vicious men."

This precious sovereign sword beheads vicious men.
Sizhen implored Zhao Yulin to forgive her father:
"My father's heart is depraved, he deserves to die,
But, please, for the sake of my dear old mother,
Be so kind and so considerate as to spare his life."

Be so kind and so considerate as to spare his life.
The Top-of-the-List willingly agreed to her request:
"For the sake of your youngest daughter I'll only
Strip you of your rank, turn you into a commoner.
Never again have the arrogance to detest others."

Never again have the arrogance to detest others.
Sizhen also addressed her husband in these words:
"The servant girl Chunlan has been very kind to me,
She loved me greatly despite my destitute poverty,
Shouldn't we take her with us to our own house?"

Shouldn't we take her with us to our own house?
The Top-of-the-List followed Liang Sizhen's advice:
"Sizhen is of course a lady of the highest category,

And Chunlan will be a lady of the second category.
Together enjoying prosperity we'll spend our days."

Together enjoying prosperity we'll spend our days.
Happily reunited the whole family went back home.
They also took her mother lady Jin with them home.
The thatched hovel was torn down, new replacing old.
Bitter was followed by sweet: they started a new life.

Bitter was followed by sweet: they started a new life.
At home he spread a banquet, receiving noble guests.
This Top-of-the-List party lasted for three full days
And he invited the local officials and all his relatives.
All things were so well prepared it was truly amazing.

All things were so well prepared it was truly amazing.
The three sisters also discussed this among each other
And they regretted that they all had spoken too rashly.
When they had prepared their presents they left home,
Hoping their dear youngest sister would show mercy.

Hoping their dear youngest sister would show mercy.
With carriers carrying their presents they left home,
And straightaway made their way to the Zhao house.
When Sizhen saw that threesome of her elder sisters,
She remembered their past encounters only too well.

She remembered their past encounters only too well:
This time around Sizhen showed them no mercy at all:
The eldest sister went to the kitchen to cook the food;
The second sister set out benches and swept the yard,
Each and every nook and cranny, without interruption.

Each and every nook and cranny, without interruption.
The third sister too was reduced to the status of a maid.
During the day she waved the fan until darkness fell;

During the night she waved the fan until bright dawn.
Not allowed to sleep by day or night she was in a fix.

Not allowed to sleep by day or night she was in a fix.
So her third sister again spoke to her in these words:
"Because I have waved this fan by now for this long,
My eyes are truly falling asleep, it's too much to bear.
Allow me to ask you, dear sister, are you feeling cool?"

Allow me to ask you, dear sister, are you feeling cool?
Sizhen thereupon answered her in the following way:
"Third sister, you are truly an expert in waving the fan;
I still remember your brazen words of earlier times.
Now my body may feel cool but my heart is still hot."

Now my body may feel cool but my heart is still hot.
Following this she spoke again to them as follows:
"The three of you insisted on uttering insulting words,
And I definitely haven't forgotten those earlier words,
So this time they will have to carry that sedan chair!"

The Top-of-the-List at this time showed no mercy:
When his three brothers-in-law had all been arrested,
It wasn't husband and wife who rode the sedan chair,
But they had brought a rock of five hundred pounds
That they had to carry, and their heads turned dizzy.

That they had to carry, and their heads turned dizzy.
The Top-of-the-List also set out with them together.
He wanted them to carry it for a stretch, and then to shake
    it violently.[22]
And if they didn't shake it, their calves were whipped.
They carried it till their shoulders were soaked in blood.

---

[22] Carriers of a sedan chair containing the statue of a god during processions will at times violently shake the chair. This violent movement is believed to indicate the presence of the divinity in his statue. The translation of this line is tentative.

They carried it till their shoulders were soaked in blood.
They made the round of east and west, north and south.
The three brothers-in-law then said with a heavy sigh:
"Had we known that carrying a sedan chair was such toil,
We should never have detested him in the first place."

We should never have detested him in the first place.
The Top-of-the-List thereupon addressed them thusly:
"My brothers-in-law, you've carried the sedan chair,
So I will now release you and send you back home,
But change your character and become decent men."

But change your character and become decent men.
Sizhen also addressed her husband in these words:
"My three sisters now have worked here quite long,
So we should release them too and send them home,
All in consideration of the affection between sisters."

All in consideration of the affection between sisters.
When the Top-of-the-List heard this, he fully agreed:
"You three sisters have suffered for quite a while,
But as we have no presents here we can offer to you,
We will give you thirty lashes with a leather whip on your legs."

We will give you thirty lashes with a leather whip on your legs.
After that beating they were allowed to go home,
And on their part the three sisters said with a sigh:
"At least he lets us escape with our damned lives,
So our brother-in-law has shown us some mercy."

So our brother-in-law has shown us some mercy.
Their three husbands also set out for their homes:
"We never should have married these evil bitches of the
  Liang family!
Because they detested their young sister Sizhen,
We ended up as the carriers of that sedan chair."

We ended up as the carriers of that sedan chair.
Now let me sing once again of that Zhao Yulin.
To the left he erected the house of the Top-of-the-List;
To the right he built the pavilion for receiving officials:
Each and every beam and rafter was totally new.

Each and every beam and rafter was totally new.
The Top-of-the-List was married to two wives:
Sizhen was blessed by the births of three sons;
Chunlan had two sons who were quite bright:
All five of them studied hard and had a career.

All five of them studied hard and had a career.
Transmitted through the ages this story is true.
I hope that the parents of sons and of daughters
All will take an example from this Liang Sizhen
And never hate the poor out of love of riches.

And never hate the poor out of love of riches.
May husbands and wives live in good harmony.
Men never should detest their wives as too ugly;
Women never should hate their men as too poor:
Staying together to the very end one is a winner.

Staying together to the very end one is a winner.
I've sung to the end the song about Liang Sizhen;
About Zhao Yulin, who was first poor, then rich.
Everyone who has listened should now be clear.
May old and young, all who listened, be blessed.

Appendix

Excerpts from *Zhao Yulin* as performed by Lu Shoumin and others

Picking up his banjo [Zhao Yulin] started out singing,
To get a feel of the mind of his three brothers-in-law.
He walked straightaway into the mansion's high hall
And sang his ballads in front of his brothers-in-law.

His three brothers-in-law were all drinking their wine,
And with one voice they made fun of this Zhao Yulin:
"You left to make a career but ended up as a failure,
You'd better jump into a river and see King Yama!"

There was one student Chen who could not bear this,
He stepped forward and greeted Zhao Yulin, saying:
"When earlier in school we were studying together,
His essays and character were respected by all of us.

Since ancient times heroes may meet with misfortune,
And my dear study friend is certainly not the only case.
Let's quickly invite him to sit down with us for a drink,
And hear from him as we sit here together with a drink."

When the three brothers-in-law saw him act like this,
They cursed him out for showing respect for a vagrant:
"You even respect a vagrant who is singing for money,
Could it be that you by any chance are of the same kind?"

Student Chen immediately responded in these words:
"All three of you, dear gentlemen, now listen clearly.
It is too bad that Yulin has fallen on such hard times,
But he still has the status degree of a flourishing talent.

One day his name may be listed on the golden poster:
It's hard to measure the sea — harder to measure a man."
When Yulin heard these words, he was very pleased,
So he sat down at the table and thanked student Chen.[23]

***

---

[23] *Zhongguo geyao jicheng: Fujian juan* 2007, 617–618.

The three brothers-in-law didn't know where to hide,
So with down-cast yes they implored him for mercy:
"Sir Top-of-the-List, if you are willing to pardon us,
We'll offer you a thousand ounces in congratulation.

May you, Top-of-the-List, blessed and magnanimous,
Not blame us, husbands of the sisters of your spouse."
When Yulin heard this, he could only laugh repeatedly
And he cursed out those three men devoid of all honor:

"Brothers-in-law, you wanted to carry my sedan-chair,
So please carry me around the four gates of the town!"
The three had no option but to shoulder the sedan chair
And to lift the thousand pounds of the Top-of-the-List.

They carried him from the eastern to the western street;
The carried him from the southern to the northern street.
They carried him around all the four gates of the city,
They carried him till blood coursed down their backs:

"Had we known that today this would be such suffering,
We should never have made fun of that person at all!"[24]

---

[24] *Zhongguo geyao jicheng: Fujian juan* 2007, 619.

CHAPTER 3

SECOND-HAND ZHANG RENTS OUT HIS WIFE

Second-Hand Zhang Rents out His Wife is the story of the complications that ensue when one poor students allows another poor student to borrow his wife so she can pose as his own in order to obtain a loan from the father of his deceased fiancée. The text is translated from the edition provided in Hu Xizhang, *Kejia zhubange yanjiu* (2010: 416–434). Hu based his edition on the text included in *Wujuban chuanben ji*, compiled and printed in 1997 by the Cultural Bureau of Wuhua District. That text was based on a performance by Wen Songman as recorded by Peng Qiang. Hu adds the information that the mountain song performer Zhou Tianhe claimed to be the author of this text.

The story of *Second-Hand Zhang Rents out his Wife* is widely known through the length and breadth of China, mostly in adaptations for the stage. A play on this topic was first recorded in 1740 in Yangzhou. Four scenes from a *Luantan* adaptation are included in the first scroll of the eleventh series of *A Cloak of Patchworked White Fur* (*Zhui baiqiu* 綴白裘), a large anthology of popular plays and scenes from the middle of the 18th century edited by Qian Decang 錢德蒼. The first of these four scenes is entitled "Borrowing a Wife" (*Jie Qi* 借妻) and shows how the poor alcoholic Second-Hand Zhang, who is trying to make money by selling cotton thread spun by his wife, runs into his old friend Li Chenglong 李成龍. Li informs him that his wife has died and that his father-in-law has repossessed her dowry because he is afraid that Li might waste it and is only willing to return it to him once he has remarried. As a result, Li now has no money to travel to the capital and participate in the metropolitan examinations. Zhang then suggests that Li should borrow his wife and present her to his former in-laws as his new bride. He cajoles his wife into agreeing to the proposal and urges Li and his wife to make the visit that very day, but be sure to return before nightfall. The second, very short scene is entitled "Paying a Visit" (*Hui men* 回門) and narrates how Li Chenglong and his friend's wife arrive at the home of his original parents-in-law, where they are detained for the night despite all their protests. The third scene, "The Double Gate" (*Yuecheng* 月城), shows Li Chenglong and his friend's wife on one side of the stage spending the night in one room and, on the other side, Second-Hand Zhang who is caught between the two closed gates of a "moon-wall",[1] cursing his wife for her infidelity. While Zhang's wife indeed tries to seduce Li Chenglong, the latter shows himself a true gentleman and spends the night sitting on a chair.[2] When in the final scene, "The Court's decision" (*Tangduan* 堂斷), a frantic Second-Hand Zhang accuses Li Chenglong in court of stealing his wife, the muddle-headed judge assigns his wife to Li, who sees the dowry of his original wife returned to him.

These four scenes together provide a self-contained comic narrative and many of the adaptations of this tale in modern and contemporary regional drama are based on these four scenes. However, in 1754 when the famous playwright Tang Ying 唐英 (1682–1755) rewrote this play as a full-length Kunqu opera entitled *A Debt of Heavenly Karma* (*Tianyuan zhai* 天緣債), he provided the play with a happy ending in which Li Chenglong passes the examinations and

---

[1] A "moon-wall" is a semi-circular wall (containing a gate) that is built in front of a city gate for added protection.
[2] Chinese literature has a long tradition, starting in the 6th century BC with Liuxia Hui 柳下惠, of men who withstand the most blatant attempts at seduction by women.

provides his old friend Zhang with money to marry a second wife. This happy ending may have been his own invention, but it also may have been borrowed from a (now lost) more complete version of the *Luantan* play. A similar ending is also encountered in some genres of regional opera. In regional opera the story circulates under a wide variety of titles, such as *The Borrowed Wife* (*Jieqi ji* 借妻記), *Selling Cotton Thread* (*Mai miansha* 賣棉紗), *One Piece of Cotton* (*Yipibu* 一匹布), and *Married to a Borrowed Wife* (*Jieqi pei* 借妻配).[3] In view of its wide popularity it comes as no surprise that this farce was also adapted in various genres of storytelling in different parts of China. In these adaptations the place of the action and the names of the characters may be changed at will.[4]

***

Second-Hand Zhang Rents out His Wife

There is no harm in telling you all kinds of silly stories,
So let me start my tune to the beat of the five-line song.
All animals and objects in this world can be rented out,[5]
But did you hear about a man who rented out his wife?
Here you have his name and surname and place of birth.

Here you have his name and surname and place of birth;
I will clearly tell you the names of the people involved.
Once upon a time there was a man named Li Tingfeng,
And this man lived in Pinghe Village in Fujian Province —
He was such a talented person, and quite handsome too!

---

[3] Fan Rong 1956; Guo Yingde 1997, 917–918; Li Xiusheng 1997, 517–518; Zeng 1989, 1212.
[4] The story also provided the plot for the first Huangmeidiao movie shot in Hong Kong in 1958.
[5] The word translated as "rented out" is *jie* 借 which in Standard Chinese only means "to borrow". In this text it used both in the meaning of "to borrow" and in the meaning of "to loan out, to rent out."

He was such a talented person, and quite handsome too!
This Tingfeng was a decent person, a noble-minded man.
His parents had taken care of the matter of his marriage:
He had been engaged to the youngest daughter of the Lius,
And once he grew up, they said, they'd become a couple.

And once he grew up, they said, they'd become a couple.
At the age of seven Tingfeng went to school, but when,
Continuing his studies, he reached the age of eighteen,
His father and his mother both passed away, leaving him
Without any help, without any support, in dire poverty!

Without any help, without any support, in dire poverty —
But Tingfeng persisted in his studies, fired by ambition.
Even though was as poor as if he had been rinsed clean,
He memorized his texts "by the stolen light from a hole",[6]
Still hoping to pass the examinations as Top-of-the-List.

Still hoping to pass the examinations as Top-of-the-List:
It so happened that the court announced the examinations.
Tingfeng very much wanted to participate in the exams,
But alas, as he was so poor, he did not have the money
And went to borrow the money from his father-in-law.[7]

He went to borrow some money from his father-in-law,
But it so happened that his fate was all set against him.
The youngest daughter of the Lius had attracted an illness
And within three days she died and met with King Yama,[8]
So when Tingfeng learned this, he lamented his misery.

---

[6] Kuang Heng 匡衡, who lived during the Han dynasty, was so poor that he could not buy his own candles, so he had made a hole in the wall of his room to study at night by the light of the candle in the neighboring room.

[7] The parents of one's fiancé can be designated as one's in-laws, even when the wedding has not yet been consummated.

[8] King Yama is the highest ruler and judge in the world of the dead.

When Li Tingfeng learned this, he lamented his misery,
But his father- and mother-in-law said to their son-in-law:
"If you now will marry a wife who'll call us her parents,[9]
I will happily give you a thousand ounces of white silver
So you can go to the capital and sit for the examinations."

So you can go to the capital and sit for the examinations —
After Tingfeng had taken his leave, he went back home,
And on the road he ran into his friend Second-Hand Zhang.
He explained the situation to him in great detail, and said
That he wanted to borrow money in order to marry a wife.

That he wanted to borrow money in order to marry a wife:
These words incited Second-Hand Zhang to some thinking.
He considered that he himself was living in dire poverty,
He was as poor as if rinsed clean, without any splendor —
A mouse without any legs cannot climb up to the beams.[10]

A mouse without any legs cannot climb up to the beams,
But Second-Hand Zhang at last came up with a thought:
Don't seek from others something you can find at home,
And he called his wife woman Liu[11] and proposed to her
He would rent her out to his friend to meet the parents.

He would rent her out to his friend to meet the parents,
But his wife did not at all agree to this proposal of his.
She vilified her husband as a stupid fool without sense:
"Who in this world ever heard about renting out a wife?
And if people knew about it, I would have no face left!"

---

[9] The Lius do not want to lose their connection with the promising scion of a prominent local family, and so suggest that he marry another woman who will address them as her parents (and be considered by them as their foster daughter).

[10] "To climb up to the beams" (*shangliang* 上梁) has the same pronunciation as "to discuss, to come up with a solution" (*shangliang* 商量).

[11] This surname Liu 劉 (second tone) is different from the surname Liu 柳 (third tone) of Li Tingfeng's father-in-law.

And if people knew about it, I would have no face left!
Second-Hand Zhang argued once again with his wife:
"That friend of mine is a man of high moral standards,
He definitely would not commit any indecency, never,
So please calm down a bit, there's no need to go crazy!

"So please calm down a bit, there's no need to go crazy!
Well in advance I'll discuss with him every little detail.
When you leave that day, you'll come back the same day,
I don't rent you out to him in order to share the same bed.
But when an old friend is in trouble one has to assist him."

But when an old friend is in trouble one has to assist him —
Eventually Second-Hand Zhang's wife accepted the idea.
Second-Hand Zhang then came to Tingfeng and reported:
"There was no place where I could borrow some money,
But I'll let you borrow my wife to go and meet the parents.

"I'll let you borrow my wife to go and meet the parents,
But there is one condition that you absolutely must obey:
Before the sun goes down, you must bring her back home —
I don't rent her out to you in order to share the same bed,
It's so you can receive the silver and take the examinations."

It's so you can receive the silver and take the examinations —
When Li Tingfeng heard this, he happily was all smiles:
"It's rare to have an old friend who is so willing to help!
You allow me to borrow your own wife to meet the parents:
As long as I live, I'll never forget your favor for one day!"

As long as I live, I'll never forget your favor for one day!
Tingfeng was now back home in the village where he lived.
At daybreak he put on a new pair of pants and a new shirt
And woman Liu also was dressed in a new set of clothes
To visit and pay their respects to his father-in-law and his
  mother-in-law.

To visit and pay their respects to his father-in-law and his
  mother-in-law.
The two of them set out on their trip together, a couple.
While on the road they talked and joked with each other
As if they had been married already for quite some time —
There was no one who realized he had borrowed a wife!

There was no one who realized he had borrowed a wife,
And so they arrived at the gate of the house of the Lius.
When Master Liu and his wife saw that they had arrived,
They hastened to welcome the young bride and also their
  son-in-law.
And hurried to pour them some tea and set out a bench.

They hurried to pour out some tea and set out a bench,
And the news about the Lius spread through the village.
Everybody said they wanted to see the substitute bride
And many said they wanted to see the recent groom.
The local relatives were all invited and filled the hall.

The local relatives were all invited and filled the hall.
Now Tingfeng was living in this place called Pinghe —
But here in this village you had a prattling busybody
And she regularly went to Pinghe to visit her relatives;
She was living next door to the Liu family mansion.

She was living next door to the Liu family mansion
And she explained his situation to the local relatives:
"That Tingfeng is as poor as if he had been rinsed clean,
So how could he have the money to bring home a bride?
Could it be that he rented a wife to meet the parents?"

Could it be that he rented a wife to meet the parents?
Quite a lot of them did not believe the story she told
And accused that busybody of spreading false rumors:
"Who in this world ever rented some woman as wife?
You're suffering from diarrhea and soiling yourself!"

You're suffering from diarrhea and soiling yourself —
But there also were some people who harbored doubt
And softly, under their breath, they said to Master Liu:
"They say that your son-in-law has borrowed a bride —
It is difficult to determine what one should believe."

It is difficult to determine what one should believe —
So Master Liu considered the matter for quite a while:
"There is no one, I think, who trusts his friend so much
He would allow him to take his wife to another village.
In a while we will be able to bring light in this matter."

In a while we'll be able to bring light in this matter.
Master Liu thereupon talked to his wife and told her:
"We will keep the groom and the bride here at home.
When darkness descends and they'll share one couch,
Then, I'm sure, they won't be fake lovebirds if they
   share one couch."

Then, I'm sure, they won't be fake lovebirds if they share
   one couch —
He ordered the boy servant and also the girl servant
To clean out a room and make sure it was speckless,
And provide it with a new blanket, new bed-curtains and
   a new bed
For the use of the young replacement bride together
   with the groom.

For the use of the young replacement bride together with
   the groom:
It just so happened that Tingfeng heard him say this,
So he said: "As soon as we have had dinner, we must go
   back home.
I must go back to read my books and practice essays
In preparation for participation in the examinations."

In preparation for participation in the examinations —
Master Liu and his wife berated the groom at length:

"This is the very first time that you come and visit us,
There are so many things that we haven't discussed!
What is the problem in staying for only one night?"

What is the problem in staying for only one night?
Tingfeng appealed to his father-in-law and also his
  mother-in-law:
"The two of us could stay here and spend the night,
But robbers have been quite rampant in our village lately,
So it wouldn't be safe if the two of us both stayed!"

So it wouldn't be safe if the two of us both stayed —
Now Master Liu told his son-in-law in clear words:
"Husband and wife came together, so return together —
You cannot go back to your village all by yourself.
If robbers steal anything, that is my responsibility.

"If robbers steal anything, that is my responsibility —
My dear son-in-law, now don't be in such a panic!
Whatever may happen, I will take care of the case:
Your father-in-law can carry an iron carrying pole."[12]
Tingfeng thereupon didn't know what he could say.

Tingfeng thereupon didn't know what he could say
And he was so upset that his heart was in turmoil:
"If this evening we have to stay here for the night,
This charade becomes true when we share a bed:
The future complications then are unpredictable!"

The future complications will be unpredictable!
Master Liu and his wife now told their son-in-law:
"Quickly take a bath and then come and have food,
But dizzy and dazed as you are, make sure not to fall
  into the bath,
That would give rise to rumors, wouldn't be right!"

---

[12] A carrying pole is made of bamboo. A carrying pole made of iron would be too heavy and too stiff for use. The father-in-law claims that he will be able to handle any difficult issue that might come up.

That would give rise to rumors, wouldn't be right!
A couple of lanterns gave a clear and bright light.
Master Liu and his wife then provided instructions
How each of them should go to the assigned room —
They hoped the young bride and her groom would
  go to bed early!

They hoped the young bride and her groom would
  go to bed early!
So that evening the two of them went to their room.
Tingfeng told the wife of his friend to go to bed first:
"I will want to read my books and practice my essays,
Who knows how soon now I will sit for the exams!"

Who knows how soon now I will sit for the exams!
Each of them experienced their own bitter suffering.
His friend's wife all evening could not fall asleep,
Her heart kept constantly pounding and thumping;
As she tossed and turned, she heaved heavy sighs.

The first watch resounded with a booming roll:
His friend's wife stretched her legs and then pulled
  them up again,
And as she called out to Tingfeng, she said: "Dear,
How come the weather today feels so very chilly?
Could it be that tonight we should expect frost?"

Could it be that tonight we should expect frost?
Tingfeng then answered her in the following way:
"If you are feeling so cold you cannot fall asleep,
There's a new padded quilt at the foot of the bed.
Whether or not you should use it, that's up to you."

The second watch resounded with a weeping wail
When his friend's wife again addressed Tingfeng:
"The mattress below me is alive with jumping fleas,

And the quilt is infested with bedbugs that bite me."
Those creatures cooperated in biting her, and again!

When drums loudly beat out the third watch roll,
His friend's wife beat on the bed without stopping.
"That old rat below the bed is way too ferocious!
I'm afraid it will jump on the bed and feed on me!"
So Tingfeng came forward and he had a good look.

In reply to her outcry Tingfeng thereupon declared:
"As soon as you beat on the bed, that rat has jumped on a beam.
And if it still has the temerity to sneak onto the bed,
I will throttle its throat, and its life will be done with.
Now sleep at ease and don't make so much noise."

When drums noisily beat out the fourth watch roll,
His friend's wife cried out she was suffering cramps:
"I cannot stretch my legs and I cannot pull them in;
Right now my whole body is covered by a cold sweat.
Please come closer — you have to take a good look!"

Tingfeng thereupon replied to her whining as follows:
"It is absolutely normal to feel a cramp in your legs.
As soon as you stretch them once, you will be fine.
It's impossible to have someone write a prescription,
As this early the doctors have not yet left their beds."

When the fifth watch was sounded, the sky turned bright:
His friend's wife's longing all night had all been in vain:
"Li Tingfeng is so noble-minded, sincere and honest!
So moral he doesn't even pick the flower that's there![13]
That fine noble-minded, sincere and honest student Li!"

---

[13] "Flower" is a common metaphor for woman.

That fine noble-minded, sincere and honest student Li —
Now let's sing of Second-Hand Zhang in their village.
How he hated his old friend Li Tingfeng and he fumed:
"He still hasn't brought my own wife back home to me,
How could I know that he would be such a scoundrel!"

How could I know that he would be such a scoundrel!
At that thought Second-Hand Zhang locked the door.
He straightaway left in pursuit through the dark night.
He didn't care that the night was dark as dark could be,
He wanted to enter the city and find his wedded wife!

He wanted to enter the city and find his wedded wife,
So he hastened on along the long and winding road.
At midnight he arrived at the gate in the city's wall,
But right as he wanted to enter, that gate was closed.
With nowhere to turn to, he was at a loss what to do.

The first watch was sounded — drums loudly booming:
At this moment, late at night, his heart was aflutter.
He considered all possibilities but saw no solution.
On the ground below the wall he lay down to sleep,
Bitten and pricked by mosquitos, in wind and frost.

The second watch was sounded, the drums a crying,
And he sighed: "That Tingfeng is such a mean cheat!
He shows a human face but has the heart of a beast.
I let him borrow my wife but he did not return her —
Single or double — that bedding bag lacks all decency!"

The third watch was sounded, sounding so coldly:
"When bamboo produces a shoot, it will lack nodes.[14]
Paint a tiger: you'll paint its skin but not its heart.

---

[14] The word for nodes (*jie* 節) also has the meanings of "norms" and "virtue."

This Tingfeng is really a person who spells disaster —
Sandalwood drenched in water turns into demons!"[15]

The fourth watch resounded throughout the world:
No lamp was burning, so he could not see a thing.
With both his feet he stepped in a pile of dog shit —
The stench was unbearable, strong enough to kill!
Like a frog that's tied up, he continued to shake.

The fifth watch resounded — the sky turned bright.
When in a moment the city gate was thrown open,
Second-Hand Zhang, as fast as his feet could carry him,
Hastily entered the city in search of his dear wife —
When he'd find Tingfeng, he'd beat him senseless!

When he'd find Tingfeng, he'd beat him senseless!
Now let's sing of the bridal room at the Liu mansion.
Tingfeng and his friend's wife that night each had slept apart,
But Master Liu and his wife were unaware of that,
They took it that the two of them had shared a bed.

They took it that the two of them had shared a bed
And treated the bride and the young groom to
   a sumptuous breakfast.
They handed Tingfeng a thousand ounces of silver:
"Now you have this silver, you two should go home.
In the future you should come regularly to visit us,
   your parents."

In the future you should come regularly to visit us,
   your parents.
The two of them departed from Liu Family Village,
And when they together arrived outside the east gate,

---

[15] Incense sticks (made of sandalwood) are called 精 in the local Hakka dialect. The same word also means "sprite" or "monster".

They were spotted by her man, Second-Hand Zhang,
Who grabbed Tingfeng, wanting to beat him senseless.

He grabbed Tingfeng, wanting to beat him senseless —
Tingfeng provided a full account, from the beginning,
And shouted, "Dear brother, don't beat me senseless!
If you eat raw beef,[16] that taste is truly awful indeed.
Your wife and I never slept in the same bed at all."

Your wife and I never slept in the same bed at all —
Second-Hand Zhang immediately replied as follows:
"Tingfeng, now don't talk such unnatural nonsense.
'Yes, one night we shared a room, but not the bed.'
Trust the cat to keep the fat — that's a damned lie!

"Trust the cat to keep the fat — that's a damned lie!
You have managed to make me completely lose my face.
Your heart and liver are completely evil, depraved!
I will take you to the court of the district magistrate,
I want to lodge an accusation to have you locked up."

I want to lodge an accusation to have you locked up —
And he pulled him along with him to the court house.
The district magistrate took his seat and asked them
Why the two of them wanted to lodge an accusation,
Whereupon Second-Hand Zhang was the first to speak.

Whereupon Second-Hand Zhang was the first to speak:
"Tingfeng and I used to be the best of friends for sure.
His family was extremely poor and bitterly suffered,
But very early on his parents had arranged for a wife.
Unfortunately that wife of his died in her early youth.

---

[16] To "eat raw beef" (which is very tough and requires a lot of chewing) is explained as a local expression for "persisting in telling lies, even when you know they are false".

"Unfortunately that wife of his died in her early youth.
It so happens that the Court will hold the examinations:
Tingfeng very much wanted to go there and take part,
But alas, because he was poor he didn't have the means,
So he wanted to borrow money from his father-in-law.

"So he wanted to borrow money from his father-in-law,
But his father-in-law then spoke to him in this manner:
'If you marry another bride who will greet us as parents,
I will provide you with a thousand ounces of fine silver.'
That money he would give to Tingfeng as his son-in-law.

"That money he would give to Tingfeng as his son-in-law,
And so Tingfeng came to find me to discuss the situation.
He wanted to borrow the money so he could marry a wife,
But I am also dirt poor and didn't have that much silver,
So I allowed him to borrow my wife to visit his parents.

"So I allowed him to borrow my wife to visit his parents,
But I set him conditions that were explicitly explained —
I told him he had to bring her back when the sun had set.
But that detestable Tingfeng didn't stick to the rules at all:
He borrowed her, and then passed the night there,
     sharing a bed!

"He borrowed her, and then passed the night there,
     sharing a bed.
As a result my position is now completely untenable.
Now my wife has passed the night together with him,
I also do not want that woman anymore as my bride
And demand that he pays me back the marriage costs!"

I demand that he pays me back the marriage costs —
The district magistrate thereupon addressed Tingfeng:
"Your friend treated you in such a magnanimous way,
He allowed you to borrow his wife to visit the parents,
So why didn't you bring her back to her own village?"

So why didn't you bring her back to her own village?
Tingfeng told his side of the story, not hiding a fact:
"As soon as we had had dinner, I wanted to go back,
But my father-in-law insisted we stay at Liu Village.
I shared a room with that woman, but not the couch."

I shared a room with that woman, but not the couch —
The magistrate slapped his table and cursed him out.
"Given the chance a man will sleep with a woman:
How could you share a room and not share the bed?
How is it possible to believe the story that you tell?"

How is it possible to believe the story that you tell?
Second-Hand Zhang opened his mouth and repeated:
"Because he has passed the night with that woman,
I implore that he pays me back the marriage costs —
With money I don't have to fear I'll have no wife."

With money I don't have to fear I'll have no wife —
Tingfeng could only take full responsibility, and said:
"My friend treated me in such a magnanimous way
That I'm happy to help him out with a certain amount,
But you have to take back your lawfully wedded wife."

But you have to take back your lawfully wedded wife —
Second-Hand Zhang thereupon answered him thusly:
"If you'd ever use a shit bucket as your rice steamer,
The rice that you cook will never be fragrant and pure,
So do not bother me with such a ridiculous proposal.

"So do not bother me with such a ridiculous proposal.
That is my honest opinion, stated as clear as can be!
Tingfeng, you should accept the magistrate's verdict:
If you pay me those three hundred ounces of silver,
I'll give you my wife — I've no feelings for her at all."

I'll give you my wife — I've no feelings for her at all.
Tingfeng so could only shoulder his responsibilities
And paid three hundred ounces of silver to Second-Hand
   Zhang.
Second-Hand Zhang signed a statement of divorce;
This was read out by the magistrate, and then all left.

This was read out by the magistrate, and then all left.
Second-Hand Zhang got three hundred ounces of silver.
When the threesome left through the court house gate,
Tingfeng was accompanied by his friend's former wife,
Whom he took to a nunnery, and there he installed her.

Whom he took to a nunnery, and there he installed her.
Sun and moon passed by as quickly as the loom's shuttle.
It happened that the time of the examinations had arrived,
So Tingfeng, buoyed with high expectations, didn't wait
And he immediately left to take part in the examinations.

He immediately left to take part in the examinations;
His Lordship the Chief Examiner ranked the essays.
After the first session test followed the second session,
After a further test in the third session, he was happy:
Reading his essays, the examiner selected our student.

Reading his essays, the examiner selected our student:
The essays by Tingfeng were outstanding and brilliant,
Superior works that showed how to order the country.
A bronze coin, often selected, gives off a brilliant light:
At his first try he was selected as the Flower-Snatcher.[17]

At his first try he was selected as the Flower-Snatcher.
The examiner, surnamed Wang, questioned him thusly:

---

[17] Flower-Snatcher" (*tanhua* 探花) is the title of the person who places third in the final ranking of passed candidates in the metropolitan examinations.

"I happen to have a daughter who just turned eighteen.
Did you, Flower-Snatcher, already bring home a bride?
I'd like to marry her to you, so you may tie the knot."

I'd like to marry her to you, so you may tie the knot —
The Flower-Snatcher answered him according to fact:
"From my earliest youth till today I've studied books,
I never brought home a bride to be my wedded wife,
All I wanted was studying books and take the exams."

All I wanted was studying books and take the exams.
Upon hearing his words the examiner happily smiled.
"You, Flower-Snatcher, have not yet been married,
And I have a daughter, whose name is Wang Juxiang.
Let's pick a good day for the two of you to tie the knot.

"Let's pick a good day for the two of you to tie the knot.
When the two of you are married, you'll be a fine match."
A good hour was carefully chosen and also a lucky day,
So on the second of the month the banquet was held,
And all guests seeing the couple voiced their praise.

And all guests seeing the couple voiced their praise:
A noble-minded girl married to a noble-minded man.
Now half a month after the wedding had taken place,
The Flower-Snatcher announced his departure to his
   parents-in-law:
"I now would like to return to my own home village."

I now would like to return to my own home village.
So the examiner instructed his daughter as follows:
"When you go there, be nice to your parents-in-law;
Ask the advice of your sisters-in-law and your aunts;
Manage household affairs with diligence and thrift."

Manage household affairs with diligence and thrift —
In this way he sent off his daughter and her husband.
While on the road, the hundred flowers all smiled

And everywhere the little birds raised their songs:
Husband and wife, this happy couple, went home.

Husband and wife, this happy couple, went home.
The Flower-Snatcher then told his wedded wife:
"We still will have many days to go on the road,
Because my home is in Pinghe Village in Fujian.
Let's take our time to leisurely travel back home."

Let's take our time to leisurely travel back home —
Let's sing again of that man Second-Hand Zhang.
After the divorce from his wife had been finalized,
He never had brought a bride back home as wife,
And each night he slept all alone in a chilly bed.

And each night he slept all alone in a chilly bed.
Without his socks, the floor felt very cold indeed!
Those with a partner don't appreciate her virtues,
Those with no wife know the length of the night:
They moan and sigh and their tears course down.

"Sigh number one: to have no wife is a disaster,
When the jug lacks water, I've to fetch it myself.
When I come to the river to scoop up some water,
Lord Frog and Sire Crab collapse with laughter.
Such a disaster: below the bed you'll only find one
   pair of shoes.

"Sigh number two: to have no wife is upsetting.
Each day I have to go into the hills to cut some kindling,
Time and again I cut my own hand with the axe.
The garrulax[18] and francolin come and tease me,
Tease me that I, being single, beat the lone bird.[19]

---

[18] This is the hwamei (Garrulax canorus), a dull-brown bird with a grey-white belly. It acquired its name ("painted eyebrows") from its white eye rims. It is famed for its beautiful singing and the male of the species is said to be bellicose.

[19] A euphemism for masturbation?

"Sigh number three: to have no wife is so lonely.
My tears course down and soak shirt and gown.
If you've something to tell, there's no one to listen
And nobody knows the many sorrows you suffer.
Such a disaster: a grass carper raised in a bucket
   that has not yet died.

"Sigh number four: to have no wife is loneliness.
There is none to take care of the vegetable patch.
This piece of land of mine is overgrown by weeds,
I haven't even planted one single kind of cabbage.
For all the shit I produce, no place needs my dung.

"As I think back and forth, I can't see a solution.
The cooking for each and every meal I now have to do
   all by myself.
As I sit and wait for the fire to start, I'll fall asleep
And in each dream I imagine my wife is coming,
But we were divorced and we can't get together.

"Sigh number five: to have no wife is a bitter pain.
Each night I am all alone, and sleep in a cold bed.
King Yama calls a meeting to discuss with ghosts:
'A dumb person marrying a wife cannot talk to her —
Now tell me whether that is the most bitter pain.'

"Sigh number six: to have no wife is unbearable.
Tears course down your cheeks, covering your face.
Whether you sleep by day or at night, no one cares.
Your cushion is slept through, the mattress broken.
When you fall ill, there's no one to find you a cure.

"Sigh number seven: to have no wife is miserable.
Every day you have to go and wash your own shirt.
You have to wash your shirt and things all by yourself,
Till your head turns light and your face turns blue,
But when you fall ill, there's none to fetch a leech.

"Sigh number eight: to have no wife is great pain:
Without a partner or mate, with no one to love you.
You are like a single lantern hanging in a temple:
Gods and ghost are aware that I have no partner —
When snow soaks my candle's pit, the heart is cold.[20]

"Sigh number nine: to have no wife makes one moan.
Wherever I go, whether coming or leaving, I am alone.
It's always one single bowl and one pair of chopsticks,
At each and every meal I eat my food alone by myself,
Even chunks of meat and sweet rice I cannot swallow.

"Sigh number ten: to have no wife is no life at all —
I never should have allowed him to borrow my wife.
I had a partner, but as a result I was left without one.
The heart was stirred in the oil container of the lamp,
Now I've cold hands and cold feet, so what can I do?"

Second-Hand Zhang each evening heaved long sighs,
And overcome by emotion he became ill, bedridden.
Those three hundred ounces of silver had been spent,
And his disease was serious, he was beyond recovery:
A mere bag of bones, his eyes falling from their sockets.

A mere bag of bones, his eyes falling from their sockets.
Now let's sing how the Flower-Snatcher told his wife:
"I have an old friend who is called Second-Hand Zhang,
We always were best of buddies, he's a man whom I trust,
So let's first go to his place to have a cup of tea with him."

So let's first go to his place to have a cup of tea with him.
When they had come to the house of Second-Hand Zhang,
He went inside and saw that his brother was on the verge of death,
So he had a doctor look at him and prescribe a medication,
And took care of Second-Hand Zhang in a perfect manner.

---

[20] "Heart" (xin 心) also designates the burning pit of an oil lamp.

He took care of Second-Hand Zhang in a perfect manner:
He bought fish and bought meat to restore him to health.
"Now today you are suffering from such a serious illness,
I will give you these three hundred ounces of white silver,
So please concentrate on nursing your body back to health."

So please concentrate on nursing your body back to health —
By his bedside he asked him what had happened, and said:
"My dear brother, when I remember how this all started out,
It was me who is to blame for all your poverty and misery,
Who is to blame for your single cushion and this cold bed.

"I am to blame for your single cushion and this cold bed —
But when I think back to that scene in the courthouse then,
I consider it your fault that you were way too hot-headed,
With the result that you are now struck down by disease
With no one to check your condition and prescribe a cure.

"With no one to check your condition and prescribe a cure.
But brother, please listen to what I will tell you clearly.
After the three of us that time had gone our different ways,
Your wife did not accompany me to my home and village,
But I had her installed in a nunnery for Buddhist sisters.

"But I had her installed in a nunnery for Buddhist sisters.
After that I promptly left to take part in the examinations.
This time when I went to the capital to sit for the exams,
I passed as the Number Three, as the Flower-Snatcher,
And the woman who is accompanying me is my wife.

"And the woman who is accompanying me is my wife.
Her name is Wang Juxiang, my examiner's daughter,
So that same Examiner Wang is now my father-in-law.
As husband and wife we have come back to the village,
It was only proper that we would come here to see you.

"It was only proper that we would come here to see you,
But we had no clue that you were bedridden by a disease.
When I remember how magnanimously you treated me,
You are entitled to share my unequaled good fortune:
We should nurse you well so you'll regain your health.

"We should nurse you well so you'll regain your health,
And once you have recovered we will visit that convent.
And when we are there, we should explain clearly to her
That it would be best for her to go back to her old home:
The two halves of the broken mirror reunited at last."[21]

The two halves of the broken mirror reunited at last.
Second-Hand Zhang happily replied in these words:
"My dear brother, you have treated me so perfectly!
Let's drop those events of the past into the wide sea,
Don't keep them all together stored up in your heart!"

Don't keep them all together stored up in your heart.
So when Second-Hand Zhang had recovered his health,
The three of them went together to the Buddhist convent,
And Second-Hand Zhang told his lawfully wedded wife:
"You should come back home with me to our village."

She should come back home with him to their old village —
But his former wife answered him in the following manner:
"When I remember what happened there in that courthouse,
I've at present no inclination at all to go back to the village.
I'll stick to my vegetarian diet here in this Buddhist convent."

---

[21] When the Chen dynasty was overrun by the Sui dynasty, Xu Deyan 徐德研 and his wife broke a small bronze mirror in two, each keeping one half. His wife was taken into the household of one of the conquering generals, but eventually the couple was reunited by means of the broken mirror.

I'll stick to my vegetarian diet here in this Buddhist convent —
But that Flower-Snatcher was a quite eloquent advocate:
"Dear sister-in-law, you and my brother loved each other,
Your love and affection as husband and wife are eternal!"
So eventually she happily agreed to leave the nunnery.

So eventually she happily agreed to leave the nunnery,
Whereupon it was Second-Hand Zhang who declared:
"My wife, now you are willing to leave this convent,
This illness of mine has been completely cured by you.
Now let me take you back home to the village with me."

Now let me take you back home to the village with me —
Together the four of them thereupon set out on the road.
Very soon they had arrived back at the Li family home;
From there they send an invitation to the Liu family village,
Inviting the father-in-law and mother-in-law for a visit.

Inviting the father-in-law and mother-in-law for a visit —
Master Liu and wife were so pleased they seemed mad.
The two of them still believed woman Liu was the bride:
"Your husband has become an official and now has returned
   to his village!"
But the wife of Second-Hand Zhang didn't dare to reply.

But the wife of Second-Hand Zhang didn't dare to reply.
Master Liu and his wife then addressed her as follows:
"Together with our son-in-law Li Tingfeng you earlier
Spent a night at our place and also shared the same bed.
Have you changed your mind now your man made it big?"

Have you changed your mind now your man made it big?
Tingfeng then stepped in and provided an explanation:
"She is the lawfully wedded wife of a friend of mine,
I only borrowed her for the purpose of my visit to you.
That night we shared the room but not the same couch."

That night we shared the room but not the same couch.
Master Liu and his wife only then understood the case.
"Second-Hand Zhang, you're a noble person and sincere,
You magnanimously allowed your friend to rent your wife.
So now you too have to consider yourself our son-in-law."

Now you too have to consider yourself our son-in-law —
Second-Hand Zhang then replied with great alacrity:
"Because my wife has already become your daughter,
It is only fitting that I now become your son-in-law!"
And he laughed so loud he couldn't close his mouth.

And he laughed so loud he couldn't close his mouth.
Master Liu and his wife then addressed him as follows:
"Second-Hand Zhang, as you are living in dire poverty,
We will also give you one thousand ounces of silver,
Wishing you and your wife eternal happiness and bliss."

Wishing you and your wife eternal happiness and bliss.
Next they said to Tingfeng and his wife Wang Juxiang
(And also to Second-Hand Zhang and his wedded wife):
"Now our whole family is together, we enjoy blessing.
The wine and the meat at our place are fragrant and pure.

"The wine and the meat at our place are fragrant and pure,
So we have set out a banquet, it's a really good spread."
The two couples now shouted together as with one voice:
"Long live our father-in-law and also our mother-in-law!"
They continued to visit each other, their mutual feelings
   sweeter than sugar.

CHAPTER 4

MORALS AND MORE

In the repertoire of bamboo-clappers songs some moral ballads would appear to have enjoyed equal popularity with the narrative songs. Hu Xizhang states that audiences were often moved to tears by performances of *When Drinking from the Low River Remember the High Ridge* (*Dihe yinshui nian gaogang* 低河飲水念高崗), and that the song was considered so highly by many families that they would never tire of hearing it and would organize the whole family to listen to performances together.[1] To what extent song such as *A Tenfold Plea to my Lover to Establish a Family* (*Shi quan qinglang ai chengjia* 十勸情郎愛成家) and *A Warning Against Gambling of the Twelve Months of the Year* (*Shieryue jie du ge* 十二月戒賭歌) enjoyed the same degree of popularity is difficult to establish. These moralistic pieces are followed by some lighter fare.

***

---

[1] Hu Xizhang 2010, 81.

*When Drinking from the Low River, Remember the High Ridge*²

While beating my bamboo-clappers, I sing the opening tune:
Remember both your parents for the hundred years of your life.
Honor and respect your father and mother for bringing you up;
When you father and mother turn old, take care of them well —
When drinking from the low river, remember the high ridge.

When drinking from the low river, remember the high ridge —
May your father and your mother enjoy good fortune forever.
When the sons and daughters are small, they take them along.
While they work at their task outside, their mind is made up;
Back home, the rice is cooked and the vegetables smell great.

Back home, the rice is cooked and the vegetables smell great.
A daughter-in-law should not curse out her mother-in-law.
These old people can eat even if they cannot work anymore.
If you are a daughter-in-law you have to consider this well:
Sweet words far surpass a simmered soup made with meat.

Sweet words far surpass a simmered soup made with meat;
If you have money, buy some meat to offer to your parents.
If they can eat four ounces of meat during their lifetime,
That beats a sacrifice of pigs and goats upon their death —
Those pigs and goats are just a big display for the show.

Those pigs and goats are just a big display for the show —
Like an axe cleaving a log of wood, I'll explain it clearly.
It may be compared to the white cabbage in the garden:
If you pull off the lower leaves, the upper leaves grow:
Generation upon generation becomes parents in turn.

---

²Luo Kequn 2000, 388–392. The text is based on the text revised by Chen Binghua 陳丙華, Yue Ren 樂人 and [Yu] Yaonan 耀南, and included in *Yuedong Kejia shange* 粵東客家山歌 (1981: 234, internal publication). Huang Ziyao 2003, 119–120 includes the first four stanzas.

Generation upon generation becomes parents in turn:
Never forget the love of your parents in raising you.
Just think of the days when your mother was pregnant:
Her hands sore, her feet weak, her expression sallow,
She even lacked the strength to ascend a high bank.

She even lacked the strength to ascend a high bank —
Don't mention chicken and wine of the Full Month.[3]
Once in her stomach they are turned into milk —
How often each day does the baby drink that milk?
As the child grows fatter, the mother loses weight.

As the child grows fatter, the mother loses weight:
How often she feeds her son with her heart-blood?
Whenever the baby cries, it will continue to cry
Until its dear mother is utterly at a loss what to do
And with her baby in her arms walks up and down.

With her baby in her arms she walks up and down.
In the eleventh and twelfth month it will be freezing,
And at midnight the baby will pass its bowels or pee.
Even in such inclement weather she will always get up
To clean up the mess and to change the baby's clothes.

To clean up the mess and to change the baby's clothes.
She is only too happy to suffer the chilly cold herself:
To the left, where it's dry, the children will be sleeping;
To the right, where it's wet, that's for the two parents.
How often have they had to sleep in a dirty, wetted bed!

How often have they had to sleep in a dirty, wetted bed!
They spend all their effort in raising sons and daughters.
As long as these are healthy and strong, it is still doable;

---

[3] The Full Month is celebrated one full month following the birth of a baby.

If they run a fever or catch a cold, this upsets the parents;
Taking them up, putting them down — at a loss what to do.

Taking them up, putting them down — at a loss what to do.
They hurry about, inviting a doctor, choosing a medicine.
As long as they have ready cash, this can all still be done,
But if they lack the money, they will scare it up anyway,
Because they want their children to be healthy and safe.

Because they want their children to be healthy and safe.
Once they can walk and run, they are always worried:
If they play with fire, afraid they will burn their hands;
If they play near water, afraid they may fall into the pond.
At each and every moment they want to protect them.

At each and every moment they want to protect them.
At New Year and festivals, when there's plenty of food,
They're afraid their small children will eat fatty pork.
They fill a bowl with chicken gizzard and chicken liver,
And feed their children one fine morsel after another.

They feed their children one fine morsel after another.
When they turn seven or eight, they go off to school;
Progressing from primary school up to senior high
They use up who knows how much money and grain.
Never forget the blood and sweat of your two parents!

Never forget the blood and sweat of your two parents!
Once he has grown up, you must find your son a wife.
The house and room have to be ready well in advance.
When you have bought the furniture and also the bed,
The cloths also have to be according to latest fashion.

The clothes also have to be according to latest fashion:
Being a father and mother means thousands of hardships!
Throughout their life they incur debts for their children;

When they pay these back, their hair has turned white.
When bamboo grows a shoot,[4] it hopes for springtime.

When bamboo grows a shoot, it hopes for springtime.
Between the rocks the flowing stream resounds loudly.
Your parents' love resembles the stream of the Yangzi;
Just think, how long can your parents expect to live?
Each should stroke his heart and question his innards.

Each should stroke his heart and questions his innards:
There are sons and daughters-in-law who are no good.
Once they have been married, they forget their origins;
It's only "husband and wife", no mention of "parents":
All delicious things they will hide in their own room.

All delicious things they will hide in their own room,
And they also have the temerity to curse their parents,
Saying, "Other people have the good sense to croak!
How is it possible that you can grow to such an age?"
And they wag their finger right in front of your eyes.

And they wag their finger right in front of your eyes.
And if you drop a bowl or break a jug in the kitchen,
They scream they want to live apart[5] or will run off
And don't care whether this may upset their parents.
When seeing this, other people all have their thoughts.

When seeing this, other people all have their thoughts.
Now all of you, when you think about this, think well.
While your parents are alive, you show no filial piety,
But once they're dead, all you'll have is the empty bed,
And no amount of crying will bring back your mother.

---

[4] "Bamboo shoot" (*sun* 笋) is very similar in pronunciation to "grandson" (*sun* 孫) (the first word is third tone, the second is first tone).
[5] Literally, "divide the household".

And no amount of crying will bring back your mother.
When your parents grow old, you have to support them.
The way in which you treat your father and mother
Will be clearly observed by your sons and daughters,
Who will follow that example in treating their parents.

They will follow that example in treating their parents.
Now my song has reached this point, I will wrap up.
May young people on hearing this be filled with joy;
May elderly people on hearing this be healthy and hale;
May families live in harmony, enjoying long blessing.

A Tenfold Plea to my Lover to Establish a Family[6]

First of all I urge you, young man, in the middle of the night
Not to lust after flowers and so cause your own downfall.
When a little frog ends up in a pond, it will drift till old age.[7]
When you're still be a bachelor in your old age whom can you blame
When you are suffering from disease and all kinds of pain?

Secondly I urge you, young man — the swallows are flying —
Make sure to do everything timely and never be too late.
Don't ever follow the example of those wandering wastrels,
Who race today to the east and run tomorrow to the west —
But who cares when they suffer from hunger in their belly?

Thirdly I urge you, young man, remember this very well:
I urge you, young man, go back home and marry a wife.
If you yourself have the cash at hand, bring home a bride.
Beat her and she is your sweetie; curse her, your wife,
Who, with tears coursing down, will wash your clothes.

---

[6] Hu Xizhang 2010, 79–80. Originally from Yu Yaonan 余耀南, *Dapu qingge zage jingxuan* 大補情歌雜歌精選.
[7] "To drift" (*piao* 漂) has the same pronunciation as "to whore, to hang out with prostitutes" (*piao* 嫖).

Fourthly I urge you, young man, who roams the world,
I urge you to go back home and plant the rice-seedlings.
It's only the fields you plow that provide the rent-rice;
There never was a darling separated from her dear lover,
Leaving him without an heir to carry the incense burner.[8]

Fifthly I urge you, young man: the sun sinks in the west —
Your own condition you should know better than me:
Once you've passed the age of thirty, you will be forty;
Once you are above fifty, old age will creep upon you.
So if you don't repent today, until when will you wait?

Sixthly I urge you, young man, think things through,
Don't hang out with the girls who dwell in red dust.
As long as Zhang has money, Zhang is a fine fellow;
As long as Li has money, Li is of course their friend:
A leaf of grain blown by the wind, a two-sided blade.

Seventhly I urge you, young man, love you own family,
Don't be like a butterfly fluttering about, seeking flowers.
Of every ten men who seek flowers, nine will collapse.
If carnal desires are too strong, your body will suffer;
If you attract a venereal disease, you'll harm yourself.

Eighthly I urge, young man, you must think straight,
Stay away from the places for gambling and betting.
People in these gambling dens are evil-intentioned;
They may not carry a sword but they still kill others,
Once you'll have lost your money, it is gone forever.

Ninthly I urge you, young man — nine times nine long —
There is an old book known as *The Western Chamber*.[9]

---

[8] The incense burner refers here to the soul tablet.
[9] *The Western Chamber* (*Xixiang ji* 西廂記) by Wang Shifu 王實甫 (c. 1300) is China's most famous love comedy. The play's male protagonist is Student Zhang 張生, who falls in love with Yingying 鶯鶯 and eventually makes her his own with the help of her maid servant Hongniang 紅娘 (Reddy). See Wang Shifu 1995.

If you hope to find a lover and wife like sister Yingying,
I'll most happily serve as your go-between Hongniang,
So you'll tie the knot of loving and loyal mandarin-ducks.

Tenthly I urge you, young man, and I've urged you often:
A good person should never hang out with evil people.
You should never share the same bed with evil people,
You should never listen to the proposals of evil people.
Live with diligence and thrift and you will be blessed.

A Warning Against Gambling of the Twelve Months of the Year[10]

In the First Month we celebrate the Arrival of Spring,
Everybody happily participates in the New Year feast.
A brother took me along to engage in some gambling
Joining him in this sin I furtively entered the gate of sin,
And after having played all day, my head felt all dizzy.

In the Second Month we celebrate the Middle of Spring.
Because I engaged in gambling I neglected green spring.
My wife went into the village, found me, cursed me out,
Shouting and screaming, creating a ruckus, until evening,
And with a distorted face she said she wanted a divorce!

In the Third Month we all celebrate Clear and Bright,
But engaging in gambling causes one uttermost harm.
You have no intention of pursuing any trade or craft,
You only hope to make millions in a high stake game —
In the dark corners of deepest hills you hope to find it.

In the Fourth Month the leaves of grain turn green —
When you engage in gambling you always want to win.

---

[10] Hu Xizhang 2010, 81–83. From Yu Yaonan, *Dapu qingge zage Jingxuan*. In the traditional Chinese lunar calendar the first three months of the year are spring, the next three months are summer, the following three months are autumn and the final three months are winter.

Brothers, uncles and cousins all take part in gambling,
As they follow the game, they stretch out their necks,
But if you cross one of them, he'll turn his face away.

In the Fifth Month we all celebrate the Double Fifth,
If you engage in gambling your life is lonely and sad.
Your friends and your relatives come to despise you;
Your parents and your wife are consumed by anger;
When your children see you, they're as cold as frost.

In the Sixth Month it is the time for harvesting grain,
If you engage in gambling, you often meet with shit.
When you come home at midnight, no fire is burning;
Stumbling and falling, you are covered with bruises;
When vomiting you will wipe it away with your hands.

In the Seventh Month we celebrate Start of Autumn.
If you engage in gambling, you are without any shame.
You sell off all fields and gardens, your house and barn,
When you want to prepare vegetables, you lack the oil,
And when you want to borrow money, you lack friends.

In the Eighth Month at Mid-Autumn we pray to the Moon,
But if you engage in gambling, you will only harm yourself.
The wok has been scoured clean and you have no rice left,
But the rice shop despite its supplies refuses to give credit,
So in desperation you dig up the sweet potatoes of others.

In the Ninth Month the chrysanthemums are blooming,
But if you engage in gambling your life is a miserable mess.
If you want to cook up a snack at night, you lack the herbs,
So in order to steal some garlic you'll sneak into a garden,
But as you grope around your fingers start reeking of piss.

In the Tenth Month we must handle the winter harvest.
Once you make a tiny profit, you feel confident again.

Again you borrow some money and set out to gamble,
But you lose both the main sum and also the interest,
So your heart feels filled up and your eyes are bleary.

In the Eleventh Month the northern wind starts to blow.
If you engage in gambling, you now feel really destitute.
You've pawned your long shirt and your padded jacket;
Winter is cruel in unlined clothes, under a thin blanket,
So you warm your cold hands and feet at an open fire.

In the Twelfth Month we all celebrate the end of the year;
You may want to buy some pork, but you lack the money.
My friends all urge me to refrain from gambling for good,
And to devote myself to plowing and sowing my fields —
A bamboo hat with a hole in the middle showing the sky.

A Nonsense Song[11]

My nonsense fantasy is truly nonsense fantasy:
In front of the house I had erected a long pole,
And on top of that pole I had built a mansion;
Encircling dragons encircled it in eighteen layers —
Nine generations under one roof: ten thousand people!

My nonsense fantasy is exceedingly original:
I have now been pregnant for ten years in all,
But yesterday afternoon I gave birth to a boy.
This morning he could go and buy tobacco,
And then talk to the boss to discuss the price.

My nonsense fantasy is way too fantastic:
Yesterday, finding a single penny, I went
To the market and bought a pregnant sow.
This morning the sow gave birth to a calf —
It was carried off into the sky by a falcon.

---

[11] Luo Kequn 2000, 387.

My nonsense fantasy is definitely fantastic:
In my mother's womb I studied martial arts.
On Mt Qingliang I performed a salto mortale.
Head into the ground, legs facing heaven —
So it took eighty old men to pull me away.

My nonsense fantasy is nonsense fantasy:
I ascended to the moon and plowed its fields.
Chang'e performed a dance to welcome me,[12]
Wu Gang offered me tea, got out a cigarette,[13]
And said he wanted to be my sworn friend.

The Five Watches of the Night[14]

The first watch of the night: I enter my darling's chamber,
Inside her room my darling is busily burning fine incense.
She burns that fine incense in a golden censer, and prays:
"May by your protection the day be short, the night long;
The day short, the night long so I here can keep my lover."

The second watch of the night: I am in my darling's chamber;
Inside her room my darling is embroidering mandarin-ducks;
With her ten slender fingers she's pulling out colored threads.
While she is pulling these threads, she's watching her lover:
Each thread longer and longer — but her love will last longer.

The third watch of the night: I am in my darling's chamber,
And inside her chamber my darling pours me yellow wine.
"This yellow wine was made by me with my own hands,
Now tonight I present it to you so you may have a taste."
One mouthful from that one person tastes even sweeter.

---

[12] Chang'e is the beautiful goddess of the moon.
[13] Wu Gang is another denizen of the moon. He is always occupied trying to cut down the cassia tree on the moon.
[14] Hu Xizhang, 137. From Yu Yaonan, *Dapu qingge zage jingxuan*.

The fourth watch of the night: I am in my darling's room,
And inside that room my darling is taking off her clothes.
When she takes off her shirt, her breasts are white like snow;
When she takes off her pants, her belly is white like frost,
As white as the Bodhisattva Guanyin of the Southern Sea.

The fifth watch of the night: I am in my darling's room,
And inside her chamber my darling shakes me awake.
"The moon is sinking on the top of western mountains,
And soon the sun will rise again in those eastern skies."
Taking me by the hands she leads me out of her room.

PART FOUR

MIGRATION AND EMIGRATION

Introduction

Migration was and is a characteristic feature of Hakka culture.[1] Once the Hakkas had settled the hilly and mountainous terrain of southeastern Jiangxi, southwestern Fujian and northeastern Guangdong, they (primarily young men) also moved on to other regions, preferably to those places where they could derive most profit from the skills they had learned as mountain dwellers. When spreading to other areas of Fujian and Guangdong and as far away as Guangxi and Zhejiang in the 16th and 17th century, Hakka communities tended to settle in hilly terrain upstream, but as close as possible to the major cities in the plains so as to benefit maximally from the burgeoning urban economies of those days. As times went by, Hakkas went farther afield. Some moved inland and settled in Sichuan, which had been heavily depopulated during the wars of the 17th century, while others moved to Taiwan as, over the course of the 18th century, limitations on the migration to that island were lifted step by step. From an early date Hakkas also emigrated to Southeast Asia, but emigration to continental and insular Southeast Asia was greatly stimulated in the 19th century by the foundation of

---

[1] Wang Gungwu, "The Hakka in Migration History", in Wang 2003, 217–238.

Singapore and by the development of plantation agriculture and mining industries as colonial administrations extended their sway throughout the region. Some (e)migrants made a fortune and the embellished stories of their success enticed many young men to also try their luck, but only too many of them discovered that working conditions away from home often were abysmal, that chances to make money were small and that the little money they made was easily lost in whoring and gambling. The settled life back home of shared poverty easily transformed itself into a society of rural bliss that they never should have left!

Not only Hakkas, but also migrants and emigrants from other parts of China such as southern Fujian, Chaozhou and other parts of Guangdong, met with hardship and pain and, from the 18th century, we can trace the development of a thematic subgenre of popular literature in all of these regions that recounts the sufferings of migrants and urges people to stay where they are. These texts run from long poems that provide an exhaustive catalogue of the hardships of migrants,[2] to longer and shorter songs in which wives urge their husbands to stay at home or long for their speedy return after they have left, always afraid they may never come back (or even marry a local woman abroad!).[3] On the Hakka side, we have both poems

---

[2] For a translation of an early Minnanese ballad warning against migration to Taiwan, see Anonymous 2013a. Most existing Chinese scholarship in this area deals with two Minnanese texts in this genre from the late 19th and/or early 20th centuries warning against migration to Southeast China. See Liu Denghan 1991; Liu Denghan 1993; Liu Denghan 2002; Liu Denghan 2005; Liu Denghan 2014; Ke Rongsan 2013. Annotated editions of these two long Minnanese ballads are provided in Zhou Changji and Zhou Qinghai 2003, 403–455; annotated editions of the longer of these two can also be found in Lin Huadong 2006 and Zheng Bingshan 2007.

[3] The first scholar to draw attentions to these songs was Zhong Jingwen 1924. Also see Zhao Jiaxin 1936. Soo Khim Wah (Su Qinghua 2012a; Su Qinghua 2012b; Su Qinghua 2013a; Su Qinghua 2013b; Su Qinghua 2014a) is engaged in a comprehensive study of these songs and ballads and has already published on the materials in Minnanese, in Hakka, in Hainanese, and from Chaozhou. These studies have been reprinted in Su Qinghua 2014b. English-language publications have focused on the songs of poems of Cantonese migrants in the US. See Hom 1987; Lai 1991; Zheng 1992; Yong and Yong 2014.

and songs that detail the hardship of those who move to Taiwan and poems and songs that describe the horrors of travel to Singapore and working in the tin mines of Southeast Asia.

As we will see in the long songs describing the migration to Taiwan and to Southeast Asia, a large role in spreading stories about the easy money that could be made on Taiwan or in Singapore was played by the middlemen who made a living by transporting migrants to their destinations. Especially the song on migration to Taiwan is explicit in its condemnation of these "headmen" (*touren* 頭人), whose function is identified by modern commentators with the "snakeheads" of recent years. These middlemen would also have been the source of information about the routes to be traveled, the precautions to be taken and the jobs that would be available. We do not have detailed records of the stories told by these snakeheads of the 18th and 19th centuries, so we do not know to what extent they went into detail about the ways successful migrants made their money. While in Minnanese we have some late ballads on the adventures of successful migrants to Taiwan (and the complications caused by success),[4] such ballads have not been preserved in Hakka. The only exception may have been a ballad on the exploits on Yap Ah Loy (Ye Yalai 葉亞來, 1837–1885), a poor Hakka migrant who eventually came to play a major role in the development of Kuala Lumpur. We know this

---

[4] Among Minnanese ballads we find titles such as *Gan Guobao guo Taiwan* 甘過寶過台灣 (Gan Guobao migrates to Taiwan) and *Zhou Cheng guo Taiwan* 周成過台灣 (Zhou Cheng migrates to Taiwan). The first text tells the story of a never-do-well from Fuzhou who eventually makes a career in the military on Taiwan and returns home in glory, while the second tells the story of a man who leaves his wife in order to set up shop in Taibei, but wastes all his money on a prostitute; when in his desperation he is about to commit suicide, he meets a man who is also about to commit suicide, whereupon they decide to go into business together. Zhou then makes a fortune in the tea business, marries his favorite prostitute, and murders his pregnant wife when she comes to Taiwan to find him. Haunted by her ghost Zhou ends by slow-slicing his prostitute wife and committing suicide. For a summary of these two ballads, see Eberhard 1972, 26: 58–60. These two legends may well have developed only by the late 19th century and do not seem to have been known in Hakka-speaking areas. The story of Zhou Cheng, his wife and his prostitute lover has repeatedly been made into a movie.

ballad only from an English translation of 1893 and cannot be sure that the ballad was originally written in Hakka. This translation and its headnote are reprinted in Appendix IV.

While the preserved long ballads warn against the dangers of (e) migration, they also provide detailed information about travel routes, sea transport, ports of debarkation and job opportunities at the place of destination. Those who were intent to seek their fortune elsewhere may well have come away from hearing or reading these ballads with the impression that success was possible as long as one was able to avoid the seductions of whoring and gambling and could rely on the assistance of friends, fellow townsmen and relatives.

CHAPTER 1

PUSH AND PULL

Scholars of (e)migration often distinguish between push and pull factors. Push factors are those aspects of life in the region of origin that make life unpleasant or even unbearable and induce people to seek a better life elsewhere. Pull factors are those aspects of a region that induce people from other regions to move there in the hope of peace and prosperity. The most common push factors are overpopulation and poverty, in combination with man-made violence and natural disasters. *A Peasant's Twelve Months* (*Nongmin shi'eryue* 農民十二月), a long poem in five-syllable lines that describes a poor farmer's life for each of the months of the year,[5] makes clear that for many peasants their daily life throughout the year, even without communal strife, warfare, droughts or floods, was never free from hunger and want, and that they often lacked the money to celebrate the most important festivals. When that even applied to peasants working their own or rented farms however, one can easily imagine that life must have been even more insecure for those who had to make a living as a laborer, a miner, a stonecutter or a peddler. *A Peasant's Twelve Months* is here translated on the basis of the Chinese text

---

[5] Poems that describe a farmer's work for each of the months of the year have a tradition that goes back to the Book of Odes.

provided by Luo Xianglin, *Yuedong zhi feng* (1936: 260–268).[6] Luo provides the following note:

> I don't know when this song originated. As early as in the Daoguang (1821–1850) and Xianfeng (1851–1861) periods the shops sold printed copies which were entitled *Mountain Songs of Seasonal Sights of Shared Prosperity* (*Qichang jiejing shange* 齊昌節景山歌). My fourth brother very much suspects that this is the work of a local literatus because, he says, its orderly exposition is very unlike that of other popular songs. I believe that even though this song may indeed be the composition of a literatus, it has now been performed and sung by all people of the district for several decades. It has already been cleansed of all awkward phrasing and its character is now identical to that of popular songs in general. The text recorded here is based on the performance by an old farmer outside the east gate of Xingning (but whose name I do not remember), and there are some small differences with the printed copies in shops.

Migration only makes sense, however, if there are other regions that offer better opportunities to make a living. All of southeast China was densely populated by the end of the 16th century if not earlier. For a while the introduction of new foods from the Americas must have offered some relief, but once the areas that had been depopulated by the wars of the mid 17th century had been filled in once again, migrants had to look farther afield. When the Manchu Qing troops had conquered Taiwan and the prohibitions on Chinese migration to Taiwan had been lifted one by one, Taiwan became an attractive destination as it offered prospects for the development of Chinese-style agriculture. Rice grown on Taiwan found an easy market in coastal cities of southeast China. From the 18th century onward Southeast Asia also attracted more and more migrants because of its gold mines and tin mines.

---

[6] The song has also been reproduced in *Zhongguo geyao ziliao* 1959, Vol. 1: 252–254, without any reference to its source or to its region of distribution. It includes Luo Xianglin's end note (anonymized), but omits his brother's suspicion that the songs might have originated as the work of a local literatus.

Soon stories started to circulate about the huge fortunes that could be made overseas. When sons returned home with boxes filled with gold and silver, a family's status was changed overnight — and all relatives hoped of course to share in this sudden wealth. One such story was encapsulated in the phrase "Three-Pound Dog on New Year's Eve; Third Elder Uncle on New Year's Day" (*Shangye Sanjingou, xiaye Sanbogong* 上夜三斤狗,下夜三伯公). It tells the story of a man who is desperately poor and has no pork to eat on New Year's Eve, but is the wealthiest man of the village on the next day because overnight his son has returned from the Southern Oceans, bringing boxes filled with silver dollars (it is never specified how this son made his fortune). The poor man carries no grudge against his fellow villagers and spreads the wealth around. Hu Xizhang, *Kejia zhubange yanjiu* 2007, 510–516 includes a bamboo-clapper song adaptation of this tale, but that was written only as late as the 1980s by the cultural cadre, mountain song activist and bamboo-clapper song performer Tang Mingzhe 湯明哲 (b. 1934).[7] I have included a translation of it here anyway, because it provides us with an example of a modern bamboo-clapper song, in which passages of prose alternate with the songs and in which some stage directions for the performance are included. Readers should also be aware that while the story is set in "days gone by" when wealth was counted in silver dollars, the author uses the terminology of the modern culture of meetings, opinions, and participation from time to time. A modern sensibility may probably also be detected in Tang's treatment of the

---

[7] For a brief biographical sketch of the many activities of Tang Mingzhe see Hu Xizhang 2010, 302–304. Upon completing high school Tang Mingzhe became a Party activist, but in 1958 he was classified as a "rightist element", a judgment that was only reversed in 1978. In the course of his work during the Land Reform Movement of the early 1950s he became acquainted with mountain songs in all their manifestations and became a skilled performer himself. For most of his life he worked in cultural agencies in Meixian, displaying great organizational capacities. He also was a prolific editor and writer of mountain songs and bamboo-clapper songs. Hu Xizhang also has published a full-length biography of Tang as *Shange dashi Tang Mingzhe zhuan* 山哥大師湯明哲傳, Beijing: Zhongguo wenlian chubanshe, 2004, which I haven't seen.

wisdom of the local God of the Soil. Hu based his edition of the Chinese text on the text included in *Tang Mingzhe zuopin zixuanji* 湯明哲作品自選集 (Tang Mingzhe's own selection of his works). It is not known to what extent Tang may have based his version on earlier adaptations of the story (which also enjoys considerable popularity in its adaptation as a mountain song opera), but at least one modern scholar has treated the text as performed by Tang as a traditional "mountain song story" with a history of centuries that exemplifies the collective mental attitudes of the Hakkas.[8]

***

A Peasant's Twelve Months

The First Month comes with the New Year,
We light incense to venerate the ancestors.
We slaughter a chicken, open a fine bottle,
And have three kinds of meat at each meal.
    In front of the gate we hang lucky couplets,
And the firecrackers resound even to heaven.
In every village the lion dance is performed,
So the gongs and drums create quite a noise.
    Married women return to their natal families,
On that day sweet rice is fried in lots of oil.
Very soon it is the middle of the First Month:
We enjoy the flower lanterns at each house.
    Shouting "Three horses" and "Four Sixes!"
We enjoy ourselves mightily, for millions.[9]
But time easily passes by and already soon
The wine is all finished, the rice all gone.
    Again we have to buy cooking rice on credit,
Like before we have to ask others for money.

---

[8] Liao Wen 2013. Liao bases his comments on a video of a performance of this bamboo-clapper song by Tang Mingzhe. As is clear from his quotations, the text of the performance departs in details from the text as presented by Hu.
[9] These two lines refer to card games and gambling.

We visit all markets, offering firewood for sale:
Again we have to shoulder that carrying pole.

In the Second Month we sacrifice at the graves:
We have to sell our grain so we can buy a pig.
Bronze drums resound with a booming noise,
Bright umbrellas are neatly arranged in a row.
    Wearing a blue gown and also a tasseled hat,
You wave your fan and also stroke your beard.
Each man receives his share of sacrificial pork,
And as they eat, their face is covered in smiles.[10]
    But very soon Excited Insects comes around,[11]
So we must consider when to plant our grains.
We harrow the fields, create beds for seedlings,
And clean out the ditches and restore the dikes.
    How often hunger forces us to tighten our belts,
But there is nobody who understands our pain!
When we sow the seeds, we don't have enough
And we also do not have the benefit of lime.
    Shrimp-chaff[12] is way too expensive as manure,
But without manure the seedling won't grow.
So if you have no money you have no choice
But to pawn your shirt, to pawn your blanket!
    Soon the old lady angrily scolds her old man,
And the old man on his side beats up his wife.
Now look at those people who have money:
They wear a long shirt and also a short gown,
    Their feet are never covered by mud because
They only order the slaves and maids around.
Too bad that Heaven is not impartial at all:
We poor people have to suffer this misery.

---

[10] These lines describe the collective sacrifices to the ancestors in the lineage temple.
[11] Excited Insects or Waking of Insects is one of the twenty-four two-week solar terms in which the year is divided. Excited Insects starts on March 5th, 6th, or 7th.
[12] Shrimp shells?

The Third Month, that is Clear and Bright,[13]
And after that Grain Rains will soon arrive.[14]
When skies are bright we harvest the wheat;
When the water drops, we gather ox turds.

When we spread manure, we add the lime,
Which bites open our face and feet all over.
When the rice seedling have grown fifty days,
They have to be transplanted immediately.

To help you out you bring in day laborers,
They create such a mess they drive you mad!
They demand three meals of rice each day;
Their daily pay is more than twenty coppers.

Rice with wheat they do not dare to taste —
It has to be white rice, pointed at both ends!
If it has been cooked they want it steamed —
They would not dare take it if it is not soft.

They want a big bowl of well-done pork,
Together with tofu and also mushrooms.
Mussels have to be mixed with shrimps;
They want salted fish and fermented beans.

You put in extra oil when frying greens —
If they are oily, they are not happy at all.
You try to please them beyond what's due,
And still they want you to raise their pay.

Today they will tell you they'll all come,
But tomorrow they have all disappeared!
Day in day out you transplant seedlings,
And the poor people collapse in laughter:

The more fields you have decided to plow,
The more anger you feel, the more spite!

The Fourth Month is a time of starvation:
The small greens are not enough as food.

---

[13] Clear and Bright (Qingming) is a spring festival at which the graves of the ancestors are visited and repaired.
[14] Grain Rains is the solar term that starts on April 19th, 20th, or 21th.

You have no potatoes, you have no yams,
In the barn there's not one kernel of grain.
  The bitter gourd is just starting to bloom,
The eggplants are only starting to sprout.
You lack the money to buy cooking rice,
And every meal consists of wheat gruel.
  You pawn her skirt, you pawn your shirt,
You sell the firewood, you sell the bamboo.
  But how nice is the life of those with rice
Who most happily sell you expensive grain:
One cup of rice costs you three *fen* of silver[15]
And the price of grain goes through the roof!
  They don't have a worry, don't have a care;
They dine not only on fish but also on meat.
Without collateral you will not get a loan:
They scheme to get your fields and house!

The Fifth Month comes with Double Fifth,
And you will go hungry for days on end.
You have finished eating all your wheat,
And the ears of grain are not yet yellow.
  People say they are celebrating the feast,
But if you don't have the cash, it's a lie!
  You don't even have a chicken to offer,
Only some eggs are laid out on the plates.[16]
There is still some pork of the Old Year,
It's now completely blackened by smoke.
  You manage to obtain two jugs of wine,
And bean leaves accompany intestines.
You select them and invite the ancestors
To these salty dishes spiced with ginger.
  The weirs have already been prohibited
And you also are not raising any ducks.

---

[15] One *fen* 分 is one tenth of a *liang* 兩 (ounce) of silver.
[16] The translation of this line is tentative.

One cup is only three tubes[17] full of rice —
For how many meals will that be enough?
  All month of the years are starvation time:
Poor people never enjoy a fine springtime.

When the rice is harvested in the Sixth Month,
Poor people have had their share of worries.
Only reluctantly they will sell the new grain:
One basket will go for five hundred coppers.
  When it's dried, they'll shout it's not dried;
When it's refined, they'll say a wind passed.[18]
You don't have the money to pay them back
And have no option but to suffer that wrong.
  Your creditor comes to collect his money,
And he talks to you till you are all befuddled:
You're offering to carry the rice to his house,
And slave till you are bent like a hunchback.
  All that is left is only one *dan* or some more,[19]
Not even enough to keep your old lady alive.
Despite the harvest you've no food to eat —
In the final analysis, you're going bankrupt.

In the Seventh Month the autumn wind is cool,
Now the foreign grain[20] has to be transplanted.
On the seventh you start making a yam garden;
You remove the hemp and gourds spread out.
  At the border of the field grow taro and lotus,
So you think of getting a young pregnant sow.
You go to each and every market all around;
You talk about the price, discuss the amount.

---

[17] A tube is one pound (catty) and a half of rice.
[18] I take these two lines to refer to complaints from buyers who complain that the seller has increased the weight of the grain by underhand methods.
[19] A *dan* 石 is a dry measure for grains, roughly equal to 120 pounds.
[20] Maize?

But nobody wants to sell if you have no cash,
And they all send you home empty-handed.
Back home nobody's willing to let you lend
Even when you offer forty percent interest.
　　With her every word your wife berates you,
These hundred scoldings equal a bastinado:
It's a disgrace and brings shame on yourself —
Only cutting your throat releases that rage.
　　You can collect the rent on hilltop ridges:
One pound of buffalo shit is one *liang* two.[21]
Leading the buffalo you scrape off the turf,
And day by day you manage so to survive.

In the Eighth Month White Dew will flow[22]
And the poor people do not have to worry.
In rows they walk and transport the yams,
At every meal they have a full pan of those.
　　The heads of the yams and the yam tubers
Fill their cups and equally fill their plates.
If at this meal you'll be unable to have them,
For sure you'll eat them at the next dinner.
　　If they are gone, you will dig up some more;
You eat all you want as they can't be stored.
Everybody is different till they are all gone;
For three days they fear they may be stolen.
　　Then, when the taro shoots have withered,
The foreign beans are ready to be harvested.
The sweet potatoes form heaps in the fields,
And the maize cobs are piled up on the land.

---

[21] The "rent on hilltop ridges" refers, according to Luo Xiangling, to ox and goat droppings. I do not understand the second line. Perhaps it is an ironic reference to the hard work involved and the small profits it brings by mentioning a preposterously high price for the manure.
[22] Whit Dew is the solar term that starts on September 7th, 8th, or 9th.

When you bring down the frigid-mist beans,
You sell them and buy some fine porcine oil.
Going to the market you wear a bamboo hat,
As an honest man you don't feel any shame.
  When the moon cakes are on sale in town,
You make a detour to go and visit Jiaying.
And when you have bought a few of those,
You celebrate Mid-autumn on the fifteenth.
  The old people will get a chunk of them,
And the little kids will also get their share.

The Ninth Month starts off with Cold Dew;[23]
You don't dare put on your summer pants.
If you can buy some high-quality cotton,
You can spin thread and weave fine cloth.
  Your blanket and your important clothes
Now still are stored over at the pawn shop.
As it turns cold, you want to redeem them,
But without cash, you just stand and stare.
  Now those mosquitoes have grown teeth,
While wasps seek shelter below the eaves.
The first ninth is the feast of Double Nine,
So where will you climb to a high place?
  To the east there is Mt. Harmony Rock;
To the south it is Cock-Spirit Monastery.
If you go to the Hill of Divine Radiance,
There's such a crowd you can't get through.

The Tenth Month is the Start of Winter;
Nobody now will see a large rainbow.
The late rice is now turning deep yellow
And the ears are hanging down in pairs.
  The wet fields have become dry fields;
When the water drops, you kill winter.[24]

---

[23] Cold Dew is the solar term that starts on October 8th or 9th.
[24] The translation is tentative as I do not understand this line.

When first you cut, the shit still is sticky,
But the load of rice should be heavy!
 The younger brother cannot lift it up,
But fortunately there is elder brother.
In brewing ale, for Strawcape Strong[25]
One suns and dries the rice, then hulls.
 If one lacks rice in making Field Red,[26]
One lends one load from the landlord.
The seed for next year is neatly sunned;
If it isn't dry, it can give rise to worms.

The Eleventh Month brings Great Snow;[27]
Each and every day the north wind blows.
It may blow the two ears off your head;
You may cut your feet and they'll bleed.
 Unless you are the window of an oven,
You fear the frost and you fear the snow.
When I see other people sowing wheat,
I also want to get finished with that job,
 Because all the different kinds of wheat
Must be planted before Winter Solstice.
The holes for wheat seeds must be deep;
On both sides there should be a furrow.
 At the end of the month at the Solstice,
The lineage hall will be quite a sight:
All members of the lineage congregate;
Pigs and goats are laid out for sacrifice.
 On the streets the crowds are numerous;
You leave early, but come home at night.

In the Twelfth Month reigns Great Cold;[28]
At the end of the year the months are done.

---

[25] Strawcape Strong is, according to Luo Xianglin, the name of a local type of rice wine.
[26] Field Red is another type of local rice wine.
[27] Great Snow is the solar term that starts on December 6th, 7th, or 8th.
[28] Great Cold is the solar term that starts on January 20th or 21st.

It may be only barely nine market places,
But each account has to be settled in full.
  When Old Year comes, creditors do too:
Poor people shouldn't take life that easy.[29]
Those who are away all want to go home;
If they don't go home, they send a letter.
  Now as soon as Old Year has arrived,
Relatives offer the prescribed sacrifices.
Every family makes the Old Year cakes,
So oil and sugar has to be weighed out.
  Radishes and "horseheads" and such —
All these things are now very expensive.
Then, on the thirtieth day of the month,
One washes his body with purified water.
  The women are at work in the kitchen,
Cooking rice, hoping to lay up a store.[30]
Boxes of candy are offered to the gods,
And at night people consult their fate.
  When the sky turns bright it's a new year,
And everybody wishes each other the best.

Three-Pound Dog on New Year's Eve, Third Elder Uncle on New Year's Day

By Tang Mingzhe

In Songkou lived in days gone by a certain Li Sanxiong,
Whose status changed overnight on New Year's Eve.
On New Year's Eve he was called Three-Pound Dog,[31]
On New Year's Day he was called Third Elder Uncle;
At once his fame was spread throughout Guangdong.

If you ask me how such a weird thing could happen,
Listen as I will sing the story from beginning to end.

---

[29] Because all debts have to be settled before the end of the year, poor people will be hassled by their creditors to pay.
[30] So they will have a store of cooked rice for the first few days of the New Year.
[31] Three-Pound Dog is a derogatory term for a very poor person, who is compared to a starving dog.

Actually that Li Sanxiong was suffering great poverty:
He had never enough to eat, never enough to wear,
And three steps out of the door he was bullied by all.

Despite his age and generation, he enjoyed no respect:
In the ancestral hall he was given the lowest position;
For weddings he wasn't invited, to funerals summoned.
He didn't dare say a word whatever he was told to do —
Three-Pound Dog eventually became his proper name.

(Prose) One day when Three-Pound Dog had no rice at all to fill the pot, he summoned all his courage and went to the rich man Uncle Geng and his wife to borrow some rice, but despite all his pleading they didn't lend him one kernel! But when he came back home walking with his head hung low and without any energy, Uncle Geng and his wife, accompanied by all their elder and younger brothers, cousins and nephews came after him, loudly shouting:

"Three-Pound Dog, you had the guts to enter our hall,
And with your stinking gall you stole that gold hairpin!
If you don't give it back to us immediately here today,
We'll cut off your hands by the wrist, chop off your feet —
Let's see then how well you can walk and run to escape!

(Prose) As if struck by lightning on a clear day Three-Pound Dog immediately said:

"Rain may hit the banana tree, its heart still lives:
I may be dirt poor, but my bones are still strong.
I never in my life did anything to be ashamed of;
I have no fear for a knock on my door at midnight:
You shouldn't brew up a soup without the meat!"

"Grasp that stubborn fool! You are the one at fault!
Boys, search his house, turn everything upside down!"
Even the wok on the stove was turned upside down;
Every old pot and pan was searched to the bottom,
But all they found were some old sweet potatoes.

(Prose) Even so Uncle Geng and his wife didn't want to let him go and they accused Three-Pound Dog by saying: "The wife of our nephew returned it only this morning to us, and nobody else has come by except for you, Three-Pound Dog, when you wanted to borrow rice, so who else can have stolen it but you?" Despite all his protestations of innocence Three-Pound Dog could not clear himself of that accusation, so he said: "Let's go to the altar of the God of the Soil and I will swear an oath to the gods: If I have stolen your golden hairpin, may we all stumble on our way."

When you have swallowed *huanglian* you can't express its bitterness:[32]
Three-Pound Dog set out on his way to the altar of the God of the Soil.
But because he was in a panic, in a hurry, his stomach filled with rage,
His head felt dizzy, his eyes were blurred and his feet were all shaking,
So he stumbled over a little dike and as a result he fell flat on his face.

Happiness and disaster, joy and misfortune: all voices rang together,
But above all sounded the shrieking voice of the wife of Uncle Geng:
"The God of the Soil shows his efficacy, Heaven is not blind after all —
Retribution followed immediately, so you stumbled into this ditch,
It's clear to all that you, Three-Pound Dog, stole my hairpin of gold!"

(Prose) From this moment Three-Pound Dog suffered this wrong of a false judgment. Now he had also acquired the reputation of a thief, people respected him even less!

Oppressed by frost and by snow he suffered vexations —
How could they sit out the Year without any good food?
When his wife had managed to buy some pork on credit,
Wang A'er came with her in order to receive his money,
And each word of that man pierced his heart like an awl.

(Prose) "Three-Pound Dog, give me the money for the pork!" "I really don't have the money to pay for the pork we bought to offer

---

[32] *Huanglian* 黃連 or China goldthread (*Coptis chinensis*) has a bitter tasting root and stem that is used in Chinese medicine.

in sacrifice to our ancestors. Please give us some slack, and I will pay you double the amount in a few days' time." "That won't do! On New Year's Eve pork is even more precious than gold, so give me back that half pound of pork!"

Three-Pound Dog was utterly at a loss what to do —
What could he do as the pork was cooking already?
Wang A'er lifted the lid from the pot and took it out,
But just as he was about to raise his foot and leave,
He overheard Three-Pound Dog muttering to himself.

(Prose) "Other people have pork to sit out the Year, but we will only have pork bouillon to sit out the Year." Once that mean Wang A'er had heard that, he immediately turned around, threw a handful of ashes into the bouillon, and angrily said: "This too has been made from my pork!" Three-Pound Dog and his wife had not even one mouthful of bouillon on the evening of the last day of the year, so they could only go to bed at an early hour on an empty stomach. But at that moment they suddenly heard someone knocking on their door. Three-Pound Dog and his wife were scared, afraid that yet someone else might come and pester them. Filled with apprehension they listened, and it seemed as if there were several people outside talking amongst each other.

Three-Pound Dog got out of bed and asked: "Who's there?
For what reason are you knocking at the gate at midnight?"
The person who was knocking on the gate shouted loudly:

(Inserted prose) "Father, it's me, your son Afa, I've come back!"
(As soon as Three-Pound Dog heard this, he immediately opened the door.) (continue in song)

Happily he welcomed his son who had come back home;
He clasped him in his arms, while his tears coursed down.

Now on the last day of the year his son had returned,
On the one side he was happy, on the other side sad.

He was happy because father and son were reunited,
Yet he was saddened by that one big pile of problems,
And he could not wipe away those clouds of sorrow.

Afa then spoke and asked his father and mother:
"What is the knotty problem that can't be solved?"
Three-Pound Dog then spoke to his son as follows:
"If you failed to make a fortune in whatever way,
People will look down on you now you came back."

Once Afa heard this, he understood the situation,
So he promptly gave his orders to those outside.

(inserted prose) "Bring it all inside!"

Three-Pound Dog lifted his head to have a look,
But he only saw four strong and sturdy porters,
Whose bodies were covered in sweat like a rain.

The four people all carried huge leather boxes;
Their poles were bending because of the weight.
They carefully put them down inside the room,
And another two loads they placed on the bed.
Afa comforted his father and mother as follows:

"Now you can dispel your sorrows and worries;
You never again will be overcome by any worry.
Once the water is clear, the rocks will appear;
Once clouds break apart, the sun comes out:
Your son has succeeded in making a fortune!"

Hearing this Three-Pound Dog was happy like mad,
And he wanted to discuss with his wife and his son
How when they joined their clansmen to offer sacrifice to the
    ancestors at midnight of New Year's Day
They might buy some stuff to make an impression,
So he summoned everyone to submit their ideas.

(Prose) Where could they buy the three meat dishes in the third watch, at midnight between New Year's Eve and New Year's Day? But Afa said: "I have a solution."

Once midnight had passed with lots of noise,
Each and every family venerated the ancestors.
Three-Pound Dog and his family also arrived,
But he was told not to enter the lineage temple:
"Outside is the place for a scumbag like you!"

With his head held high Three-Pound Dog
Strode with large steps into the lineage temple,
Placing three bowls of silver dollars on the table;
Their bright brilliance shone in all four directions.
Yet another load he put down in the middle.

When someone said that the table was wobbly,
Three-Pound Dog only smiled and said to him:
"I'll put a few silver dollars under that table leg;
I don't think I'll have to pile up three feet three —
What do I care about a few dollars more or less?"

When the others saw this, their eyes bulged out;
Only then did they know Afa had made a fortune.
Three-Pound Dog's value multiplied by hundreds:
Elder and younger generations came up to him,
And addressed him smilingly and reverentially:

[(Prose)] "Third Younger Uncle!" "Thanks!" "Third Elder Uncle!" "Thanks."

This one called him Third Younger Uncle,
And that one called him Third Elder Uncle.
"Younger Uncle" and "Elder Uncle" filled the room;
It was "Uncle" here and "Uncle" there, filling your ears:
Before venerating the ancestors they first paid their respect
  to Third Elder Uncle!

This was one time and that was a different time;
All people competed to bring them their presents.
This one sent wine and also sent chicken and duck;
That one sent pork and also sent grass carp and carp:
These were all fine supplies for celebrating New Year.

(Prose) After they had eaten their New Year's meal, the men and women, old and young, in their lineage as well as their neighbors on the left and the right all arrived to pay their respects to Third Uncle on the occasion of the New Year and paid him all kinds of compliments. Third Elder Uncle wittily joked: "Last year was a good year indeed:/Dog meat was growing faster than ever:/Last night I was only three pounds,/And today I'm already three hundred!"[33] When people heard this they didn't know whether they should laugh or cry!

Three-Pound Dog was happy at heart: on the eighth
He set out a banquet to which everyone was invited.
Each family was to send one person as representative,
All elderly people of sixty and more were also invited.
The only ones who didn't participate were the seventy-three year
   old Geng and his wife!

(Prose) When everyone was going to ask why, the daughter-in-law of Geng and his wife ran staggering and stumbling up to Three-Pound Dog to kowtow before him. As she knelt down she said: "We found the gold hairpin of my mother-in-law in the large clothes shrank. Third Elder Uncle, please forgive us for the way in which we treated you wrongly because of this event in the past." Three-Pound Dog magnanimously said: "Don't mention it anymore. Go and invite your mother-in-law to come and join us for some food. And I also have a present that I want to offer to her." Now look, there came Uncle Geng's wife!

When the meal was done, tea and tobacco were served;
Each person was also given one large silver dollar.

---

[33] "Third Elder Uncle" (*sanbo* 三伯) and "three hundred" (*sanbai* 三百) are (near-)homophonous in many dialects.

The wife of Uncle Geng was sitting in a corner,
But Three-Pound Dog then called her over to him,
And all people were watching what would happen.

(Prose) Three-Pound Dog said: "Uncle Geng's wife, my son has made a fortune, and I now have three presents that I want to offer to you". "There's no need to be so considerate!" "The first present is a towel and a face cloth so you can wash your body and wipe your face". "Many thanks"! "Because you are getting older and your eyesight is poor, the second present is a pair of gold-rimmed spectacles for old eyes which my son bought in Hong Kong. Once you wear them, your eyes will see clearly." "You really have thought of everything." "Now the third present — I wonder whether you will have any use for it and whether it is fitting or not. But if you need it, you can take it." "So what kind of wonderful present might that be?" From a leather box Three-Pound Dog fetched something that gave off a golden glare, and everyone said flabbergasted as if with one voice: "Wow, that's a big hairpin!"

Three-Pound Dog took out one big hairpin of gold,
That in the scales weighed more than two pounds!
When Uncle Geng's wife had received it, it wouldn't stick
    in her hair,
And blushing for shame she felt extremely awkward:
Now she regretted that earlier she had been blind
    in her eyes, and eyeless in her heart!

From that day on Li Sanxiong from Songkou changed
From that Three-Pound Dog into a Third Elder Uncle.
When judging people never judge them once for always:
After the fiercest winter the spring winds will come.
I remind you, dear people, remember this warning!

CHAPTER 2

DESTINATION TAIWAN

Hakka immigrants to Taiwan had been preceded by immigrants from southern Fujian who had occupied most of the western plains, pushing the aboriginal Taiwanese population into the mountainous areas of the island. The Hakka, who arrived later, mostly settled the hilly areas, not only because the plains had mostly been taken, but also because they had the skills to develop these areas.[1] As a result the Hakka found themselves caught between the often antagonistic Minnanese on the plains and the hostile "raw natives" in the mountains who continued their head-hunting ways. Conflicts between Hakkas and natives only intensified as the Hakka tried to add to their income by exploiting the resources of the mountain forests such as rattan.

The core of this chapter is a full translation of *A Sad Song about Migrating to Taiwan* (*Du Tai beige* 渡台悲歌), based on the Chinese text provided by Huang Rongluo 黃榮洛, "'Quanjun qiemo guo Taiwan': *Du Tai beige* de faxian yu yanjiu" 勸君切莫過台灣：渡台悲歌的發現與研究 in his *Du Tai beige: Taiwan de kaituo yu kangzhen shihua* 渡台悲歌:台灣的開拓與抗爭史話 1990, 22–51. The manuscript of this long song was provided to Huang Rongluo in 1986 by Zeng Jizao 曾吉造, who had bought it over ten years earlier in a village of Xinzhu district. The manuscript, written on eleven sheets of paper,

---

[1] For an introductory study of Hakka development of hilly areas in northern Taiwan, see Chuang 1989.

was slightly damaged in places, and I follow Huang's emendations for these spots. The text is written in lines of seven syllables throughout. The even lines rhyme and the same rhyme sound is maintained from beginning to end. The text must have enjoyed at least a certain degree of local circulation. Chen Jianming 陳健銘 published a fragment in 1996 that he had bought from a second-hand book seller[2] and, in 2005, Huang Rongluo and Huang Jufang 黃菊芳 obtained yet another complete version from a certain Peng Fasheng 彭發勝. In 1938, at the age of eighteen, Peng had copied the text after borrowing it from a neighbor and he was still able to recite it from memory in 2005.[3] Peng's versions closely correspond with the manuscript found in 1986 except for the closing section. The last 6 lines in that manuscript are replaced by 32 lines in Peng's versions. In these lines that author identifies himself as hailing from Lufeng in Guangdong. A translation of that final section in Peng's versions follows the translation of the 1986 text.

The ballad provides a detailed description of the miserable life experiences of Hakka migrants to Taiwan who find work as farm laborers and subsist on a diet of mostly sweet potatoes. It is difficult to pinpoint the date of the text's original composition. The description of the Hakka wives who are at liberty to take many lovers (or are pimped by their husbands) suggest to Huang a relatively early date; that of the difficulty of migrants in finding suitable work suggest to him a later date, perhaps even as late as the earliest years of the Japanese administration. As a result Huang concludes that the text most likely dates from the second part of the 19th century, but we could perhaps also entertain the thought that the poem grew over the decades as later hands added new materials.[4] We know nothing about the author(s) beyond the information that can be guessed

---

[2] Chen Jianming 1996, 61–65.
[3] Huang Jufang 2007, 24–40 prints the texts of the three versions side by side, and discusses the differences between these three versions line by line on pp. 43–63. She provides detailed annotations on pp. 70–94.
[4] Zeng Xuekui 2003 suggests that the text was written in the period 1820–1875. Chen Jianming 1996, 61–62 treats the text as reflecting the living conditions on Taiwan in the second part of the 17th century, but does not provide any evidence for such an early dating.

from the ballad. The author describes himself as one of the many victims of the snakeheads, who lure young men to Taiwan with promises of easy riches. Perhaps the author was a local teacher who never managed to return to the mainland.

A Sad Song about Migrating to Taiwan is followed by *Traveling to Taiwan to Find My Husband*. The translation is based on the Chinese text as provided in Huang Huoxing 黃火興, *Kejia qingge jingxuan yiqian jiubai shou* 客家情歌精選 1900首 (1982: 285–286).[5] The editor of that collection provides the following note:

> This set of mountain songs was sung by the people of Jiayingzhou (presently the area of Meixian) of the Qing dynasty. In those days many people went to Taiwan to make a living, to open up undeveloped areas for agriculture. This set of songs reflects the sufferings of the family members (the wives) of these masses who went to Taiwan in joining their relatives. From this set of songs one can also clearly observe the route in those days from Jiayingzhou to Taiwan: Jiayingzhou — Threerivers (Sanhe; Dabu) — Chaozhou — Liancheng (Fujian) — Xiamen (from there one crossed by boat to Taiwan) — Taiwan."

***

A Sad Song about Migrating to Taiwan

I urge you, gentlemen, never migrate to Taiwan:
Taiwan very much resembles the Gate of Ghosts.[6]
Of the thousand people who go, not one returns;
It's impossible to know whether they live or died.
In case you have the temerity to visit graveyards,
Taiwan all over has mountains of perished people.

Taiwan originally is part of the province of Fujian;
One part is Zhangzhou men, one part Quanzhou.[7]

---

[5] The text is also included in Luo Kequn 2000, 355–356; Huang Ziya 2003, 174–176. For a discussion of mountain songs related to the Hakka migration to Taiwan, see Luo Kequn 2002.
[6] The entrance to the world of the dead.
[7] Quanzhou and Zhangzhou are the two prefectures in southern Fujian, which provided the majority of early Chinese immigrants to Taiwan.

One part is settlers from Guangdong province,[8]
And one part is raw natives and cooked natives.[9]

    These raw natives live in the mountain forests;
They hunt human heads to take these with them
Into the mountains, and then drink millet wine,
Drink wine, sing a song, and celebrate together.[10]

    But the cooked natives resemble human beings,
And the Ministry appoints native administrators.[11]

The various crafts and trades there are unprofitable;
Making money, to be honest, is as hard as eating shit.
But snake-heads[12] will tell you that Taiwan is great,
That making money there is just like drawing water.

    Their words may be as glib as those of a prostitute,
But, friends, you cannot believe their stories at all!
Everywhere they talk people into going to Taiwan,
Their only thought is skimming the ones they lead.

    May none of all those snakeheads have a good death;
May they die without a son, their corpses be crushed!

Way too many people put their trust in these men,
And promptly pawn their houses, sell their graves.[13]

---

[8] The "settlers from Guangdong" are the Hakka migrants.

[9] The "raw natives" are those Taiwanese aboriginals who lived outside imperial control and maintained their native traditions. The "cooked natives" lived under imperial administration and had adopted many aspects of Chinese culture.

[10] Cf.Teng 2004, Plate 14, "Illustration of 'Raw Savages Celebrate by Drinking from a Dripping Head' from *A Qing Album of Ethnographic Illustrations* (1875)."

[11] Literally: the Ministry for the Administration of Natives appoints officials for the administration of native affairs.

[12] "Snakehead" is of course a modern term, but the Chinese expression used here refers to those entrepreneurs who made their money by talking Chinese men into migrating to Taiwan and organizing their transportation and employment. As is made clear in this text, many migrants remained in debt to these entrepreneurs for many years.

[13] Selling the graves of one's ancestors usually is the last and final step in selling one's landed properties. As long as one has not sold the graves, one has perhaps not a legal right, but certainly a moral claim to buy back one's ancestral fields.

As long as you are a single person, this can be done,
Because you have no parents or family members.

    You select a good day and also an auspicious hour;
When you walk out the door, tears fall in profusion
Because you say goodbye to neighbors and relatives
And abandon the family graves and your hometown.

    Once you have left the house and taken your leave,
You go straightaway to Hengliuyue to board the boat.[14]
The boat will take you straightway to Chaozhou city;
Each day the snakehead takes five hundred coppers.

    You transfer to a small boat for one day and night,
That takes you straightaway to the harbor of Zhilin.

    You board a small boat to find there an inn to stay;
The snakehead then discusses the price of passage;
The price for one person is one dollar and a half,
But the snakehead will take four dollars from you.

    If you bring your wife along, the price is doubled;
For each couple he makes a profit of three dollars.

Each and everyone one has to pay in ready cash;
If you don't pay in cash, you cannot board the boat.
He looks exactly like a police officer or a warden;
Displaying an angry face, he shows no mercy at all.

    Everyone has to pay the price of passage in full,
Apart from those who pay in Taiwan upon crossing.
But the big boat lies firmly moored in the harbor,
Waiting for a good wind and for suitable weather.

    It happens you have to wait for two, three months,
And people have to sell their sons and daughters.
They sell their clothes, their blankets and curtains;[15]
Waiting for the ship's departure they have no food.

---

[14] The text as edited by Huang Rongluo writes Hengjiang, but this place name does not exist in Guangdong and scholars have suggested several emendations. Peng Fasheng's text writes Hengliu which makes perfect sense in view of the identity of the author.
[15] The curtains are the bed-curtains or mosquito nets that are essential for survival in the tropics.

There are also those who beg their way back home,
Weeping tears over the injustice they've suffered.

Then there are those who stay and leave by boat,
But their sufferings on board are really gruesome.
Sea-sick, they keep vomiting, vomiting even gall,
And they lie in that boat like people about to die.
    But if you have a good wind, things will go easily:
In three days and two nights you arrive in Taiwan.
You go down from the large boat into a small one;
For one person that will be two hundred coppers.
    If you lack that money, you cannot yet disembark,
Your wife must stay behind on the boat as a surety.
As soon as you come on land, you see its misery
When you discern a few hundred thatched sheds.
    These look just like the outhouses back in China,
Are no different from the straw shacks of beggars!
When you find relatives to stay with for a while,
Their welcome already wears thin after three days.

Each and every one hopes to find some job to do,
Most likely as a hired laborer for a full year term.
It may be compared to a cattle market in China:
You are evaluated and the prices is negotiated.
    For a young and strong man it is twelve dollars;
That makes one dollar for one month of work.
If you are over forty and not that young anymore,
You only can earn five silver dollars for a full year.
    As for blanket and mosquito net, bring your own;
When they talk about a bed, you sleep in a basket.
During nighttime, without shoes, you go barefoot;
Getting outside early on never had been so hard.
    Without your own bed-curtains, mosquitoes bite;
Without your own blanket, you shiver for cold.
Now if you manage to make a new set of clothes,
You still have to make bed-curtains and a blanket.

If you add up your earnings from beginning to end,
You still owe the snakehead quite a sum of money.
If you want to leave, he keeps your blanket as pawn,
And you must work another year for twelve dollars.

On the last day of the year one prays to ancestors;
Thinking of this, your heart seems to be cut apart.
You are without parents and without any relatives[16]
And celebrate New Year at the snakehead's house.
    You can fool around from the first until the fourth,
But they dock you one thousand coppers of pay.
People who steal from you act in the same way —
Throughout Taiwan prefecture it is all the same!
    People say that Taiwan produces so much rice —
That is absolute bullshit, the lies of a prostitute!
When it's talk of food, tears gush from my eyes,
And when I hold a bowl of rice, my rage explodes:
    In one bowl of rice, there's not a hundred kernels;
It's mixed with large chunks of sweet potatoes.
At all three meals sweet potatoes nine to one,
Each bowl of rice resembles a mountain of rocks.
    In Taiwan you eat more potatoes in one month
Than you eat in China throughout a whole year.
When first you eat them, you can't let them go
And you want to keep them for a second meal![17]

You'll rarely enjoy the pleasure of oil-fried food;
For salted fish, you have to wait for over a year.
There always will be dishes of putrid dried fish:
Two big bowls at all three meals on every day.
    Want to go to a restaurant for wine and meat?
Only in your next life when you're back in China!

---

[16] The text in the manuscript in the possession of Chen Jianming starts from this line.
[17] These two lines are clearly intended ironically.

When the cock crows you rise to work till evening,
And you'll never have any snacks with your meals.
   If you want to have a hot tea with parched rice,
You had better swallow spit and suck your dick.
For all the three hundred sixty days of one year,
Each and every day is exactly like this, the same!
   Even frost and snow and the rains of typhoons
Or a burning headache is no excuse for laziness.
If you are so utterly miserable you cannot work,
And stay in bed all day, you're docked a hundred.
   Once you are slightly better, you have to work,
Even if on the road you are reeling on your feet.
To change your shirt, you wash it yourself at cockcrow;
If it is worn out, you have to repair the holes at night.

If you go into the hills to gather a load of wood,
One day will not bring you a hundred coppers.
A hundred pounds in the scales pays a hundred,
But that load is bound to bend your shoulders.
   The trips going and coming are three stretches;[18]
When you come back, it is evening or midnight.
Apart perhaps from three meals of decent rice,
All you gain extra is that you can buy a smoke.
   So alas, as a result you again work for others,
You again sign on as a laborer for one full year.

In China there are three busy periods each year,
But in Taiwan each day is as busy as busy can be.
When you have slept till only just after midnight,
Rice stampers and mortar are there in the barn.
   When three men have hulled three pecks of rice,
They call you to have a meal and bring the food,

---

[18] Huang Rongluo defines the "stretches" as the distance between two pavilions where one can take shelter against the hot sun. The distance between two pavilions would be roughly ten Chinese miles (5,5 kilometers), so "three stretches" would be roughly ten miles.

But the sweet potatoes are difficult to swallow —
How can you ever get them down your throat?
    If you eat them too rashly, you'll be burned badly,
But if you eat them later, they have no taste at all!
When you go outside, you cannot see the road,
And you hurt your toes till they all are bleeding.
    Each day, every morning it is always the same:
You work yourself to death for twenty coppers.
Now Hakka snakeheads may still be reliable,
But Minnanese boss men are truly quite hard:
    All year long there never is any bathing water;
Want to go to a bathhouse? That's hard to find.
In the end you look no different than animals;
If you have a human body, it is bound to rot.

A carrying pole measures two feet and a half:
A round bamboo pole is put on your shoulders.
It has to be sturdy, and it also has to be stiff,
And it's exactly the same as the yoke of an ox.
    Elsewhere you work the fields on your feet;
On Taiwan you work the fields with your hands.[19]
Those who work the fields must owe some debt,
And in this later life pay back for an earlier sin.
    Working the fields looks like tearing out weeds,
In my many travels I have never seen the same.
It resembles a filial son receiving his relatives;[20]
You also look like a black turtle climbing a rock.[21]
    You scratch with your hands, push with your feet,
And so work on your knees from dawn till dusk.
Your face and body are covered in mud like a ghost;
King Yama would collapse in laughter on seeing you.[22]

---

[19] Huang reads these lines as a reference to weeding.
[20] This refers to the way in which a mourning son receives the relatives who come to offer condolences during a funeral by kneeling down on the floor in front of them.
[21] The black turtle is reeves' turtle (Chinemis reevesii). The term is also used to refer to a cuckolded husband.
[22] King Yama is the highest divinity in the world of the dead.

For one day on your knees you make one hundred,
But after three days on your knees, they are worn.
At noon you are treated to a truly delicious snack:
Fried and steamed sweet potatoes fill all the plates!

Each year you kneel twice to the rice in the fields:
You also filially kneel down for the second crop.
This is a mark of the ingenuity of Taiwan people,
So there is no need for pity from people in China.
   It must be they committed a sin in an earlier life,
So in this life Heaven has them kneel in the fields.
But if you grind down the weeds with a head butt,
One year's harvest will equal that of three years.
   If the boss man doesn't understand farm work,
He is just like a water buffalo washing its horns.[23]
If you try it out for a few years, it works well:
This ingenious way deserves to be propagated.

The people on Taiwan really suffer miserably,
Even oxen in China really have an easier time.
Alas, alas! Heaven, dear Heaven!
Never trust people and cross over to Taiwan.
   You may believe the fine words of a snakehead —
Even ghosts quake on arrival in Eastern Capital![24]
When I recall in my heart all these sufferings,
Tears stream down and even fall on my breast.
   If at home you can work with diligence and thrift,
Even your boar will be able to wear a pair of pants.
If at home you manage all your affairs with thrift,
You don't need to worry you won't grow wealthy.

---

[23] The meaning of these two lines is unclear to me.
[24] Eastern Capital was the name Zheng Chenggong bestowed on Tainan after he had defeated the Dutch in 1662. This is the last line in the manuscript in the possession of Chen Jianming.

But Taiwan is not a place fit for human habitation;
You will be like a foreign duck on a seaside beach.
Like beasts, people there lack all common decency;
Once you will see that, rage rises up in your heart.

    They don't respect culture,[25] and ignore high and low:
Even actors[26] and monks are addressed as "teacher."
Farmers, merchants, sedan-chair carriers, beggars —
They all address each other as equals on meeting.

    The boys in school look like sedan-chair carriers —
It's quite a difference from my original hometown.
They do not have the slightest shred of culture:
Barefooted, bareheaded, they bow to the Sage![27]

    On cold days their head cloths cover their ears;
On hot days they tie a sweat cloth at their waist.
In this way culture and style are all demeaned;
On seeing it, the rage in my heart rises to heaven!

When fetching a bride or offering congratulations,
You won't even see a single person wearing shoes.
Barefooted, wearing a short shirt and underpants,
With a sweat cloth at their waist to wipe the body.

    At banquets they don't cede at all to their guests,
But grab the dishes as if they were hungry ghosts.
Carriers and porters are seated in the main hall,
Whereas highest ranking guests sit in some shed.

    Like animals they have no idea of high and low —
On seeing it, my heart feels as simmered by fire.
They don't care about same surname or not —[28]
It is one set of gifts and two festive banquets.

---

[25] Culture is the translation of *siwen* 斯文 ("This Way of Ours").
[26] *Dan* 旦, i.e. male impersonators of female roles who are expected to be available for sex on payment.
[27] The Sage is Confucius, who is revered in every school.
[28] On the mainland people with the same surname could not marry. Apparently this taboo was not always observed on Taiwan.

And then they have a number of dirty customs
That I don't dare mention despite my anger.
If these things would be transmitted to China,
People from Taiwan would be spat in the face!
    How can there be any husbands and wives
Who wash their bodies sharing one bucket?
They use it in hauling water and cooking rice —
If you eat it, it must rob you of three years![29]
    At New Year, they kotow and pray for blessings;
They make cakes to present to the Three Offices.[30]
If the gods are daring enough to eat those cakes,
They cannot be divine immortals from heaven.
    Burning incense they kneel till their knees are worn;
Barefooted, a head cloth — they bow to the deities.
Old Uncle God of the Soil must be very responsive:
Shrines devoted to an Old Uncle are everywhere.
    Their offerings, plain to see, are red-turtle cakes;
Those with wives, plain to see, are black turtles all.[31]

Husbands don't dare berate their wives loudly;
They allow them to seek their pleasure at will.
Of each ten husbands nine behave in this manner —
There may be one who does not follow this trend.
    When a guy enters, the husband welcomes him,
Treats him to tea and a smoke with sweet words.

---

[29] Huang explains that a bucket a woman has used for washing herself brings bad luck. Especially the blood shed by women in menstruation and child birth is considered extremely polluting.

[30] The Three Offices refer to the Offices of Heaven, Earth, and Water. As deities in charge of recording sins and administering punishments for the living, they later became associated with the punishments people will suffer for their sins upon death. Here the term may have been as a general reference to all the gods for the sake of rhyme.

[31] "Turtle" is a common designation for a cuckolded husband.

Once long ago Fan Dan's wife killed nine husbands,[32]
But Taiwan wives come complete with nine lovers.
   Three steps outside the door, these follow her;
Properly married couples even don't act like this!
As long as you have money, they love you dearly,
And each and every word is "my darling, my love!"

These women on Taiwan have sharp eyes for profit,
And observe you to see how much cash you have.
You may stay together for one full year or a half,
But how much money you have, it will be used up.[33]
   How often you rose at cockcrow, before midnight!
How many were your sufferings like a water buffalo!
Each single copper coin took three drops of sweat —
And how many coppers could you make in one day?
   As long as you are young and your body is strong,
You can slave like a buffalo for a number of years.
When fortune favors you, and things work out fine,
You still can't go whoring — it's way too much cash.[34]
   In your heart you must think of your later future,
Be aware of the years when your luck will decline.
Once you have no money left, things will change:
If you run into her on the road, she will look away.
   If you step up to her, she won't answer your greeting,
Because with the money gone, all love too is finished.

---

[32] According to a Hakka folktale from Xinzhu, Shi Chong 石崇 (249–300), the richest man of his time, had a daughter, who lost nine husbands in succession. Because of the bad luck she brought to her husbands, Shi Chong then chased her from his house. Wandering about, she encountered a young man, Fan Dan 范丹, while he was swimming and married him despite his poverty. Because of her knowledge of precious materials the couple eventually became very wealthy.
[33] In Peng Fasheng's manuscript this line is followed by the following two lines: "They want a blue shirt and a pair of black pants,/ They want bracelets for their arms, rings for their ears."
[34] These two lines have no equivalent in Peng Fasheng's manuscript.

If she speaks at all, she'll call you a good for nothing,
"A rake is useless for hanging one's shirt out to dry."

When you are suffering from a disease that is fatal,
You won't have the money to invite a good doctor.
When you'll lie in the weeds, nobody cares for you;
If you want tea or water, only ghosts will approach.
   When the illness culminates and you stop breathing,
You'll be wrapped in a mat by kind-hearted people.
When you left your home, you thought of millions,
Not knowing you would finish your life on Taiwan.

Taiwan is a one huge grave that annihilates people:
Of the hundred that go there, not one will return.
But if only each of these men could think straight,
Even Taiwan women can recover abandoned fields.
   The harvests on Taiwan are all different in nature;
In every village the women put in quite an effort.
Once they hear in the fields the grain buckets sound,[35]
They dress up in all their finery and go to the fields.
   In their hands they hold a flail for threshing the rice;
With a happy smile on their face and filled with joy.
With sweet and soft words they greet the foreman,
And the threshing benches are placed on both sides.
   When they pick up the flails, they display a smile,
Resembling jade maidens descending from heaven.[36]
With witty words they engage in banter and play,
And as a result the farm workers are filled with joy.

---

[35] When rice was harvested in earlier times, bundles of rice were first beaten against the inside of a bucket so the rice grains would fall out inside the bucket. Afterwards the rice was threshed to harvest the remaining grains. In this case the women who beat the bundles of rice with their rice-beating sticks (flails) are allowed to keep any rice they still can extract from the ears. So it is in their interest that the farmhands only beat the shelves a few times against the inside sides of the buckets before throwing the bundles to them.

[36] These two lines have no equivalent in Peng Fasheng's manuscript.

Four times they beat their bundles of laid-out rice,
Then throw them to the girls, in front of their flails.

Whereas all other goods in Taiwan are expensive,
Only a human head comes at no money at all!
The wages for one day's work are only a hundred,
So people are eagerly willing to risk their one life.
    They collect rattan for sale, they serve as braves,[37]
And take their own head into the wild mountains.
When they run into raw natives who fire their guns,
They immediately die out in those dense forests.
    The natives run over and then cut off their heads,
So they leave for the shades as headless ghosts.
It doesn't matter whether they are men or women,
Each year ten thousands enter these mountains.

But the biggest mistake was made that day long ago;
They never should credulously have come to Taiwan.
When Li Ling by mistake entered the land of the Khan,[38]
His heart always kept longing for the realm of the Han.
    With me at this moment it is also exactly the same;
My black hair already has reached the greying years.
Of course I would like to return but I have no money,
And each year here is followed by yet another year.
    Back at home my parents are now advanced in years,
And from morning till evening they weep bitter tears.
Each year the letters from home are urgent like fire;
My desire to go back each time is just like an arrow.

---

[37] In order to collect rattan they will have to enter the mountain forests that are the terrain of the "raw" natives. "Braves" refers to locally hired militia.

[38] Li Ling 李陵 was a general of the Han dynasty. In 99 BC, during a campaign against the Xiongnu in present-day Mongolia, he was outnumbered by the enemy and defeated. When the emperor learned about this, he believed Li Ling had treasonably surrendered to the enemy and had all his relatives executed. Li Ling thereupon indeed surrendered to the Xiongnu and never returned to China. The story remained popular in later dynasties.

If my father and mother die of hunger and of cold,
It would all be useless if I would make my millions.
But then it is exceedingly difficult to make money;
One never sees one who made a fortune go back.
    People want to make at least three or five hundred,[39]
But even after yet another year, they all stay put.
If they go home and say that Taiwan is wonderful,
It's the lies of a prostitute, of a common whore!

I advise you, my uncles and brothers and in-laws,
Never be persuaded to make the trip to Taiwan.
If there are ever any young men who want to go,
Beat them to death, abandon them in the wilds!
    Every sentence in my letter is based on hard facts,
And there is not a single line that's an empty lie.

Final section of Peng Fasheng's manuscript copy:

I advise you, my uncles and brothers and in-laws,
Never be persuaded to make the trip to Taiwan.
If you do not believe the words of a good friend,
Regret will come too late when things go wrong.
    If there are ever any young men who want to go,
Beat them to death, abandon them in the wilds!
If you have cash, don't go whoring or gambling;
Let each be diligent and prepare for his old age.
    If you have money you'll be a headman at thirty;
If you lack cash, at eighty you'll still carry loads.
If you want to borrow cash, you hope they'll agree,
But then you fear you won't be able to pay it back.

Every sentence in my letter is based on hard facts,
And there is not a single line that's an empty lie.
I send it to my whole family, for everyone to read,
To read carefully from the beginning to the end.

---

[39] In this case the reference will be to dollars.

If you wonder who it was who wrote this letter,
I hail from Lufeng and lived close to Hetian town.
I have written this throughout in the common dialect,
So all my relatives may read it and spread the word.

As long as you're not yet thirty, fortune may turn:
Reign in your horse, look back: the Top-of-the-List!
Once the moon is past the fifteenth, its light lessens;
Yet when dragon and tiger meet, that glory will last.
   That is the moment the fruits in the forest will ripen —
Second-Month plum blossoms only resemble silver.
Travel the roads of this world with circumspection,
Keep your mouth shut and don't speak idle words.

Remember these many words of mine very well:
I failed to avoid this bitter suffering on Taiwan.
Now if there is anyone who wants to borrow this,
Let him copy or read it and return very quickly!

Traveling to Taiwan to Find my Husband, Ten Songs

When first I set out to seek my husband in Taiwan —
Once I decided to make the trip, I borrowed money.
Earlier you said that it would be easy to come back;
Nobody knew it would be so hard to see you today!

Secondly, seeking my husband I set out on the road;
My luggage and my umbrella I was carrying with me.
I said goodbye to my uncles and to my brothers too;
Once I left home to find my husband I truly suffered.

Thirdly, seeking my husband I arrived at Threerivers.
The officials at Threerivers had all kinds of questions.
With lowered head I didn't dare speak up, and said,
Covering my mouth with a sleeve, I was seeking you.

Fourthly, seeking my husband I left Threerivers —
I had already used quite a lot of my travel money.

The people out on the streets asked each other:
Why on earth is she showing her face so in public?

Fifthly, seeking my husband I arrived in Chaozhou,
And I saw that all kinds of goods are there for sale.
But I had no desire to look at all that good stuff,
I pursued my journey in a hurry, without a pause.

Sixthly, seeking my husband I came to Liancheng,
And I arrived in that town only late in the evening.
I slept till the fifth watch and then I had a dream,
In that dream I saw you, living alone by yourself.

Seventhly, seeking my husband I came to Xiamen;
At Xiamen a bustling crowd was boarding the boat.
Only at midnight was I finally settled on that boat —
Darling, how much I had to suffer because of you!

Eightly, seeking my husband, I traveled by boat —
My many sufferings are really too much for words!
Ocean waves beat the ship, the wind was fierce —
I felt dizzy and depressed but nobody cared at all.

Ninthly, seeking my husband, I left the ship's hold,
But I had no idea, darling, where you might be.
But I had no idea, darling, where you might live;
When I didn't see you, my heart was in a panic.

Tenthly, seeking my husband, I came to Taiwan —
Darling, as soon as I saw you, the skies opened up.
When, holding hands, the two of us will go home,
Across the sea I'll have met my divine immortal.

CHAPTER 3

DESTINATION SINGAPORE AND BEYOND

Merchants and artisans from the coastal regions of southeast China had migrated to the Southern Oceans (continental and insular Southeast Asia) from an early date and some of them had amassed great wealth.[1] Hakka started to migrate to the Southern Oceans in greater numbers only in the 18th century, originally especially as miners. Gold miners on Kalimantan would establish their own independent republics (*kongsi*) between the coastal Malays principalities and the inland Dayak tribes and, in one case, chronicled their own history.[2] On Kalimantan these statelets eventually had to submit to the Dutch colonial authorities. The middle of the 18th century also witnessed the first high tide of tin mining on Banka by Chinese; Chinese miners (most of them Hakka) would also be responsible for the flourishing tin mining there in the 19th century.[3] Tin had been mined on the Malay Peninsula at least since the 16th century, but the industry would be greatly developed in the 19th century. The tin mines would continue to be a major employer of Hakka migrants

---

[1] For a comprehensive history of overseas Chinese in Southeast Asia, see Wu Fengbin 1983.
[2] Yuan Bingling 2000.
[3] Somers Heidhues 1992.

337

well into the 20th century, but as the 19th century progressed plantation agriculture was also always short of labor. The backbreaking work of hauling tin ore from the mines is mentioned time and again in the Hakka songs warning against emigration to the Southern Oceans.[4] The unlimited demand for labor in the tin mines and on the plantations was one of the major reasons for the emergence of the infamous coolie trade of the 1860s to the 1920s. Soon after its foundation in the early 19th century, Singapore developed into the undisputed center for the traffic in goods and persons throughout the region.[5]

Like the preceding chapter, the translations in this chapter start with a long poem, in this case about the hardship of migrating to Singapore and beyond. The poem is reproduced by Luo Xianglin in his collection of mountain songs, *Yuedong zhi feng* (1928: 268–280). In a note to the poems he states: "This song has most likely been written by a local literatus, but because it is very popular and identical in characteristics to other mountain songs I have included it in this collection." (p. 280). As in the long poem in the preceding chapter, the anonymous author(s) present(s) us with long catalogue of woes — from the painful parting from home, seasickness, an incomprehensible foreign language and the miserable working conditions in the tin mines, to sexual diseases.

This long poem is followed by several sets of mountain songs from various modern sources.[6] The first two sets describe the miseries of a migrant's life from the male perspective. In the next song, a dialogue song, the perspectives of the departing husband and the

---

[4] The traditional technology for tin mining in Southeast Asia is described by Somers Heidhues 1992, 6–19. Most tin ore mined in Southeast Asia consisted of alluvial deposits located close to the surface. The larger mines were open pits that could reach a depth of twenty feet and needed to be drained by water-powered pumps. Once the ore had been carried to the surface it needed to be washed and melted. Up till the end of the 19th century the Chinese miners were the most efficient producers of pure tin. It is significant to note that none of the protagonists in the Minnanese *Guofan ge* ever works in the tin mines.

[5] Yen 1986, 1–10.

[6] For a preliminary survey of these materials see Su Qinghua 2012.

wife who stays behind are contrasted. The remaining two sets are written from the perspective of the wife who stays behind. That also applies to the individual mountain songs that conclude this chapter.

***

Going Abroad

Our life in this world will only last a few decades;
Poverty and riches are all determined by Heaven.
Whatever happens has been disposed by Heaven;
No need to strive for what you'll obtain anyway.
   At the age of twice eight, when you're in your teens,
Your heart resembles the ocean, your gall the skies.
When you want to engage in some kind of business,
Your hands are tied because you don't have money.
   Each day you roam in all directions to have some fun,
For whoring and gambling, banqueting, fine clothes.
Your father and mother loudly berate you at length,
Uncles and brothers, old and young, they all chime in.
   In your heart you reach the conclusion you only can
Leave the house and go abroad to barbarian lands.
You ask your relatives and friends to come along,
But they don't have the money to pay for the trip.
   If you don't have the traveling money as a *sinkeh*,[7]
You most willingly sign a contract for three years.
You select an hour and a day for your departure,
And some uncles and cousins give you some cash.
   Your parents pray to the gods for their blessings,
To protect you so you will remain safe and sound.
   Your uncles and brothers all tell you repeatedly:
"Stay away from whoring and gambling and opium.
At home your parents are both advanced in years,
So come back to China in three years or even less."

---

[7] A new emigrant, one who travels abroad for the first time.

Having said goodbye to your uncles and brothers,
It's your lovely wife in her room — that separation!
A couple that parts: that feeling is insupportable,
And the tears that gush forth resemble a fountain.

Your pack and your umbrella you carry yourself,
You hire a man to carry your boxes and luggage.
At the County you board a boat for the Prefecture;[8]
You will go through the Pengla Rapids at Xiyang.

Form Bincun you go downriver past Songkou,
Past Threerivers and Highbank on to Hebuguan.
Once past Cai Family Garden it's the Prefecture;
At Xiangzi's Bridge you pass by the Eastern Pass.

A hundred kinds of foreign goods all pass by,
And you arrive at the seaside city of Shantou.
Several servants of the inns meet the travelers,
And take you with them to an inn to have food.

When you ask them how much passage will cost,
They immediately say it's more than ten dollars.
If you take the boat from Shantou to Hong Kong,
It will only take one single day if you go by sea.

Once when you depart by boat from Hong Kong,
Then the wide sea is boundless, no island in sight.
You don't see black birds crossing high and low,
You only see white clouds halfway up to heaven.

Those on board of the ship truly suffer miserably,
When they lie down they resemble sick patients.
For full three days they don't even eat half a bowl,
Vomiting green slime and water without any end.

The boat resembles heaven turned upside down,
Surging waves are even higher than mountains.
By the looks of it, traveling by boat is miserable,
And each and everybody prays to High Heaven.

---

[8] According to Luo Xiangling, the "county" refers here to the city of Jiayingzhou (Meixian), the prefecture to Chaozhou.

With favorable winds you sail for six, seven days,
While a journey by land would last half a year.
Then suddenly you are at White Rock Harbor,
And in the wink of an eye you're in Singapore.

When in Singapore, you'll see the city is grand
As all kinds of trades and crafts are found there.
A hundred kinds of goods are available for sale,
And the place is more beautiful than our China.

Abroad, the flower gardens are full of fine sights,
You not only have Chinese there, but also natives.
You will see that the old immigrants speak Malay;
And if you don't do so, you might as well be dumb.

But in this world there are many bright people,
Who achieve perfect mastery of foreign tongues.

The natives call those of their own kind *zhulai*;
Friends and acquaintances are called *jiaowan*.[9]
A servant there goes by the name of *maishi*;
Eating a meal there is called by them *matan*.[10]

For the natives having a talk is called *shiha*,
The word used for traveling there is *yelan*.[11]
A *niangyao*[12] is the name of a pretty young girl,
And *linyi*[13] is the word they use for a silver dollar.

The Chinese there are called by them Alingjin,
And *risu*[14] is the word that is used for tomorrow.
It is practically impossible to learn Malay fully;
When buying and selling *shilei* means money.

When Chinese arrive in those barbarian states,
The natives there in their eyes resemble demons.

---

[9] Malay: *kawan*.
[10] Malay: *makan*.
[11] Malay: *jalan*.
[12] Malay: *njonja*.
[13] Malay: *ringgit*.
[14] Malay: *esok*.

The wives of Jilin barbarians[15] pierce their noses;
The Mulaiyou barbarians[16] don't have a hairy dick.
   Jesus-men, Allah-men, and plenty of drunkards,
And also Red-Haired Barbarians and the Dutch:
Over there they have natives serve in the *police*;
The Chinese that serve as officials are *kapitans*.

When you have stayed a few days in Singapore,
You'll have spent two or three dollars on food.
Those who have relatives, seek out their brothers,
Those without relatives go on to other places.
   You hear that it is easy to make money in Aji,[17]
But also are told that Rili[18] is great for tobacco.
But these two areas both are in Dutch territory;
It's easy to go there, but difficult to come back.
   The American Gold Mountains, the Philippines:[19]
If you travel there by boat, it takes you ten days.
   Now closer by you have Danyong[20] and Malacca,
But the wages are low, it's hard to make money.
Then there are Yanggong and also Wulumeng;[21]
Both don't measure up to Large and Small Bili.[22]
   Those who have money may engage in trade,
Those without money work in the tin mines,

---

[15] Jilin probably refers to Indians. The expression is more commonly written "Jining" 吉寧, transcribing "Keling" (deriving from Kalinga, the region of origin of the first Indians in Singapore). Luo Xianglin 1936, 279 identifies Jilin as Kuala Lumpur but that does not seem very likely in this context.
[16] Malays?
[17] Aceh.
[18] Deli.
[19] The Gold Mountains refer to San Francisco. It is not clear whether "American" is also intended as an adjective of "the Philippines".
[20] This looks like a transcription of the Malay *tanjung* (cape), an element that is encountered in many place names. Quite likely Tanjongpinang on Bintan island is intended here.
[21] Yanggong refers to Rangoon. I have been unable to identify Wulumeng.
[22] Perak.

But the districts of the tin mines are in turmoil,
And many bandits rob people of their money.
   Those who are lucky are robbed of their silver,
Those not so lucky also may lose their lives.
The natives when traveling carry a scimitar;
If you don't carry a scimitar, you're not native.
   The mountains are covered by trees of all kinds;
There also are tigers and leopards and big apes,
The lower places are ordinarily filled with water;
Everywhere the high ridges are rocky mountains.
   At the tin mines you are living in thatched sheds,
Just like the outhouses back in your homeland,
Now when you first arrive in these foreign parts,
You are unused to the sights and long for China.
   Land and water in foreign lands, one hears, are bad;
For *sinkeh* it's extremely important to take their baths.
At night you can take a bath till eight or nine o'clock;
In the morning at three you again pass that ordeal.[23]
   When the weather is chilly and you lack a blanket,
Go to the riverside when the cold wakes you up.
After you have forcefully beaten your body all over,
Douse that thief with cold water again and again.
   If you take your baths but don't do it often enough,
You'll very soon be plagued by illness and disease.
Some suffer from a disease for a number of days,
But many suffer from a disease for several months.
   You also may not have the money to seek a cure —
How many people unjustly pass from this world!
In those foreign parts feelings are thin as paper:
People want money as soon as you have a request.
   When a *sinkeh* is seriously ill and needs some food,
It's hard to approach them if you have no friends.
If you don't have any ready cash at your disposal,
Even friends and relatives turn out to be useless!

---

[23] It was believed that it was essential for new arrivals to take a bath twice a day. Tin miners were made to take a bath at 4.30 am and then again at 10 pm.

While at home you thought travel would be great,
But once out of the door you are often in trouble,
And you are loudly cursed out by older workers:
"Not bathing enough, and now too lazy to work!"
   If the *sinkeh* do not listen to what they are saying,
The older workers will beat them with rattan whips.
There are also older workers who care for the *sinkeh*
And help them fill three hundred sixty days of work.
   Working in these foreign parts is often bitter toil,
Like during the Sixth Month back home in China.
Had you known these foreign parts were like this,
Would you have clamored so much to go abroad?
   While at home you didn't know about foreign parts;
Once in these foreign parts you'll remember China.
When eating you resemble a rooster seeking rice:
The food here is smelly salted fish that's fried in oil.
   Foreign parts, we've long heard, are a land of fire;
In frying and baking they don't fear fire and smoke.
Then there are *sinkeh* who do not choose their food,
And when boat-poison erupts, they resemble lepers.[24]
   At county and prefecture they arrive in thousands,[25]
They look exactly the same as dead pigs and dogs.
   Why don't you look at the company's graveyard
Each year on the festivals in spring and in autumn?
Seeing these many graves a *sinkeh* will be alarmed:
These southern regions are the Gate of the Ghosts.[26]
   Even though life and death are determined by fate,
When diseased, you still must take an effective pill.
And if your body has regained health and strength,
You should still repay the gods and thank Heaven.

---

[24] It is not clear to what illness "boat-poison" refers to. Elsewhere the symptoms are described as "oozing pus and blood by night and day."

[25] The enconffined corpses of overseas Chinese that have been transported back to China for burial in their hometown.

[26] The entrance to the world of the dead.

When the *sinkeh* will have served out his contract,
He pays the headman several tens of silver dollars.
If the tin pit has been very productive all the time,
You will pay off every penny that you owe to him.

But if the tin pit has not been productive at all,
You're left with empty hands for a full year's work.
Your friends will also invite you to visit the town,
They'll ask the headman to produce his accounts.

The headman will want you to stay for one year:
"If you want to make money, wait for next year!"
The older workers will chime in and tell the *sinkeh*:
"In one year you may hope to go up to heaven!

If things work out really well in the coming year,
It won't be a problem at all to make your fortune.
If you can do the work and put in enough of it,
You can make eight or nine dollars each month!"

Once you have a certain amount of ready cash,
Friends and brothers will all come up to you.
Your friends will get together to enjoy gambling;
Your brothers will invite you to have a smoke.

They will all ask you to go into town with them,
So loafing about you stroll through the streets.

On your head you are wearing a nice Dutch hat,
On your fingers you sport a ring made of gold.
In your hand you hold a fan which you wave,
While you smoke a cigar from the Philippines.

Now they say: "Let's go into that restaurant!"
Next they say: "Let's go and have a good time."
Once you have come to the red-light district,
The prostitutes want you to stay for the night.

They not only have iced candy and melon seeds,
But they also serve fine tea and a pipe of opium.
When the two of you talk in private on a couch,
She'll talk of a karmic bond from an earlier life.

When talking as friends in her room, having fun,
She resembles a fairy from Peach Blossom Fount.

When at eleven o'clock you lie down to sleep,
It's like a bridal room with flowers and candles.
    Naked flesh of two bodies making rain and clouds:
As if a mortal fellow encounters a celestial fairy.
That one night as husband and wife is quickly done;
The money you pay her is five or six silver dollars.
    At that time they all say that one night is worth it,
But later they realize it was hard to make that money.
How many poor people act as if they were wealthy,
While not knowing their family has been wiped out?

Because your family was so poor, you went abroad,
But now you have money you don't return to China.
In your whoring you may attract a venereal disease,
And in the end you have to pawn all your clothes.
    Your sores and boils will never get any better,
And on top of that you're plagued by jaundice.
You cannot even move three steps outdoors,
And you cry out repeatedly — truly how pitiable!
    When you have wine and meat, friends are many;
Who dares to visit you when you are in dire straits?
When day after day you are unable to do any work,
Your work badge is removed — you're kicked outside.
    Each and everyone says it is great to go into town;
There is not a single friend who gives good advice.
But once you have spent all the money you had,
You will have to beg for food from door to door.

When you had money it was great fun to spend it;
Now you don't have money, you cry out to Heaven,
While letters from home urge you to come home,
Letters as urgent as warrants issued by the police.
    In your heart you long to be able to go back home,
But it is impossible to go back without any money.
When you had cash, you didn't want to go home,
But without the money, you cannot return to China.

Suddenly you realize you have been gone for years,
And despite all your hardships you have no money.
When you think of borrowing money from relatives,
You find it hard to address them asking for help.

Had you known the misery of having no money,
You hadn't wasted it in whoring and gambling.
If a silver dollar brings in ninety eight coppers,
You need ninety coppers to buy some vegetables.

If a merchant takes dried and salted vegetables
To those foreign parts, he sells them as treasures.
At home you make do with diligence and thrift,
So why should you sail the seas and go abroad?

Going to Foreign Lands is Even Harder[27]

Even if you are poor at home, don't go abroad;
When you go to foreign lands, life's even harder.
When you go there for the first time as a *sinkeh*,
How can you manage to serve three full years?

When in those days I went abroad to make a living,
I suffered greatly when I first came to the tin mine.
Because I didn't know the business of the company,
My heart was hurt by their cold words and sneers.

At midnight, in the third watch, we got out of bed;
My fellow workers urged me on, a confused crowd.
Three hundred sixty days of work we had to fulfill —
Hating the night for its brevity, the day for its length.

I went to Folang; that was the name of a tin mine —
We had to dig out the ore and also to carry it out.

---

[27] Huang Huoxing 1982, 278–279. The text is also included in Luo Kequn 2000, 357–358; Huang Ziya 2003, 177–178.

One day of work was counted as seven full hours;[28]
Were those seven hours done, your life was cold.

Coming to talk of going abroad, I beg forgiveness:[29]
Carrying the tin ore we crossed a floating bridge.
A thousand time I crossed it, and as often safely;
If I once had lost my footing, I would have died.

The sun resembles a fire, its heat is insupportable;
While carrying a load of ore, we climbed a ladder.[30]
Our skin was burned as black as a pan's bottom —
So who can imagine all we suffered in our hearts?

The high ridges in foreign lands lack pine trees;
You only see all kind of trees with dense leaves.
Nowhere can a man be found who builds a house,
You only see those thatched sheds of the miners.

Even when you're poor, you'd better not go abroad;
During the day the heat there is truly insupportable.
At night the mosquitoes will bite you and sting you:
The day is hard to survive and the night is miserable.

Once the cock crows at midnight, you all will get up;
Eight times you douse yourself, without interruption.
If you don't douse yourself, you may develop a fever;
Dousing yourself by day and night, that's really killing.

---

[28] Most likely the "hours" here are traditional Chinese hours, which are twice as long as the modern hour. This would mean a workday of fourteen hours.

[29] The singer of the song does not want to offend those migrants who want to stay in foreign parts.

[30] The Chinese word translated as "ladder" is *tiaobang* 跳梆, which I take to be synonymous with *tiaoban* 跳板, which is commonly translated as "gangway", but probably also can be used more broadly to refer to any narrow and steep wooden gangway. In the tine mines, ladders were often made out of tree trunks.

Fine flowers cannot stay fresh for a hundred days:
To fall ill in those foreign parts is utterly miserable.
You don't have any ready cash with you to spend,
And you also have no single relative at your side.

Thinking of going abroad, I'm overcome by sadness;
A towel serves as your mat, a jacket as your blanket.
Upon your return everyone calls you an emigrant,
But nobody knows of your trials and tribulations.

For all your troubles, my friends,[31] don't go abroad:
From foreign lands you cannot go back to China.
High mountains, wide seas, and none to rely on:
Your days of bitter suffering will have no end.

While you will be abroad, your darling is in China;
The two of you each will be at an edge of the sky.
Your darling there in China will not have a partner,
While you in those foreign lands will drift about.

As Soon as You See an Aba, You are Frightened[32]

The city of Singapore looks very prosperous;
The people on the streets ride in electric cars.[33]
On both sides the glass lamps are thousands;
Chinese and foreign merchants are a million.

In Singapore they've built an iron suspension bridge;
Wu Yi has constructed it with great craftsmanship.

---

[31] Literally, "uncles and cousins."
[32] Huang Huoxing 1982, 281–282.
[33] Steam trams had serviced Singapore from 1885 to 1894. Electric trams serviced Singapore from 1905 to 1927, by which time they had been replaced by electric trolley buses (York and Phillips 1996, 5–35). First experiments with an electric tramway, however, date from 1891–1892 (York and Phillips 1996, 13–14).

Under the bridge he didn't use any supporting pillars;
He used heavenly pylons form which it is hanging.[34]

Across the bridge you come to the warehouses;
As soon as you see an *aba*,[35] you are frightened.
You'll be searched, I reckon, all over your body.
He speaks a foreign tongue you don't understand.

Once past the warehouses you walk on again;
Even when strong, southern winds are not cool.
You do not know to speak that foreign tongue;
A lively conversation here is called *langtao*.

With angle and line you angle for some *rugan*;
When you catch *rugan*, you take it to *jiaowan*.
When you come there, *jiaowan* is not at home:
Sheying jiaji and *yelan*.[36]

The most detestable thing here is the tin trucks:
Never moving to the side, coming straight down.
On Liushifutou there is really no end of them;
On purpose and deliberately — a pain in the ass!

In front of the gate of big shots flowers grow,
While our places are all taken away by them.

---

[34] This description fits the Cavenagh Bridge, a suspension bridge across the lower reaches of the Singapore River in downtown Singapore. The bridge dates from 1870. It should be pointed out, however, that the Elgin Bridge upstream from the Cavenagh Bridge in local Chinese usage is also designated as an "iron suspension bridge" (tiediaoqiao 鐵吊橋). The Cavenagh Bridge was originally constructed in Liverpool. It must be a local Chinese legend to credit its design to Wu Yi 吳義, an iron-smith from Sanzhen in Jiaoling, even though many local Chinese workmen will have been involved in the actual installation of the bridge.

[35] Aba is Malay for a policeman, in this case most likely a Sikh.

[36] Huang Huoxing identifies these Malay expressions as follows: *rugan* means "fish"; *jiaowan* means "friends"; *sheying* means "alas"; *jiaji* means "feet"; and *yelan* means "to walk".

Don't say that you and I are of no use at all —
How I hate those many high and mighty men.

I operate my business over at Jianwai,
Without a single relative to help me out.
I can't speak even half a word of Malay,
But fortunately, dear, you can teach me.

I Urge You my Boy Don't Leave for Nanyang (a dialogue song)[37]

My darling, you want to go abroad and say goodbye;
Those foreign lands are a thousand miles from China.
Crossing the oceans will mean many bitter sufferings;
You shouldn't do it — you'd better stay where you are.

Without food, without clothes — life is unbearable,
So I've thought long and hard and will go abroad.
My darling wife, don't be too worried about it all:
Once I have made money, I'll come back to China.

Time and again you say you intend to go abroad;
But once you're in those foreign lands, then what?
When you get to the Southern Oceans, life is hard —
How can you serve out the three years as *sinkeh*?

Coming down from Sanzhen, we get to Yuzi Lake —
My darling, you had better not try to make me stay.
It is really extremely difficult for me to leave you,
But alas, back here at home I can't make a living.

Those foreign lands are not the place we belong;
There you won't be plowing fields or raising ducks.
Whether we are poor or rich, we'll get through —
Brayberries everywhere are the same flower.

---

[37] Huang Huoxing 1982, 276–277.

Darling, when I hear you, my heart is in pain;
As we are holding hands, our tears don't stop.
But if I now would be following your advice,
We'll have nothing to eat and nothing to wear.

I urge you, my boy, don't leave for Nanyang;
The human heart is unpredictable like the sea.
If you leave me behind, I'll have no support —
You can't take the key, can't guard the house.

My dear wife, you talk to me in bitter words;
Now I set out, I'll meet with many adversities.
My idea has never been to leave you behind,
But because we are so poor, I've no options.

Dear, I wouldn't dare complain about poverty;
Coarse tea and bland rice are enough for me.
If you'll stay at home, poverty too will be fine:
Being together, being a couple beats millions!

My dear wife, it's no good to cry and cry on —
At most I will be gone for a number of years.
When I'll have made money, I will come back,
So our family, old and young, will be reunited.

My husband, you really have thought about it.
I have something to say, now don't take it badly:
Don't fall in love with those pretty foreign girls,
On no account cause me to come and seek you.

My dear wife, I am clear about that in my mind:
Your husband is a man who's honest and loyal.
An irregular relationship can never last for long;
Only husband and wife stay forever together.

All through the night I've talked to you, till dawn,
But to my regret I've failed to talk you around.

My tears are streaming down, falling on your body;
You're concerned about me — my guts are aching.

It is not only me who is crossing the wide oceans;
Trusting Heaven, I'll follow what fate will dispose.
When I think of my family, I can't get thru the day —
Forced to go to foreign lands I'll be carrying tin ore.

A Young Wife Seeing off Her Husband as He is Going Abroad[38]

I see off my dear darling as he is going abroad:
Please beware of evil people while on the road.
While you were still at home, all days were fine,
But out on the road you will be miserably alone.

I see off my dear darling all the way to Xiyang:
You are hurt in your heart, I'm hurt in my guts.
In future when the moon is full at Mid-Autumn,
We each will be separately watching the moon.

I see off my dear darling as far as Bingcun Village:
Furtively I stretch our my hand, pull at his clothes,
And then I softly whisper in my dear darling's ear:
Make sure to come back home within a few years.

I see off my dear darling to the Palace of Guanyin;
The bodhisattva Guanyin displays a happy smile.
I burn incense, light a candle, and make three bows:
"Protect my husband and grant him a safe journey!"

I see off my dear darling through the Pengla Rapids;
Riding a boat through these rapids is risky business.
The rocks have sharp points and the water runs fast —
Those many thoughts and worries that fill my heart.

---

[38] Luo Kequn 2000, 354–355; Huang Ziya 2003, 173–174.

I see off my dear darling all the way to Threerivers —
How hard it is to say goodbye to my darling lover!
You want to know how much my heart is suffering?
Even more numerous than the waves are my tears.

I see off my dear darling to the prefectural capital;
Below Xiangzi's Bridge I am really quite frightened.
Then there is Lord Guan, more horrific than ghosts,[39]
Scaring us in the boat so much our faces turn ashen.

I see off my dear darling all the way to Shantou city;
As soon as I see that wide ocean, I'm worried sick.
That wide ocean may be large but still has bounds,
Whereas my love for you will never reach its end.

I see off my dear darling all the way to the quay.
As he steps on the steamer, we both are bobbing.
When that steamer has left, it can easily return,
But once my lover is gone, he cannot come back.

I see off my dear darling as far as up the steamer;
When the ship's whistle blows, it rips up my heart.
When merchants return from those foreign lands,
Send me money and news, to tell me you're fine.

Hoping for My Husband's Return to China, Ten Songs[40]

First of all I hope that my husband will be in good health;
Make sure to have three meals of boiled tea and hot rice.
Rise early each morning in order to have your cold bath;
When sleeping at night, don't catch a cold — use a blanket!

---

[39] Lord Guan is the deified Guan Yu 關羽, who by the end of the Qing dynasty had become one of the most widely revered deities. He is usually depicted as a general, fully armed. See Diesinger 1984; Duara 1988; Haar 2000; Moore 2003.
[40] Huang Huoxing 1982, 280–281.

Secondly I hope that my husband will not love flowers:
By picking those flowers you'll harm yourself in the end.
You'd better not love those public women of the world —
Once your money is gone, they turn into your enemies.

Thirdly I hope that my husband won't go for gambling;
Of each ten men who love gambling, nine end up broke.
The greatest gambler was project developer Wu Sanbao,
But even Sanbao had to sell everything that he owned.[41]

Fourthly I hope that my husband will think of his family;
Most important of all, dear, don't get addicted to opium.
Once you use opium, you'll turn into a bag of bones;
You'll waste all the money you have, only harming yourself.

Fifthly I hope that my husband will write letters home;
Please, my dear darling, please remember these words.
Whenever you meet a messenger, let him carry a letter;
Seeing a letter is like seeing you already back home.

Sixthly I hope that my husband will make a fortune;
By diligence and frugal thrift that can be achieved.
By accumulating small savings you'll make it happen;
Then hire a huge boat and bring it all back with you.

Seventhly I hope that my husband will open a tin mine;
Don't fear any adversities in developing your tin mine.
Then when one day you will have collected much tin,
Load it all on a boat and take it to Mountains of Gold.[42]

---

[41] Huang Huoxing provides the following note: Wu Sanbao was a man from Xingning who made a career from gambling. In those days the following folk song circulated: Whether gambling is good or bad/ You should ask Wu Sanbao: / With his own hands he built a shopping mall, / With his own hands he had to sell it all.
[42] San Francisco.

Eighthly I hope that my husband will have a big business
And make thousands, ten thousands of ounces of gold,
So when you later come home with your gold and silver,
Oxen must carry the rattan cases, and horses the boxes.

Ninthly I hope my husband will guard against evil men:
Three steps outside the gate you have to be prudent.
First of all guard against the depredations by thieves;
Secondly guard against secret attempts on your life.

Tenthly I hope my husband will soon return to China
And then bring back home all the money he's made.
First of all, you can then be together with your darling;
Secondly, you can then be together with your parents.

A Selection of Individual Mountain Songs[43]

My darling has gone abroad so we are now separated;
Mandarin-ducks but broken apart — so truly miserable!
I've so much to say yet there's no one who talks to me,
So nobody knows all these many sorrows in my heart.

My darling is leaving today because he is going abroad,
And so doing he's leaving me here behind, here in China.
Leaving you're a young man, on your return you'll be old —
Even if you make many millions, how can we enjoy them?

My darling is living abroad and I am living in China,
So we are living each at a different edge of the sky.
I here in China do not have any matching partner,
While you there in foreign parts are drifting about.

I take out my chopsticks and beat on this bronze gong:
Hasn't my overseas husband done me great wrong?
When he lacked money he said he couldn't come back,
Now he has cash he says he is marrying a local broad.

---

[43] Zhong Junkun 2009, 168.

APPENDIX I

AN OLD AND A NEW *TEN-MILE PAVILION*

This appendix provides translations of two additional versions of the tale of *Ten Mile Pavilion*. The first text translated here is a narrative ballad printed in the 19th century that was collected by Cynthia Brokaw in the context of her research on the popular printers of Sibao in Western Fujian. This edition originally consisted of thirteen sheets, but the first sheet is missing[1] and the upper part of the left-hand side of the second sheet is damaged. This is a very simple and crude production, in which the story is reduced to a minimum. The main protagonist (called Young Master Ma 馬公子 in this version) catches a glimpse of the beautiful Liu Xiuying during a visit to town and decides to "snatch her flower" during the night. He makes his way to her room and sweet-talks his way into her bed. The lovers know they will never be able to become a couple, and Liu Xiuying not only offers to help him out financially when he does marry, but even gives him a number a practical tips on how to select a proper wife. This 19th century version of *Ten-Mile Pavilion* appears to be the direct or indirect source of all later adaptations.

---

[1] The right-hand side of the first sheet may well have been used as the title page.

The second text translated here hails from Yongding in Fujian, where it was performed by Lan Ruiteng 藍瑞騰 e.a., and recorded by Jin He 金河 and 金田 in 1990 in Zhongxiang village. The text is included in *Zhongguo geyao jicheng: Fujian juan* (2007: 605–609) as "Liu Xiuying and Chen Chunmei" (Li Xiuying yu Chen Chunmei 李秀英與陳春美). The text is followed by a short note from the editors:

> This song is also known as *The New Ten-Mile Pavilion* (*Xin shiliting* 新十里亭). Based on the relevant materials of comprehensive research into popular literature, there is both a version in four-line stanzas and a version in five-line bamboo-beat stanzas, and their content is roughly the same. This version is the five-line bamboo-beat stanza version.

The version from Yongding closely follows the text of *Ten-Mile Pavilion* translated in Part Two for the first part up to the seduction, but it omits mentioning the girl's engagement and the impossibility of a marriage. The text actually hints that the boy and the girl have fallen in love with each other at first sight because she is said to have smiled at him. The section on the couple's lovemaking is much reduced in length. The girl then sees her lover off but references to the examinations have practically all been removed and the girl ends by asking the boy to make sure a matchmaker will come and ask for her hand so the two of them can be properly married. The alternative title, *The New Ten-Mile Pavilion,* suggests that this is a deliberate rewriting in line with cultural policies of the 1950s (such as the campaign for the introduction of the New Marriage Law) and later, that turns a tale of a torrid one-night stand into a story of true and mutual love. One recent commentator accordingly characterizes *Ten-Mile Pavilion* as "a representative ballad on the pursuit of free love by people in the old society".[2] Dramatic adaptations, usually called *The New Ten-Mile Pavilion,* indeed turn the story into one of mutual love that overcomes all parental opposition.

***

---

[2] You Shengzhong 2012. "Free love" in this context means the freedom of young people to select their own marriage partner.

Ten-Mile Pavilion

[Xiuying] was dressed in a red blouse and green jacket,
And a skirt with a hundred plaits — each color so fresh!
She was fitted out like a female immortal from heaven,
Like Chang'e in the moon who descends to this world.
    When men saw how beautiful Xiuying was, [they hoped]
That Xiuying on seeing them would flash them a smile,
But she would hastily make herself scarce and go back,
Hastily moving her lotus feet outside the orchid gate.
    As soon as our hero had seen her, he was dumb-struck;
For half an hour he did not say any word [but thought:]
"If I could only be together with her behind bed-curtains,
I'd be happy to die and descend to the Yellow Springs!"[3]

When he had returned home, and had gone back inside,
All he wanted to do was to make love to this Xiuying:
"From here to her house is not more than twenty miles,
So let me be a snatcher of flowers for one time tonight."
    When the sun sank in the west and evening had fallen,
He went back to her place, all dressed up, to the gate.

...

Lightly, so lightly he pried open the door to her room.

...

When he first stroked the girl, she remained deep asleep,
When he again stroked the girl, she turned herself around.
When he stroked her a third time, she was still in a haze,
But loudly cried: "A thief!" and woke up with that shout.
    She cried out three times but there came no answer:
"Could it be that my room has produced a monster?
Could it be that robbers have broken into the house?
Could it be that a demon at midnight misleads me?
    What is the business that brought you to this house?
I will cry for help and have you arrested by servants!

---

[3] The Yellow Springs are the world of the dead.

When you're taken to the magistrate for interrogation,
Even a thousand tongues won't be able to set you free.
   Once they start to interrogate you as a common thief,
The royal law burns like an oven and shows no mercy.
So I advise you to leave this place as soon as possible,
So you will be spared the magistrate's punishments!"

When the young man heard her speak in this manner,
He was so scared his body was covered in cold sweat,
And only after a quite a while he answered her thusly:
"Intelligent young lady, please listen to what I'll say.
   I am not some bewitching demon or monster at all,
And I also am not a ghost who is out to mislead you.
I did not enter into your room in order to be a thief,
I am not such a lowlife, a person bereft of all virtue!
   I am the son and heir of the Ma family here in the city,
At twenty I'm a young man in the prime of his youth.
I am the son of a family that is both rich and noble,
My hope is to share your couch, on a single cushion.
   When yesterday I passed your family's flower garden,
I saw you, my girl, the one who aroused my desires!
From early till late my longing was focused on you,
And tonight at this hour I have entered your room.
   Now let us discuss this together, both you and me:
All I hope is that you, my girl, will do me a favor.
If you, my girl, tonight are willing to do me a favor,
I'll not forget your love, even when dead and buried."

When Xiuying heard him speak in such a manner,
She lowered her head and also did not say one word.
Only after quite a while did she answer him thusly:
"You are a student of books, yet speak such words!
   I turned sixteen this year and through a matchmaker
Have been engaged to a man who is surnamed Wang.
My husband-to-be is also the son of a noble family
And like you he is a student in the prefectural school.

I am the future wife of one who studies the books;
As an official's daughter I cannot act in this manner.
I see that you are not the son of some poor family,
But yet you want to act as a man bereft of all virtue.
   If you seduce another man's wife, it can't last long:
The royal law is hot like an oven, showing no mercy.
I urge you to go back home as quickly as possible,
We'll each have to marry our own marriage partner.
   The matchmaker's words may predestine my death,
But for raping a virgin you will be sent to the army.
Even a stalwart hero will be given fifty lashes,
So a rapist is bound to be subjected to torture!
   If I tonight would give in to your sincere request,
The two of us would equally share in the crime.
If we were arrested and led before the magistrate,
I'm afraid that we both will lose our good name!
   You are right now a person who studies the books,
So how on earth can you conceive such a desire?
Make yourself scarce, go home as quick as you can,
Otherwise you will be struck by disaster one day!"

When the young man heard her speak in this way,
He was dumbstruck and couldn't speak for a while.
Only after he had pondered her words, he replied:
"Xiuying, my dear girl, please allow me to speak.
   Wine and sex, money and honor all people love,
Even the Queen-Mother of the West has affairs!
My dear girl, if you now refuse to do me a favor,
You must be a person with innards made of iron!
   Chang'e in the moon may have sworn off marriage,
But Weaving Maiden sleeps with her Buffalo Boy.
   Fourth Sister once long ago slept with Cui Wenrui;
Seventh Sister once long ago slept with Dong Yong.
Third Sister once long ago slept with Liu Wenxi,
And the Immortal Maiden flirted with Lü Dongbin.

Green-Coat once made a pass at the girl named Liu,
And Ruilai made a pass, filled with worldly longing.[4]
While Lanying once long ago slept with He Wenxiu,[5]
Wang Shipeng once long ago slept with Qian Yulian.[6]

　　Master Peng's life was set to end at eight hundred,
But Old Zhang still had affairs at twenty thousand.
When yesterday I happened to pass by a monastery,
I saw there an arhat fondling the bodhisattva Guanyin.

　　If even gods and immortals engage in amorous affairs,
You cannot be surprised that mortal men have desires!
It is only Buddha in heaven who is clear like a mirror —
But who knows whether that is a lie or perhaps a fact.

　　Which gauze skirt does not trail along the ground?
Which tomcat is not filled by springtime thoughts?

---

[4] Ruilai is likely to be a mistake for Ruilan 瑞蘭. She is the female protagonist of the early Ming *chuanqi* play *Praying to the Moon* (*Baiyue ji* 拜月記; also known as *Yougui ji* 幽閨記, an adaptation of an earlier *zaju* play *The Pavilion for Praying to the Moon* [*Baiyue ting* 拜月庭] by Guan Hanqing 關漢卿). She is the daughter of a Jin-dynasty minister when the Mongols attack the Jin-dynasty capital. Fleeing the city with her mother, she is soon separated from her, after which she meets the student Jiang Shilong 蔣世隆 and falls in love with him. For safety's sake the couple claim to be husband and wife, but they soon end up living together as husband and wife, until she is found by her father who takes her home with him. Eventually the couple is reunited when Jiang passes the examinations as Top-of-the List. See West and Idema 2010, 70–105, "A Beauty Pining in her Boudoir: The Pavilion for Praying to the Moon".

[5] He Wenxiu 何文秀 is the male protagonist of *The Jade Hairpin* (*Yuchai Ji* 玉釵記), an extremely complicated *chuanqi* play. In some versions of later adaptations of this play, his main female counterpart is Wang Lanying 王蘭英. After this high-born young lady has bestowed her favors on He Wenxiu, the lovers are separated to be reunited after many adventures.

[6] Wang Shipeng 王十朋 and Qian Yulian 錢玉蓮 are the protagonists of *The Thorn Hairpin* (*Jingchai ji* 荊釵記), a high popular *chuanqi* play from the 14th or 15th century. Qian Yulian rejects a rich suitor and marries the poor student Wang Shipeng. When Wang passes the examinations, he refuses to marry a minister's wife and is banished to the borders. Despite the machinations of the villain, Qian Yulian remains loyal to her husband and after many adventures the couple is eventually happily reunited. See Birch 1973.

Which burning fire does not produce any smoke?
And which young man is not obsessed with sex?
   In one day you can sell a fake smile three times,
But in three days it's hard to buy one true lover.
If a man doesn't desire women, he's a silly fool;
If a girl doesn't desire a man, she's a pure idiot.
   If a snake doesn't bite a man, it is only an eel;
If a wasp doesn't sting men, it is a buzzing fly.
Even horses drop their reins to save their masters,
And dogs have the loyalty to rescue their owners.
   If animals still are filled with springtime desires,
How can you blame a young man for his passion?
I this young man am a boy who is filled by love,
So how could you, dear girl, be without feelings?
   If you, dear girl, are not willing to do me a favor,
I will die here in this room, not leaving the house.
Don't think then that I will not demand your life:
I will visit every court, requesting your presence."[7]

When Xiuying heard him speak in this manner,
[She answered:] "Dear student, please listen to me.
Your speech floors each and every human being,
Your speech brings even the deceased back to life.
   Thirty people of ancient times you've discussed,
Even those devoid of reason you fill with desire.
Fine words and crafty language: you speak so well
You now even have succeeded in persuading me.
   I have made up my mind to grant your request,
But never broadcast my name to the outside world.
A dead tree sprouts flowers because of its heart;
A dumb person won't speak even though he wants.
   Swallows carrying loam won't open their mouth;

---

[7] The young man threatens that if Liu Xiuying causes his suicide by refusing his request, he will insist on calling her as a witness when he is questioned on the facts of his life in the ten courts of the underworld.

Crows create trouble because of inside emotions.[8]
Don't tell of me to your friends and your buddies;
Don't mention my name to parents and relatives.
   Don't say that such and such a family has a girl
Who lost her virtue when you snatched her flower.
Today the two of us meet for the very first time,
I do not yet know how your heart matches mine."

With both hands he pulled aside the red bed curtains:
A pair of mandarin-ducks united in phoenix feelings:
When he had undressed, he was whiter than snow;
When she had undressed, she was whiter than frost.
   She acted the lion that lacks eyes and falls down;
He acted the bright ball that rolled atop of her body.
She pulled up the blanket and covered her lover;
Breast on breast and legs entwined they made love.
   When he put his golden pin into her lotus flower,
The girl furrowed her brow and called out to him:
"Darling, I am an untouched flower of only sixteen,
Please be careful when you go about your business."
   She resembled a dried-out field that receives rain:
A young man's devotion equals a thousand ounces!
   In the first section of the first watch their love is intense,
He resembles a dragon that sets out from its grotto gate.[9]
That dragon sports in the water to its heart's content:
"My darling, tonight you should make a special effort!"
   In the second section of the second watch their love is hot:
He resembles a ravenous tiger that is leaving the hills.
And if that tiger can dine on the flesh of swine or sheep,
It doesn't care whether it lives or dies, may lose its life.
   In the third section of the third watch their love is intense:

---

[8] Crows are hated by humans because their call is believed to be inauspicious.
[9] All rivers and lakes are home to dragons that often manifest themselves as snakes.

He resembles Zhou Cang who sets outs his battalions.[10]
When he sets out fully decided he has such great fun,
But when he returns he lacks intention to put in effort.

In the fourth section of the fourth watch their love is hot,
He resembles a honey bee that probes the flower's heart.
The honey bee probes the flower, probes it in its heart —
The young man's sophistication arouses one's heart!

In the fifth section of the fifth watch their love is intense,
But alas, the golden rooster announces that dawn arrives.
The two of them have produced a good night of romance,
But now they are separated and the two will have to part.

"The golden rooster announces dawn," the girl tells him,
And lightly embracing her lover they get out of the bed.
A handkerchief around her head down to her eyebrows —
In this way she also gets up in order to see her lover off.

She opens the leather boxes and selects some articles,
Takes out some gifts as presents for her parting lover.
She gives him one fan that is speckled with gold dust,[11]
And give him one lotus pouch of embroidered brocade.

"Theses kind of objects I can dispense with, but I cannot
Dispense with this one night of love of my darling lover.
Don't consider my gifts as too few — they may be cheap
But I come at a price of a thousand ounces of silver."

When the two of them had entered into the kitchen,
She opened a bottle of rice wine of three years old,
And she told her darling to drink without a worry —
With her own hand she poured her lover three cups.

"Those with karma will meet despite a thousand miles;

---

[10] Zhou Cang 周倉 is a famous character in the 16th century novel *Romance of the Three Kingdoms*. He is a fine warrior and a stalwart supporter of Guan Yu. In pictures of the divinized Guan Yu he is often shown standing behind his master, holding a long lance.

[11] "Speckled with gold dust" is a very tentative translation. The corresponding characters are very blurred in the original.

Those without karma even face to face will not meet.
So I urge you, my lover, now empty these three cups,
Then the two of us, hand in hand, go through the gate.
   My darling, your body is actually covered in sweat,
So how could I not be concerned about your health?
Only last night the two of us formed a couple, a pair,
But this morning we are separated, each east or west.
   In order to come here you walked a full twenty miles,
So it's proper that I will accompany you for ten miles."

She accompanied her lover to the One-Mile Pavilion;
Holding his hand she walked with him all the way.
   "In the high hall your father and mother are still alive;
To bring you up they didn't allow themselves any rest.
In the ten months of pregnancy she suffered greatly;[12]
Three years of suckling and feeding — like an ocean!
   In one day you three times drank your mother's milk;
In three days you drank her milk for nine full meals.
During the day she wiped your shit, at night your pee;
And during the night she slept with you in her arms.
   When the left side was dry, she had you sleep there;
When the right side was wet, your mother slept there.
And if you had wetted both sides of the mattress, she
Would hold you in her arms all night till early dawn.
   For three years, for five years they would nurture you,
Then hire a teacher to instruct you in the Five Classics.
By studying books you understand rites and humanity,
And the two words 'filial piety' are clearly explained.
   If you honor your father and mother, you're a filial son;
When you obey your two parents, you are a good child.
Those who are filial and obedient will have filial sons;
Those who are willful and bad will have evil offspring.

---

[12] In China a pregnancy is said to last ten months, counting from the month of conception to the month of birth.

I give you honest advice because of my love for you;
But this secret in my heart I will never tell to others."

She accompanied her lover to the Two-Mile Pavilion;
As she was holding his hand, she told her true feelings:
"Old and young in one family must live in harmony;
Family harmony is worth a thousand ounces of silver.
   Brothers shouldn't fight for the sake of their mother:
The thousand brayberry flowers grow on one tree.
In fighting a tiger nothing beats a band of brothers;
Nothing beats an army of fathers and sons in battle.
   If other people argue, you should urge them to stop;
Never should you harm other people with your words.
My dear brother, make an effort to memorize this all;
Don't think that my blabbering is only floating clouds."

She accompanied her lover to the Three-Mile Pavilion:
"Never involve yourself in affairs of right and wrong.
On no account take the case to the district magistrate —
I'm afraid that you may offend the magistrate's star.
   The outcome of a court case is overgrown weeds;
In the halls of imperial law no mercy is ever shown.
A wild wind only travels over empty-headed weeds;
A court case only victimizes evil-minded people.
   Listen like a true friend to a true friend's words:
My darling, my love, store these all in your heart."

She accompanied her lover to the Four-Mile Pavilion,
As they were walking together, she told her true mind.
"I urge you never to hang out on those flower streets,
Don't become one of those libertine wastrels and rakes.
   An affair with another man's wife can never last long,
You will have to conclude a marriage on your own.
When you are going to marry, come and inform me,
And I will provide you with several ounces of silver.

When you are going to marry, you must inspect her,
Don't stay at home and rely on a matchmaker's words.
Those matchmakers are women who are out to please,
In this world they have deceived thousands of people.
    Never marry a woman with unkempt hair or big feet:
Chewing his eyeballs out, she'll boss her master about.
One with nicely curved eyebrows makes a good wife:
She understands love and duty and will be intelligent.
    When you will marry a woman who is exactly like me,
You'll be able to live in joy and I won't have to worry.
But if the girl you will marry is quite different from me,
The two of us can only continue this affair as before!"

She accompanied her lover to the Five-Mile Pavilion:
Holding her lover's hand she told him her true feelings:
"Never commit any deed you have to be ashamed of,
And you will feel no fear stepping outside at midnight.
    Never visit the places where people gamble for money;
Once you start stealing coppers, your heart is destroyed.
When you will have sold off your movable belongings,
You will end up selling all your fields to other people.
    And if then one day you'll be without any rice to eat,
There's no one on whom to rely when hunger arrives.
When you have rice and wine you have many brothers,
But when you are in need, you won't see any of them.
    A poor man living at a busy market will see no visitors;
A rich man living in the hills has many distant relatives.
In this world it's a good thing to have money and goods;
People respect your clothes — they don't respect the man.
    Money and goods are a treasure for feeding your family;
Thousands of devious schemes cannot ensure one success.
As long as you have money, you will have many friends,
But without money when ill you'll be treated like scum.
    My dear lover, make great effort to store in your heart
All these many words of advice that I am offering you."

She accompanied her lover to the Six-Mile Pavilion;
Holding her lover's hand, she told her true feelings.
"My darling, when you came the road was pitch dark;
You were all alone by yourself, without any servant.

  Whenever a bird stirred on its nest, you were afraid;
Whenever the wind moved the grass, you felt scared.
You feared that a tiger might emerge from the hills,
Or were afraid that a storm might suddenly start out.

  I urge you, my lover, don't show off your courage
By traveling at night all alone, without a companion.
When waves are high in a storm, don't ford the stream;
Be careful when boarding a boat or riding a horse.

  If you lose your way when traveling somewhere
I back in my room would never receive the news."

She accompanied her lover to the Seven-Mile Pavilion:
"My darling, don't go after the wives of other men.
When they see you have money, they show friendship;
When they see you lack money, they turn elsewhere.

  They provide wine and food in order to entertain you;
With sweet and crafty words they'll arouse your heart.
They want you to provide them with hairpins of gold;
They want silver from you for rings on their fingers.

  They want you to provide them with clothes to wear;
All dolled-up they seem to be beckoning customers.
While healthy and strong you pursue your pleasure,
But on whom can you rely when your money's gone?

  Look only at the face of the woman who is your own,
Never try to approach the body of another man's wife.
The turtle dove is a bird that is bereft of all feeling;
A public woman is a creature that's bereft of all love.

  When you have coppers and spend them at her place,
She puts aside all shame but she lacks a conscience.
To your face she will only speak of loyalty and love,
But in her heart she already thinks of somebody else.

She showers you with sweet words and crafty lies,
But she is also afraid that her husband will find out.
The coffin is the bushel in which humans are weighed;
A lascivious woman is actually a ghost from a grave.
   The adder hiding in bamboos, or the sting of a wasp:
Nothing surpasses in poison the heart of a woman!
If you don't believe me, look around you in the village,
And you'll see how many men she will have ruined.
   Make sure to remember well the words that I tell you,
Don't dare treat them as wind passing by your ears!"

She accompanied her lover to the Eight-Mile Pavilion;
Holding hands, the twosome walked the road together.
"You are the son of a family that is rich and noble,
But don't even dare think of leaving and setting out.
   Even if you would have traveled all roads of the world,
You still would find that all kinds of business are hard,
And I'm afraid that if by chance things would go wrong,
You, all alone without a friend, wouldn't make progress.
   If you would lose your capital, things still would be fine:
A long and healthy life is the most precious thing of all.
Wealth and poverty are determined by heaven and fate:
Darling, remember well the words that I speak to you!"

She accompanied her lover to the Nine-Mile Pavilion;
While they were walking together, she told her feelings.
"My dear, I urge you never be seduced by wild flowers —
Those wild flowers have ruined thousands of people!
   Even when cold and lonely, don't go to their places;
Don't go to these women's houses for all the fine food.
A girl who loves you will know when you are lonely,
But those unfeeling whores display no understanding.
   Those whores actually are women without any feeling,
On no account should you go and visit their bordellos.
What I have been telling, my darling, is all the truth;
I've explained it to you in all detail, each little point."

She accompanied her lover to the Ten-Mile Pavilion,
And inside the pavilion she spoke her true feelings.
"I urge you, dear, don't become a traveling merchant:
When your clothes are worn, no one will repair them.
 And there is this: never, yes never smoke any opium!
That opium has ruined even the most talented persons.
That opium is really a herb that breaks one's heart —
Once you become addicted you end up as a criminal.
 I now have told you everything you need to know:
One person should never display a duplicitous mind.
You've still ten miles to go of your way back home,
Now be very careful as you make your way back."

If there are people who have been a romantic rake,
They should read *Ten-Mile Pavilion* to the very end;
They should read the full text of *Ten-Mile Pavilion*
And as long as they live on earth remember it well.

Li Xiuying and Chen Chunmei

Ever since Pangu opened up heaven and earth,[13]
Each Son of Heaven has had his own ministers.
But let's not talk of the stories in earlier writings,
Let me start out by singing of Ten-Mile Pavilion.
Now please all be quiet and listen with attention.

Now please all be quiet and listen with attention.
In Nanjing there once lived a certain Li Xiangting
Who was famed far and wide for his great wealth.
He had not only five sons but also two daughters,
And these two daughters surpassed all in beauty.

And these two daughters surpassed all in beauty.
The name of the younger sister was Li Xiuying.

---

[13] According to one Chinese origin myth, heaven and earth were made out of the body of the giant Pangu 盤古 upon his death.

Xiuying had reached the sweet age of eighteen;
Her face was quite pretty and her figure was fine:
She looked as beautiful as a heavenly immortal.

She looked as beautiful as a heavenly immortal.
Her mind was quick, her hands were nimble: a smart girl!
She excelled on the zither and in go, calligraphy and painting,
Was an expert in embroidering flowers, sketching phoenixes.
Throughout the prefecture of Nanjing she was quite famous.

Throughout the prefecture of Nanjing she was quite famous.
Let me now sing of a young man who was surnamed Chen:
In that city there lived a young man called Chen Chunsheng.
With clear eyebrows and sparkling eyes he cut quite a figure:
It seemed as if Pan An had been reborn down here on earth.

It seemed as if Pan An had been reborn down here on earth.
He was obsessed with the thought of marrying Li Xiuying.
One day when he was walking though the city of Nanjing,
It just so happened he came across the girl of his dreams —
The butterfly loves the flower through a karmic affinity!

The butterfly loves the flower through a karmic affinity:
As soon as he saw that Xiuying, his desire was aroused.
He was like a fish that has drunk water troubled by lime —
When you don't throw in alum, the water won't clear.
His only thought was to tie the marriage knot with her.

His only thought was to tie the marriage knot with her.
When he saw that the young lady flashed him a smile,
The young man watched her with wide-open eyes —
Dumbstruck like a wooden rooster he didn't move,
And overcome by love-longing he went back home.

And overcome by love-longing he went back home:
During the day he desired her, at night he desired her.

"If I could obtain Li Xiuying as my mate and partner,
I would sacrifice a huge pig's head to the divinities."
The bodhisattva makes fun of those addled by love!

The bodhisattva makes fun of those addled by love.
His servant boy asked him what was bothering him,
And the young man replied he was filled with love,
So filled with love he could not sleep at all at night:
"In vain I waste the prime years of my young life!

"In vain I waste the prime years of my young life!
I'm only thinking of that young lady Li Xiuying.
Day and night I long for her but I see no solution,
So I look so bedraggled and know no peace at all.
But I'll dredge up that needle from the ocean floor!"

But I'll dredge up that needle from the ocean floor!
The servant then lowered his voice, offering his plan:
"In such and such way you can get close to the lady.
You'll only have to give it your all for days on end —
Even an iron post can be polished into a tiny needle!"

Even an iron post can be polished into a tiny needle.
In this world one fears those whose minds are fixed.
Now his mind was made up, he left as fast as he could;
His servant boy led the way as they set out on the road,
And straightaway they came to the Li family mansion.

And straightaway they came to the Li family mansion.
He hid himself in the flower garden near the lotus pond.
Then he saw a servant girl appear, who lighted a lamp.
He explained to her his amorous purpose in great detail:
"I implore you, dear girl, to link us two with a red string."[14]

---

[14] A man and a woman who are destined to marry each other are tied together with a red string by the Old Man in the Moon according to a well-known tale from the Tang dynasty.

I implore you, dear girl, to link us two with a red string!
When the servant girl heard that, she was secretly scared:
"To help him in raping the young lady counts as a crime,
Showing up in this place this man must be filled with gall,
How could I dare help him out by providing an opening?"

How could I dare help him out by providing an opening?
But again he implored the servant girl to be of assistance:
"If you could serve as Magpie Bridge for our rendezvous,
It would resemble the union of Lady White and Xu Xian:[15]
I would be filled with gratitude for your immense favor!"

I would be filled with gratitude for your immense favor.
When that servant girl saw how true and sincere he was,
She promised she would help him out in tying the string.
With this firm idea she went back and entered the room,
And the servant boy hid himself in the shade of a willow.

And the servant boy hid himself in the shade of a willow.
The servant girl softly called and instructed the young man:
"I see that you are carrying a dagger for your protection,
Use that and softly so softly pry open the door of her room.
Then push open the door so you can get close to her body."

---

[15] Lady White (Bai) is a white snake who, after a thousand years of cultivation, has attained the ability to take on human shape. As a young widow (dressed in the white of mourning) she appears on the banks Hangzhou's West Lake and seduces the drug store assistant Xu Xian. The couple is quickly married, but it soon turns out that her presents to her husband are stolen, so Xu Xian is first banished to Suzhou, and later to Zhenjiang. There the monk Fahai tries to free Xu Xian from his infatuation with this demon, but because their karmic affinity is not yet finished, he allows him to return to Hangzhou. When the couple has been reunited there, Fahai shows up after some time and imprisons Lady White below the Thunder-Peak Pagoda near the Westlake. In later versions of the legend, Fahai waits until she has given birth to a son and it is this son who will eventually liberate his mother. Modern interpretations of this widely popular legend stress the pure love between Lady White and Xu Xian. See Idema 2009c.

Then push open the door so you can get close to her body.
Inside the room the only light was that of an oil lamp.
He wanted to say some words to comfort the young girl,
But as she didn't know him, he had no idea what to say.
So he pulled aside the bed-curtains to have a good look.

So he pulled aside the bed-curtains to have a good look.
But then that girl all of a sudden turned herself around
And cried out: "Who are you, from where do you come?
In the middle of the night you dare enter my bedroom!"
She immediately wanted to cry for help to arrest him.

She immediately wanted to cry for help to arrest him,
But the young man addressed her, explaining his case:
"I don't care for wealth and status in the world of men,
I only want to be married to you, my dear young lady!
One night as husband and wife means love for all times."

One night as husband and wife means love for all times.
When the young girl heard this, she was filled with fury.
"I advise you to immediately leave through that door.
If you don't make yourself scarce, I'll call the servants,
And then you'll find it impossible to flee with your life."

And then you'll find it impossible to flee with your life.
He politely addressed her, saying: "Please listen to me.
Dear lady, I am not a bandit and I also am not a thief,
I'm the son of a noble family and a student of books,
And my only wish is to become your wedded husband.

"And my only wish is to become your wedded husband.
At present I've just reached the young age of twenty.
I implore you, young lady, to show me some mercy,
To show mercy for me and my undivided devotion —
For all eternity I will never forget your love for me!"

For all eternity I will never forget your love for me —
The young lady pondered the matter and then spoke;
Lightly opening her red lips she said to the young man:
"You, a students of books, should behave correctly!
How can I as a decent girl throw away my virginity?

How can I as a decent girl throw away my virginity?
Once I have lost virtue and virginity I'll have no life!
My father enjoys quite a reputation here in this city;
Weighty like a mountain the law allows for no mercy:
If we are exposed, we'll suffer cruel torture in court."

If we are exposed, we'll suffer cruel torture in court.
"Smart little girl, please listen to what I have to say.
Who doesn't love wine, sex, and also rich treasure?
Even Chang'e up in the moon would love to elope;
Buffalo Boy is married to the Weaving Maiden star.

"Buffalo Boy is married to the Weaving Maiden star;
The Immortal Maiden burns with love for Lü Dongbin.
Fourth Sister once promised herself to that Gao Wenju,[16]
And Seventh Sister descended to earth for Dong Yong.
Even the arhats try to seduce the bodhisattva Guanyin!

"Even the arhats try to seduce the bodhisattva Guanyin,
And Yang Zongbao even secretly married Mu Guiying.
If even the divine immortals are conversant with love,
How can you blame a young man in this mortal world?
Please, young lady, take pity on me — I am so lonely!"

Please, young lady, take pity on me — I am so lonely!
"Moved by your love, I cannot refuse my affection —
Mandarin ducks sport on the rivers forming couples;

---

[16] This may be a mistake because the lover of Fourth Sister is usually identified as Cui Wenrui. Gao Wenju's wife is Wang Yuzhen.

Rains and clouds on Mt. Shamanka engender passion:
By oaths like mountains and seas we'll tie our hearts."

By oaths like mountains and seas we'll tie our hearts.
Inside the bed-curtains they declared their mutual love;
A karmic bond from former lives was settled this night.
Phoenixes on one branch consummated their marriage;
Sharing one couch he and she enjoyed a heavenly bliss.

Sharing one couch he and she enjoyed a heavenly bliss.
On the mandarin-duck cushion their love was unending;
There was no end to the intimate words they exchanged:
Each word more tender and sweet than the one before —
Even the moon outside the window wanted to listen.

Even the moon outside the window wanted to listen,
Because the couple seemed to soar beyond the clouds.
But all of sudden roosters started to announce dawn,
And each and every call urged the lovers to separate —
The young lady saw him off as he set out on his road.

First she saw him off past the Hundred-Flower Pavilion.
Silently, not saying a word, she couldn't let go of him.
Twittering birds and fragrant flowers, no way to let go;
She found it impossible to let go of that passionate man,
So she said to her lover: "Never, never betray my love!"

Secondly she saw her lover off past the hillside forest,
And in the hillside forest she declared her true passion:
"Fishes swimming in the rivers form couples and pairs,
Geese flying high in the sky never abandon each other.
Let me hear good news from you once you are home."

Thirdly she saw him off past the lotus flower pond:
"Even the finest flowers don't last for a hundred days.
I will be an abandoned goose at the edge of heaven,

Miserably wandering hither and thither, all alone —
I am seeing you off, but it's bound to break my heart."

Fourthly she saw her lover off past the willow village:
"A man hopes for first place, a tree hopes for spring —
So I hope that once home you will study the Classics.
If by any chance you pass the exams as Top-of-the-List,
You will become an official and I too will be famous."

Fifthly she saw her lover off past the banyan trees:
"The large branches of banyan trees give good shade.
You, my lover, should resemble such a banyan tree,
But do not offer your shade to others, only to me —
Never desire those wild flowers along the roadside!"

Sixthly she saw him off across the sun birds' ridge;[17]
The sun birds were calling, inviting the spring sun.
"Dear brother, in you springtime shows on your face,
Whereas in me springtime is hidden deep in my heart,
Craving for flower and candle, bridal room pranks."

Seventhly she saw him off across the floating bridge;
Below the bridge the river rose, full of spring floods.
"Let's board a boat and chase those spring floods —
When loving a man, love one young and handsome;
United in love, of one mind, you will stay together."

Eighthly she saw him off past the octagonal pavilion;
In the octagonal pavilion they tearfully said goodbye:
"When choosing a road, choose the Yangguan road;
Never enter an evil gate or follow a crooked path —
Be careful when making your way through the world."

---

[17] The "sun birds" are geese that migrate north in spring and south again in the autumn.

Ninthly she saw him off past the well and its pond,
Advising her lover again and again in these words:
"Don't get involved in either whoring or gambling;
Opium is a drug that will turn one into an addict —
Serving my parents-in-law I want a good husband."

Tenthly she saw him off to the Ten-Mile Pavilion.
She told her lover: "Once home, find a go-between!
A relation like dew and water cannot last very long,
Only a wedded couple sleeps together every night.
A matchmaker and marriage will fill me with joy.

"A matchmaker and marriage will fill me with joy,
Each of us should persuade their own two parents.
Don't fear evil forces that want to be a hindrance:
Seas may dry out and stones rot, but our two hearts
Will not change — a fine match for a hundred years."

Without a change — a fine match for a hundred years!
Like sailing downstream the happy event has arrived.
These lovers finally become a lawfully wedded pair;
The trumpets blare and firecrackers loudly explode,
While I have finished the song of Ten-Mile Pavilion!

APPENDIX II

AN ALTERNATIVE *GAO WENJU*

Because of its long history, the story of Gao Wenju was transmitted in many versions, each with its own plot twists. The earliest known version of the tale was a stage adaptation as a *chuanqi* play of the early Ming entitled *Gao Wenju: The Return of the Soul* (*Gao Wenju Huanhun ji* 高文舉還魂記). This play has not been preserved in a Ming dynasty manuscript or printing, but may have been preserved in a manuscript from the late years of the Qing dynasty that was discovered in 1986.[1] The manuscript, entitled *Stream and Clouds Pavilion* (*Shuiyun ting* 水雲亭) had been copied in 1868, and so may well incorporate later changes and additions. A detailed summary has been presented by Guo Yingde:

> Gao Wenju hails from the Western Capital (Luoyang). His father Gongde has died at an early age. Because the family has become impoverished he lacks the means to provide his parents with a proper burial and so borrows three thousand strings from the rich man Magnate Zhang. He then cannot but become his indentured servant, but by accident he burns down the number one storehouse. Magnate Zhang falsely accuses him of setting fire to the storehouse in order to steal its treasure. When he takes him to the magistrate for interrogation, they meet on the road with

---

[1] Ban Youshu 1992.

Magnate Wang Ji, a good friend of Wenju's father. When he learns about the affair, he magnanimously opens his purse and pays off Wenju's debts and also takes Wenju home with him. With the assent of his wife he marries Wenju to their only daughter Zhenzhen. As it happens to be the year of the metropolitan examinations, Wenju leaves his wife and travels to the capital to sit for the exams, and passes them as Top-of-the-List. Now the prime minister Wen He has two daughters. The elder, Wen Qiong, has become an imperial concubine, but the younger, Wen Zhen, has not yet been engaged. Relying on the authority of the emperor, Wen He pressures Wenju to join his household as his daughter's husband. Wenju promptly refuses the marriage proposal, and even sends up a memorial to decline the marriage, but eventually he is forced to go through with the marriage because an imperial edict cannot be disobeyed. On the wedding night Wenju explains to Wen Zhen that he already has a wife, and once she knows that she hates him. In secret Wenju entrust his loyal servant Zhang Qian to take a letter to Luoyang and bring Zhenzhen and her whole family with him to the capital. This scheme is discovered by Wen He, who has Zhang Qian captured and gets his hands on the letter. At the advice of Wen Zhen he now orders Zhang Qian to go to Luoyang and tell Zhenzhen that she on arrival in the capital first has to call on the minister. Because it is harvest time when Wang Ji receives this letter, he sends Zhenzhen on ahead together with her personal servant girl Xuexue. When they arrive at the capital it is Zhang Qian's intention to alert Wenju of the situation, but he is found out by Wen He, who has him arrested, bastinadoed, and locked up in jail. He also orders his maid Haitang to trick Zhenzhen into entering the mansion. After first having locked up Xuexue, he next accuses Zhenzhen of "breaking into the mansion of a minister." After a vicious beating, her hair is cut off and she is robbed of her shoes;[2] she is then condemned to work as a slave in the kitchen — during daytime she has to haul water; the night she has to spend spinning. But fortunately Zhenzhen manages to survive thanks to the good care of the female slave Yingchun. Wen Zhen next conspires with Haitang and the evil

---

[2] Upper-class ladies at the time bound their feet. When they were robbed of their small shoes they could not but disband their feet. As a result their large feet would mark them as servants.

slave Xingfu. Mixing crane-crest red[3] with sulfur they prepare a soup for Zhenzhen. When the latter had eaten the poison, she dies, and Haitang and Xingfu bury her body in a deep well. In order to do away with the witnesses Minister Wen has Zhang Qian and Xuexue assigned as military personnel to the Tielin Garrison in the border regions. While on the road their escorts find out about the details; they provide Zhang Qian and Xuexue with clothes and money and set them free. The God of the Three Offices[4] revives Zhenzhen with a miraculous pill and orders her to appear in a dream to Wenju to explain to him the cause of her death. When Wenju wakes up, he is so distressed that he doesn't want to live anymore. He wants to stab Wen Zhen to death but is dissuaded from doing so by Yingchun. The God of the Three Offices brings Zhenzhen back to earth, and she appeals to Bao Zheng. Judge Bao houses Zhenzhen in his office and invites Minister Wen to his place under the pretext of celebrating his birthday. During the banquet Wang Zhenzhen beats the drum to lodge an accusation and Judge Bao immediately arrests Wen He. He also has Wen Zhen, Xingfu, and Haitang brought in. When he has established the details of the murder case, he has the four of them locked up, and reports his findings to the emperor for his final decision. Wenju and Zhenzhen return home in glory, while Xuexue is married to Zhang Qian, so the whole family is now happily reunited.[5]

Gao Wenju: The Return of the Soul is known from listings in early catalogues and excerpts in Ming-dynasty drama anthologies. In the 16th century it was revised as *The Tale of the Pearl* (*Zhenzhu ji* 珍珠記), also known as *The Tale of the Pearl and the Rice-Cake* (*Zhenzhu milan ji* 珍珠米糷記). This play has been preserved in a Ming dynasty printing that has been reproduced in *Guben xiqu congkan erji*. A detailed summary of its content has been provided by Guo Yingde 郭英德:

The Luoyang student Gao Wenju (also known as Jiecheng) owes the government a debt he cannot pay. His neighbor Millionaire

---

[3] A poison prepared from the red crest of a crane.
[4] One of the divinities in charge of the underworld.
[5] Guo Yingde 1997, 93–95 ("*Gao Wenju huanhun ji*"); pp. 110–111 ("*Zhenzhu ji*").

Wang is advanced in years but still lacks a son and distributes his wealth at the crossroads in order to aid the poor and needy. When he happens to run into Wenju, he admires his bearing and features, so he pays off his debts on his behalf and takes him with him to his home where he gives him his daughter Jinzhen as wife. Later Wenju travels to the capital to take part in the examinations and passes as Top-of-the-List. The evil minister Wen Ge has a second daughter who is not yet engaged and forces Wenju to join his household as son-in-law. Remembering the love and affection of Miss Wang, Wenju secretly dispatches Zhang Qian with a letter asking her to come, but that letter is discovered by Miss Wen, who destroys it and writes a quite different letter, which she has him deliver to Luoyang. There he gets a sound beating from Millionaire Wang and his whole family. Because the oath Wenju swore when they parted as husband and wife was so intense and sincere, Miss Wang believes that Wenju certainly will not have betrayed her, so she goes to the capital in person to find him. When she arrives there, it happens that Wenju has been summoned to the Palace to lecture on the Classics and even after several months has not yet returned. Because of his grudge over the beating he had earlier received, Zhang Qian urges Miss Wen to cut off Miss Wang's hair and to rob her of her shoes and assign her the lowly task of watering the flowers and sweeping the yard. But because of the care and assistance of an older servant Miss Wang fortunately survives. When later Wenju has returned from the Palace and is resting in his study he suddenly wants to eat a rice cake. When the older servant brings it to him, he marvels it is just like the cakes that Miss Wang used to make. In the rice cake he also finds one half of a pearl, and that is one half of the pearl they cut in two when he left. Wenju questions the servant who doesn't give him a clear answer. That evening, the servant secretly tells Miss Wang to go to Wenju's study, so husband and wife finally can meet with each other. Together with Miss Wang, Wenju escapes the mansion by climbing the wall and goes to Bao Zheng to lodge an accusation. The next day Judge Bao establishes the facts and reports to the throne. Wen Ge is banished by imperial decree and Zhang Qian is beheaded, while Miss Wang is allowed to make Miss Wen her slave. Miss Wang returns to Luoyang accompanied by a Miss Wen in chains, and it is only upon the urgent pleading of Millionaire Wang and his wife that the two young women become sworn sisters who together serve Wenju.[6]

This play elicited the following acerbic comment from the late Ming drama critic Qi Biaojia 祁彪佳 (1602–1645) in his *Yuanshantang jupin* 遠山堂劇品: "This is actually *Gao Wenju: The Return of the Soul*. That work definitely was not something special, but this is even worse."[7] Despite his dismissive remark, *The Story of the Pearl* became the basis for the majority of later versions in local opera and other genres of performative literature and its influence on the bamboo-clappers song version of *Gao Wenju* is clearly observable.[8]

The *Zhongguo geyao jicheng: Fujian juan* (2007: 626–634) presents the text of a narrative ballad entitled "Gao Wenju" from Yongding, that is based on the performance of Lu Shoumin 盧壽民 as recorded by Chen Yanrong 陳炎榮 in 1987 in Kanshizhen.[9] In this version the text is subdivided into six sections. A full translation of this text is provided here to show the extent to which the treatment of the same story may vary even within the same dialect area.

***

Gao Wenju

I *The Injustice*
Ever since Pangu opened up heaven and earth
Each Son of Heaven has had his own ministers:
Some of them were loyal and capable vassals,
Others were ungrateful and traitorous fellows.

---

[6] Guo Yingde 1997, 93–95 *("Gao Wenju huanhun ji")*; pp. 110–111 (*"Zhenzhu ji"*).
[7] Qi Biaojia 1955, 132.
[8] Ma Jianhua 2003; Ma Jianhua 2006; Yu Weimin, 2007.
[9] The summary of contents of the story of Gao Wenju provided in *Zhongguo quyi zhi: Fujian juan* 2006, 168–169 follows the ballad as performed by Lu Shoumin.

But let me forgo and not sing such idle phrases,
As I start my story I will sing of a virtuous man.
This virtuous man of yore was called Gao Wenju;
He was an only son who waited on his parents.
    At the age of twice eight, which is sixteen years,
He had mastered the Four Books and Five Classics;[10]
Named a *xiucai* on the roster he was widely respected;
A student at quite a young age he was admired by all.[11]
    But alas, time was against him, his fate was unlucky:
Their next-door neighbor was the vicious Xiao Buren.
This man Xiao was a banished criminal and a vagrant[12]
Who spent his life by whoring and gambling all day.
    When he lacked money he went to the Gaos for a loan:
A tiger borrowing from a pig — that can't be explained.
But once when Master Gao refused to lend him any,
Xiao Buren, filled with rage, hatched a vicious plot.
    He ran to the prefecture and lodged an accusation,
Stating that Master Gao was in liege with bandits,
Was in cahoots with the bandits on Mt. Buffalohead,
As their patron shared in the loot — that's the truth!
    When the prefect heard this, his heart was enraged
And he loudly cursed out Master Gao as a scoundrel:

---

[10] The Five Classics are the *Book of Documents*, the *Book of Odes*, the *Book of Changes*, the *Rites* (consisting of three separate titles) and the *Annals of Spring and Autumn* (with its three commentaries). These five titles had basically achieved their present shape by the beginning of the first millennium. Tradition ascribes at least editorship, if not authorship, of these texts to Confucius. The Four Books comprise the *Analects*, the *Mencius*, the *Great Learning* and the *Central Mean*. These four texts had been selected by Zhu Xi (1130–1200) as containing the essence of Confucianism. Together with Zhu Xi's own commentaries, the Four Books became the basic texts tested in lower examinations of the Ming and the Qing dynasties.

[11] By passing the lowest examinations (held at the prefectural level) candidates were admitted to the prefectural school and would henceforth be allowed to call themselves "students". The common designation for these students was *xiucai* 秀才 (flourishing talent).

[12] One of the common punishments in traditional Chinese law was banishment to a district at a specified distance (depending upon the crime) from one's hometown.

"You were not satisfied with possessions of a million,
But still had to conspire with bandits, act the villain!"
    He threw an urgent summons-tally down on the floor,
So ordering the government runners to arrest the man.
These government runners resembled roving tigers:
Shouting and clamoring they came to the Gao house.
    Master Gao's mind and his gall were both shattered;
He was so scared that he stumbled, fell on the ground.
Old and feeble as he was, the scare was way too much:
His souls and spirits dissolved as he joined the shades.[13]
    Wenju was arrested — there was no way to escape;
He spoke up and loudly cursed out that mean bandit.
Servants and maids were arrested and taken away;
His old mother jumped into a well, so seeking death.
    The family's goods were taken, leaving bare rooms,
And the Gao mansion was locked up from that time.
When the arrested Wenju was taken to the prefecture,
Leather whips and iron chains showed no mercy at all.
    The finger presses once applied hurt his very heart;
Beaten by cudgels his back was all covered in blood.
His white shirt had, dyed by this blood, turned all red:
This student, struck by disaster, suffered such torture!
    He cried for his father and mother but they had died;
Heaven didn't answer his cries, Earth remained silent.
He had to suffer a million kinds of pain and misfortune;
He swallowed an injustice that was as big as heaven!

II *The Rescue*
Let's not sing about that student languishing in jail,
But instead of a man of that district surnamed Wang.
Master Wang was a man who was loaded with money,
But his only child was a daughter, known as Yuzhen.
    Like a pearl in their hand palm her parents loved her:
At the age of sweet sixteen, she was not yet engaged.

---

[13] Traditional Chinese physiology credits a man with three souls and seven spirits.

Many sons of wealthy, powerful, and titled families
Had asked for her hand but none had been accepted.
    He wasn't after a bride price and not after high status;
Master Wang was only after one specific kind of person:
Yuzhen was to be married to a groom of the same age,
Born in the same month, on the same day, same hour.
    Once the conditions for a match were widely known,
The soothsayers and fortunetellers were busy no end:
They checked out one person and called on the next one;
When they computed a fate, they paid special attention.
    For all their searches they could not find that man!
Soothsayers and fortunetellers were all frustrated.
    But there was one specialist called Iron-Mouth Li,[14]
Who some time before had been to the Gao mansion.
He had computed the fate of the student Gao Wenju:
Destined for glory and riches by the Star of Literature![15]
    When he took out the fate card to have a good look,[16]
Year, month, day and hour were all clearly recorded:
These were exactly identical to those of Yuzhen:
Born in the same month, on the same day, same hour!
    Mr. Iron-Mouth Li was truly overcome by pleasure;
Taking the fate card along, he went to the Wangs.
Excited as excited can be he sat down in the hall,
And there loudly and clearly reported his findings.
    He first of all explained the name and the surname:
"With neat eyebrows and bright eyes a fine student!
Alas, time is against him, he's been struck by disaster;
He was falsely accused — this wrong isn't yet cleared."
    When Master Wang had heard this long explanation,
He dispatched Iron-Mouth Li with a gift of ten ounces.

---

[14] This soothsayer will have acquired his nickname because his predictions are always true.

[15] The stars are all powerful divinities. The Star of Literature is in charge of examination success and also determines the career of civil officials.

[16] The "fate card" lists a person's eight characters, that is, the four combinations of two cyclical characters for the year, month, day and hour of a person's birth.

He had earlier heard of the name of that Gao Wenju
As a fine young student who was gifted with talents.
  His family was quite rich, but they had been framed;
It must have been fate that he was struck by disaster.
A young man down on his luck and without a house:
The perfect person to bring home as man for Yuzhen![17]
  When Master Wang thought of this, he was pleased,
And, carried in his sedan-chair, went to the prefecture.
He entered into the prefecture and greeted the prefect:
"Your Excellency, be so kind as to lend me your ears.
  Gao Wenju most certainly is not some kind of bandit,
As a student he knows the books and understands rites.
But falsely accused by others he now languishes in jail,
Suffering such a wrong, such an injustice is true misery!
  Please allow me, Your Honor, to act as his guarantor
And to ransom him with ten thousand ounces of silver.
Please be so kind as to accept these ten thousand ounces
And to release that Wenju who didn't commit any crime."
  When the prefect saw this silver, he was very pleased
And he immediately ordered the release of Gao Wenju.
Once released Wenju paid his respects to Master Wang
And Master Wang was very satisfied by what he saw.
  He took Wenju along with him when he went home,
And when his wife saw him, her face was all smiles:
"Such a handsome young man is indeed to my liking,
If he will marry our daughter, I will be quite happy!"
  The female servants were ordered to heat bath water,
Bath water for the selected groom to take a nice bath.
Once he had taken a bath he put on a new set of clothes:
All fresh and clean he now looked even more handsome!

---

[17] In traditional China the bride was expected to join the family of her husband. It was considered demeaning for a groom to marry into the family of his wife because as a rule he would give up his own surname and his children would take on his wife's surname and continue the ancestral sacrifices to her parents. While under normal circumstances Gao Wenju would not have considered the possibility of a marriage with Wang Yuzhen if this would have implied he would have to join her family, he would have little choice but to accept the offer in his present situation.

They then called Yuzhen from her room to meet him
And ordered the family servants to lay out a banquet.
With the first cup of fine wine they toasted the student:
"Escaped from disaster and misery now enjoy to the full!"
   With the second cup of wine they toasted the student:
"Study your books to make a career — make a new start!"
With the third cup of wine they toasted the student:
"Let's talk about the great business of getting married!
   This marriage bond of today is predestined by Heaven,
Our young daughter will entrust herself to this *xiucai*."
Wenju was quite startled and Yuzhen felt ashamed —
Startled, ashamed — they didn't dare raise their heads
   While their faces were flushed, their hearts rejoiced:
Their eyes exchanged glances, their hands gave signals:
   "If you feel this love and if I have this intention, we two
Will share our life till we die without ever any regret!
As we were born in the same month, on the same day
We want to die in the same month, on the same day."
   On the fifteenth of the Eight Month, at the full moon,
They then tied the marriage knot as husband and wife.
Wenju now continued to live at the place of his wife
And showed even greater determination in his studies.

III *Examination Success*
One inch of light and shadow is one inch of gold,
But one inch of gold cannot buy an inch of time.
   Wenju attacked his books with truly great diligence
And fully understood each line of the Five Classics.
He grasped the details of astrology and geomancy,
He knew the principles of government and warfare.
   He didn't have any worry about food and clothes:
The young couple was united by a lasting affection.
In the blink of an eye the time of exams had arrived,
And Wenju packed his luggage to travel to the capital.
   Yuzhen found it impossible to let her husband depart:
One night as husband and wife means love for all times.

With her eyes awash in tears she spoke to her husband,
Telling her husband: "Now please remember this well.
   While on the road make sure at all times to dress warmly,
And in cold weather you have to be even more careful.
Make sure to eat enough rice and don't eat too little;
A full stomach provides you with energy and spirit.
   Don't go and seek amusement in houses of pleasure,
Don't seek there after idle flowers and wild grasses.
When you drink strong spirits, it will hurt your body,
When you drink fragrant tea, it will give you energy.
   At the examinations compose your essays with care,
As with well-written essays you will defeat all others.
If your name is listed on the golden poster, I'm happy,
But if you fail to pass the exams, that's not a big deal.
   I only hope that after the exams you'll quickly return,
So I, your wife, won't have to worry for all that long."
   When Wenju heard this, his heart was deeply moved
Because this pampered girl was such a virtuous wife:
Each and every sentence: words of gold, phrases of jade;
Each and every sentence was filled with deepest love!
   "My father-in-law bought me free with white silver,
My pretty wife obeys me in whatever I may request:
Now if I would forget these favors and turn out a traitor,
Scoop out my heart and liver — the vile innards of a dog!"
   Wenju was ready to leave for the capital and seek fame
To glorify the ancestors and enhance his family's status,
First of all to repay his father-in-law for his great favors;
Secondly to repay his virtuous wife for her great love.
   Thirdly he hoped to pass and to become and official
To take his revenge on Xiao Buren, dissolving his rage.
Then he would offer sacrifice before his parents' grave
And the status of the Gao family would be restored.
   Husband and wife found it hard to separate at parting;
After a thousand of words there still was more to say.
Calling on Heaven and Earth they swore oaths of love,
Oaths like mountains and seas to stay faithful forever.

Taking his leave of the elders he set out on the road,
Yuzhen saw her husband off to the Five-Mile Pavilion.
All along the road she offered her heart-felt advice —
She found it impossible to let him go, let him depart.

She sawed a jade as-you-wish scepter into two parts,
So each of them could carry one half on their body —
"If you see this jade, it is just as if you see my face!
This jade will substitute for me and accompany you.

May this parting be short, may our union last long;
Briefly separated, always together: that's true love."
Let's not sing of Yuzhen who walked back home,
Let's sing of Wenju who traveled on to the capital.

Walking by day, resting at night, it was bitter toil;
But bracing rain and sun he arrived in the capital.
On the ninth of the Third the exams were started;
Candidates from all over had heeded the summons.

When the three sessions had quickly been finished,
The chief examiner selected the first three names.
These three names were placed in a golden vase;
In the Golden Hall it was presented to the emperor.

He burned incense and prayed to Heaven and Earth,
Then golden chopsticks picked the Top-of-the-List.
Next came the Number Two and the Flower-Snatcher —
The imperial choice for Top-of-the-List was Wenju!

The emperor's edict called him to the Golden Hall:
The Son of Heaven's disciple greeted the emperor!
His Majesty was pleased by his looks and his talents
And gifted this dignitary a red gown and a gold belt.[18]

Decked out in gold and jade he received the edict
To parade on horseback through the city's streets!
He was crowded by people in front and in back;
Drums resounded to heaven as he left the palace.

The common people of the city were all startled
And came in droves to watch the Top-of-the-List!

---

[18] By passing the examinations as Top-of-the-List, Gao Wenju has joined the bureaucracy and can henceforth be described as a dignitary.

IV *Selecting a Groom*

Let's not sing of the Top-of-the-List and his parade,
But let me now sing of the prime minister at court.
Prime minister at court was Grand Secretary Wen:
He held the highest rank, and his power was great.

   His only child, a daughter, had the name Wen Jin;
She was praised by all for her beauty and features.
Because at the age of eighteen she still was single,
An imperial edict: a bunted loft to select a groom!

   From that bunted loft she would throw a silk ball,
And whom the ball hit was her predestined groom.[19]
But when the young girl stood atop the bunted loft,
Holding the colored ball in her hands, she panicked.

   The crowd in front of the loft resembled an ocean:
Handsome and ugly, fat and emaciated — all a blur!
"It may be said that a marriage is fated by Heaven,
But it wouldn't do to just randomly throw that ball."

   She eyed east and eyed west, without letting go;
She looked in front and behind, raking her thoughts,
When suddenly the roar of the drums resounded
Because from afar approached the Top-of-the-List.

   His red gown and jade belt were sparklingly new;
Gold flowers had been stuck in the top of his hat.
Bright eyes and clear eyebrows: a face like Pan An;
A brilliant young man who had barely turned twenty.

   "Could I obtain the Top-of-the-list as my husband,
My good fortune would be perfect, truly unrivalled!"
With a face red behind the ears she most happily
Secretly prayed to heaven's gods to help this girl.

   She waited till he passed in front of their mansion,
Then threw the ball in the air — her heart atwitter.
Twirling and whirling the ball flew through the air,
And when it fell down, it fell on the Top-of-the-List!

---

[19] There is no evidence that such a procedure was ever used in society for selecting a groom, but in drama and fiction it is often described.

The Top-of-the-List had no idea what it might be,
Clasping it in his hand, he raised his head to look,
When shouting for joy and loudly clearing the way,
Orderlies of the minister came running up to him.

   Holding his horse by the bit they felicitated him:
"Congratulations, good fortune descends on you!
A double joy befalls you, you are greatly blessed:
Heaven wills your marriage to the minister's girl!"

   They did not pay any attention to his objections
But led his horse in exactly the opposite direction.
They led his horse into the minister's mansion
To the music of fifes and drums — a different tune.

   Minister Wen welcomed him with a joyful mien:
"Thanks to Heaven and Earth and to His Majesty:
Now my daughter will marry the Top-of-the-List,
Even I as prime minister at court can feel happy!"

   He immediately gave orders to lay out a banquet,
Lanterns and other decorations quickly appeared:
"This day today is a very lucky and auspicious day:
The marriage knot will be tied in the bridal room."

   The Top-of-the-List felt palpitations out of fright;
Wenju felt so ashamed that his face seemed on fire,
And he addressed the minister: "Please forgive me,
But I already have been married since early youth.

   To divorce one's wife to marry another is a crime,
But the crime of deceiving you, Sir, is even worse!"
When Lord Wen heard this, he could not but laugh:
"You student, you really are quite an honest fellow.

   How can a village wench from your days of poverty
Compare to a prized belle from a minister's mansion?
Selected as groom by imperial edict — it's quite legal;
So who would dare blame you, dear Top-of-the-List?

   Send a formal writ of divorce to your wife at home;
Give a thousand ounces of silver to that former wife.
You have committed no sin and show your largesse:
You act rightly in both directions, without a doubt!"

Wenju waved his hands to demonstrate his refusal:
"I, this student, am not a man like that Chen Shimei.[20]
As long as the wife of my days of poverty is still alive,
I cannot divorce her out of love for a pampered doll!"

When the minister heard this, his face turned black:
"I admonished you kindly, but you remain stubborn —
Because of his edict the emperor is the go-between:
What about the crime of contempt of the emperor?"

Once Wenju heard this, his gall was all shattered,
His lowered his head, didn't dare speak up again.
"Inferior to only one man, superior to the millions:
The authority of a minister cannot be questioned."

So he allowed them to make their arrangements:
Lanterns and characters for happiness were raised.
The groom and the bride were fittingly dressed up,
Then the newly-weds bowed to Heaven and Earth.

Thereupon they bowed to the parents of the bride;
They bowed to each other, entered the bridal room.
When others enter the bridal room, they are elated;
When Wenju entered that chamber, he was grieved.

Tossing and turning he did not sleep all night long;
When he thought of Yuzhen, his heart was broken:
"The love between us as a couple was so perfect,
And now I have turned out to be a faithless fool.

---

[20] Chen Shimei 陳世美 here serves as the archetypical example of the unfaithful husband. In the earliest known version of the tale, Chen Shimei, upon passing the examinations as Top-of-the-List appointed to high office, does not return home. When after three years his wife (Qin Xianglian 秦香蓮) eventually travels to the capital and shows up at his mansion on his birthday as a performer of songs, he first has her chased from the capital and later, on second thought, murdered. But the underworld gods, impressed by her chastity, allow her to come back to life. When her children have achieved high rank, she lodges an accusation against her husband with Judge Bao, who banishes Chen Shimei to the border regions. In more recent versions Chen Shimei has married an imperial princess on passing the examinations. He also orders the murder of his wife, but that order is not executed because the man entrusted with the task is moved by her story. Judge Bao, on the other hand, does not spare the life of Chen Shimei but has him executed.

That pretty girl here besides me is pretty indeed,
But she cannot compare to my old wife at home.
While I here in the capital enjoy all kinds of luxury,
She suffers bitter loneliness there back at home.

It is unbearable to be a traitor who forgets favors,
But my honest heart has turned into dog innards.
How could I write a writ of divorce without reason?
A thousand ounces of silver cannot buy true love.

If a thousand ounces of silver could buy true love,
The whole world would have turned upside down.
I hate Heaven and Earth, I hate my damned fate —
I never should have paraded by that bunted loft.

I am caught in a quandary, don't know what to do:
How can I, Wenju, escape from this predicament?"

V *Seeking her Husband*
Let's not sing of the misery of the Top-of-the-List,
But let's sing of Yuzhen who had stayed at home.
After her man had gone to the capital to seek fame,
A full three years had gone by in the blink in an eye.

Three years of bitter waiting, three years of hoping,
And still she had not yet seen him come home again.
Separated by mountains — no news had ever arrived,
Not a single letter had been delivered at her house.

By day and night Yuzhen only thought about Wenju;
The strands of her thought were as tangled as hemp.
She had no desire to eat even the finest delicacies,
All she swallowed was bitter tears and idle sorrows.

Day and night she burned incense before the gods,
Who displayed no efficacy and showed no concern.
The swallows in the air might form couples together,
But alas our Wang Yuzhen was all alone by herself.

Day and night she kept thinking, at a loss what to do,
Until she decided to go to the capital to seek her man.
Her father and mother opposed her, but to no avail —
Even one's parents cannot block the love of a couple!

All alone she set out on the road and left her house —
She wouldn't return unless she had found her husband!
She didn't care about storm or dew, about rain or snow;
Every day she walked on until the sun sank in the west.

Her small feet and pointed shoes made walking hard,
Her whole body felt sore and she was covered in sweat.
She didn't care for the roaring tigers in the mountains;
She didn't fear bridges across rivers made of a one log.

She wasn't bothered by forest vines ensnaring her feet,
She didn't fear the distant roads across high mountains;
Even without an umbrella she didn't fear heavy rains;
On hottest days she didn't fear lacking water to drink.

After forty-nine days she arrived in the imperial city
And there asked for information about Gao Wenju —
Everybody could tell her that that Top-of-the List
Had become the son-in-law of the prime minister!

When she heard this her heart was full of vexation;
She was both angry and sad, her heart was broken:
"While I was at home suffering such bitter misery,
You had become a high official, were living it up!

Your wife back at home was all alone and lonely,
While you in the capital pampered a pretty bride.
Without any love or any decency: a Chen Shimei;
You and that Chen Shimei make a perfect couple.

We too are one silly girl and one unfaithful man:
How come there are that many cheating lovers?"

The more she kept thinking, she more vexations;
Filled with anger and pain she came up with a plan.
A prime minister's mansion is as deep as the sea —
How would she be able to meet her faithless man?

Considering the case from all sides she had no plan;
Overcome by sorrow while the days passed all by.
Then one day she dressed as a performer of songs
And in front of the mansion's gate started singing.

The sound of the strings struck a chord in Wen Jin,
And a servant girl appeared who asked her inside.

The young lady Wen Jin was seated in the high hall;
To the singer was assigned a low bench at the end.
    She strummed the strings and she beat the clappers;
The sad sound of the strings was so deeply moving
Tears course downed before she had uttered a word —
Tears accompanied every line of the song she sang.
    "This tune is named after a person called Gao Wenju,
A vicious and unfaithful man who forgot all favors!"
    Once the young lady heard this, she cursed her out:
"You brazen hussy, you must be out of your mind —
Wenju is the son-in-law of the current prime minister,
How could you dare sing a song about that person?"
    The servant girl Yingchun hastily calmed her down:
"My mistress, don't take it seriously and get angry!
In this world many people share the same names,
Sharing surname and name they are not the same.
    How could she know the name of the Top-of-the-List?
A ballad-singer from faraway cannot know the facts.
She only needs to sing a song that has a good story,
Just allow her to sing so we may have a good time."
    Hearing this, the young lady changed her mind
And ordered the singer to sing her moral story.[21]
    Yuzhen once again started to strum the strings
And then set out to sing in a most woeful manner.
To begin she sang how Wenju had been framed,
Secondly she sang how Wenju had been jailed;
    Thirdly she sang how Wenju had been rescued
As he had the same date of birth as Miss Wang:
Master Wang wanted to make him his son-in-law
And had ransomed him for ten thousand ounces.
    Fourthly she sang how Wenju had been married,
How husband and wife were by deep love united.

---

[21] *Daoqing* 道情. This term originally denoted songs and ballads of Daoist inspiration, but later, in many parts of China, became a common term for prosimetric storytelling.

Fifthly she sang how Wenju had left for the capital,
How the as-you-wish scepter became two halves.
   But that faithless Wenju didn't care about love:
The scepter had not been joined, was discarded!"
   As she sang that ballad each note sounded so sad
It moved the Top-of-the-List in the minister's house.
"Who sings this tune that sings about my experience?
Who sings this tune in which each note draws tears?"
   With big strides he quickly walked to the high hall
And widely opened his eyes so he could see clearly.
As soon as he saw Yuzhen, he was filled by sadness
And immediately called out to his wife in this way:
   "My dear wife, when did you arrive in the capital?
Why do you perform a song in a minister's mansion?
Why didn't you come here much earlier to see me?
You never sent me even the shortest letter at all!"
   Once Yuzhen saw him, she was overcome by rage
And she loudly cursed him out as a vicious lowlife:
"For three years after you left we received no news,
While you here in the capital enjoyed the good life!
   Because of you I was filled by grief day and night,
You owe me three years of longing and desire.
I traveled these thousand miles to the capital,
Suffering unearned misery for forty-nine days.
   Because of you I suffered these many sorrows,
While you married into the minister's mansion.
Of all the many ungrateful devils in this realm
You must be reckoned the world's worst scum!"
   When Wenju heard this, his heart was saddened,
When Wenju heard this, his tears coursed down:
"My darling, you cannot be blamed for your grief;
My dear, each word of complaint is only too true.
   I had no option but to join the minister's mansion,
But in my heart, dear, I was always thinking of you.
If you don't believe me, you only have to ask Wen Jin:
In three years of marriage I never once touched her.

The minister pressured me to write a writ of divorce,
I feigned to do so but actually wrote a different letter:
One thousand ounces of fine silver I had send to you,
Telling you to find a companion, come to the capital.

We'll go and lodge an accusation at Judge Bao's office;
I'll only be satisfied when Minister Wen will be toppled."

On the one hand husband and wife were reunited,
On the other hand young lady Wen was quite upset:
"No wonder you feigned to be ill for three years,
No wonder you never touched me for three years.

No wonder you were never happy all these days,
And always moody never paid any attention to me.
For three years we were a couple but only in name,
So how should I go on living from this day forward?"

Weeping and crying she asked the minister to come,
She asked the minister to come and decide the case.

VI *The Conclusion*

"I, Wenju, was married and had a wife back at home,
I've informed Your Excellency so from the very start.
Pressured to write a writ of divorce, I didn't do so —
There's no way to cut off the love of a couple like us.

The letter I sent to my folks was discovered by you,
And the silver I had sent also never left the capital.
You only thought that a simple girl from the village
Didn't have the gall and smarts to come the capital.

You only thought your daughter's face like a lotus
Sure could tie down the body of the Top-of-the-List.
But now all your cunning has turned into stupidity:
Even you, minister, cannot hold down true lovers!"

Considering the case from all sides at a loss what to do,
He[22] had someone invite Bao Wenzheng to their place.

---

[22] Prime Minister Wen. Bao Wenzheng 包文拯 is one of the many names used to refer to Judge Bao.

And when Judge Bao arrived at the minister's mansion,
He didn't come to pronounce a verdict but to mediate.
   Wenju and Yuzhen and also Wen Jin, all three
He called one by one before him for questioning.
As a result Judge Bao highly praised Gao Wenju
As a virtuous man, true in love and true in duty.
   "Minister Wen selected a groom by imperial edict
But he should not have selected a married man.
He shouldn't be blamed for this one misjudgment,
But he has caused his daughter's pure loneliness.
   Her three years of marriage have been a charade,
She had a fine husband but was kept at a distance.
The suffering in her heart could not be described:
To whom could she disclose her bitter suffering?
   Wang Yuzhen was exceptional in her devotion;
Their love as a couple was as deep as the ocean.
Fearlessly she climbed mountains, crossed rivers,
And after forty-nine days she arrived in the capital.
   If you will abide by the ruling of my mediation,
Wen Jin and Yuzhen should become two sisters;
Together they'll wait on Top-of-the-List Wenju —
Without distinction in rank both will be Ladies.
   I now will submit a report to His Imperial Majesty,
So proper caps and stoles may be gifted to them."
Hearing this, the four of them were quite pleased
And profusely thanked Lord Bao for his wisdom.
   Wen Jin and Wang Yuzhen curtsied to each other
And addressed each other from now on as "sister".
The minister smiled while he stroked his beard,
But happiest of them all was the Top-of-the-List.

APPENDIX III

THE SLAVE GIRL'S LAMENT: A REVOLUTIONARY BAMBOO-CLAPPERS SONG

In his famous *Talks at the Yan'an Conference on Literature and Art* of 1942, Mao Zedong had demanded of all literature and art that it served as propaganda of Marxist thought in the service of the Chinese Communist Party. This applied not only poetry and fiction, but especially to drama and other performing arts that spoke directly to the (often still illiterate) masses.[1] New works, based on the struggle of the Communist Party, had to be created, while traditional titles could only be performed if their message was deemed sufficiently progressive. Following the establishment of the People's Republic of China, these guidelines were applied throughout the length and breadth of China and bamboo-clappers songs and their

---

[1] McDougall, 1980. This policy was based on the experiences of the CCP in rural areas following its retreat from the cities in the late 1920s, starting in the Soviet areas in the early 1930s and, after 1935, in Yan'an. The largest early Soviet area covered the Hakka-speaking regions of southwestern Fujian and southeastern Jiangxi, where the CCP made use of songs and ballads to spread its message. See Mao 1990, 164. Hu Xizhang 2010, 84–91 provides examples of propagandistic bamboo-clappers songs from the 1930s and 1940s.

performers were not excluded from close supervision by cultural cadres. Professional performers were organized in *quyituan* 曲藝團 (performance companies)[2] and their repertoire was scrutinized, while artists were stimulated to experiment in order to enhance the artistic level of their performances. New scripts were composed, often in the service of specific political campaigns. Such new works were closely scrutinized by the responsible cultural and political cadres and often had to be repeatedly revised before they were deemed acceptable.[3] Apparently this is also the case in the text translated here, because at the end we read a note that the present text is the fourth draft.

The Slave Girl's Lament (*Binühen* 婢女恨) was written in the context of the Socialist Education Campaign (also known as the Four Clean-Ups).[4] Following the disastrous failure of the Great Leap Forward, Mao Zedong had lost much of his political power and many of the revolutionary reforms that accompanied the establishment of the People's Communes had been scaled back. In order to reignite revolutionary fervor and strengthen socialist morality (and also to strengthen his own political basis), Mao then launched the Socialist Education Movement in 1962. In places this movement meant a close scrutiny of all local cadres, many of whom lost their position on the accusation of corruption and ideological laxity. One of the techniques to engage "the poor and lower-middle peasants" in the Four Clean-Ups and train inheritors of the Revolution, were sessions "to remember the bitter and consider the sweet" (*yiku sitian* 憶苦思甜). In these sessions, victims of "the old society" were invited to recount their misery and sufferings before 1949 in contrast to their "happy life" since Liberation in order to strengthen their gratitude to the Communist Party and demand a strict socialist morality

---

[2] The Chinese term *quyi* 曲藝 broadly covers all forms of performing art such as song, storytelling and ballad-singing, with the exception of traditional opera and spoken drama.

[3] For the fate of storytelling in the Yangzi delta since Liberation, see He 2012. The various government activities affecting bamboo-clappers songs and their performers are listed in Hu 2010, 38–42; 84–91; 109–121.

[4] Baum and Teiwes 1968; Baum 1975.

from their leaders.⁵ Disappointed with the results of the Socialist Education Movement, Mao was to launch the Cultural Revolution in the summer of 1966.

Like the earlier "speaking bitterness" (*suku* 訴苦) meetings that had been such a potent instrument in mass mobilization during the land reforms of the 1940s and early 1950s, the sessions to remember the bitter and consider the sweet would depict the evils of landlords in the blackest possible terms and, in recent years, these narratives have been criticized for their deliberate exaggeration.⁶ The sufferings of the poor, however, were only too real in the early decades of the 20th century.⁷

This translation is based on the text provided in Hu Xizhang, *Kejia zhubange yanjiu* (2010: 493–510). Hu's text was "based on a mimeographed version provided by the great mountain song master Yu Yaonan 余耀南. It was created by Yu Yaonan⁸ and Zhang Zhaoying 張照英⁹ of the *Three Men Quyi Company* of Dabu district, when in 1965 they participated in the 'Four Clean-Ups' Movement

---

⁵ On "yiku sitian" see Bulag 2010, 100–104.

⁶ Guo 2013.

⁷ See for instance Wiens n.d.c. 1930, 78–80 for the tale of a little slave girl who is maltreated by her owner until she runs away.

⁸ Yu Yaonan (b. 1938) was born in Malaysia but came to China in 1939. Upon finishing middle school he became an actor and performer in 1958, displaying a remarkable versatility in many genres. He avidly collected and acquired any kind of materials that might be useful to him in composing new songs and ballads. He had already established quite a reputation before the Cultural Revolution, but his main period of activity was the 1980s and 1990s, when he also often performed abroad (Hu Xizhang 2010, 306–310). More detailed accounts of his life are provided in Hu Xizhang, *Shange dashi Yu Yaonan zhuan* 山歌大師余耀南傳, Beijing: Zhongguo wenlian chubanshe 2004, and Hu Xizhang, *Gaoxiao dawang: shange dashi Yu Yaonan yishi* 搞笑大王: 山歌大師余耀南軼事, Beijing: Zhongguo wenlian chubanshe 2005, but I have not seen these two books.

⁹ Zhang Zhaoying (1920–2000) hailed from Dapu and finished primary school, but at the age of fifteen, lost the use of his left arm. During the Anti-Japanese War (1937–1945) he survived for a number of years by performing bamboo–clapper songs. After 1949 he became a primary school teacher, but from 1959 till 1965 he was active again as a performer (Hu Xizhang 2010, 284–285).

in Jieyang district. It was based on a story that actually had occurred in Dabu district, and was originally called *Huang Yuelian* 黃月連."[10]

***

The Slave Girl's Lament Composed by Zhaoyao 照耀 (Zhao and Yao)

I *The Sale*
The old society was a world of utter darkness,
Black clouds covered the sky, layer upon layer.
Those many poor people suffered oppression;
The wrongs they suffered were seas of blood:
Now listen as I sing the tale of Huang Yuelian.

Now listen as I sing the tale of Huang Yuelian —
These events took place before the Liberation.
Her father's name was Huang Laifa;
Her mother's name was Zhang Yutian,
They lived in Shantou near the harbor.

The family lived in Shantou near the harbor.
Her father made a living by polishing shoes.
If they had something to eat, they lacked clothes;
If they had some rice, they still lacked side dishes,
So his heart and liver were both sick with worry.

So his heart and liver were both sick with worry —
Autumn winds were blowing in the Ninth Month.
When Laifa came out in the street to do his job,
An officer with Jiang's bandits[11] stood before him —
His whole face covered with a repulsive beard.[12]

---

[10] Hu Xizhang 2010, 493–494.

[11] The national army of the Republic of China. Jiang refers here to Jiang Jieshi (Kaishek), the leader of the Republic of China since 1927.

[12] Heavy beards are not a very common feature of Chinese men, so the text seems to suggest that this officer may have been a foreigner.

His whole face covered with a repulsive beard —
He placed his leather shoes on the small bench.
Laifa immediately set out to polish these shoes,
And he polished them until they shone brightly,
Then he said the shoe soles needed some fixing.

Then he said the shoe soles needed some fixing —
Laifa was fast with his hands and not slow at all.
When he had finished these two items of work,
That bandit soldier had the gall not to pay a cent
And quickly slipped away into a small public park.

He quickly slipped away into a small public park,
But Laifa followed him and pursued him closely.
That soldier killed him without blinking an eye:
When hit by his fist in the middle of his breast,
Laifa fainted and collapsed right on the sidewalk.

Laifa fainted and collapsed right on the sidewalk.
In this world the poor people all hang together:
A worker on a tricycle brought him to his home
And carefully supported him to help him inside —
Once Yutian saw him, she was awash in tears!

Awash in tears —
She wanted to send for a doctor but had no money.
After a while he also started to give up fresh blood,
And Yutian, in a panic, knelt down before the bed —
Her heart seemed to be sliced, she couldn't speak.

Unable to speak —
On the verge of death Laifa instructed Yuelian:
"This wrong, a sea of blood, has not been avenged.
After my death I will not be able to close my eyes.
I hope that you, once grown up, will take revenge!"

Will take revenge —
That Laifa was really to be pitied after his death:
The planks of his bed were used to make a coffin,
But when people wanted to carry him to his grave,
There was no money, so they had to sell Yuelian.

The only thing they could do was to sell Yuelian —
The crimes of that dark society flood even heaven!
One moment the family consisted of three people,
Now at present the only one left was Zhang Yutian,
Who cried out to Heaven and Earth — but to no avail.

She cried out to Heaven and Earth — but to no avail.
At mealtimes she could not swallow a single bite.
When coming inside, she did not see her husband;
When going outside, she didn't see Huang Yuelian.
The more she thought about it, the more she cried.

The more she thought about it, the more she cried —
A cold wind kept soughing, the rain kept on pouring.
Thinking that from now on she couldn't make a living,
She committed suicide by jumping into the wide sea.
From that day the Huang family didn't exist anymore.

II *The Fiery Pit*

From that day the Huang family didn't exist anymore.
Let us change the subject and sing of Huang Yuelian.
She had been sold to a major landlord in Dabu district,
A big landlord and bully with the name of Qiu Peiyuan,
Who in the city of Shantou managed *Broad and Distant*.[13]

In the city of Shantou he managed *Broad and Distant*.
This landlord took her back to his hometown with him.
When little birds lack their mother, they chirp and chirp:

---

[13] *Broad and Distant* appears to be the name of a well-known shop.

Yuelian, separated from her mother, was to be pitied,
As soon as she woke up from sleep, she looked for her.

As soon as she woke up from sleep, she looked for her,
But Shantou and Dabu are each at the edge of the world.
These places are separated by ranges of high mountains.
In the morning she looked at the sun, at night at the stars,
Always longing to be reunited with her dear own mother!

Always longing to be reunited with her dear own mother.
That landlord treated Huang Yuelian in a very cruel way.
Yuelian had barely reached the house of this big landlord,
When he took out a shaving knife and shaved off her hair:
If "Baldy" would try to run away, she was easily spotted!

She was easily spotted!
The rules in the landlord's house were many and strict,
And he personally tied a hempen rope around her neck.
A hemp rope was tied around her neck, just like a cow,
And so she was led inside and locked up in a dark room.

Locked up in a dark room —
The landlord had his own weird explanation for this:
If you buy a pig or a dog, lock them up for three days,
And after three days they'll turn out to be very meek.
In this way she was locked up for three days on end.

In this way she was locked up for three days on end —
When he released Yuelian from that pitch dark room,
He told her to look after the baby, wash dirty diapers,
Make tea, sweep the floor, and fill his tobacco pipe —
She also had to feed the pigs and cut yam creepers.

Cut yam creepers —
The children of the landlord were precious indeed,
They were fed till they were fat and broad-necked.
When Yuelian had to carry them around on her back,
They weighed like a slab of stone on her shoulders.

They weighed on her shoulders —
Such a life of a female slave is truly something pitiable!
Rising from her bed at dawn she worked till nightfall,
And at night she had to stand at the side of their bed
To scratch their itch and wave the fan without any end.

Without any end —
Each night she would scratch them until after midnight.
If she scratched them too lightly, she would be cursed;
If she scratched them too strongly, she might be whipped,
Kicked by their feet and slapped in the face by their fists.

Slapped in the face —
At the age of nine she herded the buffalo in the deep hills.
She had to go despite strong winds or heavy downpours.
On cold days and over frozen fields, she led that buffalo;
If the buffalo she led did not win, she was beaten down.

If the buffalo she led did not win, she was beaten down.
At the border of cold and heat, in the lunar Eighth Month,
Yueliang was so weakened that she attracted an illness.
Now shivering, now feverish, she moaned deliriously,
And stretched out on the bed she lost consciousness.

She lost consciousness,
But the landlord loudly cursed Huang Yuelian, shouting:
"The sky is bright, the sun clear, but you sleep soundly!
This damned servant girl wants to have some time off!"
He took up a piece of vine and whipped her ferociously.

He took up a piece of vine and whipped her ferociously,
So Yuelian had no other option but to herd the buffalo.
Her arms were sore, her legs wobbly, she couldn't walk,
And while seeing many stars whirling before her eyes,
She collapsed and fell down by a dike in those fields.

She collapsed and fell down by a dike in the fields,
But fortunately that landlord's laborer Li Shugen
Noticed that Yueliang still hadn't come back again,
So he left in a hurry to search through those hills
And carried her home on his back from the fields.

He carried her home on his back from the fields,
But how extremely vicious was this Qiu Peiyuan!
When he sees how serious Yuelian's illness is,
He fears that her death might pollute the house,
So he has her carried off to the firewood shack.

So he has her carried off to the firewood shack —
Late at night, utter silence, in deepest darkness:
Rats were nibbling and screeching by her head;
Mosquitoes were biting her and flies followed —
Without a single kind person there by her side.

Without a single kind person there by her side.
This greatly upset the long-term laborer Li Shugen.
When he saw how the diseased Yuelian was suffering,
He found some vegetables and cooked them in a wok;
Once Yuelian had eaten these, she felt a little better.

Once Yuelian had eaten these, she felt a little better.
In the early morning she got up and left that room.
She felt very hungry and wanted to have some food,
But she saw that the landlord had a murderous look
   on his face:
She didn't dare go forward and approach the table.

She didn't dare go forward and approach the table.
The long-term laborer worried about Huang Yuelian,
And he stealthily handed her a full bowl of rice gruel,
Together with half a bowl of greens that were fresh:
Never ever would she forget that life-saving favor!

Never ever would she forget that life-saving favor!
At the age of ten she had to learn to hoe the fields.
As a little kid she had to deliver a grownup's work.
The urine buckets she all had to carry in her arms,
But walking it was very easy to lose one's footing.

When walking it was very easy to lose one's footing,
So Huang Yuelian secretly came up with a scheme.
Whenever the landlord would not pay any attention,
She would pour some of the shit in one of the ditches;
Only one half of the bucket was dumped on the field.

Only one half of the bucket dumped on the field:
But the wife of the landlord followed behind her,
And when she saw the shit floating in the ditches,
She cursed Huang Yuelian at the top of her voice,
And grabbed a carrying pole to give her a beating.

She grabbed a carrying pole to give her a beating:
She suffered this kind of misery for a full three years.
When Yuelian barely had reached the age of eleven,
She had to feed the pigs, tend the vegetable garden,
And pound the chaff and husk the rice without pause.

Pounding the chaff and husking the rice without end:
At Twelfth Month's end, they celebrated New Year.
The landlord had three meals of fish, wine and meat,
But by the side of the stove the laborer ad the maid
Celebrated the New Year with chunks of bare bones.

They celebrated the New Year —
The landlord with pork and all kind of sea products,
And when he discovered a woman's hair in his bowl,
He loudly cursed Yuelian for her utter lack of hygiene
And then threw boiling hot water all over her breast.

And he threw boiling hot water all over her breast,
Burning Yuelian in a way that cried out to Heaven.
Scalded all over her body, her wounds were hurting:
Standing, sitting, walking, running — all caused pain.
It took more than ten days for her skin to fully heal.

More than ten days —
On no occasion was Yuelian allowed any rest at all.
When she forgot to pick up any pig shit in the house,
The landlord would immediately be filled with rage,
And pick up the pig's shit to pour it all over Yuelian.

And pick up the pig's shit to pour it all over Yuelian.
His face dark, his nose black, he came towards her,
So she hurriedly pushed him away with her hands.
The pig's shit now flew into the face of Qiu Peiyuan,
And turd upon turd rained down exactly on his lips.

And turd upon turd rained down exactly on his lips.
The landlord set out in hot pursuit of Huang Yuelian.
Because she was still young, she couldn't run so fast,
So the landlord grasped Huang Yuelian by her braids
And janked out quite a lot of the hair on her head!

He janked out quite a lot of the hair on her head —
The devilish landlord now conceived of an evil plan.
He ran into the house in order to get a sharp knife,
And once he had that kitchen knife in his hands,
He came after Huang Yuelian, wanting to kill her.

He came after Huang Yuelian, wanting to kill her,
So Yuelian ran off and hid in the deep mountains.
During the day she lacked food and hid in the hills;
At night she sneaked off into a mountain grotto,
Collecting straw for protection against the cold.

She collected straw for protection against the cold.
Yuelian lifted her head to look up at clear Heaven:
"In the world of men there is now no way out for me,
So all I can do is to jump into a river and call it quits,
In that way I won't have to suffer all through my life."

In that way I won't have to suffer all through my life.
But after Yuelian had thought this, she thought back:
"If I now today jump into a river and die, who on earth
Will take revenge for the wrongs that I have suffered?
The bitter life of my parents will have been all in vain."

The bitter life of my parents will have been all in vain.
Neighbors caught up with her by the side of the river,
And they advised Yuelian to go back to the landlord,
And patiently wait for another three or five years —
Once a day would come that she would be avenged.

Once a day would come that she would be avenged.
Suffering patiently she suffered for six, seven years.
Huang Yuelian had then reached the age of eighteen;
With strong arms and legs, in the prime of her youth.
Now she fell in love — and with the laborer Li Shugen.

III *Getting Married*
Now she fell in love — and with the laborer Li Shugen.
They resembled a pair of bitter gourd and *huanglian*.[14]
Li Shugen then had reached the age of twenty five:
Thick eyebrows, big eyes, his shoulders iron plates.
He could handle all implements: plow, rake, roller.

He could handle all implements: plow, rake, roller.
United through labor they were a perfect marriage.[15]

---

[14] *Huanglian* is Chinese goldthread. Its bitter-tasting root and stem are used in traditional Chinese medicine.

[15] While the text uses the language of marriage, what is happening is that Huang Yuelian and Li Shugen are sleeping together.

When the red bayberry blooms, the sun is hidden:
The landlord remained in the dark as if inside a drum —
A toad living inside a jar does not know about heaven.

A toad living inside jar does not know about heaven.
The two of them had been married for half a year,
When it happened that Yuelian became pregnant.
She had already been pregnant for two months:
This was a problem that was bigger than heaven!

This was a problem that was bigger than heaven.
Yuelian then made an appointment with Li Shugen:
Wait for the third watch, when all others are asleep,
And then let's go, husband and wife, to the garden
To come up with a way for dealing with Qiu Peiyuan.

To come up with a way for dealing with Qiu Peiyuan.
Shugen promptly replied to Yuelian in this manner:
"At present there is only one possible solution for us.
Let's flee from the tiger's maw and so save our lives,
Let's run off to Fujian and survive there by farming."

Let's run off to Fujian and survive there by farming —
They talked until late at night, beyond two o'clock.
Then the landlord got up because he had to crap,
And making a little detour through the flower garden
He discovered there Yuelian together with Shugen.

IV *The Separation*
He discovered there Yuelian together with Shugen.
That deviously cunning, utterly vicious Qiu Peiyuan!
The next day as soon as the sky had turned bright,
The two of them were called to the mansion's hall,
And there he interrogated Yuelian and Li Shugen.

And there he interrogated Yuelian and Li Shugen.
The landlord, hitting the table, exploded in rage.

He accused the laborer of breaking the clan rules.
Ruining morality — his crime couldn't be pardoned:
He had the laborer arrested and made a soldier.[16]

He had the laborer arrested and made a soldier.
The wife of the landlord was even more vicious:
She selected her most pointed, her sharpest needle,
And then stabbed the eyeballs of Huang Yuelian
Till blood flowed down and covered her breasts.

Till blood flowed down and covered her breasts.
Filled with a grudge she went blind in both eyes.
When a landlord harms people, he harms them
  till bones stick out;
When cutting weeds, you also tear out the roots:
That very day Huang Yuelian was chased away.

That very day Huang Yuelian was chased away.
Huang Yuelian who was pregnant at that time
Could only stay alive then by begging for food.
Her face turned sallow and her legs swelled up;
After one step she could not take a further step.

After one step she could not take a further step.
By begging for food she survived for six months.
One day when she rested in a roadside pavilion,
Her guts started to ache — she moaned for pain,
Now the child in her belly was about to be born.

Now the child in her belly was about to be born,
No one lived at the top or the foot of the mountain.
She bit the umbilical cord through with her teeth,
And took off some of her rags to swaddle the boy;
Then she felt her way to the side of the pavilion.

---

[16]The text writes *zhuangding* 莊丁 (villager) here, which appears to be a mistake for *junding* 軍丁 (soldier). The landlord reports Li Shugen for the draft.

Then she felt her way to the side of the pavilion.
With tears in her eyes Yuelian said to her child:
"This is not because your mother didn't want you,
But because I am blind, I cannot make any living.
How I hope, son, you'll be found by a saving star."

How I hope, son, you'll be found by a saving star!
Yuelian started walking and then left the pavilion,
But when she heard the baby weeping and crying,
It seemed as if her heart was stabbed by knives:
She picked him up, and held him to her breast.

V *Weeping for her Son*
"First of all I stroke my son here in this pavilion,
I cannot see you but I stroke you with my hands.
My little son has been born so perfectly made:
His earlobes are long and his nose is so eminent!
What will happen if nobody will take you along?

"Secondly I stroke my son here in this pavilion —
Your mother's emotions are muddled as hemp.
My son, you are now just like a bamboo shoot;
Once I leave this pavilion, no leaf protects you,
How can you grow up and later see your mother?

"Thirdly I stroke my son as the sun sets in the west,
Your mother holds you tight, here in this pavilion.
Your arms and legs are trembling while you weep.
My dear darling, flesh of my flesh, you are hungry,
But I have no gruel, no water to still your hunger.

"Fourthly I stroke my son while the dusk is falling.
Your mother has been chased out of the house.
I don't have a single penny, I don't have any rice.
Ahead of us there's no house, behind us no village.
From the spring by the road I drink my own tears.

"Fifthly I stroke my son as the night is spreading,
The night wind is blowing, each gust more chilly.
A hen's little chickens still have their warm nest,
But my son at birth even lacks a bed to sleep in:
Tender grasses cannot stand the frost of autumn.

"Sixthly I stroke my son now midnight is near —
Without a companion or a friend, utterly alone.
The sky is dark, the earth is black, where to go?
East and south, west and north are all blurred.
Will the clouds ever clear so I can see the moon?

"Seventhly I stroke my son in this freezing cold.
Your mother has had no food at any mealtime.
I have not had even a single sip of ginger wine,
My head dizzy, my eyes blurry, my tongue dry,
I lack all energy — my arms and legs so wobbly.

"Eighthly I stroke my son here is this desolation.
Alone and lost and lonely here by the roadside.
Tigers do not eat the flesh of starving orphans;
Mosquitoes and flies love splendor and light:
So do not come and harm my boy in any way.

"Ninthly I stroke my son surrounded by mist —
Hatred and thirst for revenge are in my heart.
That landlord with the heart of wolf and dog
Harmed me this female slave and the laborer —
When will husband and wife ever be reunited?

"Tenthly I stroke my son while tears course down.
I place my son here by the side of the main road.
In case that you, son, have the luck to be saved,
You have to take revenge once you've grown up.
On no account can you let go of that Qiu Peiyuan!"

On no account can you let go of that Qiu Peiyuan.
Yuelian was overcome by sadness — what misery!
Her stomach was hurting as if throttled by knives,
And her heart felt as if it was boiled in seething oil:
Suffering a shock she collapsed next to the road.

VI *The Liberation*
Suffering a shock she collapsed next to the road.
After the fourth watch was gone, the fifth watch:
Guerilla forces of our army arrived at that spot,[17]
And they revived Yuelian with some medicine,
Then gave her a padded jacket and some money.

They gave her a padded jacket and some money:
Yuelian, almost dead, met with her saving stars.
She had to survive by begging until the Liberation.[18]
She wandered around for three long years on end,
Sleeping all the while in ruined roadside pavilions.

She slept all the while in ruined roadside pavilions.
Black clouds were dispersed, she saw the clear sky:
The saving star appeared of the Communist Party!
It saved the poor people from that deepest abyss:
As the new masters, they grabbed political power.

As the new masters, they grabbed political power.
Yuelian happily returned to her old hometown too,
And the people's government came to her rescue
By giving her rice and pickles and giving her money,
So she didn't need to go begging, suffering wrongs.

---

[17] The "guerilla forces of our army" refer to irregular units of the Liberation Army of the Communist Party of China.

[18] Liberation is the common term to refer to the establishment of the People's Republic of China in 1949.

So she didn't need to go begging, suffering wrongs.
The land-reform movement overturned the heaven:
A bellyful of bitterness could this day be expressed.
Yuelian recounted her sufferings, listed her grudges,
And beat down the landlord: his fields were divided.

She beat down the landlord: his fields were divided,
And the community took good care of Huang Yuelian.
She received as her part a new blanket and a jacket;
She was also assigned two big rooms of his mansion:
Mosquito-curtains of white gauze, a Jinshan carpet!

Mosquito-curtains of white gauze, a Jinshan carpet —
Once Yuelian had stood up, her face was all smiles.
She was dressed in the new jacket she had received;
The poor and lower-middle peasants cared for her,
As soon as she stepped outside, one would lead her.

As soon as she stepped outside, one would lead her:
The old and the new society were truly worlds apart.
In the old days she was rudely chased off as a beggar,
Now she was a representative in the farmers' union;
When a meeting was held, she was seated in front.

When a meeting was held, she was seated in front —
Very quickly a few years had passed and were gone,
When the province had dispatched a medical team
Which included among its staff one famous doctor
Who cured people by the millions and even more!

Who cured people by the millions and even more.
When this doctor came and had a look at Yuelian,
He diagnosed her blindness and proposed a cure.
It would only take ten days, perhaps a few more;
He would treat her gratis, she didn't have to pay!

He would treat her gratis, she didn't have to pay.
When Yuelian heard this, she was happy indeed.
The doctor promptly went ahead with his surgery,
He scraped away some layers of white membrane,
And then wrapped her face in his medical gauze.

He then wrapped her face in his medical gauze,
And after her eyes had healed for eleven days,
The doctor came and removed these bandages.
Blue rivers and green hills appeared before her:
A new heaven had opened in Yuelian's heart!

So a new heaven had opened in Yuelian's heart.
When with feeble steps she walked up to the hall,
And there saw the Chairman's portrait on the wall,[19]
Hot tears came gushing down, soaking her breast,
And she said: "You are to us the great saving star!"

The great saving star!
With concrete actions she repaid the Party's favors.
After land reform came the co-operative movement.
In every activity Yuelian competed to be in the front;
For the sake of the Revolution she hoed the fields.

For the sake of the Revolution she hoed the fields.
Let's change the subject and sing about Li Shugen.
After he had been arrested and become a soldier,
His belly was filled with hatred, a lasting memory,
And he swore he would return and take revenge.

And he swore he would return and take revenge.
The Jiang army dispatched him to Heyuan district.
While marching the troops were all tied together;

---

[19] The Chairman refers to Mao Zedong.

Every five men were tied together with one rope:
He might want to desert, but he had no chance.

He might want to desert, but he had no chance —
But Li Shugen turned out to be quite inventive.
At night they were billeted in an upstairs room.
He then tied his leg bandages to his leg bandages;
Holding on to this one long rope, he climbed down.

And holding on to a long rope, he climbed down.
In the dark of the night he escaped from Heyuan.
After walking for five days and four nights on end,
He came back to Dabu in the middle of the night,
With the firm intention of killing that Qiu Peiyuan.

With the firm intention of killing that Qiu Peiyuan.
When he arrived at that landlord's firewood shed,
He gathered eight or nine armfuls of dried rushes,
Which he all piled up in front of the landlord's gate,
And with the first lighted match he started the fire.

And with the first lighted match he started the fire.
Those burning flames reddened one half of the sky.
The landlord and his family shouted for their life,
Just like shrimps that are fried or cooked in a wok.
Grabbing the money boxes they groaned and died.

They groaned and died —
Because each and every person hated Qiu Peiyuan,
None among the masses there rushed to his rescue.
They all said that it was good riddance of bad rubbish,
And all kept on watching till the main gate collapsed.

They all kept on watching till the main gate collapsed.
Shugen did not dare stay and live in that community;
He also learned that Yuelian had committed suicide,

So he moved away to make a living by his carrying pole
Till his feet were blistered and his shoulders inflamed.

Till his feet were blistered, his shoulders inflamed.
Sun and moon move like a shuttle: one year passed.
By that time Shugen had met up with a guerilla unit,
He had joined the Revolution, engaged in struggle:
Breaching the enemy lines he was walking in front.

Breaching the enemy lines he was walking in front.
For four, five years he fought up north, down south.
Following Liberation he changed his line of work,
And was assigned for an appointment to Changting.
He then requested a leave to go home for New Year.

VII *The Reunion*
He then requested leave to go home for New Year.
Shugen met on that occasion with Huang Yuelian.
Meeting again after a long parting he was moved,
And he did not know what to say at this moment,
He had never imagined there could be a reunion.

He had never imagined there could be a reunion.
He started the conversation by asking Yuelian:
"Whatever happened to the baby you carried?
Husband and wife, we've been apart nine years,
I am sorry for all the sufferings I've caused you."

I am sorry for all the suffering I have caused you.
With tears in her eyes Yuelian told him the story:
"From beginning to end I will tell you all details —
I abandoned the child by some roadside pavilion;
In the absence of information he can't be found."

In the absence of information he can't be found.
On the next day of his return back home again,

Li Shugen spoke to the regional administration.
The region dispatched a telegram to all districts
To conduct a search in each village and hamlet.

To conduct a search in each village and hamlet:
Their son was found to be living in Dalongtian.
The adoptive parents loved the boy very much,
And had given the boy the name Liu Lusheng.[20]
He was now a second year student in school.

He was now a second year student in school.
When husband and wife arrived in Dalongtian,
And found their child and saw him in person,
Everybody was smiling, now meeting together:
At the fifteenth of the month, the moon is full.

At the fifteenth of the month, the moon is full:
Shugen carefully observed his son Liu Lusheng.
He saw he carried a fountain pen on his person
And wore the bright red scarf around his neck.[21]
His attitude and face resembled Huang Yuelian.

His attitude and face resembled Huang Yuelian.
Yuelian addressed Lusheng in the following way:
"You mother became a maid at the age of seven
While you now at the age of nine are a student.
If you make a comparison, it is hell and heaven.

"If you make a comparison, it is hell and heaven.
Remember therefore this word of your mother:
We are never allowed to forget class struggle;
Chairman Mao is the great saving star of us all:
For all eternity we can never forget his favors!"

June 17th, 1966, fourth revised version.

---

[20] "Born on the road".

[21] Indicating he is a member of the Young Pioneers, a mass youth organizations for children aged six to fourteen, run by the Communist Youth League.

APPENDIX IV

THE LOST *ROMANCE* OF THE CAREER OF YAP AH LOY

Hakka ballads on migration and emigration tend to stress the hardships of migrants. While the ballads condemn the stories told by snakeheads as lies, we have no ballads on the careers of successful migrants. However, we can obtain an impression of what such success stories may have looked like from Huang Zunxian's long poem "Overseas Merchants" (*Fanke Pian* 番客篇). This poem was written by Huang after he had served as consul-general at Singapore in the early 1890s. It begins with the description of the opulent mansion of one of the members of the Singapore Chinese business elite that has been ostentatiously decorated for a wedding celebration. Following a description of the foreign guests and their curious customs (such as whites bringing along their wives and "Persian merchants" with their turbaned heads), the poet turns to a detailed description of the sumptuous outfits of bride and groom as they are escorted to their wedding chambers, before depicting the lively party of the Chinese guests. At this moment the poem provides several vignettes of overseas Chinese who had made a fortune from scratch and it is such Singapore lore (a mixture of admiration and envy), one imagines, that must have spread widely and induced thousands upon thousands of Hakka men and women to leave their villages. One of the guests, Huang tells his readers, is a shipping tycoon who had been a poor fisherman: he had been blown to the Southern Oceans by a typhoon, but as his boat had survived the storm he had changed his line of business and soon owned tens of ships.

Dressed in white at the head of the table:
Fishing on sea, he plied the oars for a living.
A tornado once blew him down to the south,
But fortunately his junk was not damaged.
   Originally he only managed a cargo boat
That hugged the coast, visiting nearby ports,
But now he has tens and tens of steamboats
Which come and go across the oceans at will.
   He has so much silver one fears it fell from the air.
Like a coiling dragon he guards millions of strings.
For many years he now has served as *kapitan*;[1]
From early on was named head of foreigners.[2]

A second guest, Huang is informed, had been a poor miner who had struck it rich by chancing upon an endless supply of tin:

The one to the left with the dark complexion —
His father had long been working the mines,
But he returned empty-handed from treasure mountains:
Losses and gains were not enough to offset each other.
   Then suddenly he spied a peck of tin,
And that was an inexhaustible supply.
So then he was just like a dirt-poor student
Whose name is listed on the golden poster.[3]

---

[1] Dutch and British colonial authorities appointed rich members of the local Chinese business elite as leaders of their local communities of Chinese with military titles such as lieutenant, captain (*kapitan*) and major.
[2] Huang Zunxian 1981, 625.
[3] Huang Zunxian 1981, 625–626.

As Huang proceeds with his portrait gallery of successful Singapore Chinese businessmen, his tone becomes more satirical, as is brought out in the following vignette on a project developer:

Seated to his right with his a fine round face:
He truly exhibits the marks of a rich man.
But originally he did not even possess an awl;
It is only here that he started in business.
   By the seaside he occupied a stretch of land,
Cleared the open spaces of shrub and weeds....

Then the land value was counted in gold,
And now it has all become built-up streets.
He resembles a thousand-family marquis,[4]
And everywhere is called Hegemon-King.[5]
   He knows the recipes for proper eating,
And nurtures himself on the hundred tastes.
I have been told he has three minor wives
Who each in turn scratch his itching back.[6]

   Huang continues his catalogue with the portraits of a vicious rich banker and of a ruthless international import and export trader who is involved in fierce competition with westerners.
   Huang then ends his poem, which is addressed not to prospective migrants but to the government, with a plea to make a return to their home country easier for these rich emigrants because they still consider themselves Chinese and maintain Chinese customs, and can greatly contribute to Chinese economic development with their wealth. In this context he also refers to the case of the Minnanese businessman Chen Yi 陳儀, who had served as a lieutenant of the Chinese in Batavia. On his return to his homeland with his

---

[4] In the early Chinese empire a "thousand-family marquis" enjoyed an income equal to the tax payments of a thousand families.
[5] "Hegemon-King" (*bawang* 霸王) is the title adopted by Xiang Yu 項羽 (232–202) after he had succeeded in overthrowing the Qin dynasty.
[6] Huang Zunxian 1981, 626.

Macassarese wife and his huge treasure in 1749, Chen Yi was robbed of his possessions and banished to the northwestern border regions on the accusation of collaboration with the enemy.

Once there was a merchant from Dutch territories
Who came home with hundreds of sacks and bags.
When those who greedily glared liked hungry tigers
Failed to grasp these with their stretched-out hands,
He was falsely accused of collusion with the enemy
And publicly condemned as the worst villain of all.[7]

The case of Chen Yi created quite a stir throughout the region, not only because of the cruel fate he met, but also because of the huge riches he had been able to amass.[8] One wonders whether it may have served as one of the sources of inspiration for *The Tale of the Gauze Skirt* (*Luoqun ji* 羅裙記), one of the titles in the repertoire of the *guwen* performers of Southern Jiangxi. In this tale the student Zhang Yifei 張逸飛 goes abroad to pursue his studies and so impresses the local king that he is given the king's daughter in marriage. When the couple returns to China, the young bride is abducted and Zhang thrown into the water as soon as their boat docks in Canton harbor — in this case, of course, the story ends happily because the couple is eventually reunited after many adventures.[9]

---

[7] Huang Zunxian 1981, 632.

[8] Ng 1991. The Qing dynasty at the time did allow overseas trade but did not allow long-term stays abroad. In strict legal terms, Chen Yi was not allowed to return to China, but other overseas merchants had been allowed to do so (with the help of some bribery in the right places). Chen Yi had the bad luck to arrive in Fujian when the provincial authorities were very much concerned about security issues. A few years later government regulations were broadened, but apparently rich overseas merchants remained suspicious.

[9] Huang Yuying and Yuan Dawei 2008, 172. This story should be distinguished from a quite popular play of the same title, which has a completely different plot.

Among the business elite of Singapore of the 19th century, however, Hakka were almost invisible, but Huang's host points out to him one person who hails from his hometown:

A scorpion nose and shallow complexion —
That person comes from our hometown.
The south is suitable for plants and trees;
Wherever you plant them the earth is fertile.
  He planted a thousand rows of coconut palms,
The flowers of cloves bloom on all sides.
And also cardamom and black pepper
Every year yield a bountiful harvest.

...

He still smells after the night soil he carried,
But his horses and oxen are fed on grains.[10]

This would fit in with the common impression that, once the mines were exhausted, the former miners (mostly Hakka) would often turn to subsistence farming or the cultivation of cash crops.[11] The unnamed Hakka guest at the wedding party had apparently made his fortune in plantation agriculture.

The Hakka who made the most spectacular career on the Malay Peninsula, however, was Yap Ah Loy (Ye Yalai 葉亞來, 1837–1885), whose success depended very much on his martial skills. Yap was the son of a poor tenant farmer in Huizhou and, when he first came to the Malay Peninsula, he failed as a tin miner and a shop clerk. When his relatives came up with the money for his return trip to China, he gambled the money away and had to stay. His career took off when he became a body guard, after which he made money in pig-trading and struck it rich in tin-mining. He led his fellow Huizhou Hakka immigrants in their battles against local Malays and against Hakka

---

[10] Huang Zunxian 1981, 626.
[11] Carstens 2005, 90. Hakka make up the majority of rural communities of overseas Chinese in Southeast Asia.

from Jiayingzhou (Meixian) during the Selangor Wars of the late 1860s and early 1870s, ending up as the Chinese *kapitan* for Kuala Lumpur.[12] His exploits were greatly admired by nationalist Chinese in China in the first half of the 20th century and, from the middle of the 20th century, he was often touted by Malaysian Chinese as an example of the contributions of the Chinese to the development of their country.[13] Apart from biographical writings kept by the family and a biographical sketch in the colonial archives, however, one of the earliest written accounts of the life of Yap Ah Loy appears to be a Chinese ballad in seven-syllable verse penned by a Kuala Lumpur man soon upon Yap Ah Loy's death. This ballad is only known from its English translation and its headnote by a certain "C.K." on pages 184–185 of the first issue of *The Selangor Journal: Jottings Past and Present* of 1893.[14] The translator transcribes the title of the ballad as "Yap Loi Chat Shin Yin Ngi" which may be his transliteration of *Ye Lai chusheng yanyi* 葉來出生演義 (Romance of the Career of Yap Ah Loy). This translation, including its headnote, is reprinted here in full.[15]

C.K. informs us in his headnote that certain lines which might offend the surviving members of Yap Ah Loy's family had been removed from the copy placed at his disposal. Because the translated ballad starts rather abruptly without the conventional opening lines, these cuts most likely especially affected the beginning of the text in which its subject was announced and briefly characterized. The translated text offers a coherent narrative, so most likely suffered only a few or no cuts. These deletions did not necessarily result in a positive image of the hero. Sharon Carstens, a well-known scholar of the history and culture of the Chinese in Malaysia,

---

[12] Middlebrook 1951; Carstens 2005, 10–36.

[13] Carstens 2005, 37–56.

[14] The translation and its headnote have been reproduced in Gullick 2007, 527–530. Whereas Yap's name nowadays is commonly transcribed as Yap Ah Loy, C. K. uses the transcription Yap Ah Loi. In the reproduction of his translation and its headnote, I have preserved that spelling.

[15] I have been unable to locate the Chinese original of this ballad. Those surveys of Chinese literature on the Malay Peninsula in the 19th century that I have been able to locate are silent on the subject of Chinese narrative ballads, let alone their composition by local Chinese.

concludes that the anonymous author portrayed Yap Ah Loy as "a malcontent who constantly ran away from trouble, happened to be lucky in battle, but was too lazy to shoulder any real responsibility."[16] She speculates that the anonymous author may have carried a grudge against Yap Ah Loy or his sons and may have belonged to a different dialect group. She also points out, however, some mythical patterns that might be discerned in the story: one might read the ballad as "a traditional Chinese caricature of a pre-destined but unwilling ... leader."[17] One is also reminded of the many fairy tales that tell a story of a lazy boy despised by all who, after many adventures, ends up by marrying a princess and living happily ever after. The notes accompanying the translation are those of the original translator C.K. There is one clarification enclosed in brackets.

***

Yap Ah Loi

The following is a translation of "Yap Loi Chat Shin Yin Ngi," a life of Yap Ah Loi written by a Kuala Lumpur man. I am not able to vouch for the truth of every detail, but it is, I believe, as to the main facts a correct account. Many of the men who took part in the scenes referred to are still in the State. The original is in lines of seven characters, each line as a rule completing a sentence. The original has been followed as closely as such knowledge as I have of a dialect of Chinese would allow. I understand that certain passages likely to be distasteful to the relatives of Yap Ah Loi had been omitted from the copy of "Shin Yin Ngi Yap Loi Chut" which I succeeded in obtaining.

The translation may be of interest to some of the readers of the *Selangor Journal*, as giving from a Chinese point of view, an outline of some of some of the events which preceded the establishment of a British Protectorate over this State. That there were reasons other than that mentioned below for the British control being extended to the mining district over which the Captain China had power, is easily realised on comparing Kuala Lumpur as it is to-day with what

---

[16] Carstens 2005, 42.
[17] Carstens 2005, 42.

it was some 23 years ago, when, in addition to the Malay wars which distracted the country, the rival factions of Chinese were fighting against each other and collecting the most desperate characters from Southern China to make up their forces.

Yap Ah Loi

Yap Ah Loi in his early days got into trouble. He was starving for three months and more. At that time no one at home would help him and poverty forced him to go abroad. When he arrived in a foreign land his sufferings increased. Morning and night he had to bathe, and frequent bathing was not the only hardship.[18]

Finding a miner's life unbearable, he determined to go elsewhere and from Klang he ran away to Malacca.[19] Who can tell what he suffered in that town? He wants to rise, but knows not how; unable to find a living there he went to Sungei Ujong. He had no money to start in trade, but he came across Yap Ah Shak,[20] who assisted him, putting him in charge of the Gaming Farm. Now Yap Ah Loi was in charge of a farm, but he had not held that position long when a war broke out in Sungei Ujong. Malays attacked the State, and day and night men fled in sore distress. Yap Ah Loi escaped to the jungle and took refuge with some charcoal burners; but Malays came to rob their house, and he was shot in the thigh. Badly wounded, hardly conscious, he thinks he is destined to die far away in the jungle. After a time some men found him and gave him assistance, carrying him back to the town. There he was left to his own resources, and was in great distress for several months. Then his countrymen met to consider his case. As he was young and a man who in time was bound to do well, they decided to help him. Si Yiu was told, and greatly pitying him, had him carried to the kongsi,

---

[18] The Chinese in the State hold that a newcomer can only ward off fever by bathing every morning and night. Mining sinkehs are made to bath at 4.30 A.M. and 10 P.M. every day. Mining sinkehs do not as a rule possess towels.

[19] He had probably received advances and would have been detained if his intention to leave had been known.

[20] Captain China, Selangor, after the death of Yap Ah Loi.

where Si Yin's wife treated his wound and prepared his medicines. After a time the wound was cured and Yap Ah Loi stayed at the kongsi and worked as a miner. He had not been mining long before he felt a desire to go elsewhere. Day and night, discontented, he pondered what to do. Finally he ran away to Kuala Lumpur.

When he reached this State, he at first seemed no better off. He wanted to start a pig-killing business. This he did succeed in doing and in course of time made money. Now the days quickly passed, and several years went by, assured good-fortune smiling upon him. Year by year adding to his gains, his influence increased. He thought of returning to China, but people advised him to marry. At once he sent a match-arranger to the house of the family Koh.

The birth-paper was written and brought to his house, and then his birth-paper was sent to the fortune-teller. All was satisfactory, the bride was brought to the house and the marriage completed.

His bride had not long been brought home when Captain Liu, feeling his end was drawing near, thus spoke to the Sultan: "This country will shortly need a headman; if a Captain is not appointed, I fear there will be fighting." The Sultan answered: "Your words are true, I will make Ah Si Captain." Ah Si answered: "I cannot accept, Yap Ah Loi is a fit man." Captain Liu supported this, saying: "A Si is a strong, capable man." The headmen of the four races assented, and Yap Ah Loi was then appointed Captain. The Sultan's wife arrived in Kuala Lumpur and Yap Ah Loi was invested with the office.

He had not held office long when the Ka Yin Chu men[21] rebelled, following the Malay leader Lah Yah San (Raja Hasan). Yap Ah Loi was beaten and reduced to sore straits. He tried to find a way out of his difficulties and sent letters to China to bring over fresh forces. An immense number of men came over and joined him at the Klang stockades, where he was staying. He led his men against Kuala Lumpur, but driven off by the guns, he returned defeated to Klang. Now he knows not what to do; but (the Deity) Suh Yah appears in a dream to him and thus addresses him: "Within the

---

[21] A division of the Hakkas or Khes. Yap Ah Loi was a Fui Chu Hakka. [Yap Ah Loy was a Huizhou Hakka. Kah Yin Chu transcribes Jiayingzhou.]

camp there is a man to help you. His name is Yap Ah Chin. He formerly had experience in war, and can make rockets to give you victory over the Malays." Yap Ah Loi now gladly orders Ah Chin to manufacture rockets. When the rockets were properly made, he led his men on foot and on horseback against the Malays. The Malays were ready, trusting in their methods of warfare; they did not know that men who could make rockets were coming against them. One volley was fired and they were beaten. Yap Ah Loi at once returned to Kuala Lumpur. He captured 300 Ka Yin Chu men, and shut them up at the "Big Eastern Gate".[22] His brothers[23] wanted vengeance, and treacherously cut off the heads of the great number of these men.[24] When Yap Ah Loi found out what they were doing, he stopped them and saved the remainder (70 men). Before this all the Malays had run away or been killed. Peace gradually returned to Kuala Lumpur.

Yap Si[25] was in charge of Kanching. Who can tell the thirst for revenge in the hearts of the Ka Yin Chu men? A complete force of men and horses went against Kanching. Meeting Yap Si on the way they killed him by the roadside. Truly the horse of Yap Si was a good animal. It galloped to Kuala Lumpur, where it stopped and neighed three times, and Yap Ah Loi knew that something was wrong.

He went forth with his men to render assistance and found the body of Yap Si by the roadside. They took up the body of Yap Si and in sorrow bore it back to Kuala Lumpur. But the matter of Yap Si was not yet finished.

---

[22] This was a gate to the enclosure in which the house of Yap Ah Loi, the Gaming House, and other buildings stood.

[23] They had come from China with the forces mentioned above.

[24] It is said these men were taken down to the river in tens, being told they were going to bathe. Their heads were cut off near where the Java Street Bridge now stands. When the greater number had been disposed of this way, the remainder, seeing their fellow-prisoners not return, grew alarmed, and their cries caused Yap Ah Loi to interfere.

[25] Mentioned above as having refused the office of Captain.

Chong Chong[26] had now become a rebel leader. He thought nothing of wealth, his one desire was to catch Yap Ah Loi, and Yap Ah Loi was in fear. The headmen of Kuala Lumpur held a meeting. It was clear that Chong Chong was at Ampang with a large force. Wong Shiu gave his opinion that he should be attacked at once. When Chong Chong saw the attacking force he fled in fear. Yap Ah Loi then led his men back to Kuala Lumpur and went against Kanching. At Kanching he fought the Kah Yin Chu men, drove them off and gained the town. He then marched to Ulu Selangor winning back all the towns.

After these events he stayed at home and prospered much. In time the country grew prosperous and Yap Ah Loi found the work too burdensome. He invited the English[27] to look after the district, and got a large pension and lived at ease for 17 years.

It was the wish of his heart to return to China, but who can tell Heaven's reasons for opposing the desires of men? He passed away.[28] The English learnt he was dead by the flag flying at the Residency; for God, Whose power to give honour to His servants is beyond our knowledge, on that day struck and broke the flag-staff. When the English found this, they dare not raise the flag again. They held a meeting and determined to be present at the funeral and follow to the grave.

None the less the State continued to prosper greatly.

The tale is finished. May it be well mentioned in future ages! I am a writer of little knowledge, but others of greater skill may complete the lines and round the verses. Should such a man complete this work may he long prosper and his good name go down to his descendants. This is the whole story of Captain Yap Ah Loi.

C.K.

---

[26] Chong Chong had hoped to be made Captain.
[27] Literally, the red-haired men.
[28] Yap Ah Loi died in 1886.

BIBLIOGRAPHY

Anonymous. 2013a. "A Song Urging People Not to Travel to Taiwan." Trans. by Wilt L. Idema. *Taiwanese Literature: English Translation Series* 31–32: 27–34.

Anonymous. 2013b. "The Song of Peach Blossom's Competition in Magic with Master Zhou." Trans. by Wilt L. Idema. *Taiwanese Literature: English Translation Series* 31–32: 83–116.

Anonymous. 2013c. "Tale of Tang Xian." Trans. by Wilt L. Idema. *Taiwanese Literature: English Translation Series* 31–32: 225–244.

Ban Youshu 班友書. 1992. "Guju *Gao Wenju* minjian yanchuben *Shuiyun ting* de xin faxian ji qi yiyi" 古劇高文舉民間演出本水雲亭的新發現及其意義 [The new discovery and the meaning of *Shuiyun ting*, a popular performance script of the old play *Gao Wenju*]. *Wenxian* 1992 no. 1: 29–37.

Baum, Richard. 1975. *Prelude to Revolution: Mao, the Party and the Peasant Question.* New York: Columbia University Press.

Baum, Richard and Teiwes, Frederick. 1968. Ssu-ch'ing: *The Socialist Education Movement of 1962–1966.* Berkeley: Center for Chinese Studies, University of California.

Birch, Cyril. 1973. "Tragedy and Melodrama in Early *Ch'uan-ch'i* Plays: 'Lute Song' and 'Thorn Hairpin' Compared." *Bulletin of the School of Oriental and African Studies* 36, 2: 228–247.

Birrell, Anne. 1993. *Chinese Mythology: An Introduction.* Baltimore: The John Hopkins University Press.

Birrell, Anne. 2008. *China's Bawdy: The Pop Songs of China, 4th–5th Century.* Cambridge: McGuinness.

Brokaw, Cynthia J. 2007. *Commerce in Culture: The Sibao Book Trade in the Qing and Republican Periods.* Cambridge MA: Harvard University Asia Center.

Bruun, Ole. 2008. *An Introduction to Feng Shui.* Cambridge: Cambridge University Press.

Bulag, Uradyn E. 2010. "Can the Subaltern Not Speak? On the Regime of Oral History in Socialist China." *Inner Asia* 12 no. 1: 95–111.

C. K. 1893. "Yap Ah Loi." *The Selangor Journal* 1: 184–185.

Carstens, Sharon A. 2005. *Histories, Cultures and Identities: Studies in Malaysian Chinese Worlds.* Singapore: Singapore University Press.

Char, Andrew. 1982. "Social Origins of Ethnicity: The Hakka in Central Kwantung." *Stone Lion Review* 9: 53–78.

Char, Tin-Yuk (Hsieh T'ing-yü) and Kwock, C. H. (Huo Ch'ang-ch'eng). 1969. *The Hakka Chinese: Their Origins and Folk Songs.* San Francisco: Jade Mountain Press.

Chen Hong 陳紅. 2007. "Gannan Kejia guwen tanxi" 贛南客家古文探析 [An investigation of the Hakka 'old tales' of Southern Jiangxi]. *Nongye kaogu* 2007 no. 6: 195–197.

Chen Jianming 陳健銘. 1996. "Cong gezaice kan Taiwan zaoqi shehui" 從歌仔冊看台灣早期社會 [A look at Taiwan's early society on the basis of song books]. *Taiwan wenxian* 47, 3: 61–110.

Chen Zi'ai 陳子艾. 2004. "Zhong Jingwen geyaoxue jianshe licheng shuxi" 鍾敬文歌謠學建設歷程述析 [A description of the historical stages of the formation of Zhong Jingwen's folksong scholarship]. In Yang Zhe. 2004: 366–388.

Chuang Yin-chang. 1989. "Settlement Patterns of the Hakka Migration to Taiwan: The Case of the T'ou-fen Ch'en Family." *Zhongyang yanjiuyuan minzuxue yanjiu jikan/Bulletin of the Institute of Ethnology, Academia Sinica* 66: 169–193.

Cohen, Myron L. 1968. "The Hakka or 'Guest People': Dialect as a Socio-cultural Variable in Southeastern China." *Ethnohistory* 15, 3: 237–292.

Cole, Alan. 1998. *Mothers and Sons in Chinese Buddhism.* Stanford: Stanford University Press.

Constable, Nicole. Ed. 1996. *Guest People: Hakka Identity in China and Abroad.* Seattle: University of Washington Press.

Diesinger, Günther. 1984. *Vom General zum Gott: Guan Yü (gest. 220 n.Chr.) und seine posthume Kariere* [From general to god: Guan Yu (d. 220) and his posthumous career]. Frankfurt: Haag und Herchen.

Doleželová-Velingerová, M. and Crump, J I. Trans. 1971. *Ballad of the Hidden Dragon:* Liu Chih-yuan chu-kung-tiao. Oxford: Oxford University Press.

Duara, Prasenjit. 1988. "Superscribing Symbols: The Myth of Guandi, Chinese God of War." *Journal of Asian Studies* 47: 778–795.

Dudbridge, Glen. 1996. *China's Vernacular Cultures: An Inaugural Lecture delivered before the University of Oxford on 1 June 1995*. Oxford: Clarendon Press.

Dudbridge, Glen. 2004. *The Legend of Miaoshan*. Oxford: Oxford University Press. Revised edition.

Dudbridge, Glen. 2005. "The Goddess Huayue Sanniang and the Cantonese Ballad *Chenxiang Taizi*." In Glen Dudbridge, *Books, Tales and Vernacular Culture: Selected Papers on China*, 303–320. Leiden: Brill.

Dunhuang Quzixi 敦煌曲子戲 [Dunhuang song theater. 2010]. Lanzhou: Gansu renmin meishu chubanshe.

Eberhard, Wolfram. 1972. *Taiwanese Ballads, A Catalogue*. Taipei: The Orient Cultural Service.

Elman, Benjamin A. 2000. *A Cultural History of Civil Examinations in Late Imperial China*. Berkeley: University of California Press.

Elman, Benjamin A. 2013. *Civil Examinations and Meritocracy in Late Imperial China*. Cambridge MA: Harvard University Press.

Emimov, Sandra. 1975. "Folklore and Nationalism in Modern China." *Journal of the Folklore Institute* 12, 2–3: 257–277.

Erbaugh, M. S. 1992. "The Secret History of the Hakka: The Chinese Revolution as a Hakka Enterprise." *China Quarterly* 132: 937–968.

Fan Rong 繁榮. 1956. "Zhang Gudong jieqi *he* Jieqi pei" 張古董借妻和借妻配 [*Second-Hand Zhang rents out his wife* and *Marriage with a borrowed wife*]. *Xiju Bao* 12: 28–29.

Feng Menglong. Ed. 2000. *Stories Old and New: A Ming Dynasty Collection*. Trans. by Yang, Shuhui and Yang, Yunqin. Seattle: University of Washington Press.

Grant, Beata. 1989. "The Spiritual Saga of Woman Huang: From Pollution to Purification." In *Ritual Opera, Operatic Ritual: "Mu-lien Rescues his Mother" in Chinese Popular Culture*, edited by Johnson, David, 224–311. Publications of the Chinese Popular Culture Project 1. Berkeley: University of California.

Grant, Beata and Idema, Wilt L. 2011. *Escape from Blood Pond Hell: The Tales of Mulian and Woman Huang*. Seattle: University of Washington Press.

Gullick, J. M. Ed. 2007. *History from the Selangor Journal*. Kuala Lumpur: Malaysian Branch of the Royal Asiatic Society.

Guo, Qitao. 2005. *Ritual Opera and Mercantile Lineage: The Confucian Transformation of Popular Culture in Late Imperial Huizhou*. Stanford: Stanford University Press.

Guo Wu. 2013. "The Social Construction and Deconstruction of Evil Landlords in Contemporary Chinese Fiction, Arts, and Collective Memory." *Modern Chinese Literature and Culture* 25, 1: 131–164.

Guo Yingde 郭英德. 1997. *Ming Qing chuanqi zonglu* 明清傳奇綜錄 [A comprehensive catalogue of *chuanqi* plays from the Ming and Qing dynasties]. 2 Vols. Shijiazhuang: Hebei jiaoyu chubanshe.

Haar, Barend J. ter. 2000. "The Rise of the Guan Yu Cult: The Taoist Connection." In *Linked Faiths: Essays on Chinese Religions and Traditional Cultures in Honour of Kristofer Schipper*, edited by Meyer, Jan, A.M., de and Engelfriet, Peter M., 184–204. Leiden: Brill.

Haft, Lloyd. Ed. 1989. *A Selective Guide to Chinese Literature 1900–1949.* Vol. 3, *The Poem*. Leiden: Brill.

Hayden, G. A. 1978. *Crime and Punishment in Medieval Chinese Drama*. Cambridge MA: Harvard University Press.

He Jia 賀嘉. 2004. "Zhong Jingwen yu minjian wenxue jicheng" 鍾敬文與民間文學集成 [Zhong Jingwen and the Complete Collections of Folk Literature]. In Yang Zhe 2004: 485–492.

He, Qiliang. 2012. *Gilded Voices: Economics, Politics, and Storytelling in the Yangzi Delta since 1949*. Leiden: Brill.

Hom, Marlon K. 1987. *Songs of Gold Mountain: Cantonese Rhymes from San Francisco*. Berkeley: University of California Press.

Hou Jie. 2002. "Mulian Drama: A Commentary on Current Research and Source Materials." In *Ethnography in China Today: A Critical Assessment of Methods and Results*, edited by Overmyer, Daniel, 23–48. Taipei: Yuan-liou Publishing.

Hu Xizhang 胡希張. 2007. "Kai Kejia shange yanjiu zhi xianhe: qianxi Luo Xianglin de *Yuedong zhi feng*" 開客家山歌研究之先河: 淺析羅香林的粵東之風 [A pioneer in the study of Hakka mountain songs: an evaluation of Luo Xianglin's *Yuedong zhi feng*]. *Kejia yanjiu jikan* 2007 no. 2: 48–54.

Hu Xizhang. 2010. *Kejia zhubange yanjiu* 客家竹板歌研究 [A study of Hakka bamboo-clappers songs]. Guangzhou: Guangdong renmin chubanshe.

Hu Xizhang. 2013. *Kejia shange shi yanjiu* 客家山歌史研究 [A study on the history of Hakka mountain songs]. Guangzhou: Guangdong renmin chubanshe.

Hu Xizhang and Yu Yaonan 余耀南. 1993. *Kejia shange zhishi daquan* 客家山歌知識大全 [All there is to know about Hakka mountain songs]. Guangzhou: Huashan chubanshe.

Huang Changsheng 黃昌盛. 2004. "Yidu shange" 一都山歌 [Mountain songs from Yidu]. http://www.daishanyan.com/yds.htm (accessed November 4th, 2012).

Huang Huoxing 黃火興. 1979. *Tantan Kejia shange* 談談客家山歌 [Chats on Hakka mountain songs]. Guangzhou: Guangdong renmin chubanshe.

Huang Huoxing. 1982. *Kejia qingge jingxuan yiqian jiubai shou* 客家情歌精選 1900首 [1900 Hakka love songs, a careful selection]. Guangzhou: Huacheng chubanshe.

Huang Jufang 黃菊芳. 2007. "Keyu chaoben *Du Tai beige* yanjiu" 客語抄本渡台悲歌研究 [A study of the Hakka manuscripts of *Du Tai beige*]. PhD Thesis, National Chengchih Univeristy, Taipei.

Huang Rongluo 黃榮洛. 1990. "'Quanjun qiemo guo Taiwan': *Du Tai beige* de faxian yu yanjiu" 勸君切莫過台灣：渡台悲歌的發現與研究 ["I urge you, gentlemen, never migrate to Taiwan": the discovery of *Du Tai beige* and a study]. In Huang Rongluo, *Du Tai beige: Taiwan de kaituo yu kangzhen shihua* 渡台悲歌：台灣的開拓與抗爭史話 [A sad song on Moving to Taiwan: historical essays on the development of Taiwan and resistance struggle], 22–51. Taipei: Taiyuan chubanshe.

Huang Rongluo. 2005. "Zhuanzai *Jin Hudie* de chuxian" 傳仔金蝴蝶的出現 [The discovery of the *zhuanzai* story *Jin Hudie*]. *Xinzhu wenxian* 19: 57–69.

Huang Shan 黃山. 2012. "Hezhou Kejia zhubange: Hezhou minjian yinyue wenhua yishu yanjiu zhi er" 賀州客家竹板歌：賀州民間音樂文化研究之二 [The Hakka bamboo-clappers songs of Hezhou: studies on the culture and art of Hezhou popular music, no. 2]. *Hezhou xueyuan xuebao* 2012 no. 1: 54–56.

Huang Wenhua 黃文華 and Liu Xiaolan 劉小蘭. 2006. "Gannan Ningdu daoqing yishu qianxi" 贛南寧都道情藝術淺析 [An analysis of the art of *daoqing* storytelling from Ningdu in Southern Jiangxi]. *Nongye kaogu* 2006 no. 6: 212–214.

Huang Yuying 黃玉英 and Yuan Dawei 袁大位. 2008. "Gannan Kejia guwen de renwen jiazhi yu yishu tese" 贛南客家古文的人文價值與藝術特色 [The cultural value and artistic characteristics of the Hakka 'old tales' from Southern Jiangnan]. *Zhongguo yinyue* 2008 no. 2: 171–173.

Huang Ziyao 黃子堯. 2003. *Kejia minjian wenxue* 客家民間文學 [Hakka folk literature]. Xinzhuang: Kejia Taiwan wenshi gongzuoshi.

Huang Zunxian 黃遵憲. 1981. *Renjinglu shicao jianzhu* 人境廬詩草箋注. Ann. by Qian Zhonglian 錢仲聯 [An annotated edition of *Renjinglu shicao*]. Shanghai: Shanghai guji chubanshe.

Hung, Chang-tai. 1985. *Going to the People: Chinese Intellectuals and Folk Literature, 1918–1937*. Cambridge MA: Harvard University Press.

Idema, Wilt L. 2007. *Meng Jiangnü Brings Down the Great Wall: Ten Versions of a Chinese Legend*. Seattle: University of Washington Press.

Idema, Wilt L. 2008. *Personal Salvation and Filial Piety: Two Precious Scroll Narratives of Guanyin and Her Acolytes.* Honolulu: University of Hawai'i Press.

Idema, Wilt L. 2009a. *Filial Piety and Its Divine Rewards: The Legend of Dong Yong and Weaving Maiden, with Related Texts.* Indianapolis: Hackett.

Idema, Wilt L. 2009b. *Heroines of Jiangyong: Chinese Narrative Ballads in Women's Script.* Seattle: University of Washington Press.

Idema, Wilt L. 2009c. *The White Snake and Her Son: A Translation of* The Precious Scroll of Thunder Peak, *with Related Texts.* Indianapolis: Hackett.

Idema, Wilt L. 2010a. *The Butterfly Lovers: The Legend of Liang Shanbo and Zhu Yingtai. Four Versions, with Related Texts.* Indianapolis: Hackett.

Idema, Wilt L. 2010b. *Judge Bao and the Rule of Law: Eight Ballad-Stories from the Period 1250–1450.* Singapore: World Scientific.

Idema, Wilt L. Trans. 2011a. "An Eighteenth-Century Version of 'Liang Shanbo and Zhu Yingtai' from Suzhou." In *The Columbia Anthology of Chinese Folk and Popular Literature*, edited by Mair, Victor H. and Bender, Mark, 503–551. New York: Columbia University Press.

Idema, Wilt L. Trans. 2011b. "The Precious Scroll of Chenxiang." In *The Columbia Anthology of Chinese Folk and Popular Literature*, edited by Mair, Victor H. and Bender, Mark, 380–405. New York: Columbia University Press.

Idema, Wilt L. Introd. and trans. 2012. "Fourth Sister Zhang Creates Havoc in the Eastern Capital," *Chinoperl Papers* 31: 37–112.

Idema, Wilt L. and West, Stephen H. 2012. *Battles, Betrayals, and Brotherhood: Early Chinese Plays on the Three Kingdoms.* Indianapolis: Hackett.

Idema, Wilt L. and West, Stephen H. 2013. *The Generals of the Yang Family: Four Early Plays.* Hackensack NJ: World Century/Singapore: World Scientific.

Jie Yingli 揭英麗. 2006. "Kejia shange yanjiu zongshu" 客家山歌研究綜述 [A survey of the study of Hakka mountain songs]. *Minjian wenhua luntan* 2006 no. 4: 91–95.

Joniak-Lüthi, Agnieszka. 2013. "The Han *Minzu*, Fragmented Identities, and Ethnicity." *The Journal of Asian Studies* 72, 4: 849–871.

Jordan, David K. 1986. "Folk Filial Piety in Taiwan: *The Twenty-four Filial Exemplars.*" In *The Psycho-Cultural Dynamics of the Confucian Family: Past and Present*, edited by Slote, Walter H., 47–112. Seoul: International Cultural Society of Korea.

Kao, Karl S. Y. Ed. 1985. *Classical Chinese Tales of the Supernatural and the Fantastic: Selections from the Third to Tenth Centuries.* Bloomington: Indiana University Press.

Katz, Paul. 1999. *Images of the Immortal: The Cult of Lü Dongbin at the Palace of Eternal Joy.* Honolulu: University of Hawai'i Press.

Ke Rongsan 柯榮三. 2013. "Fanping qianwan bu tongxing: Minnan *Guofan ge* zhongde lishi jiyi yu quanshi huayu" 番平千萬不通行:閩南過番歌中的歷史記憶與勸世話語 ["On no account migrate to foreign countries": historical memory and words of warning in the Minnanese 'going-abroad songs']. *Minsu quyi* 179: 185–222.

Kuhn, Philip A. 2008. *Chinese among Others: Emigration in Modern Times.* Lanham: Rowman and Littlefield.

Kuzay, Stephan. 2009. "Life in the Green Lofts of the Lower Yangzi Region." In *Lifestyle and Entertainment in Yangzhou*, edited by Olivová, Lucie, and Bøhrdahl, Vibeke, 286–314. Copenhagen: NIAS Press.

Kwock, C. H. 1988. "Twelve Hakka Folksongs." *Renditions* 29–30: 17–24.

Lai, Mark H., Lim, Genny and Yung, Judy. Eds. 1991. *Angel Island: Poetry and History of Chinese Immigrants on Angel Island,* 1910–1940. Seattle: University of Washington Press.

Lai, T. C. 1972. *The Eight Immortals.* Hong Kong: Swindon Book Company.

Leong, Sow-Theng. 1997. *Migration and Ethnicity in Chinese History: Hakkas, Pengmin, and Their Neighbors.* Edited by Wright, Tim. Stanford: Stanford University Press.

Li Guisheng 李貴生. 2013. "Chuancheng yu bianyi: minjian shuochang neibu jizhi—yi Gansu Wuwei Liangzhou xianxiao *Shili ting* weili" 傳承與變異:民間說唱內部機制—以甘肅武威涼州賢孝十里亭為例 [Tradition and change: the internal system of popular prosimetric storytelling—as exemplified by *Shili ting* in the repertoire of 'Liangzhou moral examplars' from Wuwei in Gansu]. *Hexi xueyuan xuebao* 2013 no. 4: 54–60.

Li Jinfa 李金髮. 1928. *Lingdong liange* 嶺東戀歌 [Love songs of Eastern Guangdong]. Originally published 1928, reprinted in Lou Zikuang 婁子匡. Ed., *Guoli Beijing daxue Zhongguo minsu xuehui minsu congshu* 國立北京大學中國民俗學會民俗叢書. Vol. 4. Taipei: Zhongguo minsu xuehui, 1974.

Li Xiusheng 李修生. Ed. 1997. *Guben xiqu jumu tiyao* 古本戲曲劇目提要 [Classical drama: a title catalogue and content summaries]. Beijing: Wenhua yishu chubanshe.

Lian Jian'an 練建安. 2009. "Kejia minjian shuochang wenben *Zhao Yulin yu Liang Sizhen* chutan" 客家民間說唱文本趙玉麟與梁四珍初探 [An exploration of the Hakka popular prosimetric narrative *Zhao Yulin yu Liang Sizhen*]. In *Haixia liang'an chuantong wenhua yishu yanjiu* 海峽兩岸傳統文化藝術研究 [Studies on the traditional culture and art on both sides of the Taiwan Straits]. Edited by Li Weiwen 李蔚文 and Yang Jigang 楊際崗. 209–215. Fuzhou: Haichao sheying yishu cchubanshe.

Liao Wen 廖文. 2013. "*Sanjingou bian Sanbogong* chengxian de Kejia qunti xinli tezheng" 三斤狗變三伯公呈現的客家群體心理特徵 [The characteristics of Hakka collective psychology as manifested in *Sanjin gou bian Sanbo gong*]. *Nanhua ligong daxue xuebao* 2013 no. 3:111–114.

Lin Geng 林耕. 1944. *Hakka to sanka: dozoku, densetsu, minyō* 客家と山歌土俗傳說民謠 [Hakka and mountain songs: local customs, legends and folksongs]. Shanghai: Yōsukōha Chūshisōkyoku.

Lin Hengdao 林恆道. 1983. "Kejia diqu de Sanguan dadi xinyang" 客家地區的三官大帝信仰 [The belief in the Great Thearchs of the Three Offices in the Hakka areas]. *Taiwan wenxian* 34, 2: 191–192.

Lin Huadong 林華東. 2006. *Quanzhou geyao* 泉州歌謠 [Quanzhou folksongs]. Fuzhou: Fujian renmin chubanshe.

Liu Dake 劉大可. 2007. *Tianye zhong de diyu shehui yu wenhua* 田野中的地域社會與文化 [Local society and culture in the countryside]. Beijing: Minzu chubanshe.

Liu Denghan 劉登翰. 1991. "*Guofan ge* ji qi yiben: *Guofan ge* yanjiu zhi yi" 過番歌及其異本過番歌研究之一 ['Going-abroad songs' and their editions: studies on 'going-abroad songs' no. 1]. *Fujian xuekan* 1991 no. 6: 56–60, 55.

Liu Denghan. 1993. "*Guofan ge* de chansheng he liupo: *Guofange* yanjiu zhi er" 過番歌的產生和流播過番歌研究之二 [The origin and distribution of 'going-abroad songs': studies on 'going-abroad songs' no. 2]. *Fujian luntan* 1993 no. 6: 27–32.

Liu Denghan. 2002. "Lun *Guofange* de banben, liuchuan ji wenhua yiyun" 論過番歌的版本流傳及文化意蘊 [On the editions, distribution and cultural meaning of 'going-abroad songs']. *Huaqiao daxue xuebao* 2002 no. 2: 71–78.

Liu Denghan. 2005. "Zhuisuo Zhongguo haiwai yimin de minjian jiyi: guanyu *Guofange* de yanjiu" 追索中國海外移民的民間記憶關於過番歌的研究 [Retrieving the popular memories of China's overseas migration: a study of 'going-abroad songs']. *Fuzhou daxue xuebao* 2005 no. 4: 11–17.

Liu Denghan. 2014. "Changpian shuochang *Guofan ge* de wenhua chongtu he quanshi zhuti—*Guofan ge* yanjiu zhi san" 長篇說唱過番歌的文化冲突和勸世主題—過番歌研究之三 [Cultural clashes and admonitory themes in long narrative 'going-abroad songs': studies on 'going-abroad songs' no. 3]. *Huaqiao daxue xuebao* 2014 no. 2: 33–40.

Liu, Lydia H. 2003. "A Folksong Immortal and Official Popular Culture in Twentieth-Century China." In *Writing and Materiality in China: Essays in Honor of Patrick Hanan*, edited by Zeitlin, Judith T. and Liu, Lydia H., 553–609. Cambridge MA: Harvard University Asia Center.

Liu, Wu-chi and Lo, Irving Yucheng, Eds. 1975. *Sunflower Splendor: Three Thousand Years of Chinese Poetry*. Garden City NY: Anchor Books.

Liu Xiaochun 劉曉春, Hu Xizhang 胡希張, and Wen Ping 溫萍. 2007. *Kejia shange* 客家山歌 [Hakka mountain songs]. Hangzhou: Zhejiang renmin chubanshe.

Liu Zuoquan 劉佐泉. 2007. "Yibu jidacheng de mingzhu: *Yuedong zhi feng*" 一部集大成的名著:粵東之風 [An all-encompassing masterwork: *Yuedong zhi feng*]. *Kejia yanjiu jikan* 2007 no. 2: 44–47.

Lo, Irving Yucheng and Schultz, William., Eds. 1986. *Waiting for the Unicorn: Poems and Lyrics of China's Last Dynasty*. Bloomington: Indiana University Press.

Lozada Jr., Eriberto. 2005. "Hakka Diaspora." In *Ecyclopedia of Diasporas: Immigrant and Refugee Cultures around the World*, edited by Ember, Carol R., Ember, Melvin and Skoggard, Ian, 92–103. New York: Kluwer Academic/Plenum.

Luo Guanzhong. 1991. *Three Kingdoms: A Historical Novel*. Trans. by Roberts, Moss. Berkeley: University of California Press/Beijing: Foreign Languages Press.

Luo Kequn 羅可群. 2000. *Guangdong Kejia wenxue shi* 廣東客家文學史 [A history of literature by Hakkas from Guangdong province]. Guangzhou: Guangdong renmin chubanshe.

Luo Kequn. 2002a. "Geyao: Kejiaren kaifa Taiwan de wenxue fanying" 歌謠客家人開發台灣的文學反映 [Folksongs: literary reflections of how the Hakkas developed Taiwan]. *Guangdong waiyu waimao daxue xuebao* 2002 no. 3: 83–85.

Luo Kequn. 2002b. "Haiwai Kejia wenxue ji qi qianjing zhanwang: cong Huang Zunxian de 'Fanke pian' shuoqi" 海外客家文學及其前景展望 從黃遵憲的番客篇說起 [Overseas Hakka literature and its prospects: starting from Huang Zunxian's "Overseas Merchants"]. *Hainan shifan xueyuan xuebao* 2002 no. 1: 87–89.

Luo Kequn. 2004. "Kejiaren yu Malai bantao xikuang" 客家人與馬來半島錫礦 [Hakkas and tin-mining on the Malaysian peninsula]. *Jiaying xueyuan xuebao* 2004 no. 5: 79–81.

Luo Xianglin 羅香林. 1936. *Yuedong zhi feng* 粵東之風 [Airs of Eastern Guangdong]. Originally published 1936, reprinted in Lou Zikuang, Ed., *Guoli Beijing daxue Zhongguo minsu xuehui minsu congshu*. Vol. 14. Taipei: Zhongguo minsu xuehui, 1974.

Luo Yingxiang 羅英祥. 1994. *Piaoyang guohai de Kejiaren* 飄洋過海的客家人 [Hakkas who crossed the seas]. Kaifeng: Henan daxue chubanshe.

Ma Jianhua 馬建華. 2003. "Mingchu nanxi *Gao Wenju* ji qi gaixieben" 明初南戲高文舉及其改寫本 [The early-Ming *nanxi* play *Gao Wenju* and its adaptations]. *Xiqu yanjiu* 63 (March 2003): 50–66.

Ma Jianhua. 2006. "Lun *Gao Wenju Zhenzhu ji* de minjian secai" 論高文舉珍珠記的民間色彩 [On the popular features of *Gao Wenju Zhenzhu ji*]. *Yishu baijia* 2006 no. 5: 25–30.

Mair, Victor H. 1983. *Tun-huang Popular Narratives*. Cambridge: Cambridge University Press.

Mair, Victor H. and Bender, Mark, Eds. 2011. *The Columbia Anthology of Chinese Folk and Popular Literature*. New York: Columbia University Press.

Mao Zedong. 1990. *Report from Xunwu*. Translated, with an Introduction and Notes by Thompson, Roger R., Stanford: Stanford University Press.

McDougall, Bonnie S. 1980. *Mao Zedong's "Talks at the Yan'an Conference on Literature and Art": A Translation of the 1943 Text with Commentary*. Ann Arbor: Center for Chinese Studies University of Michigan.

McLaren, Anne E. 2010. "Folk Epics from the Lower Yangzi Delta Region: Oral and Written Traditions." In *The Interplay of the Oral and the Written in Chinese Popular Literature*, edited by Børdahl, Vibeke and Wan, Margaret B., 157–186. Copenhagen: NIAS Press.

McNaughton, W. 1971. *The Book of Songs*. New York: Twayne.

Middlebrook, S. M. 1951. "Yap Ah Loy," *Journal of the Malayan Branch of the Royal Asiatic Society* 24, 2: 1–127 (reprinted as Middlebrook, S. M., *Yap Ah Loy, 1837–1885*. Edited by Gullick, J. M., Kuala Lumpur: Art Printing Works, 1983).

Miska, Maxine. 1993. "Drinking the Blood of Childbirth: The Reincarnation of the Dead in Hakka Funeral Ritual." In *Bodylore*, edited by Galloway Young, Katharine, 88–107. Knoxville: University of Tennessee Press.

Moore, Oliver. 2003. "Violence Un-scrolled: Cultic and Ritual Emphases in Painting Guan Yu," *Arts asiatiques* 58: 86–97.

Moser, Leo J. 1985. *The Chinese Mosaic: The Peoples and Provinces of China*. Boulder/London: Westview Press.

Mulligan, Jean. Trans. 1980. *The Lute: Kao Ming's P'i-p'a chi*. New York: Columbia University Press.

Ng Chin-keong. 1991. "The Case of Chen I-lao: Maritime Trade and Overseas Chinese in Ch'ing Politics." In *Emporia, Commodities and Entrepeneurs in Asian Maritime Trade, c. 1400–1750*, edited by Ptak, Roderich and Rothermund, Dietmar, 373–399. Stuttgart: Franz Steiner Verlag.

Nienhauser, Jr., William, H. Ed. 2010. *Tang Dynasty Tales: A Guided Reader*. Singapore: World Scientific.

Norman, Jeffrey. 1988. *Chinese.* Cambridge: Cambridge University Press.
Ōki Yasushi and Santangelo, Paolo. 2011. *Shan'ge, the 'Mountain Songs': Love Songs in Ming China.* Leiden: Brill.
Ono Kazuko. 1989. *Chinese Women in a Century of Revolution, 1850–1950.* Edited by Fogel, Joshua A. Stanford: Stanford University Press.
Oxfeld, Ellen. 2004. "'When You Drink Water, Think of the Source': Morality, Status and Reinvention in Rural Chinese Funerals." *Journal of Asian Studies* 63, 4: 961–990.
Pan, Lynn. 1991. *Sons of the Yellow Emperor: The Story of the Chinese Overseas.* London: Mandarin.
Pan, Lynn, Ed. 1999. *The Encyclopedia of the Chinese Overseas.* Richmond: Curzon.
Paton, Michael John. 2013. *Five Classics of Feng Shui: Chinese Spiritual Geography in Historical and Environmental Perspective.* Leiden: Brill.
Peng Suzhi 彭素枝. 2003. *Taiwan Liudui Kejia shange yanjiu* 台灣六堆客家山歌研究 [A study of Hakka mountains songs from Liudui on Taiwan]. Taipei: Wenjin chubanshe.
Puk, Wing-kin. 2009. "Reaching out for the Ladder of Success: Outsiders and the Civil Examinations in Late Imperial China." In *Marginalization in China: Recasting Minority Politics*, edited by Cheung, Siu-keung, Tse-Hei Lie, Jospeph, and Nedilsky, Linda V., 21–34. New York: Macmillan.
Qi Biaojia 祁彪佳. 1955. *Yuanshantang Ming qupin jupin jiaolu* 遠山堂明曲品劇品校錄 [An annotated edition of the "Rankings of Ming *chuanqi* plays and Rankings of *zaju* plays from the Distant Mountain Hall]. Edited by Huang Chang 黃裳. Shanghai: Shanghai chubanshe.
Qiu Chunmei 邱春美. 2003. *Taiwan Kejia shuochang wenxue zhuanzai yanjiu* 台灣客家說唱文學傳仔研究 [A study of 'stories', Taiwan's Hakka prosimetric storytelling]. Taipei: Wenjin chubanshe.
Qiu Chunmei. 2008. "Kejia zhuanzai *Chen Baibi* canben de yuwen tantao" 客家傳仔陳白比殘本的語文探討 [A linguistic study of the preserved fragments of the Hakka ballad *Chen Baibi*]. *Chuangxin* 2008 no. 1: 95–98.
Ramsey, S. Robert. 1987. *The Languages of China.* Princeton: Princeton University Press.
Rusk, Bruce. 2012. *Critics and Commentators: the* Book of Poems *as Classic and Literature.* Cambridge MA: Harvard University Asia Center.
Schimmelpenninck, Antoinette. 1997. *Chinese Folk Songs and Folk Singers: Shan'ge Traditions in Southern Jiangsu.* Leiden: Chime.
Schipper, Mineke; Ye Shuxian and Yin Hubin. Eds. 2011. *China's Creation and Origin Myths: Cross-Cultural Explorations in Oral and Written Traditions.* Leiden: Brill.

Schmidt, J. D. 1994. *Within the Human Realm: The Poetry of Huang Zunxian, 1848–1905*. Cambridge: Cambridge University Press.

Schneider, Laurence A. 1971. *Ku Chieh-kang and China's New History: Nationalism and the Quest for Alternative Traditions*. Berkeley: University of California Press.

Shepherd, John Robert. 1993. *Statecraft and Political Economy on the Taiwan Frontier 1600–1800*. Stanford: Stanford University Press.

Shi Nai'an and Luo Guanzhong. 1980. *Outlaws of the Marsh*. Trans. by Shapiro, Sidney. Beijing: Foreign Languages Press.

Skinner, William G. 1997. "Introduction." In Leong, Sow-Theng. *Migration and Ethnicity in Chinese History: Hakkas, Pengmin, and Their Neighbors*, edited by Wright, Tim, 1–18. Stanford: Stanford University Press.

Somers Heidhues, Mary F. 1992. *Bangka Tin and Mentok Pepper: Chinese Settlement on an Indonesian Island*. Singapore: Institute of Southeast Asian Studies.

Soo Khin Wah, see Su Qinghua.

Soymié, Michel. 1965. "*Ketsubon kyō* no shiryōteki kenkyū" 血盆經の資料的研究 [A study on the materials concerning the *Xieben jing*]. *Dōkyō kenkyū* 1: 109–166.

Su Qinghua 蘇慶華. 2012a. "Kejia zuqun guofan Nanyang de gongtong lishi jiyi: yi Kejia *Guofange* wei tantao zhongxin" 客家族群過番南洋的共同歷史記憶以客家過番歌為探討中心 [The common historical memory of the Hakka migrating to Southeast Asia: with a focus on the Hakka 'going-abroad songs']. *Haijiaoshi yanjiu* 2012 no. 1: 103–114.

Su Qinghua. 2012b. "Nanyang guofange de lishi jiyi he fengtu tese—yi Nanyang Minsheng qiaoxiang liuchuan de *Guofange* wei tantao zhongxin" 南洋過番歌的歷史記憶和風土特色—以南洋閩省僑鄉流傳的過番歌為探討中新 [Historical memory and regional characteristics of the 'going-abroad songs' from Southeast Asia: focusing on the 'going-abroad songs' circulating in the home districts of Fujian migrants to Southeast Asia]. *Nanyang xuebao* 66: 1–21.

Su Qinghua. 2013a. "Pasi bulaifan: Hainan zuqun *Guofange* yanjiu" 怕死不來番:海南族群過番歌研究 ["If you are afraid to die, don't come to foreign lands": a study of the 'going-abroad songs' by Hainanese]. *Chengda zhongwen xuebao* 42: 221–241.

Su Qinghua. 2013b. "Wunaihe, chui tianguo: Chaozhou guofange yanjiu" 無奈何炊甜粿:潮州過番歌研究 ["There's no way out but to go abroad": a study of Chaozhou 'going-abroad songs']. *Nanyang xuebao* 67: 57–72.

Su Qinghua, 2014a. "Guangdong guofange yanjiu: yi Zhujiang sanjiao linjin yanhai diqu Yueyuxi guofange wei li" 廣東過番歌研究: 以珠江三角鄰近沿海地區粵語系過番歌為例 [A study of Cantonese 'going-abroad songs': as exemplified by the Cantonese-dialect 'going-abroad songs' from the coastal regions of the Pearl River Delta]. Unpublished paper.

Su Qinghua, 2014b. *Su Qinghua lunwen xuanji disiji: Guofange yanjiu* 蘇慶華論選集第四集過番歌研究 [Selected papers of Su Qinghua, Vol. 4, Studies on 'going-abroad songs']. Kuala Lumpur: K.L. Commercial Book Co.

Teiser, Stephen F. 1988. *The Ghost Festival in Medieval China.* Princeton: Princeton University Press.

Teiser, Stephen F. 1994. *The Scripture of the Ten Kings and the Making of Purgatory in Medieval Chinese Buddhism.* Honolulu: University of Hawai'i.

Teng, Emma Jinhua. 2004. *Taiwan's Imagined Geography: Chinese Colonial Travel Writing and Pictures, 1683–1895.* Cambridge MA: Harvard University Asia Center.

Tian, Xiaofei. 2011. *Visionary Journeys: Travel Writings from Early Medieval and Nineteenth-Century China.* Cambridge MA: Harvard University Asia Center.

Tuohy, Sue. 1991. "Cultural Metaphors and Reasoning: Folklore Scholarship and Ideology in Contemporary China." *Asian Folklore Studies* 50: 189–220.

Van Zoeren, Steven. 1991. *Poetry and Personality: Reading, Exegesis, and Hermeneutics in Traditional China.* Stanford: Stanford University Press.

Waley, Arthur. Trans. 1996. *The Book of Songs: the Ancient Chinese Classic of Poetry.* Ed. with Additional Translations by Allen, Joseph R.; Foreword by Owen, Stephen; Postface by Allen, Jospeh R.. New York: Grove Press.

Wang, C. H. 1974. *The Bell and the Drum: Shih Ching as Formulaic Poetry in an Oral Tradition.* Berkeley: University of California Press.

Wang, C. K. 1984–1985. "Lü Meng-cheng in Yüan and Ming Drama." *Monumenta Serica* 36: 303–408.

Wang Gongwu. 2003. *Don't Leave Home: Migration and the Chinese.* Singapore: Eastern Universities Press.

Wang Senran 王森然. 1997. *Zhongguo jumu cidian* 中國劇目辭典 [A title dictionary of Chinese plays]. Shijiazhuang: Hebei jiaoyu chubanshe.

Wang Shifu, 1995. *The Story of the Western Wing.* Translated with an Introduction by West, Stephen H. and Idema, Wilt L.. Berkeley: University of California Press.

Wang Yan'an 王焰安. 2005. "Ershi shiji shangbanye Guangdong Kejia minjian wenxue souji qingkuang gaishu" 20 世紀上半葉廣東客家民間文學搜集情況概述 [A general description of the situation of the collection of Hakka folk literature in Guangdong in the first half of the twentieth century]. *Jiaying xueyuan xuebao* 2005, October, 87–90.

Wang Yan'an. 2006. "Ershi shiji shangbanye Guangdong Kejia minjian wenxue yanjiu gaishu" 20 世紀上半葉廣東客家民間文學研究概述 [A general description of the situation of the collection of Hakka folk literature in Guangdong in the first half of the twentieth century]. *Minzu wenxue yanjiu* 2006 no. 1: 158–161.

Wen Ping 溫萍. 1992. *Kejia shange tansheng* 客家山歌探勝 [The superior qualities of Hakka mountain songs]. Shenzhen: Haitian chubanshe.

West, Stephen H. and Idema, Wilt L. 2010. *Monks, Bandits, Lovers and Immortals: Eleven Early Chinese Plays*. Indianapolis: Hackett.

Wiens, F. J. n.d. *Fifteen Years among the Hakkas of South China*. n.pl.

Wu Fengbin 吳風斌. Ed. 1983. *Dongnanya huaqiao tongshi* 東南亞華橋通史 [A general history of overseas Chinese in Southeast Asia]. Fuzhou: Fujian renmin chubanshe.

Wu Xiaoli 巫小黎. 2001. "Li Jinfa he ta de *Lingdong liange*" 李金髮和他的嶺東戀歌 [Li Jinfa and his *Lingdong Liange*]. *Xinwenxue shiliao* 2001 no. 02: 64–65.

Wu Yuantai. 1993. *Pérégrination vers l'est* [Pilgrimage to the east]. Trans. by Perront, Nadine. Paris: Gallimard.

Wu Zhenqing 吳振清. 2007. "Luo Xianglin suocang Huang Zunxian shiwen shouji" 羅香林所藏黃遵憲詩文手迹 ["Autographs of Huang Zunxian in the collection of Luo Xianglin"]. *Wenxian* 2007 no. 4: 119–126.

Xue Shan 薛汕. 1985. *Shuqu sanji* 書曲散記 [Notes on popular song]. Beijing: Shumu wenxian chubnshe.

Yang Erzeng. 2007. *The Story of Han Xiangzi: The Alchemical Adventures of a Daoist Immortal*. Trans. by Clart, Philip. Seattle: University of Washington Press.

Yang Zhe 楊哲. Ed. 2004. *Zhongguo minsuxue zhi fu: Zhong Jingwen shengya, xueyi ziji yu xuejie pingshu* 中國民俗學之父 鍾敬文生涯學藝自記與學界評述 [The founding father of Chinese folklore studies: Zhong Jingwen's life, his own record of his scholarship and his standing in the scholarly community]. Hefei: Anhui jiaoyu chubanshe.

Ye Chunsheng 葉春聲. 1996. *Lingnan suwenxue jianshi* 嶺南俗文學簡史 [A short history of the popular literature of the Lingnan region]. Guangzhou: Guangdong gaodeng jiaoyu chubanshe.

Yen Ching-hwang. 1986. *A Social History of the Chinese in Singapore and Malaya 1800–1911*. Singapore: Oxford University Press.

Yung, Bell and Yung Eleanor S., Eds. 2014. *Uncle Ng Comes to America: Chinese Narrative Songs of Immigration and Love*. Hong Kong: MCCM Creations.

York, F. W. and Phillips, A. R. 1996. *Singapore: A History of its Trams, Trolleybuses and Buses.* Volume One. *1880s to 1960s.* Croydon, Surrey, UK: DTS Publishing.

You Shengzhong 游生忠. 2010. "Minjian chuantong changben *Shiliting dujie*" 民間傳統唱本十里亭读解 [An interpretation of *Shili ting*, a popular traditional ballad]. *Sanming Ribao* 三明日報, November 19th, 2010. http://smrb.smnet.com.cn/shtml/smrb/20101119/15123.shtml (accessed June 15th, 2014).

You Shengzhong. 2012. "Minjian changben *Zhao Yulin* manhua" 民間唱本趙玉林漫話 [About the popular ballad *Zhao Yulin*]. http://www.fjsen.com/d/201212/14/content_10104789.htm (accessed May 15th, 2014).

Yu, Anthony C. Trans. 1977–1983. *The Journey to the West.* 4 Vols. Chicago: The University of Chicago Press.

Yu Weimin 俞為民. 2008. "Nanxi *Gao Wenju* kaolun" 南戲高文舉考論 [A study of the southern play *Gao Wenju*]. *Xiqu yanjiu* 77: 1–17.

Yü, Chün-fang. 2001. *Kuan-yin: The Chinese Transformation of Avalokiteśvara.* New York: Columbia University Press.

Yuan Bingling. 2000. *Chinese Democracies: A Study of the Kongsis of West Borneo.* Leiden: CNWS.

Yuan Ke. 1993. *Dragons and Dynasties: An Introduction to Chinese Mythology.* Selected and trans. by Kim Echlin and Nie Zhixiong. London: Penguin/Beijing: Foreign Languages Press.

Yung, Judy, Chang, Gordon H. and Lai, Him Mark. Eds. 2006. *Chinese American Voices: From the Gold Rush to the Present.* Berkeley: University of California Press.

Zeng Bairong 曾白融. Ed. 1989. *Jingju jumu cidian* 京劇劇目辭典 [A title dictionary of Peking Opera]. Beijing: Zhongguo xiju chubanshe.

Zeng Xuekui 曾學奎. 2003. "Taiwan Kejia *Du Tai beige* yanjiu" 臺灣客家渡台悲歌研究 [A study of the *Du Tai beige* by a Hakka from Taiwan]. MA Thesis, National Hsinchu Teachers College, Xinzhu.

Zhang Zhiyao 張志姚. 1981. "Kejia shange gaishu" 客家山歌概述 [A general description of Hakka mountain songs]. In *Yuedong Kejia shange* 粤東客家山歌. Meixian, 4–16.

Zhao Jiaxin 趙家欣. 1936. "Guanyu Nanyangke de minge" 關於南洋客的民歌 [About folksongs on migrants to Southeast Asia]. *Tian di ren* 4: 62–63.

Zheng Bingshan 鄭炳山. 2007. *Zheng Bingshan qiaoshi wenji* 鄭炳山僑史文集 [Collected articles by Zheng Bingshen on the history of overseas Chinese]. Hong Kong: Xianggang shehui kexue chubanshe.

Zheng, Su De San. 1992. "From Toison to New York: *Muk'yu* Songs in Folk Tradition," *Chinoperl Papers* 16: 165–205.

Zhong Jingwen 鍾敬文. 1924. "Nanyang de geyao" 南洋的歌謠 [Folksongs from Southeast Asia]. Originally published in *Geyao zhoukan* 歌謠周刊 70 (November 1924); reprinted in Zhong Jingwen, *Zhong Jingwen Minjian wenxue lunji* 鍾敬文民間文學論集 Vol. 2, 324–327. Shanghai: Shanghai wenyi chubanshe, 1985.

Zhong Jingwen. 1927. *Kejia qingge* 客家情歌 [Hakka love songs]. Originally published in 1927 as *Keyin qingge ji* 客音情歌集 [A collection of love songs in the Hakka dialect]. by Beixin shuju; reprinted Shanghai: Shanghai wenyi chubanshe, 1991.

Zhong Jingwen. 1994. "Liu Sanjie chuanshuo shilun" 劉三姐傳說試論 [An exploration of the legend of Liu Sanjie]. In Zhong Jingwen, *Zhong Jingwen xueshu lunzhu zixuanji* 鍾敬文學術論著自選集, 299–327. Beijing: Shoudu shifan daxue chubanshe.

Zhong Junkun 鍾俊昆. 2009. *Kejia shange wenhua yanjiu* 客家山歌文化研究 [A study of the culture of Hakka mountain songs]. Harbin: Heilongjiang renmin chubanshe.

Zhongguo da baike quanshu: yuyan wenzi 中國大百科全書語言文字 [The great Chinese encyclopedia: language and writing]. 1988. Beijing: Zhongguo da baike quanshu chubanshe.

Zhongguo geyao jicheng: Fujian juan 中國歌謠集成福建卷 [Complete collection of Chinese folksong: Fujian province]. 2007. Beijing: Zhongguo ISBN zhongxin.

Zhongguo geyao jicheng: Guangdong juan 中國歌謠集成廣東卷 [Complete collection of Chinese folksong: Guangdong province]. 2007. Beijing: Zhongguo ISBN zhongxin.

Zhongguo geyao ziliao 中國歌謠資料 [Chinese folksong: source materials]. 3 Vols. 1959. Beijing: Zuojia chubanshe.

Zhongguo quyi zhi: Fujian juan 中國曲藝志福建卷 [The gazetteer on minor performative arts: Fujian province]. 2006. Beijing: Zhongguo ISBN zhongxin.

Zhongguo quyi zhi: Guangdong juan 中國曲藝志廣東卷 [The gazetteer on minor performative arts: Guangdong province]. 2008. Beijing: Zhongguo ISBN Center.

Zhou Changqi 周長楫 and Zhou Qinghai 周青海. 2003. *Xinjiapo Minnanhua suyu geyao xuan* 新加坡閩南話俗語歌謠選 [A selection of Minnanese popular expressions and folksongs from Singapore]. Xiamen: Xiamen daxue chubanshe.

Zhou Heping 周和平. Ed. 2007. *Diyipi guojiaji feiwuzhi wenhua yichan minglu tudian* 第一批國家級非物質文化遺產名錄圖典 [An illustrated compendium of the first group of national level 'intangible cultural heritage' genres]. 2 Vols. Beijing: Wenhua yishu chubanshe.

Zhou Jianxin 周建新 and Zhou Li 周琍. 2003. "*Yuedong zhi feng*: Kejia chuantong shehui jingji yu fengsu de shengdong touying" 粵東之風:客家傳統社會經濟與風俗的生動投影 [*Yuedong zhifeng*: moving reflections of the economy and customs of Hakka traditional society]. *Nanfang wenwu* 2003 no. 4: 60–64, 95.

www.ingramcontent.com/pod-product-compliance
Lightning Source LLC
Chambersburg PA
CBHW052342230426
43664CB00042B/2645